Stars, Stripes, and Italian Tricolor

STARS, STRIPES,
AND
ITALIAN TRICOLOR

The United States and Italy,
1946–1989

LEO J. WOLLEMBORG

Foreword by Richard N. Gardner

New York
Westport, Connecticut
London

Library of Congress Cataloging-in-Publication Data

Wollemborg, Leo J.
    Stars, stripes, and Italian tricolor : the United States and Italy,
1946–1989 / Leo J. Wollemborg.
      p.   cm.
    Includes bibliographical references.
    ISBN 0–275–93141–2 (alk. paper)
    1. United States—Foreign relations—Italy. 2. Italy—Foreign
relations—United States. 3. United States—Foreign
relations—1945– 4. Italy—Foreign relations—1945–1976. 5. Italy—
Foreign relations—1976– I. Title.
E183.8.I8W65   1990
327.73045′09′045—dc20   89–16217

Library of Congress Catalog Card Number: 89–16217
ISBN: 0–275–93141–2

First published in 1990

Praeger Publishers, One Madison Avenue, New York, NY 10010
A division of Greenwood Press, Inc.

Printed in the United States of America

∞

The paper used in this book complies with the Permanent
Paper Standard issued by the National Information Standards
Organization (Z39.48-1984).

10 9 8 7 6 5 4 3 2 1

Copyright Acknowledgments

Stars, Stripes and Italian Tricolor is a translation, abridgment, and adaptation of the author's earlier work, *Stelle, Striscie e Tricolore*, published by Arnoldo Mondadori Editore in 1983. Material is used with permission of Arnoldo Mondadori Editore, Milan, Italy.

Material taken from the author's articles in *Il Progresso Italo-Americano* reprinted courtesy of Sedint Società per Axioni, Rome, Italy.

Material taken from the author's articles in the *Washington Post* reprinted courtesy of the *Washington Post*.

Material taken from the author's articles in *Freedom at Issue* reprinted courtesy of Freedom House, New York, New York.

Articles taken from the January 28, 1949; April 22, 1949; May 8, 1949; June 3, 1949; and March 24, 1950 issues of *Commonweal* © Commonweal Foundation.

The following articles are reprinted by permission of THE NEW REPUBLIC: "Italy and the New Frontier," by Leo J. Wollemborg, June 12, 1961, © 1961, The New Republic, Inc.; "Italy and the Berlin Crisis," by Leo J. Wollemborg, October 9, 1961, © 1961, The New Republic, Inc.; "The New Frontier and The New Italy," by Leo J. Wollemborg, September 10, 1962, © 1962, The New Republic, Inc.; "Italy Between Governments," by Roy Meachum, January 10, 1970, © 1970, The New Republic, Inc.

TO DINA
Without her love and help
this book could not have
been written

Contents

Abbreviations

ITALIAN POLITICAL PARTIES AND LABOR ORGANIZATIONS

CD,CDS	Democrazia Cristiana, Democristiani
CGIL	Confederazione Generale Italiana del Lavoro
CISL	Confederazione Italiana Sindacati dei Lavoratori
MSI	Movimento Sociale Italiano
PCI	Partito Comunista Italiano
PLI	Partito Liberale Italiano
PRI	Partito Republicano Italiano
PSDI	Partito Social-Democratico Italiano
PSI	Partito Socialista Italiano
UIL	Unione Italiana del Lavoro

Foreword

Richard N. Gardner

One week after the election of President Kennedy in November 1960, young leaders of the Christian Democrats, Republicans, Social Democrats, and Socialists met in Italy to celebrate the event. What brought them together, Christian Democrat leader Franco Malfatti told Leo Wollemborg, "was the feeling that, as we struggle on to make our country at last into a modern democratic nation, we can now look forward, once more, to a rendez-vous with America."

The search for the right kind of "rendez-vous," the most appropriate form of relationship, between postwar American diplomacy and Italy's complex and fragile domestic politics is the fascinating and important story that Leo Wollemborg tells here as no one else has and no one else could.

For the last 40 years, Wollemborg has observed and chronicled the tortuous course of Italian politics and U.S.-Italian relations from his unique vantage point in Rome as a U.S. journalist who returned to his native Italy after the defeat of Fascism. During this time he came to know and interview almost every Italian leader of importance from Gronchi, Nenni, Saragat and La Malfa to Moro, Fanfani, Andreotti, Forlani, Craxi, and Berlinguer. With a single exception, he interviewed, and was on close terms with, every U.S. ambassador in Rome. On his regular trips to Washington, he took soundings on the attitudes toward Italy of senior administration officials and congressional leaders. He even managed to interview three U.S. presidents on the subject of Italy before they became president—Carter, Reagan, and Bush. He also gained access to confidential documents bearing on U.S.-Italian relations, including the historic presidential decision paper on Eurocommunism and Italy approved by President Carter on March 14, 1977, which is published in this book for the first time.

Mr. Gardner served as U.S. ambassador to Italy from 1977 to 1981.

For forty years, in short, Wollemborg has played a unique role as the premier U.S. journalist interpreting Italy to the United States and the United States to Italy. His thoughtful contributions have appeared in the *Washington Post*, the *Wall Street Journal*, and *Freedom at Issue*, on our side of the Atlantic, and in *Il Tempo*, *Il Messagero*, and *Oggi*, on the Italian side. In this book we have his first-hand, authoritative account of Italian-American relations as they unfolded from the early postwar period right down to the present time, drawn from his writings of the moment, from his personal recollections, and from his unequalled file of newspaper clippings and government documents. The result is an invaluable chronology of events that is at once a gold mine for historians and an adventure for the general reader, who can enjoy the dramatic effect as the story of Italian politics and U.S.-Italian relations is told from a contemporary viewpoint.

Two decisive "turning points" in postwar Italian politics occupy the center stage in this valuable book. The first is the famous "opening to the left" of the early 1960s, which brought the Socialist party of Italy, previously in electoral alliance with the Communists, into a governing coalition with the Christian Democrats, Republicans, and Social Democrats. As Wollemborg points out, "this was the first concrete step in a far-reaching realignment of Italy's political forces aimed at isolating the largest Communist party in the west and forming a stable governmental majority resting on a wider and solid foundation of popular support."

The center-left governments of the 1960s may be criticized for many excesses in labor legislation and wasteful public expenditures, but the only alternative, a center-right coalition with the then extremely conservative liberals and depending on parliamentary support from the neo-Fascist MSI, would have polarized Italian society, blocked needed social and economic reforms and resulted sooner or later in a Communist-Socialist government dominated by the former.

Wollemborg gives high marks, rightly in my view, to President Kennedy and his advisers for recognizing these realities and giving the green light to the center-left in 1961–1963, reversing the futile policies of Ambassador Clare Booth Luce, who wanted a Christian-Democratic alliance with the Monarchists, and of Deputy Chief of Mission Outerbridge Horsey, who, a few years later, was so hostile to the Socialists (and Republicans) that he considered a government dependent on the support of the neo-Fascists a better way of protecting U.S. interests.

The second "turning point," which is analyzed in the last part of Wollemborg's book, was the failure of the Communist party's efforts, after its electoral successes of 1972 and 1976, to form a "historic compromise" government with the Christian Democrats in 1977–1978. Since this period coincided with my service as U.S. ambassador to Italy, I am particularly pleased by the painstaking accuracy with which Wollemborg describes the events. He was a trusted confidante of mine during these years, and no one outside of the official embassy family is in a better position to tell the story accurately and to provide the necessary historical context. Let me take this opportunity to add a few observations of my own.

⌐When President Carter was elected in November 1976, Italy was, as Zbigniew Brzezinski, then national security adviser, warned him in an early memorandum, "potentially the greatest political problem we now have in Europe." In the last months of the Ford administration, the Communists achieved their all-time high in an Italian election, 34.4% of the vote. They were extending their hegemony in every important area of Italian life—the schools, the press, the judiciary, the trade unions, regional and local governments. It seemed inevitable to many experts that they would soon enter the government in a "historic compromise" coalition with the Christian Democrats, eventually compromising both Italian freedom and the country's support of the Western Alliance.⌐

⌐In this crisis atmosphere, the Carter Administration was pressured with bad advice from two extremes of the U.S. political spectrum. From the right came demands for the United States to take a direct role in stopping the Communist threat, through covert operations if necessary. But the president, supported by Brzezinski and Secretary of State Cyrus Vance, wisely rejected that option. In the presidential decision paper of March 14, 1977, he ruled out the financing of Italian political parties, the manipulation of Italian political events, and trying to dictate to the Italians how they should vote.⌐

⌐In making that decision, the president and his advisers were obviously influenced not just by moral considerations but by the counterproductive effect of past efforts of this kind in Italy. Early in the Nixon years, as the Congress's Pike Report disclosed, large sums of money were given by the U.S. Embassy in Rome to a right-wing general who subsequently ran for parliament on the neo-Fascist ticket. Wide publicity was also given in Italy to reports that another covert financing operation was discussed and then aborted in the Ford Administration. Both of these episodes helped the Communist party to gain support as the defender of the country's sovereignty against "American domination."⌐

⌐Incautious statements were also made by U.S. officials during this period that appeared to threaten Italy with reprisals if it gave the Communist party a governing role. These had no visible positive effects. During the Nixon-Ford years, the PCI gained in two national elections, raising its vote share from 26.9% to 34.4%, while steadily extending its influence in key sectors of national life.⌐

⌐The other bit of bad advice to the Carter Administration came from the other end of the political spectrum. A small group of academic specialists in Italy argued that the PCI's accession to power was both inevitable and desirable. The inevitability was "proved," they argued, by the fact that in all recent elections the PCI had won more than its share of the youth vote (they refused to admit the possibility, now realized, that Italian youth would turn away from the Communists to other parties). The alleged desirability of PCI entry into government was also "proved," in the view of these specialists, by the argument (also disproved by history) that worker peace and control of terrorism could only be obtained by giving the Communists a share of power.⌐

President Carter rejected this kind of advice as well. In the same March 1977 memorandum, he determined that the United States should make clear to the Italian people that, while America would not interfere with their democratic right to choose their leaders, it would exercise its right as a friend and NATO partner to express a clear preference not to see Communist Parties in allied governments. This was stated plainly in public six times between May and December 1977.

A first public statement, on April 6, 1977, misfired when, in an attempt to please François Mitterrand, then in an electoral alliance with the French Communist party, the State Department declared opposition only to allied governments "dominated" by Communists. The error was corrected three weeks later on April 25, when President Carter stated that the United States preferred that its Western allies "continue to be democratic and that no totalitarian elements be influential or dominant." Brzezinski, on October 9, was particularly blunt, saying, "We do not wish the Communist parties to come to power in Western Europe."

During these difficult months, the U.S. Embassy in Rome launched a major effort to win the confidence of Bettino Craxi and other leaders of the Italian Socialist party, which, after its electoral debacle in 1976, had reverted to the position that it would only join an Italian government together with the Communists. The Embassy also cultivated assiduously leaders of the non-Communist left who had previously been neglected—political figures, journalists, scholars, artists, and trade union officials. When I learned in December 1977 that some Christian Democratic leaders (not Moro or Andreotti) were contemplating the possibility of bringing the PCI into the government, I urgently asked President Carter to authorize another stronger statement of our foreign policy preferences. One reason I considered this to be necessary was the well-orchestrated disinformation campaign of the Communists and their supporters to persuade the Italian people that the Carter Administration had no objection to a PCI governing role. I was summoned to Washington, and after a meeting with the President and National Security Council, the State Department issued a declaration on January 12, 1978, saying: "We do not favor such (Communist) participation and would like to see Communist influence in any Western European country reduced."

After this statement, plans to share power with the Communists were dropped. In the 1979 elections, the PCI suffered its first postwar electoral setback, slipping to 30.4% from 34.4%. The party has been on the downhill slope in national elections ever since, and barring an economic collapse or incredible mismanagement by the non-Communist parties, the Communists' role in Italian life will continue to decline. Italy is now—and will very likely continue to be—governed for the foreseeable future by the "pentapartito," a five-party alliance of the Christian Democrats, Liberals, Republicans, Social Democrats, and, most essentially, the Socialists.

It may be asked why I feel so strongly, as Wollemborg evidently does too, that Communist entry into the Italian government in 1977–1978 would have been such a misfortune for both Italy and the United States. It is true that under Berlinguer, the Communist party abandoned the policy of "NATO out of Italy, Italy out of NATO." But Berlinguer's party, while accepting Italy's membership in NATO in principle, continued to practice to oppose every Italian action that could help NATO to achieve its defense objectives.

During my years in Italy, for example, the Communists opposed fulfillment of NATO's agreed 3-percent real increase in annual defense spending, sought to shut down the U.S. submarine facility at La Maddalena, Sardinia, and urged a 50-percent reduction in the area available for use by NATO forces in the militarily critical Italian northeast. It also opposed the deployment of the cruise missiles in Comiso, Sicily.

Certainly the Communist party under Berlinguer criticized the Soviet Union's invasion of Czechoslovakia and its ruthless suppression of Solidarity in Poland. Yet the Communists continued to endorse Soviet-sponsored "wars of national liberation" in Latin America, Africa, and Asia, and spoke warmly of Soviet allies such as Cuba and Vietnam. Berlinguer regularly trooped to Moscow to issue joint communiqués denouncing the activities of "imperialist, militarist and reactionary circles"—meaning, of course, NATO and the United States.

While occasionally critical of the Soviet Union, Berlinguer was always careful to place it on a higher moral plane than the United States. In an interview with Oriana Fallaci in 1980, he declared that of the two superpowers only the United States could truly be called "imperialist." During the Carter years, Communist leaders even tried to persuade the Italian people that the Central Intelligence Agency was behind the Red Brigades and the murder of Aldo Moro.

On economic issues, Berlinguer and the Communist-dominated trade union flirted briefly with moderate policies in 1976–1977 but returned to intransigent opposition to two fundamental reforms necessary to reduce Italy's double-digit inflation—altering the wage indexation system and cutting excessive social spending. When FIAT dismissed redundant workers in 1980, in an effort to restore the company's international competitiveness, Berlinguer stood at the FIAT gates in Turin and called for worker occupation of the factories.

With the failure of the "historic compromise" in 1977–1978 and the subsequent decline in Communist influence, the basis was laid for the "second Italian economic miracle" of the 1980s and Italy's extraordinary performance as a strong and reliable NATO ally. Italy's decision to join the European Monetary System, its modification of the inflationary wage indexation system ("scala mobile"), its deployment of cruise missiles (which made possible the INF agreement), and its subsequent acceptance of the F–16s from Spain—all of these important decisions were opposed by the Communist party and none of them would have occurred had the PCI joined the Italian government.

Obviously, the credit for the decline of Communist power in Italy and the spectacular recovery that followed belongs exclusively to the Italian people and their leaders. But the balance could have been tipped in the wrong direction if the United States had tried to block the PCI by counter-productive and improper interference in Italy's internal affairs, or if we had supported the Communists in their demands for a governing role. These conclusions, I believe, are very well documented in Wollemborg's account.⌋

⌐One final observation is in order. U.S.-Italian relations for most of the last 40 years have been dominated by questions of domestic Italian politics rather then by foreign policy questions. Thus our relations with Italy have been fundamentally different from our relations with France, Germany, the United Kingdom, and other Western allies. This anomaly was due to the power of the Italian Communist party and Italy's fragile sense of nationhood. Fortunately, all this has now changed. ⌐

Wollemborg cites early on a monograph by Lloyd Free and Renzo Sereno entitled, "Italy: Dependent Ally or Independent Partner?" For much of the postwar period Italy was, in fact, a dependent ally. Those who would understand why it has now become, at long last, an independent partner will find the answer in this excellent book.

Stars, Stripes, and Italian Tricolor

The author (right) with Christian Democratic president Giovanni Gronchi in 1956.

1

Big Choices and a New Coat of Paint for the Old House

Under pressure from international events, the Truman administration developed and began to implement quickly its approach to the new, democratic Italy which was working its way out of the disastrous heritage of Fascism and World War II.

Following the collapse of the wartime alliance between the Western democracies and the Soviet Union, the United States was driven and to a large extent forced to take over in areas, like Italy, where British influence had been traditionally paramount. The United States alone could provide the military counterweight to Soviet pressure and the large scale economic aid necessary for the reconstruction of Western Europe.

By late 1946, the main planks of the U.S. "Italian policy" were in place. They were to remain basically unchanged for a long time while undergoing, of course, more or less timely and appropriate adjustments.

In Italy, a fairly clear-cut alignment of forces emerged from the June 1946 general election, the first free national consultation since the downfall of the Fascist dictatorship. The Christian Democrats (CDs) won a significant plurality (35 percent of the votes), but were confronted by a leftist alliance which included the Socialists, with just over 20 percent, and the Communists with more than 19 percent. This was the big confrontation the outcome of which would determine the course of Italian affairs for a long time, although other groups (Republicans, Liberals, Monarchists and Neo-Fascists) were in a position to play a role. Outside of the Communist and pro-Communist left, openly aligned to the Soviet side, only the Catholic church, with its far-reaching network of parishes, could and did provide the basis for a mass party. Moreover, the moderately reform-minded program drafted by the CD leadership could appeal to the industrial workers of Northern Italy and to the Southern peasants who otherwise would support the Communist party (PCI) and its Socialist allies (PSI).

Some political circles in the United States also looked forward to the rise of an Italian Social Democratic party similar to those which had grown up elsewhere in Western Europe long before World War II and were now showing new strength. The opportunity came when most PSI leaders, prompted by the myth of "working class unity" and by the expectation that the Soviet army would soon become the dominant force throughout Europe, chose to play second fiddle to the PCI rather than position their party as a "third force" between the CDs and the Communists. With encouragement and financial support from the U.S. unions and from the Truman administration itself, many PSI representatives and about one-third of the Socialist voters split away formed a Social Democratic party under the leadership of Giuseppe Saragat. The split was finalized early in 1947, a few days after CD premier Alcide de Gasperi's return from a visit to Washington. The next step was the "unloading" of the Communists and of their Socialist allies from the government. De Gasperi waited a few more months mostly because he wanted to get the PCI's support for enshrining in the new Republican constitution the Concordat concluded in 1929 between the Vatican and the Fascist regime. Toward the end of 1947 the battle lines were clearly drawn. In the general election of the following spring, Communists and Socialists ran on a joint ticket under the label of "People's Bloc." The CDs led a centrist coalition which included Social Democrats, Liberals, and Republicans.

Doubts and concern over the outcome were still strong in Washington in March 1948 when I came back to the United States after four years of military and government service in Europe. If the leftist alliance won the election or proved strong enough to control strategically vital regions in Central and Northern Italy, the balance of power would be dangerously tilted to the East, especially in Southern Europe and in the Mediterranean, just when Tito's Yugoslavia was moving away from its close allegiance to Moscow. Even if the PCI and its allies secured only a plurality of the votes, congressmen and administration officials wondered, wouldn't President of the Republic Enrico De Nicola call on a leftist rather than on a CD leader to form the new government?

Shortly after my return, I was introduced to the group of "Italy watchers" which met on most Fridays in a Washington restaurant. These "Italian lunch-eons," I reported in the weekly *Il Mondo* (October 21, 1950), were attended by 10 to 20 specialists from government departments and agencies who had been looking for opportunities to compare notes outside of official meetings and watertight bureaucratic compartments. Quite often one of the regular participants brought along a guest speaker, usually a newspaperman or a scholar just back from Italy. Some two weeks before the Italian election, I told the group that the alarmed and alarming assessments and prospects bandied about in Washington were not justified. The CDs would benefit from the vigorous efforts under way to "get out" the Catholic vote and from the inclination of many conservative groups to rally behind De Gasperi's party as the only effective bulwark against a leftist victory. Some help would come from the recent pronouncement of the Western powers in favor of the return to Italy of the city of Trieste which in the closing days of the war had been taken over by U.S. and British troops to forestall a Yugoslav occupation. The recent takeover of Czechoslovakia by a Communist-dominated regime had been a rude reawakening for those Italians who might have been lulled by the "soft sell" long practiced by PCI leader Palmiro Togliatti to ease the way for a leftist victory at the polls.

These forecasts I reported in a special issue that the weekly bulletin *Economic News from Italy* published on the eve of the election: "The CDs will . . . win at least as many seats in Parliament as the 'People's Bloc' . . . and thus remain the strongest single party in the country. . . . The parties represented in the De Gasperi government should be able to total about 300 out of the 574 seats in the Chamber of Deputies" and a similar majority in the Senate. It would be up to these parties and first of all to the CDs "to face the urgent economic and social problems which . . . are bound to remain paramount for a long time to come." This meant implementing long overdue tax and land reforms as well as a thorough over-hauling of the bureaucratic apparatus and of the economic system itself in order to "improve the lot of the most destitute and forgotten groups . . . farm laborers especially in the South . . . most civil servants left defenceless before the on-slaught of inflation . . . small industries which have been allowed to wither and die . . . and labor's stepchildren, the unskilled workers." De Gasperi's task in tackling such reforms would be "more difficult" because his centrist coalition included "both the non-Communist Left and the moderate Right whose views on social and economic issues are notoriously far apart."

Actually the CDs came close to polling an absolute majority of the votes, scoring what I called "an oversized victory" (*The Commonweal*, April 22, 1949). "Millions of Italians, who under normal circumstances would have voted either for some rightist party or for some moderate left-of-center outfit, cast their ballots for De Gasperi's party as the only available alternative to Communism." The new Social Democratic party got 7 percent of the votes. Despite the rather poor performance of the Republicans (PRI) and of the Liberals (PLI) who ran under the label of National Bloc, the centrist governmental coalition won the support of 62 percent of the electorate, twice as much as the Communist-led Popular Front.

"During the first months of 1948," I wrote in *The Commonweal* of January 28, 1949, "Italy was featured in the American Press as the hottest battleground of the cold war against Communism." As soon as the democratic forces won a decisive majority at the polls, U.S. political circles "thought they could relax and turn their attention to other trouble spots." To be sure, some people in Washington felt that it would not be enough for Italy to just keep "coasting along." U.S. aid should be used to stimulate the Italian government to "do more," to mobilize effectively the national economy's resources and productive capabilities. Such was the basic concept of the *Country Study: Italy* submitted to Congress by the Economic Cooperation Administration (ECA) early in 1949. It was largely drafted by Bruno Luzzatto who, after having been compelled to leave Italy in the face of the anti-Semitic policies of the Fascist regime, had already held and would later on hold important public assignments in the United States. The study acknowledged the need to continue to keep inflation under strict control but placed strong emphasis on ''a bolder policy of public investments.''

In Italy, the most vocal proponents of such an approach were the *"profes-sorini"* (little professors) of the CD left wing, notably Giuseppe Dossetti, for a short while vice-secretary of the party, and Amintore Fanfani, then labor minister and later on several times premier, foreign minister, and party leader. As I reported in *The Commonweal* (March 24, 1950), they conceded that the deflationary measures and strict credit controls introduced in late 1947 by then minister of the budget Luigi Einaudi had checked the runaway rise of prices, stabilized the Italian currency, and promoted significant progress toward balancing the national budget. They argued, however, that the price paid for these achievements had been too high and questioned the wisdom of clinging to a policy that kept the Italian economy in low gear. Unemployment continued to hover around 10 percent of the labor force, underemployment remained widespread, and a rise of investments and economic modernization were hobbled by underutilization of available resources. Even U.S. aid could not be fully absorbed (Italy had lost about 75 million dollars of the 1948–1949 allocations and some more might be lost in the near future).

An open conflict developed between the CD left-wingers and the new budget minister Giuseppe Pella—handpicked by Einaudi for the job after his own election to the presidency of the Republic in May 1948. De Gasperi sided with Pella, thus tilting the balance against the ''professorini.'' The premier's stand had a major influence in Washington as well, where the prevailing inclination was to ''place all bets on a single horse (the CD party) and a single jockey (De Gasperi),'' as I summed it up. The head of the ECA mission to Italy, Leon Dayton, continued to advocate a more dynamic operation of the Italian economy, but his efforts were blocked not only by De Gasperi but by the U.S. ambassador to Rome, James Dunn.

In earlier years, De Gasperi had served well the interests of his own party in addition to the twin causes of Italian democracy and the country's cooperation with the United States (and other key nations of the West). Even after the 1948 election, the premier had played a largely positive role, upholding public order and free institutions at home and making Italy a reliable and active partner in the Atlantic Alliance and in the budding process of European integration. For U.S. political leaders and administration officials, so often grilled by congressional committees on so many pressing and unpleasant matters (from the ''loss'' of China to the chronic political instability in France), it was a great relief to be able to point at Italy ''this good friend and ally who gives us no headaches!''

The tendency to identify U.S. policy in Italy with support to the CDs and to De Gasperi personally colored the U.S. approach to labor issues as well. This led U.S. representatives to press hard for the immediate confluence into a new national union of all the workers who were no longer willing to accept the

Communist-cum-Socialist leadership of CGIL, the single, all-embracing labor organization revived during the heyday of the anti-Fascist unity against Mussolini's regime and its Nazi bosses.

In the summer of 1948, conditions were ripe for setting up a mainly Catholic national union (CISL). Many Social Democratic, Republican, and independent labor leaders and workers, however, strongly resented U.S. efforts to force them to join right away the new organization in which they would be a minority. When two years later those leaders and workers moved out of CGIL, it was to form a national union of their own (UIL) which made a point of stressing its independence not only from CGIL but from CISL as well. CISL itself was bound to assert its autonomy from the government and from the CD party when they appeared more and more disinclined to attend to their own pledges of social and economic reform. The claim to autonomy by a mostly Catholic organization was a source of resentful surprise, almost a scandal, for De Gasperi. As usual, the premier's feelings and reactions were shared and underwritten by the U.S. Embassy.

In U.S. political journalistic, and even cultural circles, there was little awareness of the danger that in Italy political stability might turn into stagnation or that the reconstruction drive itself would result in a substantial restoration of old economic and social structures. There was even less realization of the danger of missing a great opportunity to broaden and consolidate the foundations of Italy's democratic institutions and to give them an updated capability in a country that had had so little experience of democracy and expected so much from it.

Impressions and perceptions brought back by Americans flocking to Italian art cities and tourist resorts did not help. "A short time ago, as the plane of a foreign airline was approaching an Italian airport," I reported in *The Commonweal* (April 22, 1949), "the hostess told passengers: 'You are about to land in the country that has won the war.' After a few days' stay in Italy, the average tourist is inclined to agree. In hotels and restaurants, he has found excellent food and service. Trains are running on time (even without Mussolini). . . . You can have the most wonderful six-course dinner (wine included) for as little as three dollars, but it takes the average Italian worker two days to earn that much money. You can have a suit made to order from the best material for the equivalent of 70 dollars, but it would take the average white-collar worker a month's salary to pay for that suit. Labor is still Italy's cheapest commodity—to the fortune of the few who have the money to hire labor and to the misfortune of the many who have only their labor to offer for hire.

"As a country," I continued, "Italy has always been very good for the rich, very bad for the poor. Economic and political power has always been vested in very few hands: mostly landowners in the south, big business and industrialists in the north. A professional class of politicians (drawn mostly from the swollen ranks of the lawyers) provided a parliamentary veneer. The system was topped by the monarchy and propped by the Army and by an evergrowing, pervasive bureaucracy. The Catholic Church, always very powerful in the country, had a working agreement with this paternalistic regime long before it officially recognized the Italian State in 1929.

"Millions of peasants toiled in the fields, procreated and died without taking any part in the country's political life. Emigration was the only chance to improve their dreary lot. At the turn of the century, a socialist movement was born in the growing industrial towns of the North. In later years, this movement was to give birth to several political organizations of the Left and the extreme Left (including the Italian Communist Party); but its main body was to remain faithful to a moderate brand of socialism, with a basically bourgeois leadership and a natural aversion to violence.

"Came the First World War. Italy emerged a victorious but tired and embittered country. . . . A small group of professional nationalists managed to turn their disappointment over the peace settlement into a national calamity. Too busy moaning over the 'imperial' war they were supposed to have lost (and which they had never intended to fight in the first place), many Italians forgot to rejoice over the national war they had won.

"This feeling of frustration, the economic and social consequences of the war and the dread aroused by the Bolshevik revolution in Russia, set the stage for Fascism. . . . Mussolini's victory was gained over democracy much more than over Communism. And . . . it was a victory by default and desertion. The forces that should have stood for freedom just were not there or turned up in the Fascist camp. Mussolini 'marched on Rome' in a sleeping car.

"Eventually, Fascism plunged the country into another World War. The people had no say in this decision; it aroused mixed feelings among the forces of wealth and tradition which had so powerfully helped Fascism to power. . . . After three years of war [these forces] threw Mussolini overboard. . . . Too late to save the country from foreign occupation, from destruction and misery. Too late to save the Monarchy itself."

Following the CD triumph in the April 1948 election, De Gasperi and his collaborators behaved much like a landlord who, confronted with a house calling for basic alterations . . . is afraid that the replacement of some rotten beam may cause the collapse of the whole structure. So he gets busy applying a coat of paint to the rusty front door, fixes a couple of leaking pipes, but postpones sending for the contractor, hoping that somehow the old building will last another winter or two."

The price paid by the nation (and by the CD party itself) was very high because at the time De Gasperi's power and prestige and overall political and social conditions would have made it possible to move boldly to narrow the traditional gaps between Italy and the more advanced Western societies. "Within the CD camp, factional strife and personal rivalries, set aside during the 1948 electoral campaign, had not had the time and opportunity for a strong revival as yet. To the minor partners in the centrist coalition, the premier's authority was a guarantee that they would be able to preserve a relatively autonomous role despite the overwhelming power of the CD party. . . . Stunned by the utter failure of their strategy, the Communists were going through a period of uncertainty and frustration. Many Socialists were bitter toward their Communist allies who had exploited to the full their party's greater strength and efficient organization to secure a disproportionately big share of the parliamentary seats obtained by the joint ticket of candidates fielded by the leftist coalition. On the right, the feeling that De Gasperi had 'saved' Italy from Communism was widespread even among the representatives of social groups and economic interests which had not voted for the CD or had done so with great reluctance. . . . Accordingly, they were willing or at least resigned to accept the sacrifices that the premier might deem necessary to demand from them in order to consolidate the fruits of the April 1948 election.''

Most important, the outcome of the election had opened the way for developing a modern and flexible system of political parties. The CDs were in a position to form a governmental majority with the Social Democrats or with the Liberals, while the Republicans could join either coalition. The coming to power of a government based on cooperation between CDs and Social Democrats would signal the determination to give priority to a gradual but effective program of social reform and economic expansion. Once such a center-left coalition had achieved some of its major aims, it would become possible and even advisable to usher in a period of consolidation to be presided over by a government based on collaboration between CDs and Liberals. The voters would have a choice between a center-left and a right-of-center coalition both made up of parties which, whatever their differences on other issues, shared a deep commitment to free institutions at home and to Italy's ties to the West.

Democratic prospects in Italy could be further improved by a timely appeal to those ''many Socialists, led by former Interior Minister Giuseppe Romita, who felt that they had been the victims and the dupes of the so-called 'unity of action pact' with the Communists. . . . At the same time, they thought that a strong and reunited Socialist Party could still play an important role holding the balance of power between the CDs and the Communists.'' These Socialists, I further reported in *The Commonweal* (January 28, 1949), were ''either snubbed or pressed too hard into becoming overnight anti-Communist.'' Several more years were to elapse before the majority of the PSI drew away from the alliance with the PCI and was ready and eligible for participating in a governmental coalition with traditionally democratic and pro-Western forces. Romita himself delayed his walkout and eventually was able to take along only a relatively small group of Socialists.

De Gasperi displayed real statesmanship when he overruled his fellow CDs who claimed ''all the power'' for their party, and called instead on Social Democrats, Republicans, and Liberals to share in the government. It was neither wise nor far-sighted, however, for the Premier to insist that *all* these parties join the Christian Democrats in the ruling coalition. Much worse, De Gasperi exploited this condition of affairs and the mistakes of the minor center parties themselves not only to neutralize their conflicting pressures but to play them off against the wings of his own party. Dossetti, who was then the leader of the CD left-wingers, told me time and again: "De Gasperi blames us on the ground that we demand reforms that 'not even the Social Democrats are asking for!' " In the same way, the Premier used the Liberals to foil the requests of the conservative sectors of his own party. The eminently foreseeable result was to further strengthen the trend toward stalemate and *"immobilismo,"* a term that became fashionable in those years to describe the performance or lack of performance by the De Gasperi governments.

Under the circumstances, all the resentments and disappointments that rightly or wrongly could be related to the handling or mishandling of national affairs, found no outlet except in a protest vote for leftist or rightist parties representing a more or less radical opposition to the country's democratic system and international commitments.

In the regional elections held in the island of Sardinia (May 8, 1949), the CDs lost one-third of the votes they had polled a year before. These losses did not benefit the other partners in the national government but Monarchists and Neo-Fascists as well as the Communists and their Socialist allies. The Sardinian returns, I reported in *The Commonweal* (June 3, 1949), showed that "by failing to take concrete action on the necessary social and economic reforms . . . the present CD leadership has failed to deprive the Communists of their most effective political weapon."

In the following autumn landless peasants, often led not only by Communist activists but by local parish priests, began moving into large, poorly cultivated estates, especially in Southern Italy. The government's answer was a confused mix of police action against the squatters and new, vague promises of early land redistribution. Only after more bloody clashes between police and peasants in Calabria, the government approved a bill whereby some 110,000 acres of Calabrian land would be turned over to the peasants. It took another full year to begin to implement these pledges. At the same time, I wrote in *Collier's Yearbook* (covering the year 1950), even this belated and meager beginning confirmed that "land reform in Italy involves . . . a large-scale program of public works (roads, aqueducts, housing, schools, etc.), and the granting to the peasants of easy term loans which alone can enable them to live on and improve their assigned plots."

A special agency *Cassa per il Mezzogiorno* (or Fund for The South), created in the same year, was to carry out a ten-year program intended to close the long-standing economic and social gap between Southern and Northern Italy. The task proved much longer, harder, and more expensive than anticipated. Meanwhile a comprehensive tax reform began to take shape after more than two years of research and debate. Its key feature was the introduction of a progressive income tax to replace most of the 70-odd direct levies still on the books. The overall goal of the reform was a more equitable distribution of the tax load (at the time, the government derived some 75 percent of its income from sales taxes, custom duties, and state monopolies on salt, cigarettes and matches, while direct taxation accounted for less than 25 percent).

Significant progress was made in doing away with the custom barriers that hampered Italy's foreign trade. Long opposed by many industrialists accustomed to operate in the "hothouse" of a traditional protectionism, the liberalization, promoted mainly by Republican foreign trade minister Ugo La Malfa, strengthened Italy's commercial ties as well as her political links with the major industrial democracies of the West. It also prompted a much needed modernization of the Italian productive machine laying the groundwork for a rapid expansion of the national economy. The expansion, however, was disorderly, unbalanced, and precarious. There was no purposeful approach to the problems of apportioning the increased production between exports and the domestic market, the investments among the more or less dynamic industrial sectors and between industry and other branches of the national economy, or the benefits of economic growth among the country's social groups and regions.

The Christian Democratic party, I wrote in *The Reporter* (June 26, 1951), was "a rainbow with a spectrum ranging from a faint pink to a Fascist black, or at least gray. . . . On the Left, . . . the little professors combine Catholic Action training, academic background, impatience to get things done, and a deeply religious interest in the welfare of the poor. . . . They find natural allies . . . in the predominantly CD CISL, Italy's second largest labor federation. About fifteen CD deputies, ranged around Giovanni Gronchi . . . since 1948 President of the Chamber of Deputies usually join the left wingers in criticizing the government's conduct of economic affairs. In political matters, however, Gronchi and his followers manage to flirt with the nationalistic Right while winking at the Communistic Left. Their favorite theme is . . . a more 'Italian' policy—a handy formula which might mean loosening Atlantic Treaty ties [and] forming a 'national union' government supported by the Communists. . . . Gronchi himself seems ready to ride any horse, of any color, that might carry him to the premiership. . . . The rightists are a motley crowd, with a composite background. Some have traditional interests, others newly won positions, to defend. Almost all are hostile to new-fangled notions of economic and social democracy and vaguely nostalgic for the good old times of Fascism and pre-Fascist monarchy."

The CD party, moreover, included several personalities whose influence was not determined primarily "by the parliamentary votes they control. . . . There is Interior Minister Mario Scelba, Italy's strong man and the Communists' No. 1 enemy. On occasion, Scelba has come out against the Neo-Fascists with equal bluntness, but his bill to curb their activities was blocked in the Senate last November and has been forgotten since. There is Attilio Piccioni, a party wheelhorse and former secretary general, who is now Minister of Justice (Rome wits have nicknamed Piccioni 'the Queen Mother' because he is reported ready to head a regency should De Gasperi step down). There is Guido Gonella, a former editorial writer for the Vatican paper *Osservatore Romano* and still very close to the highest Vatican circles."

The Civic Committees, I recalled, had been established a few months before the 1948 general election "under the leadership of Luigi Gedda, then chief of the Men of Catholic Action.'' They played a significant role in getting out the Catholic vote. After the victory at the polls, Gedda disappointed many CD leaders by refusing to disband the Civil Committees even while insisting that they are not a political party. ''Still much of his strength comes from the support of powerful Vatican circles who feel that the CDs may not prove 'clerical' enough and who, on general principle, do not like to put all their eggs in a single basket. . . . In recent [local] elections, the Civic Committees called for the election of 'honest, efficient, patriotic administrators,' regardless of party affiliations. While Gedda clearly draws boundaries on the left, he leaves them rather open on the right.

''To keep this patchwork confederation together,'' I concluded, ''would be quite a job under any circumstances and for any length of time. De Gasperi has managed to do it for over five years. . . . But only too often the difficulties of the Italian situation, the rocking balance of power within the party and De Gasperi's own disposition have combined to make inaction and postponement the line of least resistance. Even the government's determined anti-Communism . . . has failed to carry the attack to the heart of the enemy positions. . . . The CDs have not tackled the social and economic issues which the Communists exploit but did not invent. A motto concocted by Rome wits for the CDs runs: 'Never do today what you might have a good excuse for not doing tomorrow.' ''

By running joint tickets of candidates in the local elections of May–June 1951, the centrist alignment managed to wrest from the PCI and its Socialist allies control of such important cities as Milan, Turin, Genoa, Venice, and Florence. But the CD plurality dropped to 37 percent, while the leftist coalition made a net gain of 500,000 votes. A year later, a second round of local elections was held mostly in Southern Italy. There the CD losses benefitted mainly Monarchists and Neo-Fascists: ''Land barons and conservative businessmen fanned and exploited the vague nationalistic aspirations of the populace and its primitive attachment to the dethroned House of Savoy. . . . Militant royalism found a colorful leader in Achille Lauro, a wealthy Neopolitan shipowner who became president and financial mainstay of the PNM (*Partito Nazionale Monarchico*). . . . The Neo-fascist MSI (*Movimento Sociale Italiano*) found it easier and politically more expedient to softpedal the Republican and Socialistic motives inherited from the last-ditch Social Republic established by Mussolini in northern Italy in 1943–45'' (*Collier's Yearbook*, 1952).

Clearly, the policy of reforms had been undertaken too late and its implementation was too slow and uncertain to destroy the credibility of the charges hurled against the centrist government by the leftist parties or the appeal of their promises. But it was enough to arouse alarm and hostility among the powerful interest groups which clung to an outdated and almost pre-capitalistic conservatism. The center coalition parties ended up by falling between two stools. The general election of 1953 registered, for the first and so far the only time in postwar Italy, a defeat for all the partners in the governmental lineup (CDs, Social Democrats, Liberals, and Republicans), and significant gains for all the opposition parties (Communists and Socialists, Monarchists, and Neo-Fascists).

The outbreak of the war in Korea changed the nature of U.S. aid programs to Western Europe. The new approach did not disavow the importance of a continued strengthening of economic and social structures in democratic Europe but emphasized preparation and cooperation aimed at guaranteeing military security. I wrote in *Il Mondo* (October 20, 1951) how these developments highlighted "the mistakes of the overly cautious policy," which had given priority to "salting away" gold and dollar reserves, whose purchasing power was to be curtailed by rising international prices (especially of the raw materials required to fuel Italian industry), rather than to the expansion and modernization of the country's productive plant, whose worth was sharply increasing. "We must not take steps too long for our legs," I was told by Domenico Menichella, who had succeeded Einaudi as Governor of the Bank of Italy. As far back as November 1949, Menichella maintained that it would have been easier and more beneficial for the Italian economy to absorb U.S. aid if it had been distributed over a longer period, "possibly ten years." "You know," I replied, "we choose a president every four years." It seemed unlikely, if not altogether out of the question, I further pointed out, that economic assistance to Italy (and to other beneficiaries of the Marshall Plan) could be continued, at the same level, beyond the current four-year period.

By an ironic paradox, the larger appropriations, which had been denied to the proponents of a bolder program of economic expansion, were finally authorized to finance the strengthening of the military machine and the buildup of stocks of strategic raw materials in the wake of the Korean War. At the same time, the disturbing returns of the 1951–1952 local elections persuaded the government to approve at last sizable investment programs intended to expand production and reduce unemployment. But this shift came too late to affect substantially the outcome of the impending general election.

2

Mrs. Luce Goes to Rome While Italy Regains Self-Confidence

In spite of so many warning signals, the severe setback suffered by the centrist coalition in the election of June 7, 1953, was a hard, largely unexpected blow for U.S. political circles. In the race for the Chamber of Deputies, the governmental coalition got over 49 percent of the votes, failing by a very narrow margin to qualify for the seat bonus provided by the new electoral system (branded as "the Swindle Law" by the opposition parties). Yet the working of the old law (a proportional representation somewhat corrected in favor of the big parties) allowed the coalition to win altogether 303 seats out of 590. In the Senate race the center parties polled 50.2 percent of the votes and secured 125 seats out of a total of 237. The Christian Democrats' share of the popular vote dropped to just over 40 percent compared with 48.5 percent in the 1948 general election. Social Democrats and Republicans lost about one-third of their following and the Liberals lost almost one-fifth. The PCI won 22.7 percent and the PSI 12.7 percent in the poll for the Chamber of Deputies. Their combined share thus reached 35.4 percent compared with 31 percent in 1948. Minor leftist groups got 2 percent. In the Senate race, Communists and Socialists received just over 33 percent and the small leftist parties about 3.5 percent. The Monarchists polled about 7 percent, more than doubling their 1948 vote, but failed to achieve control of the balance of power. The Neo-Fascists got about 6 percent.

"By and large," I reported in *Collier's Yearbook 1953*, "the election's outcome appeared to be a setback, but not a defeat, for the democratic parties." For U.S. officials and broad sectors of U.S. public opinion, however, it was a traumatic experience. Its impact was further magnified when De Gasperi proved unable to put together yet another government. Saragat, stung by the large losses suffered by his party, hastened to proclaim that the returns demanded an understanding with the Socialists. The latter, however, "would not give up their 'unity pact' with the Communists.'' De Gasperi sought next the benevolent neutrality of the Monarchists, but ''they held out for bigger prizes than the Premier could or would offer—backtracking on land and tax reform and promises of direct participation in the government.''

After Attilio Piccioni failed, too, to put together a center coalition government, President Einaudi turned to outgoing budget minister Pella, who formed a care-taker, minority cabinet including only CDs and a few ''independent'' experts. It managed to survive thanks to a motley combination of forces and attitudes: ''Neo-Fascists and Social Democrats abstained. . . . Only Socialists and Com-munists voted against, but theirs too was a 'sweet no.' Liberals, Republicans, Monarchists, and CDs voted in favor,'' although the latter stressed that the new Cabinet must confine itself to the urgent administrative matters on hand, pending a decision 'clarification' of the political situation.''

The Pella government got involved in a sharp confrontation with Yugoslavia on the Trieste issue. When Tito was reported ready to annex outright the sector of the contested area already administered by Yugoslavia, Pella moved some troops to the frontier. Pella's approach gave impetus to nationalistic feelings in Italy. De Gasperi and other CD leaders ''did not dare to precipitate a Cabinet crisis,'' but made it clear that the party continued to oppose ''a consolidation of Pella's government.''

In the wake of a trip home by Clare Boothe Luce, who a few months earlier had been appointed ambassador to Rome by the Eisenhower administration, a spate of columns and dispatches in the major U.S. papers described Italy as ''an ally in distress'' and even wondered whether she was about to become ''a lost ally.'' The main emphasis was on the danger that the PCI might ''take over'' in the near future or at least gain enough additional votes to ''overtake'' the CDs and become the number one political force in the nation. By her pessimistic assessment of Italian conditions and prospects, Mrs. Luce probably reckoned that she could not be held accountable if the worst forecasts materialized, but could maintain to have reached quickly, and courageously voiced, an unfortu-nately all-too-true diagnosis. If things took a turn for the better, she could claim credit for snatching victory out of the jaws of defeat.

A long-standing, active membership in the Republican party and the influence of her husband's publishing empire gave Mrs. Luce excellent political contacts and easy access to the Eisenhower White House itself. An activist temper led her to display too much zeal, especially in the pursuit of newly discovered causes such as Catholicism, to which she had been converted in the late 1930s. During a private audience with Pope Pius XII, according to a story circulating in Rome, the lady embarked upon a long discourse in praise of Catholicism. When the pontiff finally managed to put in a few words of his own, he could only say, ''But, my dear child, I am *already* a Catholic!''

Mrs. Luce ''adopted'' Italy with a sincere warmth and dedication. On the whole her role was positive in promoting a constructive solution of the delicate and complex problems related to the future of Trieste, in turn the key to relations between Italy and Yugoslavia. Italy might have got a better deal if in the early 1950s De Gasperi had realized that time was not working in favor of his country and had accepted the risk, inevitably connected with any reasonably workable settlement, of fueling street demonstrations and electoral maneuvers by nationalistic and Neo-Fascist groups. By and large, the accords concluded in October 1954 represented the best that Italy could realistically achieve at the time, or hope to achieve later on.

In our long and fairly frequent talks, Mrs. Luce displayed a remarkable intelligence, perhaps more lively than deep. On occasion she could exhibit a surprising degree of realism and even more surprising capacity for self-criticism. "What this country [Italy] needs is some New Deal," she told me more than once. When we met once again several years after the end of her mission to Rome, she recalled that we had sharply differed on the prospects for a turn to the left-of-center in Italy, and told my wife: "You know, your husband was right when he predicted that such a turn would take place and that its consequences would not be necessarily bad."

Mrs. Luce was deeply aware that the sizable cuts in the economic assistance to Italy were weakening the ability of the United States to influence Italian affairs. It was too much to expect, however, that she would draw the conclusion that a "lower profile" U.S. presence was becoming advisable. Perhaps other U.S. officials in Rome were responsible for the statements issued shortly after Mrs. Luce's arrival that hinted none too discreetly that U.S. aid might be discontinued if the leftist and/or rightist opposition parties gained ground in the forthcoming election. But it was right after her trip to Washington in early 1954 that significant changes were announced in the program whereby the United States financed the production in Italy of military goods for her armed forces. Henceforth these offshore procurement contracts would be denied to factories where Communist-dominated unions continued to poll a majority of the workers' votes. The whole program of economic assistance to Italy became more controversial. Even more harmful was the crude spotlighting of the U.S. intention to use economic aid not only to strengthen Italy's international commitments but to condition domestic developments which could be viewed, at most, as indirectly bearing on these commitments. As I reported in the *Washington Post* in May 1955, even top leaders of the democratic unions, such as "Giulio Pastore, secretary general of CISL, and Italo Viglianesi, UIL general secretary, expressed preference for a more flexible approach." They also cited "episodes of virtually open collusion between management and Communist officials in rigging shop steward elections in order to secure or retain American contracts."

Mario Scelba, a source who could not be suspected of being anti-American or soft on Communism, told me a couple of years after the end of his premiership (1954–1955): "Mrs. Luce was always urging us to 'do something about the PCI.' So in December 1954 we made public an anti-Communist program, or rather an anti-Communist proclamation. By its very nature, it was bound to be less productive than the measures that I had already introduced, without so much fuss, to restrain the activities of many organizations and economic corporations controlled by the PCI."

Mrs. Luce's ideas played a significant role in shaping the approach taken by President Eisenhower when he met the Italian premier in Washington (March 1955): "I tried to explain," Scelba told me, "how and why the fight against Communism in Italy can and must be conducted firmly and steadfastly but always with democratic means and methods. Only by staying within these limits and by implementing, with the help of adequate aid from abroad, economic and social policies aimed at improving the standard of living of our people, could we achieve gradual but concrete results in the battle against Italian Communism." Top representatives of the U.S. administration, however, "evidently felt that our government did not display all the desirable vigor in such a battle." Scelba went on: "Eisenhower suggested, for instance, that the municipal Council of Bologna (the biggest Red stronghold in Italy) be disbanded. I replied that should we have solid legal grounds to do so, we might as well outlaw the PCI as a whole, something obviously out of the question. In the United States, I told Eisenhower, the truly dedicated Communists were probably less than 50,000 and sympathizers did not reach half a million, yet the Administration had not deemed it possible to outlaw the communist party as such. Would it appear advisable or possible to do so if the Communists in the United States were 40 millions, proportionately as many as there are in Italy?"

The feeling that the centrist governments were "soft" toward the PCI had surfaced a few years earlier, notably among U.S. officials most attuned to the views prevailing at the top of the Catholic church. The Vatican encouraged efforts to promote a right-of-center alignment to prevent a leftist victory in the Rome municipal elections. The operation collapsed because of strong opposition from the minor center parties as well as by many CDs. At the same time, Gedda, recently appointed by Pius XII to head Catholic Action, seemed bent on forming "a second Catholic party," nationalistic and conservative, as a counterweight and eventual alternative to De Gasperi's "liberal-minded" Christian Democracy. "In the closing weeks of the 1953 electoral campaign, Catholic Action and the Civic Committees added to their basic anti-Communist line an open endorsement of De Gasperi's center policies and outspoken denounciations of Monarchism and Neo-Fascism." It was probably too late, however, I pointed out in *Collier's Yearbook*, to dispel fully the doubt that "powerful Catholic forces would welcome a shift of the government axis to the right."

During my trips to the United States and from my contacts in Rome, I gathered that in the closing years of the Truman administration some U.S. officials began to look with greater interest at Social Democrats, Liberals, and Republicans. Yet, these parties continued to be viewed as "auxiliary units" able at most to patrol the flanks of the CD battleship: the whole task force, I was told, would remain under the command of De Gasperi, "the only Italian leader whom the West can truly respect and trust."

"The situation is certainly serious, but there is no immediate danger that Italy will go Communist or . . . will be paralyzed as an effective partner of the Western alliance. A few months of honest and efficient government, committed to a policy of vigorous anti-communism and of social and economic progress, may be sufficient to turn the tide," I wrote in the final paragraph of an article that took most of the front page of the *Washington Post* editorial section on February 14, 1954. The article, friends in Washington told me, had a strong echo because it answered "many of the questions being asked in this town." Reactions were favorable in Rome, too, although the article was mostly ignored by the major Italian papers' U.S. correspondents, who readily reported on the alarmist comments on Italy by U.S. media. Mrs. Luce invited me to lunch and asked many questions about the arguments made in the article.

In my opinion, the political instability and the troubles of the last few months did not stem so much from the outcome of the June 1953 election, but rather from a slow process that had developed "over the years when Italy was enjoying a much vaunted political and economic stability which too often covered a condition of democratic stagnation." This had helped a resurgence of the rightist parties, but the "most significant feature has been the gradual emergence of the Social Communists from the political and psychological isolation to which they were confined in 1948–1949.

"In a recent conversation with a top American representative here," I continued, "former Premier De Gasperi is reported to have blamed his June setback on 'Churchill and Trieste.' To be sure, the British prime minister's campaign for a Big Four meeting and possibly a security pact with the USSR helped to convince many voters that they could safely vent their prejudices and resentments, which were mostly directed against the party in power. Also, the Allies' uncautious and unfulfilled pledges to return Trieste to Italy weakened De Gasperi's position on an issue . . . close to the hearts of many Italians. . . . The fact remains that on the Italian home grounds Togliatti's men have generally outpointed De Gasperi's, or at least they have committed fewer errors in playing their admittedly easier role of 'outs.' . . . Despite its remarkable post-war recovery . . . to a large extent Italy is still a country, as the old saying goes, where '50 million people are governed by 5,000 in the interest of 500.' " The Communists "monopolize the protest vote, channeling dissatisfaction against the democratic government; they exploit real or alleged cases of government inefficiency, graft, favoritism, and petty intolerance (and only too often they have something to go on).

"The Communists are always on the job. They alone seem to have realized that in this era of mass movements and universal suffrage, politics is an everyday business, not a three-week job on the eve of a national election. . . . At the time of the Calabrian floods last fall, Communists took the lead of joint action by all Calabrian members of Parliament . . . to demand large scale government relief. At the time of the Trieste incidents last November they posed as the stoutest defenders of 'Italian national rights and dignity' and joined up with Neo-Fascist agitators in attempting to turn students' demonstrations into anti-British and anti-American riots. In the industrial North, they stress their championship of the

worker in overalls. In the destitute and peasant South, their watchword is ex-
propriation and redistribution of all land to farm laborers. To the prosperous
tenant-sharecroppers of Central Italy, they promise further improvement of a
situation giving them most of the benefits of land ownership without its burdens.
In Rome, they espouse the grievances of the too numerous but generally un-
derpaid civil servants." PCI leaders stress that theirs is "a constitutional and
patriotic party, mildly progressive in social and economic matters, full of respect
for Italian traditional 'values' including Catholicism.

"A large, perfectly disciplined party organization and plenty of money are
naturally indispensable for carrying out this diversified operation. . . . The Italian
Communist party, the largest this side of the Iron Curtain, has more than
2,500,000 members, 400,000 trained workers, 10,000 local branches and 52,000
plant and block cells. . . . It has been widely reported that large funds have been
coming from the other side of the Iron Curtain especially around election time.
The PCI and its affiliated organizations are well able to finance their own activities, however. There are membership dues, of course, and frequent special
assessments for the party press, for special needs and emergencies, for 'solidarity'
drives on behalf of strikers, etc. Communist members of Parliament are required
to kick back to the party a percentage of their salary, while many truly dedicated
party officials are satisfied with the pay of an unskilled laborer. There are the
contributions reportedly paid by some industrialists as insurance against the future
or as 'protection' against strikes in their factories. It is an open secret in Italy
that trade with the Soviet-dominated countries is monopolized by Communist-
controlled corporations to which even government-controlled concerns have been
reportedly compelled to pay fees in order to sell beyond the Iron Curtain."

Right now, I emphasized, the first major objective of the PCI "is the continued
erosion of the minor center parties . . . which enables the Communists to increase
their pressure on Christian Democracy for 'an end to the cold war on the domestic
front' and for 'a new political departure in line with the June returns.' In Italian,
that means giving the Communists and fellow traveling Socialists a share in the
government. . . . Should the CDs resist, they would have to seek the alliance of
the Monarchist and pro-Fascist Right and pay for it with the abandonment of
social and economic reforms. Such a shift would make all moderate positions
untenable and give Togliatti an excellent opportunity to present his favorite
formula—the Popular Front—as the only alternative to a 'clerico-Fascist, reactionary regime.' "

The only thing that could "spoil Togliatti's game" was the formation of "a
strong Center coalition. . . . Admittedly, the four Center parties can count on
very narrow majorities in Parliament. . . . But efficient government operation
should provide opportunities to widen such majorities by leading from strength—
the strength of a solid bloc of unquestionably democratic votes. . . . It would be
rather awkward for [Socialist leader Pietro] Nenni to oppose, solely on grounds
of foreign policy or of solidarity with the Communists, a Center government

effectively 'moving toward the Left' in economic and social affairs.'' Of course, I concluded, such reassuring prospects were ''predicated upon the Center parties' maintaining close solidarity and internal discipline and giving the country concrete evidence that they have learned the lesson of the June returns.''

A few days later, a new government based on a revived cooperation among these parties was formed with Scelba as premier. ''It is about the best solution that we could reasonably hope for under the present circumstances,'' I told Mrs. Luce. She listened to my arguments, shook her head and said, ''All this is fine and quite logical. But, believe me, Leo, we won't be able to have governmental stability and democratic security in Italy until and unless we manage to bring into the majority that bloc of 40 Monarchist votes.'' (This was the total number of Monarchist representatives in the Chamber of Deputies.) On the basis of their own record, I replied, Monarchist leaders did not seem apt nor ready to cooperate constructively with the minor Center parties nor with the sizable sectors of Christian Democracy itself. The Monarchists, moreover, were far from being ''a bloc.'' ''Let's keep them out of the government, out of reach of the related perks and privileges,'' I went on, ''and within six months their party will split. It will take only a little longer for some of their representatives and, most important, for quite a few of their voters to turn to a democratic party, notably the CDs and the Liberals.'' Four months later, there was a break between the two top Monarchist leaders, Achille Lauro and Alfredo Covelli, and each of them ended up heading a splinter party of his own. Within the next few years both parties ceased to represent a relevant political force.

Mrs. Luce, however, kept toying with the idea that the right could make a useful and possibly decisive contribution to solving Italian problems. I remember, for instance, her enthusiasm about the new symbol of Lauro's party, ''a golden lion on a blue field.'' Many of her mistakes could be traced to the fact that she paid to the opinions of some circles and individuals an attention quite out of proportion with their ability to read and interpret, let alone influence, Italian trends and events. It was notably the case of the group that edited the weekly *Il Borghese*. They were brilliant ''cultural operators,'' often amusing, but more inclined to the cutting repartee than to thoughtful analysis, to skepticism than to constructive proposals. Their contempt for contemporary Italy was pervasive enough to make them hanker after her Monarchist and even Fascist past. Flattered by the interest shown by the U.S. ambassador, they were willing to return the flattery but also ready to look patronizingly upon her from the heights of the Italians' ''thousand-year-old wisdom.'' They were equally ready and even eager to criticize her and to vent their basically anti-American feelings as soon as the lady's (and Washington's) approach did not conform to their likes and dislikes. They resented the fact that the United States failed to use ''the policy of the whip,'' in their opinion the only effective way of dealing with the Italians. The Americans should have turned their backs on De Gasperi, Scelba, and other CD leaders as well as on the ''eternally wavering'' minor partners of the center coalition (to quote the well-known journalist Indro Montanelli). The capital sin of all those Italian politicians and parties, *Il Borghese* maintained, was to keep at arm's length the rightist forces instead of welcoming them as indispensable partners in the effort to prevent a Communist takeover.

The other side of the same coin was Mrs. Luce's failure or refusal to perceive the significant changes underway in Italy and the related role of people like Nenni, Gronchi, and Enrico Mattei, the head of the state oil and gas agency, ENI *(Ente Nazionale Idrocarburi)*. A maverick within his own party, Gronchi had managed to become a rallying point both for dissident CD groups and for sizable sectors of the leftist and rightist opposition to the Center coalition. As speaker of the Chamber of Deputies, moreover, Gronchi had gained widespread support among the members of Parliament who, in April 1955, would be called upon to choose the new president of the Republic.

Early in 1954, control of the Liberal party was taken over by a conservative group who felt that the centrist coalition had almost outlived its usefulness. The new secretary general of the party, Giovanni Malagodi, told me: "Whenever a difficult problem came up, Bruno Villabruna, my predecessor at the party's helm, always said: 'Let's hear what Saragat and the Republicans think about it.' " Villabruna had indeed emphasized the issues on which the minor center parties were closest, particularly when it came to a confrontation with their all-too-big CD partner, while soft-pedaling the matters that set them apart, notably economic and social policies. Malagodi did the opposite, in the hope that his party would gain votes among Monarchists and Neo-Fascists as well as among CD right-wingers. The Liberals, he argued, would then be able to persuade and if necessary force Christian Democracy to accept them as the only ally both indispensable and sufficiently strong to put together a working government majority. Such a design was bound to fail, as I told Malagodi time and again. The PLI could hope to expand its following substantially only if it made truly sizable inroads into the CD electorate. If this took place, I added, the CDs would seek to recoup their losses by stepping up the political and electoral competition with the Liberals rather than by accepting an alliance with them (and this duly happened after the 1963 general election). Such a transfer of votes, anyway, would not change the national balance of power since a combination of CDs and Liberals would continue to fall far short of a majority large enough to govern. The "new course" undertaken by Malagodi's PLI could and did only contribute to slow down and eventually paralyze the operation of the Scelba government at a time when the survival of the ruling coalition was threatened by the new rifts that developed among the CDs after the Fanfani faction seized control of the party at the Naples National Congress (June 1954). Fanfani's all-too-obvious ambitions made for increasingly difficult relations with premier Scelba as well as with the minor parties in the governmental coalition, and aroused strong concern and resentments among the CD forces, which were excluded from the party's ruling bodies but retained a significant following within its parliamentary groups. These forces included more or less organized factions and individual politicians of disparate backgrounds and views. They shared a clear-cut hostility to both Scelba's centrist government and to Fanfani's designs. The maneuvers under way in the CD camp puzzled most Italian "experts" in Washington. One of them asked me, "What's the position, today, of people like Guido Gonella and Giulio Andreotti?" "I don't know," I shot back, "but I know that you won't find them wherever Fanfani stands." Gonella and Andreotti (a longtime lieutenant of De Gasperi) were generally identified with the CD right wing, but did not hesitate to play a key role in electing a left-winger like Gronchi to the presidency of the Republic in order to defeat Fanfani's candidate for the job.

Mrs. Luce was shocked when I told her that Gronchi had "at least a 50 percent chance to become Italy's next Chief of State." My arguments did not convince her nor the other U.S. newsmen who attended the lunch she had organized to pick our brains on the eve of the presidential election. Mrs. Luce was so evidently upset by Gronchi's victory that Roman wits hastened to comment on her subsequent illness by saying, "She is suffering from gronchitis." Dispatches from Rome to *The New York Times* and *The Christian Science Monitor* reflected all too clearly the ambassador's worries about the new president's reported inclinations toward neutralism in foreign affairs and "socialistic openings" in domestic politics.

Gronchi himself mentioned these reports and comments during his first meeting with a foreign newsman after his election to the presidency: "This kind of reaction," he told me, "might be understandable from the public abroad but journalists should know better." Gronchi maintained that he had voiced "long before the issue of my election to the presidency came up" his support for the Atlantic Alliance and for Western cooperation and solidarity. "I made this position clear to Mrs. Luce herself back in the Fall of 1953, the only time I had the pleasure of talking with her," Gronchi noted with a smile which was half sour and half ironic. "Anyway," he went on, "no one in Italy today, the Communists excepted, is opposed to our participation in NATO." "Not even Nenni?" "Not even Nenni," Gronchi shot back, "and I hope that I can be credited, at the very least, with being somewhat less of a leftist than Nenni."

On that occasion as on many others, a nationalistic note was clearly perceptible in Gronchi's words. Like other aspects of his concepts and ambitions, this nationalism was marked by a good deal of wishful thinking. But it also reflected some facts of life that were taking shape in Italy. The country had emerged with amazing speed and vigor from the ruins of war and, thanks to her vitality and imagination, appeared able to reduce substantially the gaps that set her apart from the leading Western democracies. The origins and characteristics of the consequent "new found sense of nationalism and self-confidence . . . and aspiration to independence" were the subject of perceptive research carried out in 1955–1956 by Lloyd Free and Renzo Sereno. It was published by the Institute for International Social Research of Princeton under the title, *Italy: Dependent Ally or Independent Partner?* As I pointed out in *Il Mondo* (December 12, 1957), the work showed clearly that the revived "nationalistic feelings" were not a monopoly of more or less isolated individuals like Gronchi or Mattei. Free and Sereno emphasized that the answer to the question mark featured in the title of their book would be provided not only by the Italians themselves but by the Americans' ability "to shift their basic outlook toward Italy from one which has looked to Italians suspiciously like that of the *boss* to that of the *partner*."

"I did criticize De Gasperi's hurry in leading Italy to join the Atlantic Pact," said Gronchi during our conversation. "A decisive factor was De Gasperi's strong feeling that he represented a defeated country. Yet, Italy could have waited for a more favorable time to negotiate our participation in the alliance, possibly getting something in return, say with regard to our former colonies." Anticipating one of the main thrusts of his presidency, Gronchi stressed that Italy was entitled to "a more equal treatment and standing" within the Atlantic Alliance. "In practice, the alliance is run by three countries: the U.S., Great Britain, and France. No one demands or expects that Italy should play a role comparable to the United States, but more consideration could and should be given to a country which has 50 million people and such a geographic and strategic position."

On the eve of the CD National Congress of June 1954, the new president recalled, he had told me that a "more dynamic" approach was urgently needed in domestic affairs. Far-reaching economic and social reforms must be carried out quickly, but he was "more convinced than ever" that they could not be "endorsed, let alone supported, by the Liberal party." No positive contributions could be expected from the Communists, either. Implementation of a purposeful reform program, Gronchi went on, was not only required on grounds of social justice, but would "precipitate a crisis within the PSI. This would pave the way for drawing many Socialists away from the PCI, and for enabling them to play a constructive role in governing the nation."

In the *Washington Post* on May 8, I outlined the circumstances and the maneuvers which had combined to make Gronchi a "natural" choice for the presidency. His election had again "brought into the open the conflicts and rivalries, both within the CD camp and among the center coalition parties, that had been simmering beneath the surface of political stability offered by the Scelba government. At the same time, the motley conglomeration of forces that had backed Gronchi's election could not "provide the foundation for a stable government or consistent policies. . . . The center coalition formula remains the only combination that can count on a narrow but fairly stable democratic majority . . . favoring continued collaboration with the West."

As to Gronchi himself, I pointed out, "attempts at preemption from right and left should not only neutralize each other but make him even more determined to stand off all of them and to steer his own course." I also stressed that "the opinions and intentions attributed to Gronchi in this story" reflected "accurately" his views and actually represented the gist, approved by Gronchi himself, of our recent talk. Gronchi, I wrote, "has certainly shown more inclination than most other CDs to test the real intentions of the Nenni Socialists and their proclaimed willingness to help speed the country on the road to social and economic reforms.

At the same time, his background as a Catholic politician and union organizer, as well as his public statements, bear witness to his conviction that Communism represents a deadly threat to free labor and to the liberties of all citizens. His role in helping to steer the NATO and WEU (Western European Union) treaties through the House, in the face of bitter Red opposition, should be sufficient indication of his stand on basic foreign policy issues.''

In subsequent talks with representatives of the U.S. administration and Congress, I bolstered these assessments and forecasts with additional information drawn from my contacts with the new Italian president and his aides. The result, friends in Washington told me, was to strengthen the arguments and the position of those officials and politicians who felt that Mrs. Luce's reactions to Gronchi's election were ''unwarranted'' and even ''hysterical.'' A few weeks later, Johnny (John W.) Jones, director of the State Department's Office of Western European Affairs and formerly first secretary in the Rome Embassy, made a short visit to Italy. Jones deplored what some U.S. correspondents, notably Arnaldo Cortesi of the *New York Times*, had written about Gronchi's election. Mrs. Luce herself seemed to come around fairly quickly to acknowledging two basic facts: ''With this President we must live and deal for seven years,'' she told me during one of our first meetings after Gronchi's election. The ambassador added that ''perhaps the devil'' was not ''as nasty'' as she herself had figured him to be.

Mrs. Luce made a determined effort to make sure that Gronchi's visit to the United States, a major aspiration of the Italian president, would be arranged fairly soon and produced good results. When the visit took place, less than one year after Gronchi's election, Mrs. Luce stressed that the Italian chief of state had impressed President Eisenhower and Americans in general most favorably. She went so far as to state that the visit had ''put Italo-American relations on higher and more secure foundations than they have ever been.'' This was an obvious exaggeration. However, the statements Gronchi made in the United States, both in public and in private, contributed to further whittling down of the diffidence and the concern which his election had aroused in Washington.

On February 26, 1956, the day before Gronchi's arrival in the U.S. capital, the *Washington Post* ran a long article largely based on an interview and other talks I had with him during the previous week. President Gronchi reaffirmed ''Italy's loyal and active commitment to NATO'' as well as his conviction that ''if Western leaders want to give substance to a genuine Atlantic Community, the decisions of common interest must be discussed by all partners rather than taken . . . by a sort of Directorate of the major NATO powers.'' Gronchi spelled out a concept that conveyed the gist and the spirit of his approach to both international and domestic issues: ''We must stop thinking about what the Communists are doing and start thinking, instead, about what we are *not* doing.'' The West ''should offer the German people concrete evidence that the problem of their country's reunification has really A–1 priority on its agenda. . . . By offering the USSR adequate guarantees that German reunification would not jeopardize Soviet security and asking in return for Moscow's acceptance of truly free elections in a reunified Germany, the Western powers . . . would place the Soviet leaders in a painful dilemma: either see a reunified Germany gravitate inevitably toward the West, or admit before the tribunal of German and World opinion that the true Soviet aim is not security against a rebirth of German militarism but 'sovietization' of both Eastern and Western Germany. Some fresh approach should also be devised to the issue of arms' reduction. The trend toward an 'atomic stalemate' gives conventional weapons back much of their importance and makes more urgent the need to control them.''

Gronchi stressed time and again that Italy was ''able and entitled to make a more active contribution'' to the dynamic policy he advocated for the West. Articles appearing in the U.S. press in the wake of Gronchi's election to the presidency, ''freely described him as favorable to taking the fellow traveling Socialists and perhaps the Communists themselves into the government, as well as to steering Italian foreign policy in the general direction of neutralism. These articles gave the Italian Reds the opportunity to denounce 'arrogant American meddling in Italian domestic affairs' and to point at corroboration of their claim that the new president was indeed favorable to their views and aims. . . . Four weeks ago, Edmund Stevens of *The Christian Science Monitor* . . . quoted Gronchi as favoring, in effect, a Popular Front with the Nenni Socialists, recognition of Red China and its admission to the United Nations, and sharply criticizing U.S. foreign policies as too rigid and narrow. A flat denial was immediately issued by the president's office. Gronchi himself told me that in the conversation, which should have remained confidential anyway, he had merely pointed out that '' 'in the long run it would not be advisable or possible to stick to a wholly negative approach to a nation of 700 million people.' '' But the story was picked up by several other U.S. papers including the magazine *Time*. ''Italian people in general,'' I went on, ''including those who do not share the views attributed to Gronchi, have been deeply disturbed by those polemics on their president especially since they came on the eve of his official visit to Washington.''

In the interview with the *Washington Post*, Gronchi also said that ''the Nenni Socialists need not be invited into the government. But they should be given the opportunity to differentiate themselves from the Communists.'' The Socialist leaders ''must now be put to a real test, . . . by the democratic forces taking bolder, aggressive action to eradicate those economic and social inequities on which Communism thrives. Should the Socialist leaders condition their support to such a policy to a loosening of Italian loyalty to the Western alliance and to democratic institutions, they would stand exposed as more interested in promoting Communist subversion and Soviet domination than in the welfare of Italian workers. But should the test prove successful, it would provide Italy with the broad political foundation necessary to at last launch a full-scale attack upon her chronic problems.

''Unemployment and underemployment are the most urgent of those problems,'' Gronchi stressed. ''Their solution . . . is the key both to domestic stability and to a more active and positive Italian partnership in the Western Community of nations.''

Top level Italian government documents that I have been the first outsider to read provide significant insights into key areas of agreement and disagreement between Gronchi and leading U.S. representatives. During a meeting between the Italian president and Secretary of State John Foster Dulles, which took place in Rome on October 22, 1955, and was attended by Italian foreign minister Gaetano Martino and ambassador Luce, both sides stressed that ''the determination of the Italian government to defend democratic institutions is above any doubt,'' and that ''the relations between Italy and her allies rest on a foundation of absolute loyalty and mutual trust.'' There was also full accord on the need to ''strengthen the organization of the Atlantic Pact by broadening solidarity among its members to the economic, cultural and social fields as provided by art. 2 of the Pact.''

Other ideas and initiatives championed by Gronchi were bound to appear potentially dangerous or at best premature. The Italian president himself pleaded guilty to being ''too far-sighted'' and told me time and again that ''in politics, the worst sin is to be right too soon!''

He advocated the formation of an ''international consortium'' to run aid programs to developing countries which should be set up by the West and open to Soviet participation: ''Look at the Middle East, for instance,'' he told me repeatedly in the late 1950s. ''The Soviets are already there and the consortium might well be a useful tool to control and channel their activities. Should Moscow try to wiggle out, we in the West would be in a position to get full credit for the undertaking and to denounce the Soviet behavior just as it happened when the USSR prevented the Eastern European countries from sharing in the benefits of the Marshall Plan.''

Another pet project of Gronchi's was a plebiscite allowing both East and West Berliners to choose between the status quo and turning the former German capital into a united free city. A reference to such a proposal during Gronchi's visit to Moscow in February 1960 triggered one of Khrushchev's celebrated tantrums. It was the Soviet leader's way to advertise his displeasure over the performance of the Italian president who, contrary to his reported neutralism, was championing Western principles including ''the Berliners' right to choose freely their future.'' On the eve of the visit, Gronchi himself had told me: ''Recent articles in the Soviet press seem to indicate that the leaders of the USSR look at me as a neutralist or a Kerenski. If this is true, they are in for a big disappointment, just as it has been the case with others who, in Italy and abroad, shared such views!''

Gronchi was a steadfast opponent of including Italy in the orbit of a Paris-Bonn axis. Such inclusion, urged by the French government, especially in the late 1950s and early 1960s, would have had ''at least two unacceptable consequences: the Atlantic Alliance would break up and Europe itself would split into two groups,'' the Italian president told me on the morrow of his meeting with de Gaulle in June 1959 (Gronchi's firm stand on the issue was fully shared by other major proponents of a center-left coalition government in Italy, such as Nenni, Fanfani, Saragat, and La Malfa).

Gronchi gave strong support to the policy of cooperation on an equal footing with the oil rich countries of the Third World inaugurated by Enrico Mattei. Mattei's initiatives, in Italy and on the international front, met with bitter aversion in Washington. With the coming to power of a Republican administration, many key posts were entrusted to people close to the big oil corporations. A major case in point was the new under secretary of state, Herbert Hoover, Jr. Traditional ties with powerful private groups and strong hostility to public intervention in economic affairs prompted large sectors of the U.S. media to attack sharply Mattei and the Italian state oil and gas agency, ENI. *Time* and *Fortune* were in the forefront of the attack.

The promoters of these attacks were among the standard-bearers of the most outspoken anti-Communism but provided ammunition for the PCI's claims that "the campaign unleashed by the oil trusts against the government agency is backed by the State Department and represents another shameless interference in Italian domestic affairs," I reported to the *Washington Post* on March 6, 1955: "The Communists' nationalistic cries fall on sensitive ears. The oil debate is having a disturbing effect on wide sections of public opinion, including many of the supporters of the Scelba center coalition government and quite a few of America's best friends in Italy. Many CDs deeply resent attempts by conservative and Neo-Fascist newspapers to smear Mattei as pro-Communist."

Mattei was not pro-Communist any more than he was anti-American. My notes on the many conversations that I had with him from 1949 to 1962, the year of his death in a plane crash, show that Mattei did not turn anti-American even when his battles with the major oil corporations reached their climax and Washington's backing for their stand appeared most determined. Mattei did not mince words in denouncing these corporations' hostility to Italy, which he in- stinctively identified with himself, nor in deploring that it should be often shared by representatives of the U.S. administration. But he also told me, time and again: "I'm not only convinced that Italy and the U.S. must be close friends and allies, but I wish to cooperate with the American oil companies themselves in Italy and elsewhere whenever this can take place on the basis of honorable compromises safeguarding the interests, the independence, and the dignity of my country."

Such statements may be discounted because they were addressed to a U.S. newsman. Mattei was intelligent enough, however, to realize that his best assets were frankness and sincerity, particularly when dealing with the only corre- spondent for a major U.S. daily who at the time tried to understand and convey the "other side of the story"—the facts and arguments that explained how and why Mattei had become involved in battling the big oil corporations and their allies in Italy, and above all why his approach was winning sympathy and support not only among Italian politicians but in wide sectors of Italian public opinion. In most cases, moreover, subsequent developments and timely cross-checking with information from other sources, Italian and American, bore out the truthfulness of his statements, whether they concerned his projects in Egypt, Iran, and other oil rich countries; the circumstances and motivations of his accords for importing Soviet crude in Italy; or his purposes and influence in Italian domestic affairs with special regard to his relations with Gronchi, Nenni, and Fanfani.

"The old cliche about pouring oil on troubled waters was never more appropriate," I wrote in the already quoted article in the *Washington Post*: "The first step, thoughtful Italians agree, is to dispel the poisonous atmosphere of personal and political polemics. Then the issue can be tackled on a more technical plane, where a reasonable compromise should not be impossible. . . . "

By Italian law, all underground resources are the property of the State. In the Po Valley and in other areas, "a law passed in early 1953 . . . gives exclusive oil and gas rights to the government agency ENI. . . . Five years ago in Sicily, the regional government passed special legislation offering generous inducements to attract private investment, both Italian and foreign. In the rest of Italy, mining legislation passed in 1927 remains in force, and that offers no guarantees for private development of successful private explorations. New legislation now pending in Parliament . . . embodies many features of the Sicilian legislation, although less generous to private enterprise, and it quite definitely provides for extending the scope of ENI.

"No one, except the Communists," I concluded, "wants the state monopoly extended to the whole of Italy. Mattei himself and local representatives of the American oil companies told this writer that the main provisions of the bill pending before Parliament are acceptable, although some details could be revised after careful study of comparable foreign legislation."

Mrs. Luce referred favorably to my article (and not only in talking with me). A meeting between the ambassador and Mattei had apparently encouraging results. During a trip to the United States, the president of ENI secured sizable loans from some banks and opened up promising prospects of cooperation with independent oil producers. Even some administration officials came to see him, as one of them told me at the time, as "the only force that can generate some real competition in the Italian economy. The man often talks and acts like a case fit for a psychiatrist, but he is also somewhat of an industrial genius."

But the major international companies (and their Italian partners) apparently concluded that it was no longer worthwhile to enter into large scale commitments in Italy and that an acceptable compromise could not be reached with Mattei, anyway, following enactment of the new legislation granting ENI a privileged position in the mainland regions outside its areas of monopoly in the Po Valley. A tug-of-war developed, moreover, between Mrs. Luce and Henry J. Tasca, director of the U.S. Operations Mission to Italy and minister for economic affairs in the embassy. In private conversations, she accused him of trying to outflank her on the right and he said much the same about her. The practical result was to stiffen U.S. hostility against Mattei.

The latter stepped up his activities abroad after apparently coming to the conclusion that large oil deposits could hardly be located in Italy. He achieved significant successes in Egypt and other Third World countries, including Iran, thanks to an approach keyed to partnership with the local governments. It was a novel development and a direct challenge to the major oil companies that a few years before had haughtily dismissed Mattei's bid for a modest share in their club. Concern and resentment about the "Italian upstart" grew on the part of these companies and their allies in U.S. political circles. Inordinately proud of his successful forays in Iran and elsewhere, Mattei became increasingly unwilling to look equally upon the moves and countermoves of his rivals especially when they in turn proved successful. In Libya, some big U.S. companies, reportedly backed by representatives of the U.S. administration, managed to win exploration rights in a large area that Mattei, benefitting from the good offices of the Italian Foreign Ministry, believed to have secured for ENI. On that occasion, I heard his furious outburst, against those Americans "who seek to thwart me by spreading the word that we Italians cannot be trusted or that we lack the ability and the means to deliver on our commitments." But he was also quick to point at "the new and hopeful prospects" that the Kennedy presidency was opening up for Italy in matters of major domestic and international importance. Shortly before his death, Mattei told me that he was again hopeful not only to reach an amicable settlement of the conflicts with the U.S. oil companies but to develop with them a fruitful cooperation. The kind of agreements he envisaged were similar to those which were actually concluded a few years later by his successors at the helm of ENI.

By the late 1950s, however, the "Mattei issue" had become part of a much broader controversy bearing directly on *political* developments in Italy and on her relations with the United States. It revolved around the prospects and consequences of drawing the Nenni Socialists (or at least most of them) away from the Communists and into a governmental partnership with the CDs and such other parties as the Social Democrats and the Republicans. Out of personal conviction and because of his links with Gronchi, Fanfani, and Nenni, Mattei gave support and financial backing to such an operation, which was anathema to powerful political and journalistic groups in the United States. They dubbed it "opening to the left," a definition that reflected only too clearly their feeling that it was bound to pave the way for a Communist takeover in Italy (and perhaps not in Italy alone). U.S. officials, who held key posts in Washington and in the Rome Embassy, refused to accept the possibility that the operation would take place anyway and could turn out to be an "opening to the West" by the Socialists, notably in foreign affairs, at least as much as an "opening to the left" by the CDs in domestic and notably economic and social affairs.

After my first in-depth conversation with Nenni (May 1953), I pointed out in *The Boston Post* that in the early postwar years the Socialist leader had "managed to turn a very neat trick. In line with the widespread cult of 'working class unity,' he has been the loyal ally and occasionally the willing stooge of the

Communists. Yet, much more widely than Togliatti, he is accepted as an 'Italian' leader and the standard bearer of the homespun traditions of good old pre-Cominform Italian Socialism." As a result, Italy was the only country in free Europe where the majority of the Socialists remained allied with the Communists. At the same time, Nenni enjoyed "personal sympathies and a personal 'sphere of influence' extending way beyond the right-hand boundary of his party." De Gasperi realized that Communist power would suffer a deadly blow and the future of Italian democracy could be best assured "if the large sectors of the working class militating under the Socialist flag could be won over to cooperation with the Center parties; moreover, the prospect of a 'deal' with Nenni helped the premier to keep control of the balance of power against the more conservative groups in the Catholic camp and within his own CD party." The same prospect gave Nenni a modicum of 'autonomy' vis à vis the Communists and powerfully contributes to his own personal prestige. "The latter point is of special importance to Nenni since the Socialist party's machinery is largely controlled by people . . . who are generally considered as 'Togliatti's men.' Here lies the main explanation for Nenni's determined efforts to have his party run its own separate slate of candidates in this election rather than merge with the Communists into an electoral 'People's Bloc' as in 1948."

This was the background, I summed up, of Nenni's current efforts "to capitalize both on the formal 'autonomy' of his party and on the apparent slackening of the cold war" in the wake of Stalin's death. In foreign affairs, he was talking about "a non-aggression pact with the USSR . . . to counterbalance Italy's adherence to the Atlantic Pact which, Nenni hints, may be accepted as an accomplished fact but should be given a strictly 'defensive' interpretation."

In domestic affairs, "Nenni offers to support De Gasperi against resurgent Fascist movements and against pressures from the 'clerical Right.' If necessary, Nenni adds, the PSI may be ready to share again in the government, even without the Communists." Yet the fact remained that if, right after the end of World War II, "Nenni had refrained from underwriting so completely Togliatti's line, he would have kept all of the Italian Socialist forces together and, by cooperating on a footing of equality with De Gasperi's CDs, he could have helped the country move more speedily on the road to economic and social reform."

Most disturbing was Nenni's insistence that the prospects of the Socialists' loosening their ties with the Communists could materialize only if in the impending general election the ruling center coalition failed to win a majority of the votes and therefore full control of Parliament. According to Nenni, a victory of the Center would perpetuate the absolute CD control over the government and favor, at the same time, control of the majority party by its more reactionary groups. "Nenni can legitimately hope," I wrote, "to win back all the votes and the seats that the PSI lost in 1948 to the benefit of the PCI. . . . This, however, may have only long term favorable implications. . . . As Saragat and other Social Democratic leaders have pointed out, Nenni's verbal 'flirtations' with democracy have never jeopardized his basic loyalty to the Communist line. It may well be," I concluded, "that developments on the international scene and/or on the Italian domestic front will shorten the distance; but even so, it would still be up to the Socialist Mohammed to go to the democratic mountain and not the other way around."

Two and one-half years later, I reported in the *Washington Post* (Dec. 25, 1955) that the issue of a collaboration between the democratic forces and the Nenni Socialists had become "the major theme for debate in Italian political circles and especially within the CD Party. . . . The hope that Nenni would eventually break with the Communists and take most of his followers into the democratic camp . . . blossomed as never before in the milder international climate of last summer," which made "Nenni's arguments sound both more appealing and more plausible." From his recent trip to Moscow and Peiping, Nenni "brought back alluring prospects for expanded Italian trade with the Chinese . . . and the first public indication of a softened (Soviet) attitude toward Italy's admission to the U.N. The fact that Nenni, just before leaving and just after his return, was received by foreign minister Martino, premier (Antonio) Segni and President Gronchi, inevitably helped to build him up . . . as 'the Italian Attlee'— the leader of a 'constitutional' and 'loyal' opposition who tomorrow may have a voice in the government."

In domestic affairs "the very ambiguity" of Nenni's latest slogan "Socialist alternative," I further reported, "fits the current Italian situation like a glove. An increasingly large number of people who would never vote Communist are becoming impatient with the performance of the present centrist coalition. Others, while disgusted with the negative results of the Communist approach, lack confidence in the minor center parties and are opposed to an all-Christian-Democratic regime. . . . 'Our ultimate goal,' Nenni says, 'is naturally a Socialist society. We do realize, however, that its establishment in a country like Italy must be a long and gradual historical process. In the meantime, we aim to extract from the present Italian society all the possible down payments in the field of democratic and social progress.

"Quite a few CD politicians would prefer to share power with Nenni rather than with the minor center parties for whom they have little love or respect. Moreover . . . the Nenni Socialists have twice the combined parliamentary strength of the three minor center groups. . . . According to other Christian Democrats, an understanding with the Socialists is the only way to build the broad political foundation for a more dynamic social and economic policy. A center government has too slim a majority and, moreover, depends on the votes of the conservative Liberals. And president Gronchi thinks that 'Operation Nenni' can be pulled off without bargaining away either the defense of Italy's democratic institutions or her loyalty to the Western alliance. . . . There are also many Christian Democrats to whom any rapprochement with Nenni is anathema. Some of them, like other conservatives, appear to oppose it as a threat to economic vested interests rather than to Italian liberties. Others are quite sincere in branding Nenni a Communist Trojan horse. Last but not least, there is the Catholic Church's traditional opposition to alliances with Marxist parties.

"The Communists," I continued, "have been following the activities of their brilliant Socialist ally with growing uneasiness. . . . They have their own men in key positions of the Socialist Party and are said to provide some of the funds for its operation. Also, Communist boss Togliatti has served notice that he would 'go over Nenni's head' if the latter made a deal with the Christian Democrats. But could he really make good on his threat? How long could the Communists afford to vote for a government loyal to democracy and to the Western alliance and bent on speeding up the eradication of those social and economic conditions upon which Communism thrives?"

A few days later I put the question to Nenni himself, who replied: " 'Go over the head' and other similar expressions are just words. What matters are facts, the nature and methods peculiar to each party. The Communists could vote in favor of some bills introduced by a government supported by us. But they could hardly afford to do so for a long time and in each instance; otherwise, they would stop being Communists."

Publication of the full text of Khrushchev's indictment of Stalin, I noted in the *Washington Post* (September 23, 1956), gave Nenni "the opportunity to question openly 'the very structure of the Soviet State' and to proclaim that 'the Italian workers' movement must place itself unreservedly on a plane of democratic and Socialist struggle.' " The nationwide administrative elections of May 27 had shown that sizable sections of the Socialist electorate not only wanted to promote their party's full autonomy from the Communists but favored reunification with the Social Democrats led by Saragat. "The lesson of the polls was not lost on Nenni, or on Saragat, or on the French and British Socialists who had long been seeking reunification of Italian Socialist forces through a break of Nenni's loyalty to the Communist line. Nenni and Saragat met in the French Alpine resort of Pralognan August 25 and agreed to agree. . . . "

"To be sure," I continued, "the official positions of the two parties still look quite distant. Also, Saragat is meeting some resistance from his own rightwingers, skeptical about Nenni's sincerity (while leading left-wing Socialists have criticized Nenni for going too far and too fast and generally oppose any development likely to endanger relations with the Communists)." Powerful economic groups, moreover, feared that a reunified Socialist party would represent "a threat to their vested interests" because it should be able to power "a vigorous drive for social and economic reform. In today's Italy, however, that does not mean state socialism but eradication of still semi-feudal aspects of the country's economic and social structure."

In foreign affairs, Nenni seemed "to be pouring generous dashes of Western water into the Red wine of his original neutralism. 'We are in the West, we live in the West,' he says, accepting on this basis the principle of 'Western solidarity.' He also admits that the United States, called in twice in the last 40 years to help save European liberties, has acquired an 'historic title' to military bases on the Continent. He still rejects, however, what he calls 'all-out Atlantism.' ''

The biggest reservoir of Nenni votes, I added, "is the largely Communist-controlled CGIL (General Confederation of Labor). His followers firmly refuse to quit it, although they are pledged to work for a merger of all unions (Communist, Socialist, and Catholic) into a single organization independent of party controls."

Following the PSI National Congress in Venice, I reported in the *Washington Post* (February 19, 1957): "[Nenni] has crossed the Rubicon heading for democratic territory, but many of his Socialists are still floundering in midstream or have stayed on the Communist side of the river." In his opening speech to the Congress, "Nenni squarely laid responsibility for the Hungarian and Polish events to the Soviet Union and its satellites, and pledged Socialist action to 'spare Italy similar experiments and tragedies.' He formally denounced pacts providing for unity of action and consultation with the Communists. And he called for early reunification with the anti-Communist Social Democrats. . . . Nenni reasserted the traditional Socialist loyalty toward neutralism . . . He accepted the strictly defensive and geographically limited interpretation of the Atlantic Alliance, and endorsed the European integration idea but insisted that it must take place 'outside military blocs.'

"Nenni's speech was enthusiastically received by an overwhelming majority of the Convention. . . . But secret-ballot elections for the new Socialist Central Committee gave Nenni's men only a third of the seats." Nenni's "severe setback" had been engineered by young officials staffing the party apparatus. They feared that "too speedy a reunification with the Social Democrats may wreck the party machine; above all, they balked at surrendering control of the machine to Nenni's men. Yielding on this point, Nenni was able to [win] reappointment as General Secretary, but failed to secure for his followers a clear-cut majority in the party's policy-making bodies."

The outcome of the Congress, I concluded, showed that "to quote Nenni himself, left-wing Socialists need some time yet to digest the new course chartered by their leader. . . . At the same time, the party displayed a remarkable disposition to break all political ties with the Communists and shake free of Moscow's control of foreign policy. . . . Several days later the Socialists took their first step in that direction. During a parliamentary debate on Euratom and the European Common Market, they [abstained] in accordance with the decisions made at the Venice convention. The Communists voted against."

A few months later, "the long simmering crisis within the pro-Western center coalition . . . erupted," I reported in the *Washington Post* (May 7, 1957). The downfall of the Cabinet headed by Premier Antonio Segni "was precipitated by the Social Democratic leader, Giuseppe Saragat. . . . Left-wing Social-Democrats have . . . insisted that their party quit the government to . . . pave the way for Socialist reunification. With the Social Democratic Convention coming next month, Saragat would have risked a split in his party and perhaps have lost control altogether if he insisted both on remaining in the government and opposing any negotiation with the Nenni Socialists.''

The government crisis was long, confused, and marked by ''paradoxical gyrations,'' as I wrote in the *Washington Post* on July 14. The new, all Christian-Democratic government headed by Adone Zoli ''submitted a program intended to win the benevolent abstention of the Socialists and ended up by surviving, thanks to Neo-Fascist votes.''

Under the circumstances, the projects and choices of Christian Democratic secretary general Fanfani took on added significance. Several meetings with him and his closest collaborators provided me with some clear-cut indications: ''Fanfani,'' I told friends during a visit to Washington in April 1958, ''is looking forward to an outcome of the forthcoming general election which would make it advisable and possibly necessary to form a government including his own party, the Social Democrats and the Republicans and intended, more or less openly, to lay the groundwork for collaboration with the Socialists.''

The increase in the Christian Democrat vote, the gains by the PSI, and the failure of the Liberals to make inroads into the right-wing CD electorate, encouraged Fanfani to carry out his plans. ''A government coalition including our party, the Social Democrats, and the Republicans,'' he told me a few days after the returns were in, ''is the only combination which appears both realistic and promising.'' The CD leader made clear that he intended to take over the premiership himself and to ''widen the initially narrow majority of such a government by persuading the Socialists to abstain.'' He stressed, however, that ''things are not ripe yet either within our party or in the Socialist camp.'' One of his top aides added: ''It is the Socialist fleet that must enter into our harbor, but it is up to us to ready the harbor to welcome them.''

3

Interplay between Italian Domestic Politics and Foreign Policy

Recent developments spotlighted "the interplay between domestic and foreign affairs in current Italian politics," I wrote in the *Washington Post* (January 6, 1957). "Since the beginning of the [Suez] crisis, some CD groups (notably those closest to Fanfani) have shown a marked sympathy for Nasser's position. . . . The other CDs, as well as Liberals, Social Democrats and Republicans . . . pointed out that Nasser had violated international agreements and provoked France and Great Britain and especially Israel." After the latest NATO meeting in Paris, "sources close to Fanfani again accused foreign minister Martino, a Liberal, of being in effect 'too pro-European and not enough pro-American' and demanded a 'rethinking' of Italian foreign policy. Martino retorted that Italy must remain solidly anchored to both 'the Atlantic alliance and the solidarity with the European West. . . . ' Centrist groups . . . maintain that the 'rethinking' of Italian foreign policy . . . advocated by Fanfani and his friends would be tantamount to 'turning Italy's back on Europe' and possibly embarking upon a bilateral relationship with the United States—in order to pursue pipe dreams of political prestige and economic expansion in the Mediterranean and Arab world, somewhat along the lines of Franco Spain." These groups, I continued, "fear that the demand for such a 'rethinking' may be part of Fanfani's scheme to 'outflank' the present allies of Christian Democracy on the domestic terrain. The new course advocated by the CD Secretary, they say, can appeal to the pro-Fascist extreme Right (traditionally anti-French and anti-British) over the heads of the Liberals. It also appears less distant from some positions of the Socialist Left than from those occupied by the Saragat Socialists. In any case, they conclude, Fanfani's moves are creating fresh differences in the democratic camp and can only offer the Italian Communists a much-needed opportunity to divert attention from their present plight [over the Soviet repression in Hungary].

Fanfani and his friends reject those charges. In turn, they charge Liberals, Social Democrats, Republicans and many CDs with 'mental laziness.' '' *Il Popolo*, the official daily of the CD party, wrote on December 23, 1956, that, like the United States, ''Italy must dissociate herself from the outdated positions and conceptions still prevailing in other West European countries. Only thus will she be able to actively participate in the new course of U.S. policy and play in the Mediterranean and Arab world a role 'befitting a country of 50 million people.' ''

On March 16, 1957, the vice-president of the United States, Richard M. Nixon, met in Rome with president Gronchi. The meeting was attended by the new U.S. ambassador to Italy, James D. Zellerbach, by Italian premier Segui, and by foreign minister Martino. According to a secret report, revised and approved by Gronchi himself, the Italian chief of state emphasized the importance of ''collaboration among Western nations'' being extended to relations with the emerging countries with special regard to the Middle East. ''In this area,'' Gronchi said, ''it does not seem a good idea for the United States to appear isolated in confronting the Soviet Union. The size itself of America, together with her already big interests in the area (let's just think about oil), can command respect but arouse inevitably diffidence. It would be more effective, therefore, if the United States should present itself in the Middle East together with other nations, notably from Western Europe. . . . France and England right now would not be welcomed by the countries directly interested [in view of their recent intervention in the Suez Canal Zone]. But Italy, one of the U.S. allies which has the greatest interests in the Middle East from a security standpoint as well, could usefully become one of the first nations to make an active contribution.''

Nixon displayed a remarkable disposition to agree, at least verbally, with the main ideas and aspirations outlined by Gronchi: ''I'm particularly happy to note that during the most recent experiences we have seen things 'eye to eye.' '' Nixon continued: ''It would be actually most useful if in the Middle East we could act in closer cooperation with Italy and with other major countries more directly concerned. I do not think that such an important problem should be dealt with anymore by just three powers. . . . You have put your finger on one of the biggest problems, the difficulty for France and England to be welcomed in that part of the world. . . . Gronchi's idea to look right away into the possi-bilities of a collaboration with some European countries is correct and should be explored.''

Gronchi further emphasized that Italy's participation in the ''Working Group'' on German problems would be ''indispensable if that body should become per-manent''; the main purpose, he pointed out, must be ''to avoid the spreading in Italian public opinion of the suspicion that our country gets less consideration than France.'' Here again the vice-president of the United States was generous with acknowledgements and assurances: ''As one of the major European powers, Italy should not only be consulted but take part in every decision involving a European dimension. I'll make a point of calling attention in Washington to what I believe to have been an oversight [Italy's exclusion from the recent meeting of the Working Group in Washington], which should be corrected."

Encouraged by his talk with Nixon, Gronchi completed and signed the next day a personal letter to President Eisenhower that had been in the works for some time (the Italian president referred to it during a meeting with Mrs. Luce on November 13, 1956). Some excerpts of the letter were quoted for the first time in an interview that Gronchi gave me in November 1971 for the Italian weekly, *Oggi*. I was also the first outsider to gain knowledge of the text of the letters exchanged between Gronchi, Segni, and Martino.

The main passages of Gronchi's letter to Eisenhower read as follows:

Dear Mr. President,
Recent events in the Mediterranean have dealt a rather serious shock to Italian public opinion. The fact that France and England should have resorted to force has left a large number of Italians dubious as regards both the value in an emergency and the inherent efficiency of the Atlantic alliance. . . . There is agreement in estimating that Italy should receive from her allies the consideration she feels she is entitled to as a result of the responsibilities she has to meet in complying with the obligations placed upon her by the Treaty.

Two further events have afforded consistency to this state of mind: the "Eisenhower doctrine" and the "Working Group" convened in connection with the problems of Germany.

(1) *The Eisenhower doctrine.* The action undertaken by the United States [for the defense of the Middle East] is considered most timely, for it stands as a firm warning to Russia in an area where so many French and English positions have been weakened or lost. . . .

Italians are also well aware that such action was taken in an emergency and that any previous consultation with America's Atlantic allies would have proved indeed difficult, particularly subsequent to the course followed by England and France. It is felt here, however, that in our mutual interest the individual action of the United States should now find completion in a closer measure of collaboration. . . . This could well be achieved through consultations aimed at constantly establishing the highest possible measure of common agreement between America and her Western allies. . . .

Support in the economic rather than the military field may well prove the more important factor in a gradual process of safeguarding the countries of the Near and Middle East from Soviet Russia. At the same time it would seem clear that those countries would more willingly receive support from a combined American and European source than from the United States alone. . . . One may indeed be fond [of] a giant, but one is all too often inclined to be rather frightened of him, too. And some who behold your oil interests in the East may construe, however unfoundedly, that it is monopolies that are now being sought.

. . . The problem is of course rendered more difficult by the impossibility for such countries as England and France to join at present in a collaboration of this kind. But a useful beginning could be made with some other European countries. . . . Italy feels she can validly claim to enter upon such a collaboration, enjoying as she does wide sympathies both among the Arabs and with Israel. . . .

Public opinion is aware of the special situation created here by the presence of NATO bases. To safeguard freedom and peace by far the greater number of Italians are willing and ready to face any sacrifice and risk which the Alliance should require of them. At the same time . . . they deem it a right they cannot relinquish to their allies that they should not be faced with situations which they have not been called upon to discuss in proper time and to determine freely in the frame of their Constitution.

People here readily understood the reasons which prompted the Secretary of State's recent words in Paris, when he declared that the United States could not engage indiscriminately upon prior consultations with their Atlantic allies because of the complexity of America's world-wide interests and of the varying policies required in the pursuit of these over widely distant areas.

But it is felt here that Mr. Dulles's statement could hardly be accepted if referred to any section of the Mediterranean, because some NATO countries, and Italy in particular, are interested in the whole area covered by this sea, even where territories technically outside the Alliance are concerned. . . . Italian interests here are not merely economic but bear directly on the country's security.

(2) *Working Group*. It now appears clear that this is an organization which may well prove to become permanent as designed to promote mutual and continuous consultations among the four countries. . . . The problems of German unity, and indeed all problems connected with relations between Germany and the other countries of this Continent, are undoubtedly overall *European* problems. . . . It is not, therefore, considered sufficient here that we should be kept informed of discussions in the "Working Group." Italy, it is felt, should take part in these directly and be afforded the opportunity of jointly confronting problems, freely and at the right time and before agreements or decisions be arrived at as between the remaining members of the Group. . . .

The above remarks are of course in no way suggested by any feeling of mistrust whatsoever. . . . Rather, they are prompted by the conviction that treaties acquire a deeper value when they cease to be instruments negotiated between Governments, and become agreements which reflect the feelings and outlook of public opinion in the countries they bind. . . .

I have termed these remarks "personal" because, as you know, responsibility for the pursuance of my country's policies rests with the Government. But I cannot but feel I am under a moral obligation of acquainting you with some of the chief trends of opinion among Italians as a whole, as deduced by me from continued close observation.

The Italian Foreign Ministry "held up" the president's letter instead of forwarding it to Eisenhower. This decision was apparently taken by the Ministry's secretary general, ambassador Rossi Longhi, and endorsed both by foreign minister Martino and by premier Segni. The president of the Republic wrote to Segni and Martino complaining that his confidential letter "to another Chief of State" had been held up without even notifying him. Martino and Segni sought to pacify Gronchi on this point, but maintained that the premier and the foreign minister were "responsible for the political initiatives and pronouncements of the Chief of State" and that "the message addressed to the President of the United States had not been agreed upon with the Government nor submitted to its approval." A long memorandum signed by Segni but obviously prepared by ranking Foreign Ministry officials recommended many changes in Gronchi's letter which in effect would have emasculated it. The memorandum, moreover, rejected flatly the "extension of the commitments stemming from the Atlantic alliance and from the WEU (Western European Union)," which, according to the Foreign Ministry, were implicit in Gronchi's suggestions of an Italian role in implementing an aid program in the Middle East as well as in the "working group" on German problems.

Eventually, Gronchi yielded, however, unwillingly, and his letter was not forwarded to Eisenhower. The *New York Times* correspondent in Rome, Arnaldo Cortesi, reported on April 12 that Gronchi's letter was sharply critical of some aspects of U.S. foreign policy including the "Eisenhower doctrine" and recent statements by Secretary Dulles, and supported the setting up of a neutral zone extending across Europe from north to south. According to Cortesi, Gronchi had always been lukewarm toward the policy of close friendship with the United States and far from enthusiastic about current efforts to create a united Europe.

It is hard to say how far Cortesi's dispatch reflected information originating with Italian sources obviously acquainted with and hostile to the views conveyed in Gronchi's letter and how far it should be attributed to Cortesi's own opinions or possibly to his imperfect understanding of facts and circumstances. Unquestionably, the spirit and specific parts of the letter were reported and interpreted in such a way as to provide a distorted picture of the Italian president's views and to credit the charges of neutralism and intrusiveness leveled against him by some political circles in Rome.

On the eve of his departure for Washington, Premier Fanfani, who had taken over the Foreign Ministry as well, gave me an interview (*Washington Post*, July 27, 1958). "Today, as yesterday," Fanfani said, "the guiding star of Italian foreign policy is the fullest and most effective Atlantic solidarity. . . . Such a solidarity does not rule out and in fact demands the frankest exchange of views within the alliance which will be all the more efficient as each of its members is both more capable and enabled to make its own positive contribution to the common policy with due regard, of course, to its strength, geographic position and specific interests in the problems under consideration.

"In the Middle East, today's most pressingly important theater, Italy occupies a frontline position in the Western alignment just behind those Middle East outposts which are today being subjected to the heaviest and most direct Soviet pressure. At the same time Italy has no colonies (this is one of the historical circumstances that bring our political position closest to that of the United States and of Western Germany) and therefore is in a better position to show interest in the national aspirations of other people without arousing distrust or suspicion. Furthermore, the Middle East and the Mediterranean basin are among the areas that lend themselves most naturally to the development of Italian trade relations."

To a question about the oil deal just brought off in Morocco by the Italian state agency ENI, Fanfani replied that "the issue of Italian oil enterprises in the Middle East and in Africa, like any other issue related to our sharing in the economic development of the underdeveloped countries, can always be examined in a spirit of friendly cooperation. The need to coordinate the undertakings of the allied countries in this field appears especially urgent today since oil is now over and above its obvious industrial importance a key factor of security for all the free people.''

Speaking off the record, Fanfani added: "Any attempt to achieve a political solution, intended to bring stability to the Middle East and to the Southern shores of the Mediterranean, must take realistically into account the presence and the strength of Arab nationalism as well as the danger of turning it into a tool of the Soviet policy of expansion and subversion. Contrary to the opinion of many Italians, I've always felt that the U.S. policy toward Tito's Yugoslavia has served well the West because it has helped the swing to neutralism of a country which belonged to the opposite camp. When it comes to Nasser, the West must be likewise realistic enough to admit that if an ally is better than a neutral, a sincere neutral is better than an adversary.'' Fanfani also recalled that, during his trip to America in the summer of 1956, Washington's political circles had "unfortunately" dismissed his suggestion that the United States act promptly to promote an agreement in the Middle East to forestall a French and British armed intervention against Nasser's Egypt. More recently, he had come to believe that the U.S. administration had realized the need to take upon itself "a primary responsibility" in the Middle East: "the area has become truly vital for the West which must now be defended on the Nile as much as if not even more than in Berlin.''

According to Italian secret documents, the Middle East was frequently discussed by president Gronchi and ambassador Zellerbach. On October 10, 1957, the ambassador stated that the U.S. administration fully recognized the importance of an Italian contribution to restoring "a healthy situation in the Middle East.'' Zellerbach went on to say that he had discussed with foreign minister Pella "the possibility of developing a joint economic program in the Middle East" and added: "Secretary of State Dulles has suggested that Pella develop such ideas and talk them over with me in the hope of actually drafting such a program.'' When Gronchi mentioned the oil issue, Zellerbach said: "I have ascertained that an Italian entrance into this field of competition does not meet with objections not only from my government but from several of the big corporations themselves.'' The Italian president replied: "I can take fully into account what you're telling me, but I must add that quite often the actions of your oil concerns are backed by American diplomatic representatives. We feel that the behavior of these corporations does a great disservice to the United States. Just when the British and French 'imperalism' has come to an end in this sector, the 'imperalism' of the North American corporations is getting under way.'' Gronchi said that he was quoting "opinions voiced in friendly Arab countries like Iraq," and added: "a frank discussion of the issue between our two governments is advisable. . . . Personally, I feel that, if the Americans should ask us to set a good example by allowing more room to private initiative, foreign or national, especially in the Po Valley, we might even consider a revision of the legislation on the books, provided we are given a different treatment outside Italy.''

In a speech titled, ''Italy's Place in the Atlantic Alliance,'' delivered in San Francisco on November 19, 1958, Zellerbach said: ''Italy is committed politically to the West and economically to the Community of Europe. . . . Both in the West and in the world, Italy intends [now] to play a more active role.'' In the Italian view, Zellerbach went on, quoting recent statements by Gronchi and Fanfani, such a role could not and should not develop only in Europe but with regard to Latin America and ''above all'' in the Mediterranean and in the Middle East. ''I am thus in agreement,'' the ambassador stated, ''with those who feel that we need to be aware that a change is taking place in Italy. I am not in agreement, however, with the gloomy view some take of the nature of the change. In my opinion, Italy's new confidence in foreign affairs clearly means more strength, not less for the Atlantic alliance. . . .

''In her relations with the United States and other nations of the West, Italy is vigorously determined to be consulted on all matters in which she considers she has an interest. Now consultation is a difficult and time-consuming process which cannot be reduced to a routine formula. . . . Mr. Fanfani is right, however, in his insistence that it is the lifeblood of the Alliance. . . . Italy's friendly advice is well worth listening to. If she feels able today to offer it on a wider variety of issues, we are the gainers thereby. . . .

''It may be argued,'' the ambassador added, ''that although Italy's commitment to the West remains complete it is becoming only one of several principles which guide Italian policy. This opinion completely mistakes the nature of the Atlantic Alliance. . . . Had a total identity of foreign policies been a prerequisite, I doubt that the alliance would ever have been formed. I am sure it would not have survived Suez or any of half a dozen other matters on which its members have not seen eye to eye. NATO is on the contrary made up of countries of diverse interests and traditions, which are united in the defense of the most important interests of all—peace, justice, and freedom. Diversity is NATO's greatest asset. To the common council each member brings an independent contribution of viewpoint, experience, and strength.''

Looking ahead, Zellerbach continued: ''While it is unlikely, it is not inconceivable that in the unforeseeable future some aspect of American and Italian foreign policies may fail to coincide. . . . The possibility, however, should not be cause for alarm. Italians have the good sense and good will to recognize that American foreign policy has to deal with a vast variety of questions in a complicated world. They rely on their policy to serve the causes of peace and order. Italy has given the United States her friendship and confidence. I think we have every reason to accord Italy's policy an equal trust.'' The ambassador concluded: ''Today, Italy is determined to bring her full measure of strength to the solution of a broader range of the Free World's problems. . . . We should welcome her readiness.''

Zellerbach carefully confined his public remarks about the ongoing changes and rising expectations in Italy to their significance with regard to foreign affairs. But these changes and expectations were obviously bound to have an impact on political developments in Italy herself. In turn, the country's course in international affairs would be affected to the extent dictated by the traditionally close interaction between Italian domestic politics and foreign policy.

Two broad alignments took shape and confronted each other. According to one of them, implementation of a far-reaching program of "reform and progress" was required to strengthen the foundations of Italian democracy as well as to help the country to pursue a more dynamic international role which would respond to her burgeoning aspirations as well as to a far-sighted concept of Western solidarity. According to the other side, far-reaching reforms of Italy's social and economic structures would be dangerous not only by themselves but because their implementation would help the coming to power of leftist forces committed to leading the nation down the path to neutralism and possibly all the way into the Soviet camp.

Several officials of the State Department's Office of Intelligence and Research (OIR) made up one of the early components of the first alignment. This office pointed at prospects and made suggestions which often proved to be more far-sighted and realistic than the views and assessments of other sectors of the department, notably the country and regional desks which must generally concentrate on matters of more immediate relevance. Similar divergencies emerged gradually within other departments and agencies interested in Italian affairs.

Labor leaders close to Walter Reuther, president of the United Automobile Workers, felt that Nenni and other Socialists deserved sympathy and support because of their sincere efforts to make the PSI wholly independent from Italian and international Communism and able to help give Italy a democratic and progressive-minded government. I remember several long talks with Walter Reuther's brother, Victor, who was in charge of the UAW's international relations department, and with Augusto Bellanca, an Italian-American who had a leading role in one of the largest clothing workers' unions. Bellanca was an old and close friend of Nenni's. Sympathizers included notably Daniel L. Horowitz, an expert on the Italian union movement who was Labor attaché in Latin America, U.S. representative at the U.N. International Labor Office, and later on U.S. consul general in Naples; and John T. Dunlop, professor at Howard and a top expert on labor relations, who was secretary of labor in 1973–1974. For a long time, however, hostility to any "opening" to the PSI prevailed in the U.S. labor movement because of the stand taken by AFL–CIO president, George Meany, by his adviser on international affairs, Jay Lovestone, and by their representatives in Europe and in Italy, Irving Brown and Harry Goldberg. Union officials of Italian origin who had played a significant role in the Socialist split of 1947 were at best lukewarm toward the Nenni Socialists; such was notably the case of Luigi Antonini and later on of Vanni Montana. In the mid–1950s only some congressmen of Italian origin (Emilio Daddario and Victor Anfuso) were aware of the crisis of the Center coalition and of the opportunities offered by the evolution among the Italian Socialists.

Such awareness could be stimulated and enlarged only by a day-in day-out effort to develop, both in Italy and in the United States, a steady flow of information and personal contacts. An exceptionally intelligent and useful work was performed by Victor Sullam, one of the Italians who were compelled to emigrate by the anti-Semitic campaign of the Fascist regime and who in due course became U.S. citizens. Sullam held several governmental posts mostly related to the programs of economic aid to Italy. He also lectured at the School for Advanced International Studies of the Johns Hopkins University. Sullam and I were in constant communication until his untimely death in 1972. He introduced me to several State Department officers, notably Tom Fina and John Di Sciullo of the OIR, and to CIA officials operating on the overt side of the agency such as Joe Zaring, his wife Dorothy Jane and Dana Durand. Through Sullam I also met Roger Hilsman, chief of the foreign affairs division of the Library of Congress, who later became director of OIR and Government professor at Columbia University, and James King of the Institute for Defense Analysis. Sullam introduced King and other friends in Washington to Fabio Luca Cavazza and other leaders of the research and publishing group *Il Mulino* of Bologna, which at the time was promoting a working collaboration between progressive-minded Catholics and secular forces in Italy and seeking grants from U.S. Foundations for its program of political and social studies. I had the opportunity to introduce Sullam and other friends interested in Italian affairs to leading representatives of U.S. political and academic circles, notably Arthur Schlesinger Jr., who was to become a ranking adviser of President Kennedy. When I met him in June 1957, Schlesinger already felt that U.S. policies toward Italy required a thorough updating. In subsequent years, he became more and more convinced that the United States would greatly benefit, directly and indirectly, from the coming to power in Italy of a coalition based on collaboration between Christian Democrats and Socialists.

However, many key posts, notably in the State Department, continued to be held or controlled by officers whose ideas about Italy and contacts in Italy had crystallized in the early postwar years. They looked to the right rather than to the left when the shortcomings of the center governments became all too evident. Foremost among them was Outerbridge Horsey, a tough, hard-working career officer, who served in the Rome Embassy from 1948 to 1952, was again assigned to Rome as deputy chief of mission in 1959, and retained the post until the fall of 1962. As Schlesinger recalls in his book on the Kennedy presidency (*A Thousand Days*, Riverside Press, Cambridge, 1954, p. 416), Horsey was largely responsible for the "prolongation" of the "obsolete" policy of "unrelenting American opposition to the center-left coalition in Italy." Horsey carried out a no-holds-barred campaign to "select out" of the Foreign Service a young officer, George Lister, who had dared to contradict him and tried to carry his case to the ambassador. Assigned by the embassy to follow developments in the Italian

Socialist camp, Lister had become convinced that a PSI participation in the government was both inevitable and in the U.S. interest. A last-minute intervention by the White House saved him from being kicked out of the Foreign Service. Not even the backing of people like Averell Harriman, however, could prevent Lister's career from being negatively affected by his having been "right too soon" on an issue that pitted him against a higher-ranking official like Horsey. "If you refrain from coming out for an approach that is new and therefore at least potentially controversial," several other officers told me over the years, "you run no risks. But if you stick your neck out, there will be always somebody who will hold it against you even though in the meantime facts have proved you right." Only too often, moreover, conservative-minded groups in the Foreign Service and in other departments and agencies resorted to such slogans as "continuity" and "non-interference in other countries' affairs" in order to give support to the forces committed to the *status quo* in Italy.

These forces included powerful economic groups as well as representatives of the Liberal party and the CD right wing whose opposition to Gronchi and Fanfani was rooted in domestic even more than in foreign policy grounds. They also included top officials of the Italian foreign Ministry who played a key role in blocking Gronchi's letter to Eisenhower but were moved out or set aside to the benefit of younger officers after Fanfani became premier and foreign minister.

It was an open secret in Rome that those officials and their friends had largely inspired the columns by Cyrus L. Sulzberger that appeared in the *New York Times* in the late fall of 1958. According to Sulzberger, a "purge" of NATO's friends in the Italian Foreign Ministry had been carried out by younger officials belonging to the CD left wing and known as the "Mau-Mau" (a nickname made notorious by African rebels in Kenya) because their last names began with the letter "M". Sulzberger also asserted that Gronchi, widely known for his leftish and neutralist bent, favored an alliance between the Christian Democrats and the Socialists led by Nenni, "an adversary of NATO." According to Sulzberger, Fanfani, too, seemed ready to loosen Italy's ties with NATO and to flirt with neutralists like Nasser. Mattei, the main backer and financial angel of Fanfani's CD left wing, advocated friendly relations with the Arabs for the sake of their oil deposits. Ambassador Zellerbach's speech in San Francisco, Sulzberger further alleged, had been widely read in Italy as underwriting the new neutralist-minded course of Italian foreign policy. If approved by Secretary Dulles, the speech would signal an actual U.S. inclination to commit suicide.

Sulzberger's columns were prominently quoted by the right-wing Italian press, while Communist papers charged once again that Italian foreign policy was "subservient" to the United States. The Italian ambassador to Washington, Manlio Brosio, was a steadfast supporter of NATO and could hardly be suspected of harboring sympathies for "openings to the left" or for Gronchi or Fanfani. But he sent a letter to the *New York Times* denouncing several of Sulzberger's allegations as unfounded and bound to arouse doubts about Italy's loyalty to the Atlantic Alliance and to weaken rather than strengthen the alliance. At a news conference, Dulles himself stated that the United States was looking with favor upon Italy's policy of closer relations with Arab countries. Nothing in NATO, the Secretary of State added, prevented a member from seeking to establish closer relations with countries in other areas: indeed the United States, while a firm member of NATO, had sought to build closer relations with countries in areas outside the North Atlantic region (November 26). Two weeks later, the *New York Times* itself ran an editorial which in effect refuted the substance of Sulzberger's columns, although it avoided direct reference to them (how could the paper disown openly a member of its owners' family?). The editorial praised the Italian role in NATO adding that it was perfectly possible for a Mediterranean country like Italy to pursue a policy of friendship toward the Arab world while continuing to cooperate with her partners in the Atlantic Alliance. The doubts voiced recently about Italy's loyalty to NATO, the editorial pointed out, could be traced back, in part, to the political opposition to Premier Fanfani, notably from the right wing of his own party.

In effect, many of the economic and social planks of Fanfani's "New Dealish" program "alarmed powerful economic vested interests as well as conservative groups," I reported in *Collier's Yearbook* (1958 and 1959). This was notably the case when the government tried to check the rise in the cost of living by breaking "the monopoly of entrenched groups of municipal food markets operators and other middlemen. . . . Time and again, several CD representatives in Parliament, while supporting Fanfani on roll calls, helped to defeat government-sponsored measures on secret ballots. These same conservative groups and interests sparked the charges, widely echoed at home and abroad, that Fanfani, in order to gain Socialist support for his shaky domestic position and for his plans for a more active foreign policy, was ready to embark upon a neutralist-minded course. "Actually," I further reported, "Fanfani's government placed Italian airfields at the disposal of American forces moving into Turkey and Lebanon during the 1958 crisis that followed the revolution in Iraq; it also made a Sicilian base available to the U.S. Sixth Fleet and agreed to the setting up of IRBM launching sites (for Jupiter missiles) on Italian territory. . . . Even Fanfani's visit to Cairo, which finally took place in January 1959 and represented perhaps the most controversial aspect of the Italian 'new course,' was thoroughly discussed beforehand with Italy's major allies."

Meanwhile, however, the Fanfani government's position and prestige had been sapped by the maneuvers of CD "snipers" in Parliament and by the more overt actions of such prominent party representatives as former premier Scelba and former premier and foreign minister Pella. Hostility to Fanfani was further fueled by his insistence on keeping both the premiership and the party secretary-ship as well as by his rather authoritarian temper and the high-handed methods of some of his lieutenants. In November 1958, dissident CDs joined with the extreme left and the extreme right to defeat the party's official candidate for the presidency of the regional government in Sicily and to elect one of their own group, Silvio Milazzo.

Fanfani, on his side, clung to power under circumstances that prevented his government from carrying out any substantial part of its program and thus from gaining any additional support.

Nenni himself told me during the National Convention of his party, held in Naples at the end of January: "It would be not only politically unworkable but useless for us to try to salvage a government which is on the brink of collapse because of the contradictions within its majority and of its consequent inability to implement even the limited economic and social measures it had pledged to carry out."

These domestic developments, reflecting largely the infighting within the CD camp, brought about Fanfani's twin downfall as premier and party leader. Early in March, I met a still embittered Fanfani who listed angrily names and mistakes of all those he blamed for his misfortunes. Key members of the CD majority had "betrayed" him after years of "working together to gain control of the party and then rebuild it." Gronchi had failed to give Fanfani more effective support "against our common enemies," while Nenni had not realized "the urgent need to sustain a government committed to preparing the ground for Socialist participation in the ruling coalition."

Segni and Pella, who had again taken over the premiership and the foreign ministry, seemed now ready to endorse ideas and aspirations similar to those propounded by Gronchi and by Fanfani himself. Significant and persistent differences concerned Segni's and Pella's reluctance to Italy's playing the role of "a bridge" between the West and the Arab world and their inclination to support or at least go along with the policies of Gaullist France. Such was the gist of the information I gathered from private talks and interviews with Segni and Pella before their visit to the United States at the end of September 1959. Much the same picture emerged from their meetings in Washington, as well as earlier in Paris, with President Eisenhower and the new Secretary of State, Christian Herter.

According to secret Italian documents, Segni emphasized Italy's "primary interest" in participating in the East-West Summit which was scheduled for the spring of 1960 (and was cancelled by Khrushchev after a U.S. U–2 was shot down over Soviet territory). The premier mentioned his country's "first-line position in the defense of freedom in Europe," and "4 percent increase of Italian military appropriations over the next five years," the deployment on Italian soil of medium-range U.S. missiles, the size of the Italian population, "greater than France's, equal to Britain's, and second in Europe only to Germany's," and Italy's "special geographic position in direct contact with East European countries, a few tens of miles from Soviet bases in Albania, as well as between the West and the African and Middle East countries. . . . Our nation's position as an exposed outpost," Segni concluded, "has been confirmed by the threats that the Soviets have made openly against us."

Eisenhower agreed that "Italy is fully and unquestionably entitled to be heard on matters relating to disarmament and security." The negotiations under way with the Soviet Union, however, concerned the Berlin question and more broadly the issues left open by the war and in this connection "the victorious Powers have special responsibilities and special rights." Segni replied that the forth-coming conference would deal with problems of major importance for Italy, first of all the issue of German reunification: "Should Italy's allies show that she was considered a minor partner, they would hand the Communists a very effective weapon." Eisenhower said that he was fully convinced of the importance that "a solidly democratic Italy has for the whole West." Right now, however, the issue on the table was Berlin. Segni apparently decided to make the best of it and thanked the U.S. president "for the assurance that Italy will not be kept out in the event that the conference should extend to problems other than Berlin."

Segni also asked Eisenhower whether de Gaulle had again brought up the issue of a "Directorate" within the Western alliance. Eisenhower replied that the issue "is not only asleep (as Segni had said) but very, very sick." The U.S. president stated "emphatically" that he would never "take part in a restricted group pretending to rule the world." Should there be problems in Africa or in Asia that would be of special interest to a certain group of allied or friendly nations, Eisenhower went on, he would be glad to discuss them with "three, four or more of these nations." Segni hastened to say that he was fully satisfied and most grateful for "the firm stand" taken by the U.S. president.

Foreign minister Pella reaffirmed Italy's readiness to participate in a multi-national undertaking to organize, under the overall guidance of the United States, a large-scale program of economic aid to underdeveloped countries.

He also mentioned in cautious terms Gronchi's idea to invite the Soviet Union to join in the undertaking. But Eisenhower ruled out "flatly" any such invitation which was bound to prove "unrealistic" as long as a "climate of political trust has not been created between East and West." The American president shared, at least in part, another view propounded by Gronchi: "While Great Britain, France and Belgium," Eisenhower said, "have special responsibilities in some territories where they should concentrate their efforts, the U.S., Germany and Italy have more freedom of action."

When Eisenhower visited Rome and met with Gronchi, Segni, and Pella, I reported in the *Washington Post* (December 8), "According to high Italian sources, the major fruit [of the meetings] has been 'distinct progress' toward a bigger Italian contribution to a Western alliance made more efficient and updated to face both the opportunities and problems connected with the thaw in the cold war. . . . The Italians hope to gain a greater voice in Allied councils now that President Eisenhower has specifically confirmed American sympathy for their aspirations. As government circles here emphasize, disarmament—like European security and unlike Berlin and a German settlement—is one of the broad issues which were not contemplated in the Potsdam agreements and therefore cannot be considered as the specific province of the Big Four. It may be added that Italy has no Algerias or Berlins of her own. Accordingly, she appears in Italian eyes particularly fitted to perform as 'a factor of equilibrium' in furthering a united Western approach to the problems of East-West negotiations and of aid to underdeveloped countries.''

Official Italian documents that I was able to read several years later, bear out this report and provide further information on the topics discussed during Eisenhower's visit to Rome.

The U.S. President stated that Italy, as a member of the special Ten-Power Committee on Disarmament, was entitled to have her say on the problems of European security which in turn were linked with other aspects of the forthcoming East-West summit. ''Even though Italy is not a signatory of the Potsdam accords,'' Eisenhower went on, ''she has just as great an interest as the others in peace and stability in Europe. . . . Italy is our candidate'' to take part in any Allied talks which should extend beyond the special case represented by Berlin. Eisenhower further pledged that the United States would help to overcome the well-known French dislike for Italian participation. Gronchi's idea to explore ways and means for turning the whole of Berlin into a free city was thoroughly discussed. The U.S. President said that he would like to ''put Khrushchev on the spot'' with a proposal acceptable to ''the Germans, the West Berliners and all of us.'' He pointed out, at the same time, that on the basis of past experience, notably of his own talks with Khrushchev at Camp David, it would be hard, if not impossible, to secure ''adequate guarantees'' for Berlin as a free city. Gronchi stated that his impending visit to the Soviet Union would provide an opportunity to ''explore in depth Khrushchev's real thinking'' on Berlin and other matters. The Italian president added that ''the only purpose'' of his visit to Moscow was to discuss such issues with the Soviet leader and to inform ''our allies'' of these discussions.

Gronchi had been obviously told that Eisenhower strongly opposed any form of ''institutionalized'' collaboration with the Soviet Union in providing aid to developing countries. The Italian president suggested a more flexible approach which would make use of existing organizations, ''for instance, the OEEC (Organization for European Economic Cooperation). . . . The issue of Soviet participation could be resolved with the required caution: the USSR would not be invited to join the OEEC but the problem should be examined on a case-by-case basis with special regard to countries and areas where Russia has already penetrated and therefore a competition with it is already in effect. In these cases the usefulness of associating the Soviet Union is obvious, also as a means to control its actions, at least in part.'' Eisenhower replied: ''I like the suggestion about the OEEC but I would like to have Japan too as an associate'' (in the aid program to developing nations).

Both Gronchi and Segni stressed that ''Italy must insure the defense not only of her Northern and Eastern land frontiers but of the Adriatic coasts threatened by the Soviet military preparations in Albania.'' Gronchi did not refer to the possibility that attacks, or threats of attack, by the Soviets be coordinated with ''subversive actions'' organized by the Italian Communists. In his opinion, this was essentially a matter of Italian domestic politics. Yet, he was fully aware that the problem existed and referred to it in a conversation we had right after Eisenhower's visit to Rome and on several other occasions. The Italian president told Eisenhower that "despite the recent four percent increase in our military budget, we have not even managed to reach 100 percent readiness status for the nine Divisions earmarked for NATO. In the event of war, the Italian military command would be confronted with a hard choice: move to northern Italy the few organized units currently located in other parts of the country, which would be left defenseless, or be unable to protect effectively the Po Valley, thus jeopardizing the whole defense of the European West, since France would be compelled to fight not only on the Rhine but on the Alps as well."

Gronchi and Segni asked for additional U.S. aid to strengthen Italy's conventional armaments. They agreed, at the same time, to complete quickly the deployment of the U.S. Jupiter missiles, although this could be "expected to raise domestic problems" as Segni put it. Eisenhower noted that "the deployment of the missiles has changed Italy's situation because it is now possible to strike from her territory both for defense and retaliation." He stressed that the United States had already undertaken heavy financial commitments at home and abroad, but promised that Italy could continue to rely "on the friendly collaboration of the United States for the necessary strengthening of her military forces."

4

Moro Speaks Up on Italy's Future

On the day following Eisenhower's visit to Italy, the *New York Herald Tribune*'s Rome correspondent Barrett McGurn wrote that Italy's determination to continue to play an active role in NATO might be undermined because traditionally pro-Western groups were seeking, for considerations of domestic politics, an accord with Nenni. The latter had criticized Stalinism and the Soviet behavior in Hungary but had not dropped his requests for the withdrawal of U.S. forces from Europe and for a neutralist Italian position (December 8). A few months later, *The Reporter* carried an analysis by Claire Sterling under the headline: "A dead end in Italy's politics" (June 9, 1960). The long dominant Christian Democrats had "become incapable of making any decision," Sterling wrote. Recent attempts to move toward a deal with Nenni had "almost wrecked the party" and the CDs "fell back on the solution they dislike most: a government wholly dependent on the Neo-Fascists in parliament." On his side, Togliatti had "made it plain that . . . any solution favored by Nenni will get the Communists' votes 'requested or not, welcome or not.' " What loomed ahead, Sterling concluded, was "at best . . . a numerically weakened [CD] party, far more in need of Nenni than it is now. At worst, the prospects would be first a right-wing Sacred Union and in the end, almost fatally, a Popular Front."

As late as the spring of 1961, when CDs and Nenni Socialists were clearly heading toward governmental collaboration, Cortesi claimed that the outcome of the PSI convention in Milan had represented such a severe blow for Nenni's prestige that he might soon be replaced as party leader, a development making it much more unlikely that Socialists would move into "the center area" (*New York Times*, April 1, 1961). As I had already pointed out in the *Washington Post* (March 26), "the most significant and novel feature of the Socialist position," as it had emerged from the Milan convention, was (instead) adoption of "the platform drafted by Nenni which calls on the party to turn its back more firmly on its former Communist allies and to move toward collaboration with the pro-Western Christian Democrats." To be sure, "the pro-Communist wing [of the PSI], which can rely on all-out financial and organizational support from the Communists while the 'autonomists' continue to be hard up for money, has managed to reduce the margin of Nenni's majority in the party down to a bare 55 percent." However, this majority had backed Nenni's argument "that the existence of a strong Communist party, closely linked to Moscow and to the policies of the Soviet Union, delays rather than hastens the modernization of Italian social and economic structures and the country's progress toward a democratic and Socialist society." Nenni further stressed "that a collaboration with the Christian Democrats is necessary to 'strengthen Italian democratic institutions against the attacks from the Right and to promote that democratic stability which alone can allow a peaceful struggle for socialism.' "

As I had reported in the *Washington Post*, August 7, 1960, Nenni had told me time and again "that the United States, having been called upon twice to save European liberties, first from German militarism and then from Nazi-Fascism, has acquired a historic title and a vested interest in European freedom and security."

In domestic affairs, Nenni told me in March 1960 that "the ideological break" between Socialists and Communists must be widened to political matters even if it meant a split in his own party. The PSI must be ready to back a government of Christian Democrats, Social Democrats, and Republicans "which would undertake concretely to turn Italy, I don't say into a Socialist society, but into a modern Western democracy. If we could begin now to implement the required reforms, the favorable economic outlook would permit to start improving the standard of living of the working masses without denting too deeply the privileges of the well-to-do. There would also be a margin for error, for the mistakes which otherwise might prove fatal but are almost inevitable when you embark upon a new political course."

Within the CD camp, the evolution under way in the PSI was looked upon with growing interest even by leading members of the groups that had brought about Fanfani's downfall early in 1959 and in the fall of the same year defeated his bid for a comeback at the party's National convention in Florence. In the *Washington Post* of November 24, I called attention to the increasingly significant role played by Aldo Moro who, back in February, had been elected party secretary by the CD factions that had turned against Fanfani. Moro's almost unanimous reelection to the party leadership following the Florence convention reflected his reaffirmed "sympathy for a social-minded approach" and his willingness "to go farther" than wanted by most of his original backers "in meeting Fanfani's terms during the dramatic negotiations which preceded the election of the new party executive."

A few weeks later, I had the first in-depth talk with Moro. Far from resorting to the tortuous, occasionally ambiguous speechmaking, which was considered his trademark, he outlined with impressive frankness and clarity prospects and assessments which were to find an equally impressive confirmation in the events of the next several years.

Moro spelled out right away the differences between the party's policies and the position of the government. "Our party," he told me, "is a composite political formation featured by social motivations that are strong among the rank and file and perhaps even stronger among its cadres. Many of our voters hold somewhat different views. I would not call them conservative, but they are certainly inclined to be very cautious, if not reluctant, toward changes. Here is the key to many of the differences between the outlook of our party and of our parliamentary groups. The government, moreover, must take into account the other parties whose support is necessary to achieve a majority in Parliament. Our party, instead, must reaffirm its traditional, determined opposition to all kinds of totalitarianism even if this highlights the diversity from the government's position" (the all-Christian-Democrat Cabinet headed by Segni depended on the votes not only of the conservative-minded Liberals but of the Monarchists and Neo-Fascists).

Acceptance of rightist backing by the Segni government, Moro stressed, reflected "a condition of necessity," the lack of workable alternatives. The crisis of the center coalition, he went on, had "emerged before the 1958 election" and was due "essentially to the fact that the individual center parties, primarily the Liberals but also the Social Democrats and the Republicans," were trying to put more emphasis on their specific identity. Therefore, "a return to centrism looks most difficult not to say impossible. Saragat," Moro emphasized, "has come out repeatedly against resuming the collaboration with the Liberals. His stand is wholly understandable in view of the increasingly conservative policies adopted by the PLI in the last few years and of the severe electoral losses suffered by the PSDI as a consequence of, or at least in connection with, its participation in centrist governments." Moreover, "Saragat seems now to have given up his opposition to an agreement with the Socialists and appears ready to take again into consideration a closer relationship and perhaps a reunification of the two parties. The Republicans go even farther: they look forward to a center-left government with us and with the PSDI and want the Socialists included in such a new ruling coalition even if it should be able to rely on a sufficient majority in Parliament without them."

Answering a direct question, Moro stated flatly: "At this juncture, there are no workable and in any case no positive alternatives to a center-left coalition including the Socialists." This coalition "might be presented as a sort of updated centrism in so far as it would involve the return to a set up which would exclude the two extremes, the Communists and the Rightists."

Moro added carefully: "Not all the conditions are yet ripe for such a realignment of political forces which, in any case, could not be a painless operation." (Nenni had used the same expression in talking with me some months earlier.) "For the PSI," Moro spelled out, "the logical consequence of a governmental collaboration with us will be a split on its left. The size of the split will not reflect the current balance of power in the Socialist camp (58 percent for Nenni and 42 percent for the leftist opposition). Nenni and his friends, however, cannot realistically expect to lose only a fringe, say 10 percent, of the party.'' Moro was aware that he would have to confront his own party's "Catholic hinterland," namely the forces which could mobilize fairly large sectors of the CD electorate against an accord with the Socialists. He felt, however, that the party would suffer "some electoral losses" but no "organized defections."

"If no concrete progress is made soon toward bringing in the Socialists," Moro further warned, "Nenni and his friends will be forced to fall back into the Communists' arms or to surrender control of the party to the left-wingers." It could not be expected, either, that a right-wing minority would "walk out of the PSI and move toward the center, much as Saragat did in 1947," or that the Social Democrats themselves would gain at the polls if the PSI, frustrated in its hopes for a governmental collaboration with the CDs, should move closer again to the Communists: "Even the most autonomist-minded groups within the Socialist electorate, however disappointed by the failure of Nenni's efforts to reach an agreement with us, would feel that these efforts had been sincere and earnest; they could not expect, either, to be more successful in reaching such an agreement if they disavowed Nenni, let alone if they walked out of the party." Moro's assessments directly contradicted those U.S. officials who argued that the only possible and desirable developments were "minor splits to the right" in the Socialist camp or "defections of PSI voters to the Social Democrats."

Moro concluded, "I'm confident that Nenni and his followers will manage to hold fast at least for a few more months and that in the mean time conditions will ripen enough to allow a first 'coming together' of Socialists and Christian Democrats. I'll spare no efforts to make sure that the dialogue between the two parties goes on and makes progress."

The quickening prospects of such a dialogue gave new impetus to the mobilization of all the forces opposed to an "opening" to the Socialists. In May 1959, for instance, the archbishop of Palermo, Ernesto Cardinal Ruffini, a well-known sympathizer of the Franco regime in Spain, sought to indoctrinate me in the dangers that any "opening to the left" in Italy would involve for the United States. The cardinal maintained that "the Socialists are the worst Communists because they represent the apparently reasonable and peaceful face of the same movement." A few months later, premier Segni told me: "If Fanfani tries to implement his plan to form a government backed by the Socialists, at least 200 of our representatives in Parliament will stage an open revolt."

This background helps to explain the failure of the attempts made in the spring of 1960 to put together a tripartite government (CDs, Social Democrats, and Republicans) which would have the PSI's support in Parliament. At the same time it emerged that in the most authoritative church circles opposition to an opening to the Socialists was not as rigid and widespread as it was still claimed to be by the adversaries of the opening. The change was largely the result of

Moro's patient efforts to "coach Italian bishops and members of the Curia [the church's central organization] on the new facts and circumstances of Italian political life," some of his closest collaborators told me at the time. In that spring of 1960, one of those collaborators was dispatched to the Vatican to get direct word about the stand of the church's top leadership. According to well placed Italian and Vatican sources, the secretary of state, Domenico Cardinal Tardini, replied: "As clearly pointed out by Pope John XXIII, the Vatican does not feel that it should interfere in Italian political affairs. Since we have been asked to give an opinion, however, there will be no objection from us to the formation of a center-left government provided that this be actually deemed to be the necessary or anyway the most advisable solution and that such a government can rely on a majority of its own" (namely, would not depend, completely and from the very beginning, on Socialist support). Several years later, Moro told me that such information was substantially correct.

A stern warning against pursuing the policy of collaboration with the Socialists was conveyed to the Christian Democrat leader by Giuseppe Cardinal Siri, then president of the Italian Episcopal Commission, through the archbishop of Bari, the capital of Moro's electoral district. A PSI representative, well acquainted with the CD leaders, told me at the time: "If De Gasperi had received such a warning, he would have wept and possibly complied, but Moro stood fast."

Not only president Gronchi and other ranking CDs, but well informed Vatican sources, notably the assistant editor of *Osservatore Romano*, Federico Allesandrini, told me shortly afterwards: "It was a mistake to seek a previous and formal blessing for a specific political operation. The Vatican would have been more likely to underwrite, more or less tacitly, an already accomplished fact or to give a more flexibly positive answer if the question had been put in more general terms." Gronchi himself, however, had instructed the Italian ambassador to the Holy See, Migone, to inquire about the Vatican's attitude toward the kind of government, made up of CDs, Social Democrats, and Republicans, and backed by the Socialists, that Fanfani was trying to put together. On the afternoon of April 22, the president told me a few days later, Migone managed to talk with the Pope. John XXIII reaffirmed the decision not to interfere in Italian domestic affairs, adding that he did "not oppose" the projected solution, "provided, of course, that the proper safeguards be adopted." The ambassador hastened to convey this information which Gronchi read as "a green light." But just a few minutes earlier, Fanfani had officially told the president of the Republic that difficulties and opposition within the Christian Democrat Party forced him to give up the task of forming a center-left government.

The Rome correspondent of the *New York Times* reported that the Vatican had vetoed the formation of a government willing to accept the outside support of the Socialists. "These reports are incorrect," I was told flatly by Alessandrini, a man known for his reliability and close personal contacts with top Vatican circles.

It was only an apparent paradox that decisive progress toward a government role for the Socialists, was promoted by the conservative-minded leadership of the PLI. By withdrawing support from the all Christian Democrat Segni government, I wrote in the *Washington Post* (February 23, 1960), "the Liberals . . . precipitated a decisive 'moment of truth' in Italian politics." Their move spotlighted "the basic choice which confronts the country as a result of the divisions in the traditional democratic alignment: a more clearcut shift to the right, involving the twin dangers of a semi-fascist regime and of a Red-controlled popular majority, or a turn to the Left, based on the hope that the Socialists led by Pietro Nenni will actually prove themselves eligible as members of a new democratic majority."

The downfall of the Segni cabinet did not pave the way for a revival of the center coalition, as the Liberals hoped, but for repeated attempts to put together combinations more or less open to the Socialists. The failure of these attempts gave president Gronchi the opportunity to push through the formation of a government intended to reflect directly his views and projects. This government, headed by CD Fernando Tambroni, a ranking member of earlier cabinets, should operate, Gronchi told me at the time as well as in later days, "as a bridge" toward an early participation of the Socialists in running national affairs. I was present when Gronchi phoned Tambroni to urge him to seek the support of the Socialists rather than of the Neo-Fascists. At the same time, however, Nenni was telling me that the distrust aroused among the Socialists by Tambroni's personality made it impossible for them to give him any support; moreover, Social Democrats, Republicans, and many Christian Democrats led by Fanfani's friends, were bitterly hostile to the new premier. Eventually, Tambroni won the required votes of confidence in Parliament only thanks to the backing of the Neo-Fascists.

"The important role which the Neo-Fascists were allowed to play," I summed up in *Collier's Yearbook* (1960), "gave the Communists an effective issue and threatened to split the country down the middle. . . . The danger to Italian democracy posed by this situation became manifest with the bloody riots which swept many parts of the country in July taking a toll of 11 dead and more than 1,000 injured." This alarm bell, I wrote in the *Washington Post* (July 15), convinced "most democratic leaders" of "the urgent need for a fresh start which, while not fully satisfactory from the standpoint of their individual parties, might at least break a vicious circle which can only benefit the two extremes, the Communists and the Neo-Fascists. Accordingly, both the conservative-minded Liberals and the progressive-minded Social Democrats and Republicans have announced their readiness to support a new all-Christian Democrat government which would reject all ties with the Neo-Fascists. Nenni himself has pledged not to oppose such a government." Former premier Fanfani, I concluded, "appears the most likely candidate to head the new government."

When this government was actually formed on July 26, Saragat told me: "We . . . avoided the worst and can now prepare the better." The "better" was the formation of a center-left government still headed by Fanfani which would have the support of the Socialists. Such a government, Saragat stressed, would reaffirm "Italy's full loyalty to the Atlantic alliance and back vigorously American and British policies on all matters concerning East-West relations. . . . The only thing we're willing to offer to the Communists is a guarantee that we'll continue to fight them with democratic means and methods, provided of course that they refrain from illegal activities." The projected center-left government, Saragat went on, would be committed to "a forceful drive to meet the aspirations of the working masses. This policy should be carried out even if there were no Communists in Italy because it reflects the requirements of social justice; at the same time, it is the best means for fighting effectively against Communism and defeat it."

In meetings with U.S. officials, in Rome and in Washington, I outlined the characteristics and motivations of the accord that was shaping up between CDs and Socialists. Only too often, however, the answer was: "We do not believe that such an accord is likely, let alone impending. In any case, there is the danger that by becoming engaged with Nenni we'll end up in bed with Togliatti." "Nenni cannot be trusted," I was also told time and again. It did not help to stress that what matters in politics is not whether this or that leader can be trusted but to ascertain whether and to what extent "his interests parallel ours." In the specific case, I pointed out, we should assess, without preconceptions but without forgetting, either, Nenni's pro-Communist past, the opportunities provided by his efforts to persuade the majority of the PSI to accept the conditions required for an alliance with parties solidly committed to a pro-American policy. To be sure, no political operation can ever be expected to be 100 percent successful, or riskless." But an excellent opportunity was at hand for broadening and consolidating popular support for Italy's democratic institutions as well as for her secure anchorage to the West.

Too many U.S. representatives, however, kept turning a deaf ear to these suggestions and arguments. It was the bitter experience, too, of a man like Vittorio Valletta, the chairman of the board of Fiat, who enjoyed great prestige in the United States and easy access to Washington's top political circles. "I had very limited success," he told me in late 1959, "when I stressed that, whatever Nenni's positions and responsibilities may have been in the past, the key point today is that he is fighting, against heavy odds, to draw the bulk of his party away from the Communists. Isn't it in the interest of the United States, too, to have him succeed?"

In those waning days of the Eisenhower administration, the lack of effective guidance from the top gave a free hand to those officials who were most determined to lock the Socialists out.

The result was not only to give encouragement to those Italians who opposed the coming to power of a center-left government but to provide ammunition for the long-standing campaign by Communists and fellow travellers to portray the United States as the natural ally and possibly the prompter of rightist forces, Neo-Fascists included. During the short tenure of the Tambroni government some Italian papers reported, without drawing any denial, that American diplomats met frequently with representatives of the most militant Catholic right wing and of the MSI itself. U.S. officials in Rome were instructed to shun not only the Socialists but leaders of the traditionally pro-Western and democratic groups which, according to the embassy, were "dangerous radicals" and "troublemakers bent on rocking the boat." Even a man like La Malfa, who had been a member of De Gasperi's centrist governments and could hardly be suspected of holding subversive or pro-Soviet views, was denied time and again the opportunity, as he told me himself, to meet with high ranking U.S. officials.

This condition of affairs was bound to have worrisome consequences for the future of Italian democracy and for U.S. interests, I argued in talks with representatives of U.S. political and cultural circles, as well as in several articles in the *Washington Post* and in *The New Republic*.

To begin with, I pointed at "the apparent paradox" of a country where an impressive economic growth had taken place in recent years while the ruling Christian Democrats and the other traditionally pro-Western parties had "lost one million votes despite the large increase in the overall electorate" and "the Communists have gained two million votes" (*Washington Post*, June 11, 1961). Public opinion polls supported the view that these shifts of votes did not reflect a strengthening of pro-Soviet or neutralist trends, but the disappointment and resentment aroused by the pro-Western parties' domestic policies among voters who at bottom continued to look with sympathy at the United States and at the cause of Western solidarity. But this state of affairs underlined the dangerous impact of the spreading perception that U.S. influence in Italy was "mobilized in favor of conservative groups and big economic interests." To progressive-minded Italians, such an approach by U.S. officials was "the more surprising since it would be necessary to go back a generation or longer to find an American counterpart of the kind of *status quo* which Italian conservatives strive to maintain—a *status quo* directly responsible for keeping the Italian Communist party the strongest in the West" (*The New Republic*, June 12, 1961).

The main key to the Italian puzzle, I further wrote, "is the great discrepancy in the rates of material and civic progress. Italy may have all the caparison of a democracy, but neither its social and institutional structure nor its administrative practices have been brought in line with those of the modern Western democracies. . . . The country still lacks an equitable and effective tax system; a foresighted approach to land tenure and agricultural problems; antitrust legislation; efficient regulatory agencies in the fields of power, trade, labor relations, etc., and a modern educational system. At the same time, the tremendous development of television and other communications is bringing home to more and more Italians the great gap between the formal ideology which is supposed to guide the country's affairs and their daily experience of the way those affairs actually are conducted" (*Washington Post*, June 11, 1961).

I gave specific examples of the imbalances and bottlenecks responsible for the fragility of the current economic boom so indiscriminately hailed at home and abroad.

"In Milan, industrial expansion offers good job opportunities to young people from the countryside, like Luigi. But Luigi must spend six hours a day in a slow and overcrowded train to get to and from work or else move into one of the shantytowns which ring the city.

"Roberto lives in an old building not far from the automobile plant where he works. But he points at the expensive apartment houses which have recently sprouted across the street. 'I may be making 150 dollars a month and that's not bad,' he says. 'The owners of that land, however, must have made millions by selling it, with no effort and no risk, and they paid very little in taxes, too, I bet.'

"Francesco, a young industrialist down in the deep South, plans to use foreign-made parts for a new line of products for export and wants to benefit from drawback arrangements on import duties. He is told that the case must be referred to Naples and then to Rome, so that he won't get a reply for several months at best.

"Riccardo is one of the many Italians who, having saved some money, decided a year ago to get into the booming stock market. After a further rise last summer, the bottom fell out of the market in the fall. The big, wise boys had already raked in their profits; Riccardo, like most of the small fry, lost his little capital and now gets furious if somebody mentions 'the Italian economic miracle.'

"In Italy, corporations are required to provide so little data about their activities that a major chemical combine which sought to have its shares listed in New York, had to supply the Securities Exchange Commission with ten times as much information as it gives its Italian stockholders.

"Legislation was passed a few years ago to tax at least the most speculative kind of capital gains, but its implementation was first blocked by a stockbrokers' strike and then practically voided by a peculiar interpretation officially endorsed by the same ministry of finance which was supposed to enforce it."

"In a Sicilian village," I reported in *The New Republic* (June 12, 1961), "the great hopes aroused by the building of a dam turn sour when the precious water wastes away because neither the landowners nor the government authorities have provided for the necessary canalization network. In another village, the canals have been dug, but the water supply is tightly controlled by the Mafia."

"Another source of irritation," I wrote in the *Washington Post* (June 11, 1961), "is the attitude of too many government representatives who still consider the 'ordinary' Italian as a subject of the state rather than a fellow citizen.

"It would be unfair to say that Italy's democratic governments have done nothing to correct conditions which enable the Communist Party to pose not only as the champion of social and economic reform but as the good fighter in the battle against arbitrary authority, against public graft and mismanagement, and against attempts to hush up scandals and abuses. But any major drive to modernize the country's outdated institutions has been blocked by conservative elements in the center coalition. Their veto power is based on the small majorities held by the Center in the national and local governments and this explains why they stubbornly oppose any shift in the political alignment, even if it involves a widening of the democratic area and isolation of the Communists. There has been a chance to bring about such a shift ever since a large segment of the Nenni Socialist Party began to turn away from the Communist alliance. To be sure, Nenni still maintains some ties with the Communists, mainly in the labor field, and still refrains from endorsing unambiguously Italy's pro-Western policies. But the democratic forces have not given sufficient indications that they are ready to go to work for social and institutional reform and Nenni needs to hold out at least a concrete prospect of such reform in order to lead his followers into collaboration with the 'bourgeois' parties.''

Under the circumstances (I further wrote in *The New Republic*, June 11, 1961), the election of President Kennedy aroused great expectations: "One week after the election, a group of some 200 Italians—members of Parliament, labor leaders, social scientists, intellectuals in general—met to celebrate the event. They were mostly people in their 30s and 40s, representing a wide political spectrum: Christian Democrats, Social Democrats, Republicans, Radicals, Nenni Social-ists. What brought them together—as pointed out by Franco Malfatti, a young Christian Democrat close to Fanfani—'was the feeling that, as we struggle on to make our country at last into a modern democratic nation, we can now look forward, once more, to a rendez-vous with America.'

"In today's Italy," I went on, "a delicately poised balance may be tipped if American influence, which in past years has appeared to be working on the conservative side, should now shift to the progressive side.''

The democratic and pro-Western coalitions which governed after 1947, I recalled in *The New Republic* (September 10, 1962), reflected an old Italian tradition whereby "governments have been to the right of the electorate.'' [These coalitions] could be labelled as 'centrist' insofar as they were anti-Communist and anti-Fascist, but their majorities did not truly represent the center of the political spectrum since they excluded over one-third of the electorate on one side (those who voted Communist or Socialist) but only one-tenth on the other (those who voted Monarchist and Neo-Fascist).

"The only way to have corrected this situation would have been to strike a bold course of social and economic reform designed to appeal to the bulk of the Communist and Socialist voters. Some tentative stabs were made at such old issues as the development of the southern part of the country, land tenure and the revamping of the cumbersome, outdated and generally inequitable tax system. But under mounting conservative pressure within the coalition, progress was too little and came too late to meet pent-up demands. The government coalition suffered a slow but steady erosion on its left flank and was able to hold on to a slim majority only by gaining ground on its right, at the expense of the declining Monarchist movement. Even the great economic expansion of recent years, unattended by adequate social progress and institutional modernization, failed to produce political dividends for the government coalition.

"This state of affairs aroused a fitful concern in American diplomatic circles, which reached peaks of anxiety on the eve of each election but quickly gave way to a feeling of relief when it turned out that somehow the government parties had managed to scrape through once more. It didn't seem to matter much that the domestic policies of the pro-Western governments not only drove more and more voters into the arms of the Communist left but tended to identify the U.S. and the Atlantic alliance with an outdated *status quo* in Italy herself.

"In retrospect," I went on, "it is easy to conclude that progressive-minded Italians expected too much too soon," when the Kennedy administration came to power. Yet, "months went by before they could notice any change in the American approach to Italian affairs. . . . Over and above bureaucratic lags there was a lag in thinking, a failure to read and properly interpret the implications of the material and psychological changes that were taking place in Italy."

A year after John F. Kennedy came to the White House, Italy acquired "a new kind of government—one still controlled by pro-Western forces but one looking to the Nenni Socialists for the parliamentary support required to put across a New Dealish program of social reform and institutional modernization. Through most of those months, however, leading Italian politicians were left under the impression that many U.S. officials did not believe such a change would actually occur, or that they continued to harbor strong misgivings about it. Only at the last moment was this impression partly corrected. No wonder Roman wits cracked: 'We have always been told that Vatican diplomacy is very slow and cautious; on this one it has beaten the Americans by six months at least!'

"More recently there has been a gradual widening of American contacts with the democratic left," and these have not been confined to people holding official positions but have included some "Nenni Socialists who have played a major role in loosening their party's ties with the Communists." The gap between Italian political reality and its perception by U.S. diplomacy has been narrowed. Yet, there is still a tendency on the part of U.S. officials to emphasize the difficulties and risks of a center-left approach rather than its advantages and achievements. This tendency is strengthened by the coverage of Italian events by some of the major U.S. newspapers and magazines.

"On foreign policy, progressive and pro-Western Italians feel that the present government should by now have dispelled all suspicions that the support of the Nenni Socialists would mean a shift toward neutralism. They are not sure that U.S. diplomacy fully appreciates how able and willing the present Italian government is to take a constructive interest in such major international issues as British participation in the European Communities, the further development of European economic and political integration, the coordination of Western nuclear defense, and aid to the underdeveloped world (here Italy, thanks to her own fresh experience as an 'emerging country' can offer a unique contribution).

"Above all progressive Italians are wondering why, at the very moment when their country strives at long last to bring about reforms and institutions broadly similar to those adopted in the United States a generation ago, the representatives of the New Frontier have not grasped with both hands the opportunity to enhance American prestige by expressing great interest in what the Italian government is trying to do. . . . In past years, there has been little if any effort to correct the often-distorted image of the United States, projected by the large circulation Italian press, which may be independent of political parties but not from economic interests. America has been publicized as a technological giant rather than as a leader seeking modern democratic solutions to basic social and economic problems. To quote . . . a knowledgeable Italian, the U.S. Congress is better known through the reports of the Internal Security Subcommittee than through the reports of the Anti-trust Subcommittee. In the last few months some progress has been made, but speeches by embassy representatives or by visiting Americans are still more likely to dwell on the 'U.S. Customs Court' or 'The Hero in Hemingway' than on tax enforcement, the Tennessee Valley Authority or the Food and Drug Administration.

"In short," I concluded, "the U.S. in Italy is today less easily taken by the kind of Italian conservative who denounces as Communist even a proposal to allow the government to check on bank accounts for income tax purposes. What is still urgently required is to sharpen the U.S. image as a model of that forward-looking, social-minded capitalism that Italy increasingly wants and needs."

The strains and contrasts over the updating of the traditional U.S. policy toward Italian affairs developed into "a fight," as Robert Kennedy told me in April 1968, recalling his own role in that fight. A significant episode took place in early March 1961 when Averell Harriman visited Rome as special envoy of the president in Europe: "The visit," I reported in the *Washington Post* (March 9), sparked new charges by the Communists that the United States "wants its European allies to pay a large share of the alliance's costs." Neo-Fascist and Rightist papers claim that "Washington is unhappy over several aspects of Italian foreign policy and particularly over the Italian contribution to Western aid to the underdeveloped countries." According to them, American dissatisfaction was already voiced in the message sent by President Kennedy to premier Fanfani in connection with Harriman's visit. This has been denied by government sources [and] those who have read it can confirm that the message merely mentions current international problems as the subject of Harriman's talks here. Nevertheless, the Rightist press insists that American criticism 'is aimed at those very politicians, like Fanfani, who have sought to pass themselves off as supporters and interpreters in Italy of the left-of-center approach artfully attributed to the new American President'. [Neo-Fascists and right wingers were] 'worried that the new wind from Washington will actually favor enactment' [of the reforms propounded by the Italian progressive-minded forces].

"Gronchi and Fanfani had already told me about their hopes that Harriman's visit would inaugurate a period of better understanding and closer cooperation between the two countries.'' Gronchi praised warmly the overall policies outlined by the Kennedy administration as aimed at promoting ''a more active and co-ordinated contribution by each Western nation to an effective performance of the alliance in the political, military, and economic field. ''I am reaffirming,'' the Italian president told me, ''our readiness to mobilize part of our national resources in favor of the emerging countries whose growing importance I've stressed in my address before the American Congress in February 1956.'' Gronchi called ''stupid and provincial'' the members of the Italian government who opposed an increase of economic aid to developing nations, notably to Somalia. Fanfani called them ''the Scots of Italy.'' He let me read the message that Kennedy had sent him through Harriman and said: ''Right after Kennedy's election, I sent him a private letter to assure him that Italy will operate more actively to promote a more effective Western solidarity and to increase assistance to the emerging nations.''

Both the president of the Republic and the premier, I reported in the *Washington Post* (March 16), favored ''a dynamic and substantial Italian role in the new approach to joint aid and defense propounded by President Kennedy. . . . The Italians have warmly greeted Harriman's acknowledgement that fuller mobilization and more efficient use of the country's resources must give proper consideration to domestic requirements, particularly in the still depressed South. The more forward-looking Italians see this as a most welcome confirmation that the Kennedy Administration intends to reidentify the United States with the forces of world economic and social reform, escaping the label of standpat capitalism which Communist propaganda has sought to pin on the U.S. . . . Those Italians are just as conscious that today's greatest problem is to reduce the discrepancy of living standards not only between the citizens of each country but between rich and poor nations. . . . As Fanfani stressed to me, 'higher standards of living in the Mediterranean basin, particularly, mean new outlets for the budding industries of the Italian South.' ''

Further light on the meetings between Harriman and top Italian leaders comes from secret Italian documents. ''The earlier U.S. administration,'' Harriman is quoted as saying, ''devoted too many efforts to mere stopgap responses to crisis situations abroad. Communism has made concrete advances in the last few years because we have failed to take into account the social revolution under way in the world.'' Harriman recalled the stand taken by Gronchi on the issue and mentioned the Italian president's forthcoming trip to Latin America: ''In the last ten years,'' Kennedy's envoy continued, ''we have had no real policy in that region. The South American leaders, on their side, do not seem aware of the revolutionary social changes that are taking place on a world scale. That's why I attach so much importance to the visit there by a statesman like you who is so well known for his constant commitment in favor of the 'common man.' I also hope that you will have the opportunity to meet our ambassadors in those countries. This will be doubly useful: the local leaders and the local populations will have a confirmation that we work together, and President Kennedy will benefit from what he'll learn about your views.''

When Kennedy's envoy raised the issue of Communism in Italy, the following exchange took place. Gronchi: ''The situation is at a standstill . . . '' Harriman: ''This is exactly what you told me five years ago, but I still see that Communists and Socialists share the same bed.'' Gronchi: ''It is an exceedingly slow evolution. But it is not a delusion to say that some progress is taking place, however slowly. I would say that they no longer share the same bed, but rather the same home.''

As further reported in my article in the *Washington Post*, Gronchi and Fanfani also told Harriman that the Italian government favored the projects for placing under direct NATO control some nuclear weapons ''such as Polaris missiles aboard submarines and tactical land-based missiles.''

The opponents of any ''opening to the left,'' still strongly entrenched in the Rome embassy, were determined to ''pilot'' visiting firemen from the States. Their main concern was to block or limit the contacts between representatives of the U.S. progressive-minded circles and Italian politicians (and foreign observers) favorable or at least not prejudicially hostile to a government role for the Socialists. All kinds of obstacles were raised, for instance, to a meeting between Nenni and Senator Hubert Humphrey. (Humphrey himself told me about this some years later.) And it was only thanks to Alfred Friendly, the managing editor of *The Washington Post* and a long time friend of Harriman's, that Kennedy's envoy had the opportunity to ''listen to the other bell''—as Friendly himself put it when he told me that he had persuaded Harriman, over the embassy's opposition, to see me.

The meeting took place late in the evening of March 11 in Harriman's suite at the Excelsior Hotel on the Via Veneto. With Harriman there was only the then colonel Vernon Walters, who was military attaché at the embassy and had acted as interpreter for Kennedy's envoy in the talks with Italian leaders. Walters, who later became vice director of the CIA, special envoy for the Reagan administration, and lately ambassador to the United Nations, did not take part in the conversation except for some remarks which highlighted his familiarity with the Italian events, recent and less recent.

Harriman asked for my opinion on the Italian situation and prospects. I sought to place the search for a political solution of the ''Italian case'' against the background of the troubles, requirements, and capabilities of a country that was going through a period of vigorous but disorderly economic expansion and was affected at the same time by a persistent governmental instability and by an equally persistent backwardness in the social and administrative sectors. Harriman asked several specific questions mostly about the Nenni Socialists and their relations with the Communists on one side and with the Christian Democrats on the other. In the end, he summed up his own assessment by saying, ''I see:

great economic growth, no political progress. Something is not working and must be corrected."

As I heard soon afterwards from friends in Washington, Harriman had concluded that there was no workable, let alone promising alternative to a center-left government: the United States would hurt its own interests if it continued to oppose any opening to the Socialists and thus contributed to pushing them back into the arms of the Communists.

In the conversations I had with him over the several following years, Harriman voiced unfailingly his sympathy for government coalitions in which the Socialists would participate "together with the Christian Democrats and other traditionally 'Western' parties." After those coalitions came to power, he voiced strong appreciation for their commitment to reformist programs as well as to a foreign policy keyed to supporting the Kennedy rather than the Gaullist approach to European and Atlantic matters. As pointed out by Arthur Schlesinger in his already quoted book, *A Thousand Days*, Harriman played a key role, especially after his appointment as under secretary of state for political affairs, in "turning around" U.S. diplomacy and notably those U.S. officials who had opposed Socialist participation in the Italian government.

5

The Italian Center Left, Gaullism, and the Kennedy Administration

On the eve of a visit to Washington, in June 1961, Premier Fanfani told me that he was looking forward to meetings with a U.S. president "strongly sympathetic toward the implementation in Italy of far-sighted programs of reform and modernization . . . which would strike at the very roots of Communist influence." The Italian premier praised "Kennedy's commitment to identify the U.S. and the West in general with the aspirations to social and economic progress which are on the rise throughout the world."

Opponents of the "opening to the left," still active in the Rome embassy and in several Washington offices, emphasized the need that President Kennedy be "most cautious" when talking with Fanfani on Italian domestic politics. The fact that the Italian premier was accompanied by foreign minister Segni, notoriously far from favorable to the "new course" in Italy, did not make any easier an in-depth review of these matters. On the other hand, the "position papers," largely prepared by Schlesinger, influenced the president's statements during his meetings with Fanfani. The Italian premier returned to Rome more convinced than ever that the White House looked favorably on his views and programs.

"Quite a few Italians, including some government leaders," I wrote in the *Washington Post* (September 29, 1961), "increasingly feel that their country, whose economic and industrial capacity has recently expanded more rapidly than any other in the West, should play a more prominent role in Allied councils and in foreign affairs generally."

"While Italy enjoys equal status with France and West Germany in the European Community," I further noted in *The New Republic* (October 9), "her official standing in older Western organizations such as NATO is that of a lesser partner and there is a tendency to treat her as the stepchild she was in 1949. Growing Italian sensitivity on this point has been taken into full account by

Soviet diplomacy'' as witnessed by an invitation to Fanfani to visit Moscow and the "subsequent messages sent him by Premier Khrushchev. The USSR has sought to use Italy as a communication channel in the conflict over Berlin and possibly thereby to weaken NATO's united front. It has also pressed for closer commercial ties between the two countries and with some effect since major Italian private and government-controlled concerns are interested in finding new outlets for their soaring industrial output. The Russians are aware, too, of the sharpening rivalry between the Italian state oil agency, headed by the dynamic Signor Enrico Mattei, and the major Western oil companies.''

Drawing on my talks with the Italian premier as well as with other leading CDs who did not particularly care for him or his policies, I reported that Fanfani had not given the Soviet premier "reason to hope that Italy would waver in allegiance to her allies. At the same time, Fanfani came back fully convinced that Khrushchev, obsessed by the danger of a resurgence of German 'aggressive militarism,' was determined to consolidate by every means at his command the division of Germany. But Fanfani also felt that there was 'an appreciable margin for negotiation,' probably in the area of new guarantees for the freedom of West Berlin and possibly for giving the whole city an international status." Accordingly, the Italian premier urged the Western allies to explore "the possibility of negotiations, in the conviction . . . that things would get worse if they were left to drift." (A few days later the construction of the wall between East and West Berlin actually got under way.)

Fanfani told me shortly afterwards that he had immediately informed the allies "and first of all the U.S. representatives" of the gist of his talks with Khrushchev. He added: "When the Soviet premier sent me a personal message on August 24, I communicated right away not only its substance but direct quotes on its most relevant sections to President Kennedy. He sent me a personal message voicing warm appreciation for the information I had provided and more generally for my efforts to promote a peaceful solution of the crisis over Berlin."

Feeling, however, that inadequate attention was paid to his suggestions, Fanfani was "overly peeved, just as he had been overly flattered by Khrushchev's adroit references to the increased weight and international standing of Italy," I further noted in *The New Republic*. "Nor were feelings soothed when Secretary Rusk, in announcing plans to confer with Chancellor Adenauer at the latter's vacation place in Northern Italy, failed to indicate a desire to meet with the Italian premier." (The meeting was quickly arranged after the Italian displeasure had been called to the attention of U.S. officials in Rome.)

"At the end of August, an unfortunate note issued by the Italian premier's office . . . in effect stated that the worsening of the situation (notably the sealing off of East Berlin) might have been avoided if the Western allies had heeded Fanfani's recommendations. The note caused an uproar in Italy.

"In part, the uproar came.from people sincerely fearful of any deterioration in the relations between Italy and the NATO powers. But it also reflected an attempt by Fanfani's political adversaries and by all Italian right-of-center forces to carry out a major operation of a domestic nature. Their purpose was to smear all the proponents of an understanding with the Nenni Socialists as tainted with 'neutralism' and thus to bring about a crisis which would pave the way for a right-of-center regime as the only one allegedly capable of ensuring Italy's loyalty to the West. Rumors were spread to the effect that the attempted operation was viewed sympathetically by some French, West German, and American circles.'' The maneuver failed and the uproar "largely subsided,'' I concluded, ''thanks partly to the public reaffirmation of Italian dedication to NATO made by the government.''

Yet, such interplays between foreign policy and domestic politics contributed to slow down the final phase of the process leading to a Socialist participation in the government. In Italy, Moro and Fanfani, as well as Saragat and La Malfa, had come to distrust Gronchi and his intentions deeply as a result of the latter's role in connection with the Tambroni government. They sought therefore to put off any move to speed up the coming to power of the new coalition until the end of the year when the president of the Republic, having entered the last six months of his mandate, would lose the right to dissolve Parliament and the related ability to influence decisively the outcome of a political crisis.

During a temporary assignment to Washington, Horsey continued to lobby vigorously against "the opening to the left.'' According to my well-informed friends in the U.S. capital, ''one day Horsey talks tough and says 'This marriage will not take place.' The next day, he sounds conciliatory and tells the supporters of the center-left: 'In the final analysis, our positions are not so different. But things in Italy have taken a turn for the better, the CDs are recouping ground, a good centrist majority is still possible and anyway there is no hurry to throw ourselves and help throw Italy into Nenni's arms.' ''

Ambassador Frederick Reinhardt, whom I had met in New York shortly after his appointment to Rome, appeared uncertain and at the same time jealously eager to uphold his prerogatives as the Number 1 representative of the United States in Italy. The antagonism between the State Department and the president's personal advisers was already becoming a feature of the management or mis-management of U.S. foreign policy. According to Schlesinger and other members of the White House staff, the administration should come out clearly in favor of the political operation intended to sanction the Socialists' separation from the PCI and their entry into the democratic orbit, as was pointed out in a memo by McGeorge Bundy, Kennedy's special assistant for national security. Such pressures angered State Department officials and pushed them to display their lack of sympathy for the center-left approach and its supporters.

In November 1961, Richard N. Gardner, who had recently been appointed deputy assistant secretary of state for International Organizations, came to Rome. Dick had married the daughter of Bruno Luzzatto, an old friend of mine (and author of the already quoted *Country Study* on Italy prepared by the ECA in 1949) and was on friendly terms with Vic Sullam. A lunch was organized for Gardner at the home of the economic counselor George Ainsworth and was attended by Reinhardt, by a ranking CD member of Parliament, Mario Ferrari Aggradi, and by Egidio Ortona, the top expert on the United States in the Italian diplomatic corps. The host made a rather nasty remark to the effect that my views, favorable to the center-left, were published in the *Washington Post* without my name. "But Leo's reports from Rome carry his byline," Ortona retorted. "Yes, but what about the editorials?" Ainsworth insisted. "You should know," I interjected, "that writing editorials is not part of my correspondent's job." But Ainsworth tried to have the last word: "I thought that things were not like that because the *Washington Post* editorials on Italy reflect entirely your approach," he told me. "Well, it means that they trust my reports from Italy," I concluded.

Reinhardt tried to keep Gardner "under surveillance" by sending an embassy representative along whenever Gardner met with Italians holding official positions. This made it very difficult, not to say impossible, to discuss frankly and fully the aspects and prospects of the Italian political situation on which conflicting views were known to exist in Washington and within the State Department itself. It was notably the case, Gronchi himself told me, with a meeting between the president of the Republic and Gardner that I had arranged on a private basis. Embassy officials also tried to talk Gardner out of a meeting with La Malfa. Gardner was not deterred and I was able to arrange a lunch for the three of us in a Rome restaurant. "I'm particularly happy to meet you," La Malfa told Gardner right off the bat, "because for the last several years I have been denied the opportunity to talk with ranking American representatives." The Republican leader illustrated the domestic and international facts and circumstances that made useful, in fact urgently necessary the coming to power of a center-left coalition. Deeply impressed by La Malfa's arguments and worried about the embassy's attitude, Gardner hastened to discuss both topics with Schlesinger and other officials interested in Italian affairs.

A few weeks later, Sullam and other friends confirmed to me that during their private meeting at the White House in June, Kennedy had told Fanfani: "On our side, there are no objections to a role for the Nenni Socialists in the ruling coalition should this be considered helpful to Italian democracy."

By the end of the year, such an approach had become official policy which could be conveyed to Italian representatives. USIS officials assigned to Italy were told to "cultivate" the Socialists. Among the White House staffers, Walt Rostow joined Schlesinger in supporting the "opening" to the Socialists. Much the same views prevailed at the OIR under the leadership of its new director, Roger Hilsman, and among career diplomats who were in a position to influence policies concerning Italy (a notable instance was Bill Tyler, deputy assistant and later assistant secretary of state for European Affairs).

"Unless Reinhardt has become blind and deaf," Sullam wrote to me in November, "he should know by now which way the wind is blowing here." The ambassador did read the signals from Washington. Within a few days he met with Fanfani and Moro whom I had advised that the time had come to speak up clearly. Both told the ambassador that they were determined to promote "in the near future" Socialist participation in the governmental majority while assuring him that the operation would be carried out with "all due caution."

In late November Moro stated publicly that "the main issue" before the forthcoming CD national Congress was "the formation of a left-of-center government" relying on "the parliamentary support of the Nenni Socialists."

As I reported in the *Washington Post* of November 25, "Moro spelled out, much more clearly than ever before, that he does not see 'any concrete and stable alternative to such a government.' Those statements appear the more significant because they were made during a press conference that television brought into the homes of an estimated 10 million Italians."

Moro stated that "he does not envisage an 'opening to the left,' but something very different: a parliamentary collaboration with the bulk of the Nenni Socialists who . . . would thus be encouraged to break their remaining ties with the Communists. The CD leader expressed the opinion that this kind of working understanding with Nenni Socialists will not run into a veto by the Church. Unquestionably the attitude of powerful groups of the clergy has been softened by the encouraging results of the collaboration that has been in effect for some time between Socialists and CDs in important local administrations. Moro made it clear that Socialist support will not be purchased with concessions on foreign policy matters. At the same time," I concluded, "he joined such other stout pro-Western politicians as the leaders of the Social Democratic and Republican parties in voicing confidence that the 'ideological neutralism' still professed by the Nenni Socialists will not prevent them from supporting the progressive-minded domestic policies of a left-of-center government fully committed to the continuation of Italy's pro-Western course in foreign affairs."

In other reports to the *Washington Post* (November 22 and December 7), I pointed out that "the shock waves" originated by the recent Moscow congress of the Communist party of the Soviet Union and by "the further downgrading of Stalin have not only shaken the Red rank and file, but have also cracked the solid front that the Italian Communist leadership had maintained even when it was confronted with the first de-Stalinization back in 1956." However, "returns from local elections held in recent weeks in many parts of Italy show that Communist tickets continue to attract the support of one of four Italians.

"An explanation of this paradox," I went on, "is offered by Saragat. He says: 'It is useless to hope that the problems of de-Stalinization and the fresh disclosures about the crimes of the Communist regime will automatically produce electoral shifts [until and unless] the democratic forces prove concretely that they can fulfill the widespread popular demands for social progress and institutional modernization.' "

As I reported in the *Washington Post* of December 17, Nenni acknowledged that Italy's links with NATO represented an accomplished fact which "has been endorsed by a majority of the voters in all recent elections." Speaking to the Foreign Press Association in Rome, Nenni spelled out that Italy should follow an approach "closer to that of President Kennedy than to that of French President de Gaulle." The formation in Italy of a left-of-center government, enjoying the support of the Socialists, would not hamper but favor European integration, founded on democratic and supernational principles rather than on "a confederation of nationalistic countries as advocated by the Gaullist regime. . . . Nenni stated that his party's main purpose is to help bring Italy's social and institutional framework in line with the requirements of 'the current high rate of industrialization and increase in production.' He specifically mentioned the urgent need to develop and modernize the Italian school system, to crack down on tax evasion in the high brackets, to give better protection to the rights of the workers and of their unions, to extend local self-government, to step up public investments in the still depressed South, to place the electric power industry under public control and to strengthen in general the government's regulatory powers and agencies."

The Rome correspondents of the *New York Times* and of the *New York Herald Tribune* continued to label Nenni and his party as "frankly neutralist." The projected new government, backed by the PSI, would be "the most Socialistic . . . Italy has had since World War II," Barrett McGurn wrote in the *Herald Tribune* (December 30), adding, quite inaccurately, that "the Republicans, despite their name, are markedly Socialistic too."

In reporting on the CD congress, which took place in Naples at the end of January 1962, both the *Herald Tribune* and the *Associated Press* gave prominent play to the pronouncements by representatives of the party's conservative minority, notably former premiers Pella and Tambroni and defense minister Andreotti, who opposed a deal with Nenni as likely to turn Italy into a neutral country and to "open the door to a Socialist-Communist rise to power."

After the congress endorsed by a large majority the center-left approach, a *New York Times* editorial insisted on the risks involved in the "opening to the left," but admitted that the CDs remained loyal to NATO and to the integration of Europe (February 7).

In the *Washington Post* of February 2, I pointed out that the decision by the CD congress to endorse "a working collaboration with the Nenni Socialists" marked "the first concrete step in a far-reaching realignment of Italy's political forces aimed at isolating the largest Communist party in the West and forming a stable governmental majority resting on a wider and solid foundation of popular support. The outcome of the congress represents a great personal success for Moro, who managed to rally almost 80 percent of the party membership to the new policy. The right-of-center Liberals will be dropped [from the ruling coalition]. The Nenni Socialists will have no seats in the cabinet, but will back the government on domestic issues and abstain on foreign policy votes." In the Socialist camp, I further reported, "a strong faction still opposes any move aimed directly or indirectly against the Communists. Among the CDs, the center-right groups have reiterated their opposition to any deal with Nenni."

This opposition was bound to collapse when it failed to rally substantial support within the Catholic hierarchy. Alfredo Cardinal Ottaviani, an outspokenly conservative prelate, "publicly denounced those CDs who 'in order to promote their own interests' favor an agreement with the Socialists and to that effect 'are shamelessly bartering away, among other things, the freedom of the school,' a reference to the request for direct state aid to Catholic schools. It now appears," I further wrote in the *Washington Post* (February 19), "that the attack has failed and, if anything, backfired. Premier-designate Amintore Fanfani and the CD party secretary are going ahead with their plans, reaffirming that the party must have autonomy in political matters.

"Pope John XXIII, meanwhile, has pointedly refrained from granting Cardinal Ottaviani, who head the Congregation of the Holy Office, the customary weekly audience. Ever since the election of Pope John, a perceptible change in the Vatican's attitude has led Roman wits to remark that 'the Tiber has become wider,' referring to the river that runs through the city leaving the Vatican on one side and the Italian government's headquarters on the other. In recent months, there have been indications that the Vatican has not only adopted a line of less direct involvement in Italian politics but, if anything, looks in a direction opposite to that advocated by Cardinal Ottaviani. The latter has long been known for his sympathies for the Franco and Salazar regimes."

At the same time, "such papal pronouncements as the encyclical *Mater et Magistra* have offered positive confirmation that the church is now emphasizing the social aspects of its traditional doctrines. In its cautious way, the Vatican has thus managed to convey the definite impression that, contrary to what would have been the case a few years ago, it is now viewing at least with benevolent neutrality the contemplated experiment of collaboration between CDs and Nenni Socialists."

The quickening prospects of the coming to power of a left-of-center coalition produced embarrassed and wavering reactions from the PCI leadership. As I reported in the *Washington Post* on December 24, 1961, the Communists were "stepping up their long-standing attempts to undermine Pietro Nenni's position and his hold over the Socialist party. Their main tool is the pro-Communist wing of Nenni's own party. Their main line of attack is the charge that Nenni is ready to collaborate with the 'bourgeois' parties on terms which, far from promoting the interests of the Italian workers, will 'contribute to consolidate the CD regime and help Western Imperialism.' The official Communist daily this week strongly denounced the article written by Nenni for the American magazine *Foreign Affairs*, particularly his acceptance of Italy's membership in the Atlantic Alliance and his stand on Berlin and German reunification."

The Italian Communist leaders were also pursuing "a much more insidious" approach. "They now accept as a 'step in the right direction' the social and economic program the Nenni Socialists have outlined as a platform for their future collaboration with the CDs and with the minor left-of-center parties, but add that implementation of such a program 'requires the united efforts of the whole Italian workers' movement,' which means the active participation of the

Communists. Rightist and conservative forces have immediately seized upon the Communist move as confirming that 'you can't do business with Nenni without letting Togliatti in, too.' But the democratic forces,'' I went on, ''have been equally quick to expose what Saragat brands as a combined maneuver by the Communists and by the conservatives. Saragat stresses that the aim of the proposed left-of-center government is not only to promote social and economic reforms but to strengthen 'Italian political democracy.' Accordingly, such a government will slam the door even more firmly in the face of the Communists unless they ''disavow political totalitarianism,' that is, cease in effect to be Communists. Much in the same way, the official Nenni Socialist daily *Avanti* states that if the Communists really want to help promote a progressive social and economic policy they must first 'recognize the indissoluble bond between socialism and democracy.' To that effect, 'it is not enough for the Italian Communists to admit what they call the mistakes of Stalin and of Stalinism.' They must also acknowledge 'their historical mistake of 40 years ago' when they walked out of the Socialist party and 'split the Italian workers movement in order to ape the Soviet model.' ''

Yet the Communist leaders' maneuvers found some response among Americans who had not yet given up the fight against the center-left. *Time* (March 2) alleged that ''Togliatti heartily endorsed Fanfani's opening to the left.'' Actually, Togliatti and other PCI chieftains had already served notice (as I reported in the *Washington Post* on December 26, 1961) that their party ''will oppose any government which, however progressive-minded in social and economic matters, maintains Italy's ties with the West'' thus confirming that ''all the tactical flexibility of the Italian Reds disappears as soon as the foreign policy interests of the USSR are involved.''

Six weeks later, just when the new Fanfani government was taking shape, Togliatti ''pushed his flexibility on domestic matters to the point of asserting that the Communists would be satisfied, as a first step, with less far-reaching reforms than those demanded by the Nenni Socialists. By this approach,'' I noted (*Washington Post*, February 16, 1962), ''Togliatti seeks to hold over the new government the threat of a favorable vote or at least of an abstention by the Communists in Parliament. Togliatti emphasized again,'' I continued, ''that no changes in domestic matters can prove really fruitful if they are not attended by specific and concrete changes in foreign affairs, 'such as, for instance, a refusal to continue to make Italian territory available to the Americans for their nuclear weapons and bases.' ''

As it was eminently predictable, the Communists ended up by voting solidly in the opposition in the vote of confidence to the new left-of-center government— and so did all the right-of-center parties from the Liberals to the Neo-Fascists. The significance of the Socialist abstention, I pointed out (*Washington Post*, March 11), was underlined by Nenni who ''pledged to use his party's present pivotal position to back 'unreservedly' the government's program of social and economic reforms.

"For the first time the veteran Socialist leader spelled out publicly that such support would be available to insure implementation of those reforms not only over conservative opposition but also against any maneuvers by his former allies, the Communists. This pledge was reaffirmed by the Socialist leader after premier Fanfani earlier today had once more reasserted Italy's 'full loyalty to her political and military obligations within the Atlantic Alliance.' "

Meanwhile I had also reported (*Washington Post*, February 23) that Italian political leaders looked "for signs of a change in the American attitude toward Italian domestic politics" following the coming to power in Rome of "the first left-of-center government. In the early Eisenhower years," I recalled, "ambassador Luce was known to favor a shift to the right designed to bring into the governmental alignment what she called 'the solid Monarchist bloc.' Subsequently, the Monarchists have been so badly battered by electoral defeats and internal splits that they no longer represent an organized political force. With some exceptions, however, U.S. representatives continued to convey, through their political and social contacts, the feeling that the best forces with which to work were to be found in the conservative camp." Even after the coming to power of the Kennedy administration, "there has been" a continued "lack of interest in extending contacts to parties that might play a role in the next government, like the Nenni Socialists," or even "to left-of-center groups within the incumbent governmental coalition—the Social Democrats and the Republicans" (and here I referred to La Malfa's experience). "Only in the last few weeks, the feeling has begun to spread that Washington might look with benevolent neutrality and perhaps with sympathy upon a government which, while still controlled by staunch pro-Western parties, would rely upon the Socialist votes in Parliament to put across, over conservative opposition, a program of social reform and institutional modernization. But many Italian politicians are still under the impression that U.S. officials continue to harbor too many misgivings about the current turn in Italian political affairs."

According to friends in Washington, a "counteroffensive" had been unleashed by State Department officials traditionally hostile to any "opening to the Socialists." These officials were reportedly inspiring press attacks against the center-left coalition like those found in the columns by Constantine Brown in the *Washington Star*. The climate in the Rome embassy reflected, at best, a cold detachment with regard to the coming to power of a left-of-center government: Reinhardt himself had taken off for a long holiday leaving the helm in Horsey's hands.

Following the publication of the article, embassy officials hastened to assure me, on Reinhardt's behalf, that relations with all the traditionally democratic and pro-Western parties had never been neglected, even when one or the other of them was not represented in the government. Particularly at the present juncture in Italian politics, I was further told, the embassy did not intend to "cultivate" conservative groups to the detriment of progressive and reform-minded forces. I was later told by friends in Washington that in his cables to Secretary of State

Rusk, Reinhardt complained that I was accusing the embassy of privileging contacts with conservative circles in Italy. My articles, I told the embassy officials who had approached me on Reinhardt's instructions, reflected the assessment, shared by other observers in Rome and in Washington, that too many U.S. diplomats were still reluctant to accept the fact that, contrary to their expectations, a center-left government had been formed in Italy and that its politics would be helpful rather than detrimental to U.S. interests.

When Schlesinger came to Rome during the same days and was informed about Reinhardt's and Horsey's behavior, he told me: "This unfortunately confirms that the coming to power of the center-left takes place not against us but without us."* Schlesinger continued to feel that the opening to the Socialists provided "a good opportunity" both for Italian and for U.S. interests and therefore deserved to be strongly supported by Washington. I fully agreed but pointed out that, even under the best of circumstances, the social and economic reforms championed by the new government would represent a rather belated answer to Italy's problems and requirements. Implementation of the reforms, moreover, would meet with strong opposition within the center-left coalition itself. Accordingly, the general election due in the spring of 1963 was likely to register some losses for the CDs while the PSI would hardly make substantial gains. On the other hand, I further told Schlesinger, my latest talks with Nenni made me even more confident that Socialist participation in the ruling coalition would "not create problems with regard to Italy's foreign policy. There might be some trouble," I added, "only if additional NATO bases should be planned in Italy or if the project for an allied nuclear force should be carried out under conditions allowing West Germany to develop some atomic arms of its own." "But this is out of the question," Schlesinger replied flatly.

A meeting with Nenni, which was a significant item on Schlesinger's agenda in Rome, took place under circumstances that did not favor a quiet, thorough exchange of views. Their talk was interrupted by urgent phone calls related to the choice of the members of the new Fanfani government, a topic of major interest for Nenni, for La Malfa and other Italians whom Schlesinger met on that occasion. By and large, anyway, the meeting was satisfactory for Nenni, mainly because (as the Socialist leader told me shortly afterwards) Schlesinger's parting words were, "All of us look forward to seeing you soon in America." An early trip by Nenni to the United States was a project born in political circles close to Senator Humphrey. Friends in Washington told me that it aroused strong negative reactions by State Department officials. In my opinion, I told those friends as well as Schlesinger, it was a good idea but its implementation seemed "premature" (as it turned out, the trip took place almost three years later).

Before leaving Rome, Schlesinger kindly told me that my articles in the *Washington Post* and our private talks were most helpful in providing top Washington officials with "timely and reliable information about what's going on in

---

*Schlesinger used the same words in his report to President Kennedy (*A Thousand Days*, p. 879).

Italy which we don't find in the official cables from Rome.'' He asked me to advise promptly about any developments or prospects that might require the White House's attention.

"During its first months in office," I reported in *Collier's Yearbook* for 1962 and 1963, the new Fanfani government "acted on matters that previous center and center-right governments had ignored or failed to tackle effectively—distribution of free textbooks, increases in social security benefits, and liberalization of theater and movie censorship . . . the first revision of legislation dating back to Fascist days. It next secured passage of measures of more far-reaching significance—a unified secondary school system, to provide equal education to all children under 14; a 15 percent withholding tax on dividends intended to supply more information on stock ownership and thus curb tax evasion.''

The outcome of the local elections held in June was a disappointment for the opposition parties. They "had hoped that the formation of the new center-left coalition would cause many CDs to vote for parties on the right and many Socialists to vote for the Communists. Instead, the limited CD losses were more than offset by the gains made by Social Democrats and Socialists, largely at the expense of the Communists.

Nationalization of the electric power industry (except for small producers) was the most controversial plank of the new government's program. In my opinion, it represented a primitive tool of public intervention which, however, found some justification under the circumstances still prevailing in Italy. In my writings for the U.S. press and in talks in Washington and New York with administration officials, congressmen, economic experts, and labor leaders, I pointed out that in Italy there was nothing comparable to U.S. antitrust legislation. True, the Italian state already held stock control in a number of large electric power concerns it had taken over during the economic crisis of the 1930s. But in most of those cases the Italian government had been playing a very limited role in managerial decisions. Much in the same way, I further noted in the *Washington Post* (June 20, 1962), "electric power rates have long been set by a governmental body, but its rulings have been largely influenced by figures and arguments originating with the major private companies. As a result, the rates charged to Italian consumers, with the exception of the big industrial users linked or friendly with the major producers, are high in relation to other aspects of the Italian economy and to rates in the U.S. and other Western countries. Average per capita consumption is still one fifth of that in the U.S., one half of the West German average, and two thirds of the French figure. The high prices and the different rates charged by the producers have worked to the disadvantage of the areas and economic sectors that would most need cheap power (the Italian South, agriculture, and small users).''

On the assumption that the government would not have decreed "outright nationalization,'' the PCI propaganda apparatus "had been readying a major two-step drive. It would stress that not even a center-left government supported by the Nenni Socialists could or would strike a direct blow at the powerful combine of vested interests and privileges centering on the big electric companies; and it would point at this failure as additional proof that no government combination excluding the Communists could ever take effective action against 'the big private monopolies which have actually ruled Italy before Fascism, under Fascism and after Fascism.' Now the Communists have been thrown off balance.''

Secretary of State Rusk's attitude toward the center-left had seemed to reflect mostly the diffidence still widespread among U.S. officials as well as their resentment about the ''undue activism'' of White House staffers favorable to a government role for the Italian Socialists. This background added significance to Rusk's statement at the end of his visit to Rome in late June: ''It has been the easiest and most satisfactory stopover so far in my European trip.'' On Berlin and the general issue of East-West relations, I continued (*Washington Post*, June 25), ''the Italians fully endorse American determination to 'keep talking' with the Soviets. U.S. representatives voice high praise for Italy's role in the disarmament discussions held recently in the United Nations and in Geneva. Italian leaders reportedly stated their conviction that the whole issue of a multilateral nuclear force for the West must be approached and settled 'only within the framework of NATO.' In other words, Italy continues to oppose the setting up of 'subgroups' within the alliance.'' The Italians also ''stressed their determination to pursue a European political unity broadly based on supernational principles; they further oppose any attempt to promote, even as a first step, such limited schemes as the so-called Fralit (from the combination of the first two letters in the French spelling of France, Germany, and Italy). The Italian leaders reiterated that they intend to do their utmost to facilitate a full and early British membership in the European Economic Community.''

Nenni had already confirmed to me that the new Fanfani government would follow a foreign policy ''closer to that of the Kennedy administration than had been the case with earlier Italian cabinets. The same will be true of the next government that we hope to form with the direct participation of our party after the general election due in the spring of 1963.''

During the crisis over the deployment of Soviet missiles in Cuba, Nenni did not share the pro-Soviet and anti-American views expressed by other Socialists and notably by the pro-Communist wing of the party. Saragat himself told me: ''Nenni has gone further in backing U.S. policies than I've done myself.'' (Saragat had wondered initially whether the U.S. decision to impose a quarantine involved a violation of Cuba's sovereignty and therefore of international law.)

The course followed by the center-left coalition in international affairs became even more of an asset for the Kennedy administration because of the sharpening differences with Gaullist France. At a dinner I organized for Al Friendly in late November, Fanfani stated, ''Continued French opposition to an early agreement allowing Great Britain to join the European Economic Community would set in motion a chain reaction which would not only threaten Europe's economic capabilities but endanger political relations with the U.S. and hence the West's own security. . . . British participation in the EEC is required by the interests of Italy and of the West in general. It would enable us to proceed with the construction of European political unity on broader and more balanced foundations and to guarantee, at the same time, the closest ties between the U.S. and a politically unified Europe."

Friendly noted that the Italian premier's approach and outlook "coincided perfectly" with Kennedy's concept of an Atlantic partnership resting on the twin pillars of the United States and Europe. "I know and I'm happy about this coincidence," Fanfani promptly answered. "Italy is the only major continental nation whose views are so close to those of the U.S."

According to the Italian premier, de Gaulle wanted "to weld quickly West Germany to France. The general feels, correctly, that Adenauer's successor will be more sympathetic toward the British and less likely to support the Gaullist plans for developing a Franco-German 'hard core' of Europe and thus enabling the French President to become the leader of the whole Western Europe and its spokesman in discussing world affairs with the U.S. and the Soviet Union." Both de Gaulle and Adenauer had "invited Italy, time and again, to join in a 'three-power Europe' which would leave the British to fend for themselves and confront the Benelux countries with the dilemma of staying out in the cold or following the lead of the three major continental powers. This invitation has been addressed to me personally by de Gaulle early last spring, by Adenauer a few days later when I visited him at the Northern Italian resort of Cadenabbia, and again by French Premier Georges Pompidou and Foreign Minister Maurice Couve de Murville in mid-September when we met for the opening of the Mount Blanc tunnel. I have turned down those offers," the Italian premier concluded, "because the proposed three-power combination would split rather than unite Europe and endanger rather than strengthen the close ties that exist and must continue to exist between the West European nations and the U.S."

In reply to another question, Fanfani stated: "Italy continues to oppose any proliferation of national nuclear deterrents. . . . De Gaulle himself must admit that an independent French nuclear deterrent is not only terribly expensive but can never become truly credible. Of course, he wants an atomic force of his own to enhance his country's prestige and bargaining power. In any case, such a force can hardly increase the West's overall capabilities to deter aggression while it will continue to represent a divisive factor within the Atlantic camp. Only the United States, the Italian premier emphasized, "can shoulder the responsibility for maintaining a nuclear deterrent sufficiently strong to meet the requirements of the whole Atlantic Alliance. Italy favors, in principle, the development of a multilateral NATO nuclear force closely integrated with American atomic power and, of course, feels that she, too, should have a voice in the eventual use of such a joint NATO force."

Earlier in the fall, Nenni had proposed that the partners in the center-left coalition undertake to work together not only beyond the general election scheduled for the following spring, but until the next one due in 1968. In order "to achieve political stability on the national and regional levels," I reported in the *Washington Post* (October 19 and 21), "The PSI would join formally with the pro-Western Christian Democrats, Social Democrats, and Republicans in a new government to be formed after next spring's election." The program of the Fanfani Cabinet, I continued, "includes the establishment of regional self-government throughout the country. Within this new framework, the Socialists will be ready to join with the [national] government parties, rather than with the PCI, in all regional administrations, including those to be set up in areas like Tuscany, Emilia and Umbria, where Socialists and Communists together command a majority." This proposal was approved by the Socialist Central Committee over the bitter opposition of the party's pro-Communist wing and in the face of sharp attacks from the Communists. All of them, I further reported, read Nenni's move as a confirmation that the PSI leader and the majority of his party are heading for 'a total break' with the Communists, a charge promptly echoed by the Soviet press. According to friends in Washington, U.S. political circles and President Kennedy himself paid special attention to those two articles in the *Washington Post* because "they spotlighted some aspects of Italian politics that were "ignored or neglected by other U.S. press reports."

Nenni's proposal, however, met with strong opposition or ill-concealed hostility from moderate and conservative groups within the CD camp which had never stomached the opening to the Socialists and wanted to undermine Fanfani's hold on the premiership. "These groups," I wrote (*Washington Post*, December 19), "fear that a strengthening of the center-left combination would negatively affect their power and ambitions. Accordingly, they urge the CD leadership to refrain not only from accepting Nenni's bid for a long-term alliance but also from carrying out completely, before the general election, the program of the present center-left government itself. Here are the makings of a governmental crisis. Should it actually take place, both the Communists and the rightist opposition would receive a major psychological boost, while the center-left coalition would go to the polls in a state of disarray."

The crisis was staved off thanks to a compromise which, however, involved putting off enactment of the new regional system until after the election. "The CDs have given us strong motives for opening a crisis," Nenni told me, "but I have been against doing so mostly out of foreign policy considerations. I have advised Fanfani to go ahead with his impending visit to Washington despite the tensions that have developed within the center-left coalition. It is of paramount importance to have in Italy a government which, as I'm sure Fanfani will tell Kennedy, is determined to stand up against De Gaulle's plans with regard to the political organization of Europe and the security of the West."

Saragat told me during the same days: "We cannot forget about de Gaulle's great qualities or his role in the fight against Nazism or in solving the Algerian problem. Yet one of his major mistakes concerns Italy. I certainly hope that Italy will never be called upon to choose between Europe and America. But if it should come to this, I would choose America and so would the overwhelming majority of my countrymen, with the only exception of the Communists and of the Neo-Fascists. America, the alliance with America are essential for our security and for our freedom which for us have priority over everything else.''

A few days before Fanfani's departure for the United States, I reported in the *Washington Post* (January 14): "The differences within the Western alliance over the British role in the economic and political organization of Europe and the nuclear defense of the West'' had confronted ''many sectors of Italian public opinion . . . with the moment of truth. The Italian conservative forces, in which many U.S. diplomats had long put their faith, have shown that they share the views of de Gaulle rather than those of the Kennedy administration. The Milan daily *Corriere della Sera*, leading spokesman for the Liberals and for other Italian conservative forces, published a front-page article Saturday by its foreign policy expert, Augusto Guerriero, which branded as 'insensate' the strategy which 'the Americans are now trying to force upon the Alliance.' Such a strategy, Guerriero wrote, does not guarantee that Europe will be effectively defended.'' On the other hand, I continued, ''the attitude of the groups making up the present majority has confirmed that a center-left government is the kind of Italian regime which can be relied upon to take the approach closest to that of Washington on the major problems confronting the alliance.''

I happened to be in Fanfani's office when he received word that de Gaulle had made new, harsher statements about NATO and signaled his determination to veto British entry into the European Common Market. The news led the Italian premier to spell out, in terms of indirect but obvious polemics with those statements, ''the spirit which will guide him in the impending talks with President Kennedy,'' I reported in the *Washington Post* the next day (January 15). ''We Italians hope,'' Fanfani told me, ''that the friends of the U.S. in Europe will continue to be most numerous, but in any case we intend to remain, more than ever, in the very front ranks among those friends.'' Listing the main topics to be discussed between the Italian premier and top U.S. leaders, I underlined Italy's strong feelings that ''a nuclear force for Europe must be both closely integrated with America's atomic power and placed under a truly 'collegial' control within the overall framework of NATO, that is, should not be under the control of any 'restricted directorate.' The Italians continue to hope that the joint efforts of the U.S. and of most members of the Common Market will still succeed in securing British membership in the European Economic Community and eventually in a European political union. But in the event that those efforts should fail, Italy, while remaining a member of the Common Market, would be forced to come to the conclusion that no acceptable form of European political union is possible, at least in the foreseeable future.'' According to the present Italian leaders, ''the current French approach to the European problems threatens to introduce a major factor of division within the Atlantic Alliance, in addition to encouraging dangerous authoritarian trends in continental Europe itself. As against those dangers, they would look to closer relations with Great Britain and, above all, would reassert most vigorously their support for American leadership of the alliance.'' The toast delivered by Kennedy at the dinner for the Italian premier was read in U.S. political circles as ''an official blessing'' for the center-left, despite the efforts by ambassador Reinhardt and some state Department officials to water it down. An editorial in the *Washington Post* (January 19) pointed out that the communiqué on the talks between Kennedy and Fanfani ''did not say and could not say'' that the U.S. administration looked with favor upon ''the important domestic experiment aimed at bringing the Nenni Socialists into the democratic family.'' The editorial further stressed that under Fanfani's leadership, Italy had not only continued her exceptional economic expansion but adopted a policy that should spread more widely its benefits and further isolate the Communist party.

When the French refusal to let Britain join the Common Market was formalized, Italian ''resentment'' mingled ''with a growing realization that vigorous countermeasures are required to prevent de Gaulle from forcing through his political and military concept of Europe,'' I wrote in the *Washington Post* (January 30). The latest developments had called ''attention'' to the proposals made recently by La Malfa ''for the formation of a European alignment including Italy, Britain and the Benelux countries'' which would work out ''a policy of its own'' in direct ''contrast with de Gaulle's approach on all matters pertaining to the organization of Europe, development of a multilateral nuclear force for the West, relationship between Europe and the United States and the future of the Common Market itself.'' The policies of such an alignment ''would be based on the closest solidarity with the U.S. and would enable the democratic forces in West Germany to neutralize the negative effects of the French-German treaty signed last week by de Gaulle and chancellor Adenauer.

''The Vatican press has also voiced increasingly deep concern over de Gaulle's policies. In an almost unprecedented attack against the policies of a Catholic chief of state, *Osservatore della Domenica*, the Sunday edition of the Vatican paper *Osservatore Romano*, wrote in its latest issue: 'Atlantic solidarity, which has protected so far the security of Western Europe, is now in serious danger. . . . One is strongly tempted to conclude that if a de Gaulle had not existed as a force expressed or endured by the French people, Soviet diplomacy could not have found anything better to split what it calls the capitalistic world.' ''

The chairman of the Senate Foreign Relations Committee, J. William Fulbright, quoted this *Washington Post* article on the floor and had it printed in *The Congressional Record* of January 30, 1963.

Some sections of the U.S. press, however, kept harping on old charges and prejudices. For *Time* (June 29, 1962), Nenni was still a ''powerful fellow traveling Socialist'' for whom nationalization of the electric power industry represented a ''step toward the end of free enterprise in Italy.'' The magazine *Reporter*, whose editor Max Ascoli reportedly felt snubbed by the Italian premier, asserted that the formation of the Fanfani government backed by the Socialists was a maneuver ''that could gently bring Italy close to a semi-neutralist position.'' In the same issue (March 15, 1962), correspondent Claire Sterling wrote that the new Italian government represented a "difficult and dangerous adventure" because it would be "answerable for its conduct to a party [the Socialists] that dislikes the very idea of NATO. Under these circumstances, it is hard to see how Italy can avoid a change of posture within the Atlantic alliance—marked enough to deprive the alliance of the solidarity it often lacks but surely needs."

Barrett McGurn, winding up his assignment as Rome correspondent for the *New York Herald Tribune*, asserted that Italy had now "a government based on an alliance with pro-Communists" (June 29). Two months later, a *New York Times* editorial charged that Italy had broken away from the Western alignment at the 17-power Disarmament conference in Geneva and attributed the breakaway to the growing Socialist influence on the Fanfani government. The editorial drew an immediate, flat denial from the State Department (August 17). When some agreements were achieved at the conference, moreover, the "constructive" Italian cooperation with the United States and other Western allies was warmly praised by top representatives of the Kennedy administration (April 6, 1963).

Some well known U.S. newspapermen, however, began to show increasing interest and understanding for current developments in Italian domestic politics and for their international significance.

In December 1962, Walter Lippmann met in Rome with several Italian leaders and some foreign observers, including myself. Shortly afterwards, he wrote in one of his columns (*New York Herald Tribune*, December 28): "In Italy today there is being carried on a trial run of the only visible alternative to a Gaullist Europe. It consists of an alliance between Democratic Socialists and Christian Democrats. . . . if the alliance can be consolidated . . . there will be a solid majority for a democratic progressive government." Four months later (April 26, 1963), Lippmann emphasized that "at the national level, though not so completely in the localities, the Nenni Socialists have broken away from the Communists and have openly denounced the undemocratic totalitarianism of the Communist party." At the same time, the CDs had "drawn away from the right and from the far right."

During my visits to Washington and his trips to Italy, I met regularly with Drew Pearson. In a column published in the *Washington Post* on September 11, 1962, Pearson praised the economic and social reforms implemented or planned by Fanfani "in return for Socialist backing" to his government and for lining up "their large block of votes behind NATO and the American policies." Yet, Pearson went on, Fanfani's efforts had "horrified" certain career officers in the U.S. Embassy, notably Horsey "who has long consorted with the right wing in Rome and who has sent reactionary reports to the State Department, frowning on Fanfani's tactics of wooing the Socialists." On the eve of the election in Italy, Pearson emphasized that the accord between CDs and Socialists had removed the danger of a victory at the polls by a Communist-Socialist coalition which otherwise would have been inevitable in view of the gains made by the left and of the losses suffered by the CDs in the last 15 years.

6

JFK Advocates a Government Role
for the Italian Socialists

The outcome of the 1963 general election in Italy was greeted with composure in Washington. U.S. political circles were learning to look at developments in Italy with a mature perception which eschewed emotional reactions to specific episodes to concentrate on substantial longer-term considerations and prospects. The Communist gains and the CD losses (to the benefit of the Liberal party) prompted some officials to say: ''I told you so!'' But these individual comments did not have any real follow-up, largely thanks to the growing impact that Harriman's appointment as under secretary for Political Affairs was having on the department's bureaucracy. The climate had changed in the Rome embassy, too, where Horsey had been replaced by Francis Williamson. Reinhardt himself had apparently realized that the game was up and ill health was pushing him more and more to the sidelines.

In a press conference a high-ranking official of the Kennedy administration endorsed the efforts made by the Fanfani cabinet to promote a wider and more balanced popular participation in the democratic system. The current phase of transition in Italy, the spokesman went on, would inevitably be accompanied by difficulties and political controversy, but there was no alternative to the center-left approach in view of the situation obtaining in Parliament and above all of the opportunity to reabsorb into the democratic area a large share of the Socialist electorate (April 27).

In a cable of CISL secretary general Bruno Storti, Walter Reuther stressed that the center-left coalition could still rely on a parliamentary majority even thought its first test at the polls had come before it had the time to carry out its economic and social program (May 4).

These statements represented an effective counter to the campaign undertaken by some sectors of the Italian press. Girolamo Modesti, Washington correspondent for *Il Resto del Carlino* of Bologna and *La Nazione* of Florence, claimed that the outcome of the Italian elections had caused concern and doubts in U.S. political circles and announced that President Kennedy would cancel his visit to Rome and make only a stopover in Milan during his forthcoming European tour (May 1, 4, 7). Former ambassador Roberto Cantalupo asserted that Washington was no longer betting on the center-left in Italy but now looked with favor on a Europe shaped along Gaullist lines (*Il Giornale d'Italia*, Rome, May 19).

Lippman wrote: ''While the Fanfani coalition has lost some seats in Parliament, it is still very considerably stronger than any other combination which could be put together.'' It remained to be seen whether the Nenni Socialists, at their forthcoming National congress, ''will divorce the Communists completely'' (*New York Herald Tribune*, May 3). An editorial in the same paper stressed that the coalition headed by Fanfani ''won the national election (though by a smaller majority) and undoubtedly will retain the government''—a ''central point . . . much more significant (though less dramatic in the headlines)'' than ''the gain of the Communists (about 3 percent) and the small advance of the Liberals on the right.'' According to a *New York Times* editorial, ''The Communist gains were disturbing but the CDs retained a plurality of the votes. The Socialists would continue to support a government coalition of CDs, Social Democrats, and Republicans, although only the forthcoming PSI National Congress would chart the party's future course'' (May 2).

The editor of *The Reporter*, Max Ascoli, attacked President Kennedy for coming out in favor of Fanfani's ''opening'' to the Socialists. Ascoli argued that the ''opening'' had not produced ''a diminution of Communist strength'' but rather helped the PCI to gain ground and move into a better position to promote a Popular Front in Italy and contribute to its establishment in other major European countries (June 20). In an earlier issue of the same magazine, Claire Sterling contradicted her own recent assessments. She admitted that ''about two-thirds of the Socialists [were ready] to make their break with the Communists final'' and that in foreign policy the positions of the Socialists largely coincided with those of the British Laborites and of the Kennedy administration itself. But Sterling wondered whether the Socialists (and Fanfani himself) would enclose the multilateral nuclear force for NATO and other policies of the Kennedy administration (May 23).

Likewise, Arnaldo Cortesi acknowledged retrospectively that the Fanfani government had accepted all the policies in which the United States was particularly interested. He insisted, however, that Italy might slide into neutralism if the Nenni Socialists exploited the CDs' increased dependence on their support. Cortesi further asserted that Nenni had pledged ''not to break with the Communists'' (May 6). According to the *United Press*, the PSI intended to rejoin the Communists in the opposition since the center-left was ''dead'' (May 9).

The bias of some sectors of the U.S. press and their inability to understand Italy and Italian politics emerged most flagrantly when the conflicts within the Socialist camp led to the failure of Moro's first attempt to form a new center-left government. ''Epitaph for the *Apertura*,'' crowed *Time* and added: ''Shut tight was the risky opening to the left'' (June 26). ''Opening to nowhere,'' chimed in *Newsweek* (July 1). According to a *New York Times* editorial (June 20), the strengthened Socialist left-wing might defeat Nenni in the next congress. In that event, the Communist-Socialist alliance would be revived, precipitating a crisis of domestic and foreign significance. The *New York Times* advised President Kennedy to drop his plans for an early visit to Rome which was ill-advised ''even before the Italian election.''

As soon as the election returns were known, I pointed out in the *Washington Post* (May 1) that, despite the gains scored by the Communists and by the Liberals, the center-left coalition was still ''the only combination capable of commanding a large and fairly solid majority in the new Italian Parliament.'' The Communists' gains at the expense of the PSI had been ''made much easier by the CD leadership's failure to push the 'New Dealish' program agreed upon with the Socialists when the center-left government was formed in February 1962.

''The Liberal surge,'' I added, ''reflected the success of a well organized and well financed effort, backed by powerful sectors of the press, to play upon the fears aroused by the center-left approach among the conservative segments of the CD electorate. The CDs gave ground on their left as well, probably because some of their supporters became impatient over the party's failure to press more boldly on the road to social reform.''

The Communist gains at the polls, I further reported in the *Washington Post* on May 15, should be seen in the context of spreading protests fed by practical rather than by ideological factors and circumstances. As shown clearly by the Letters to the Editor column of one of Italy's best papers, *La Stampa* of Turin, these protests concerned mainly the rises in cost-of-living for outstripping salary and pension increases, ''graft and mismanagement of public money'' and the taxes ''that hit the small fry, while the big ones do as they please.'' These were long-standing conditions. I concluded, ''that post-war Italian democracy has failed to tackle effectively; and the recent material progress has made Italians more aware and less tolerant of the shortcomings in their country's social and civil structure.''

Top Vatican circles, I wrote in the *Washington Post* on May 13, are reliably reported to have concluded: ''The losses suffered by the CDs and the gains made by the Communists represent a setback and a warning for the Italian democratic forces, but are not a disaster; the Communists . . . have been the main benefi-ciaries of the all-out attacks launched against the CDs from most quarters of the political alignment and notably from the right; the rightist and conservative groups have further helped the Communists by speeding wholly unfounded reports that recent moves by Pope John XXIII indicate a softening of the church's attitude toward Communism.'' (The audience granted to Khrushchev's son-in-law, Alek-sei Agiubei had been played up by the U.S. press as well, in connection with political developments in Italy.) ''Christian Democracy remains the dominant political force in Italy and must be encouraged to pursue a forward-looking course in economic and social affairs and to strengthen the moral and material fabric of its organization in order to match the efficiency of the Communist machine.''

From conversations with top CD and Socialist leaders, I gathered that the first move would be an attempt "to install Aldo Moro as the head of a new center-left Italian government. Moderate and conservative CDs have indicated that they will support another center-left government only if Fanfani leaves the premiership. Saragat has also underlined the need to make some major changes in the top governmental posts (*Washington Post*, May 14).

"No significant change should be expected in Italian foreign policy," I continued. "Many spokesmen for the rightist forces are not only stepping up their criticism of the Kennedy administration, which they blame for having favored the center-left in Italy, but are offering fresh evidence of their sympathy for many of de Gaulle's ideas. Most outspoken are the Neo-Fascists, but some conservative spokesmen have taken a similar approach. For instance, a newly elected Liberal senator, writing in the rightist Rome daily, *Tempo*, charged today that 'the American President has pushed his support of the dangerous center-left experiment . . . to the absurd point of favoring, as a pawn in the game against Paris, a tendentially neutralist Italy over an Italy fully committed to the Atlantic alliance' '' (*Washington Post*, May 8).

On the Socialist side, Nenni told me, foreign policy was "not a problem, so much so that I have left out all references to our party's traditional neutralism in the draft platform that I submitted to our Central Committee as the basis for the negotiations intended to insure our support to a new center-left government. In domestic affairs we don't want more than was promised to us at the time the Fanfani government was formed, but we need more solid guarantees that the promises will be kept."

For many years, Riccardo Lombardi had been point man in the effort to draw the Socialists away from the Communists. But CD reluctance to implement key reforms agreed upon with the Socialists, made Lombardi increasingly skeptical about the prospects of the center-left coalition. Shortly after the April 1963 election, he told me: "The center-left has been the most intelligent operation undertaken in Italy since the end of World War II; unfortunately, it has been undertaken with a delay of several years, as it happens only too often in our country. . . . Ideally, we should have had the opportunity to devote the first two or three years of the center-left to far-reaching reforms and modernizations of the Italian administrative, fiscal and financial structures. This would have given us the key tools to carry out the program required to do away with our chronic geographic and social imbalances and to insure, at the same time, a steady economic growth. But the first center-left government has been compelled to face all these problems together. Today, the problems are just as urgent or more so, while the country's condition has deteriorated economically and psychologically."

Lombardi pinpointed correctly the main roots of the troubles that were to beset the center-left governments and the nation itself over the next years and decades. But he seemed unable to provide effective answers. "Personally," he further told me, "I feel that our party can well afford to wait for a couple of years and still have the opportunity to give the center-left a new lease on life under more favorable or at least less unfavorable circumstances. Meanwhile the CDs would be left to their own devices and our party would not shoulder its share of responsibility for a governmental policy which could hardly be in line with our program and in fact would be bound to antagonize the workers and their unions to the exclusive benefit of the Communists."

Eventually Lombardi decided to block Nenni's plan to support the new center-left government to be headed by Moro. I continued to feel, however, that the basic political outlook had not been altered and that negotiations to form such a government would be resumed and successfully concluded in the near future. On the morrow of the split in the PSI majority and of the consequent collapse of Moro's attempt, I reported that the task of putting together a new cabinet had been given to the CD speaker of the House, Giovanni Leone. His only chance, apparently, was "to persuade Socialists, Social Democrats and Republicans to give outside support to an avowedly caretaker government . . . by presenting [it] as a bridge toward a new center-left combination that might be put together in the fall if by that time all the parties concerned are ready to reach an agreement along the lines advocated in recent days by Moro" (*Washington Post*, June 20).

Two weeks later Leone formed "a minority all-Christian-Democratic government" which was expected to win quick approval in Parliament thanks to "the abstention of the Social Democrats, Republicans, and Nenni Socialists. Communists and Neo-Fascists will vote against the government and so will the conservative Liberal Party. . . . In the Socialist camp, the pro-Communist wing demanded again last night that the party line up with the Communists in voting against the Leone government, but the majority of the party rallied behind Nenni, who pointed out that the defeat of the Leone Cabinet would open the way to a dangerous radicalization of the political struggle. . . . Even Riccardo Lombardi, leader of the dissident group which only two weeks ago torpedoed the agreement with the CDs, argued that the Socialists must abstain on the vote of confidence. Lombardi tried to explain his recent revolt against Nenni's leadership by maintaining that the party will be in a better position to negotiate a fresh agreement with the CDs after its National congress scheduled for October 25–29" (*Washington Post*, July 4).

The latest developments, however, had been a painful experience for Nenni. "The battle is lost or almost lost," were his first words when we met again. I replied that this bitter assessment was understandable, but I also listed facts and circumstances that made it unwarranted or at least premature. While professing deep concern over the party's conditions and about the prospects of the next Socialist congress, Nenni affirmed his determination to "do all I can to rally a majority numerically adequate and politically committed to relaunch and consolidate the center-left coalition. I'm prepared to face the new and more violent attacks that the Communists will unleash against me as soon as we Socialists reach a solid accord with the CDs and participate in a government which will confine and isolate the PCI into the opposition." An open break with the pro-Communist wing of his own party, Nenni went on, was "an inevitable and even healthy development." Nenni strongly criticized Lombardi's behavior: "He did not disagree from the way I conducted the negotiations with Moro until the last moment when he torpedoed them."

The agreement he had reached with Moro, Nenni added, left unsettled only two relatively minor issues relating to urban zoning regulations and to the powers of a new agency to promote agricultural development. In reply to a specific question, the Socialist leader told me that his party had not raised any objections when Fanfani, during his visit to Washington in January, had accepted in principle the project for a multilateral nuclear force for NATO (MLF). "We Socialists," Nenni said, "prefer that atomic weapons be a monopoly of the U.S. and of the Soviet Union. This would not only avoid a most dangerous nuclear proliferation but favor an accord or at least a better *modus vivendi* between the two major Powers. Since, however, such a monopoly is no longer possible, the multilateral force can help to check nuclear proliferation at least in Europe." Nenni stressed that both Italy and Great Britain must participate in the MLF which otherwise would appear "an undertaking in which only the Germans would share with the Americans."

Nenni praised once again President Kennedy's championship of close relations between the United States and a Europe which "must proceed toward political unification and include Great Britain rather than develop along the nationalistic and authoritarian lines favored by de Gaulle." The Socialist leader said he strongly hoped to meet the U.S. President who was expected to visit Rome early in July. The latest information from Washington led me to believe that the meeting would take place. Some last minute hitch might still develop, mainly because president Segni, who would play host to Kennedy, was known to dislike the "opening" to the Socialists. Accordingly, I only told Nenni that, in my opinion, the White House and political circles in Washington looked with sympathy at the constructive role that the PSI, under Nenni's own leadership, had played in recent years and would hopefully continue to play.

The meeting took place on the evening of July 1 during the reception given for Kennedy in the gardens of the Quirinale Palace, the official residence of the Italian president of the Republic. I remember quite well how Togliatti and Malagodi, leaders of the two main parties opposed to the center-left, waited in the wings with all too apparent impatience and concern while the talk between Kennedy and Nenni went on, way beyond schedule. And I remember how moved and elated Nenni was, as he recalled a few days later and even many years afterwards, that Kennedy had not only invited him to come to the United States but had displayed a warm interest for the significance of the center-left, "actually for 'operation Nenni' as the President chose to call it," Nenni added with obvious satisfaction. I was also told by Schlesinger and by Bob Komer (at the time on the White House staff) that Kennedy had been deeply impressed by Nenni's personality and "lucid views."

Meanwhile the talks between the top Italian and U.S. leaders had "confirmed once more that the agreement between the two countries on all major international issues is not even marred by the differences of method and emphasis that exist between other members of the Western alliance. Despite the admittedly provisional character of the Leone government," I reported in the *Washington Post* (July 5), "the consensus in both Italian and American quarters after the visit here by President Kennedy" was that Italy intended to "make a major contribution to help implement the 'strategy of peace' outlined by the President in his [recent] speeches. . . . The reaffirmed Italian support for plans to organize a multilateral atomic force for NATO stems from political rather than from military considerations. From a strictly military standpoint, the Italian leaders feel that their country is perfectly safe under the umbrella of American nuclear power. But they also feel that the proposed multilateral force can: (1) help control the proliferation of national atomic forces; (2) offer the European partners of the alliance a higher degree of coresponsibility for the measures intended to safeguard the security of the Western community as a whole; (3) provide a further stimulus to the integration of Europe, including Britain, 'within the framework of the interdependence between the U.S. and Europe itself'; (4) give the Soviet Union further evidence that the Atlantic Alliance is guided by 'the utmost sense of responsibility' and therefore strives to commit as many as possible of the countries with potential atomic capabilities to participate in multilateral arrangements rather than proceed independently with the development of those capabilities."

In September, Schlesinger asked me, through Vic Sullam, to provide a detailed and confidential assessment of the prospects of the Socialist congress. I replied that a "moderate optimism" was warranted: "Nenni and Moro are sincerely committed to form and support a center-left government." On the other hand, there were persistent reports but no definite evidence that powerful French, West German and Dutch economic groups, allied with conservative forces in the United States, had decided to join the fight against the coming to power of a full-fledged center-left alliance in Italy—an event which would jeopardize the success of their plans to secure control of continental Europe and thus thwart the efforts of the Kennedy administration and of the other supporters of a united Europe including Great Britain. The Socialist congress, in my opinion, would register a strengthening of Nenni's majority which, however, would fall short of 60 percent of the PSI; Lombardi's faction would still be able to play an important role in the balance of power within that majority and possibly with the party itself.

The PSI members of Parliament, I also pointed out, had abstained on the vote on the defense budget which called for a 10-percent increase over the preceding year. As I reported in the *Washington Post* (September 21), Socialist spokesmen had "recognized that the continued large-scale military expenditures by both the Western and the Eastern countries make an adequate defense budget 'a realistic requirement' for Italy, too."

With regard to MLF, I further wrote to Schlesinger, "asking the Socialists to say 'yes' or 'no' right now, will probably produce a negative result." Apart from the position that may be taken by Lombardi's group, "the recently improved relations between the Italian Socialists and the British Laborites make it even less likely, not to say impossible, that the PSI will publicly underwrite Italian participation in the MLF as long as the British Labor party sticks to its present, strongly negative stand. On the other hand, if a noisy and untimely debate on the issue can be avoided, the position of many Socialists will soften after their party gets into the government (and much the same may well be the case with the British Laborites after they get back in office)."

At the PSI Congress, a majority "of almost 60 percent," I reported in the *Washington Post* (October 31), "authorized direct participation by the party in a coalition government with the pro-Western CDs, Social Democrats and Republicans. As underlined by Nenni today, this means that the majority of the Socialists are determined at last to join actively in the effort to turn Italy into a modern democracy, without letting themselves be hamstrung any more by a doctrinaire 'class' approach. Time and again, since the Socialist Party was first formed in 1892, its refusal to share in the government with the 'bourgeois' forces was responsible for 'lost opportunities' to strengthen democratic institutions and promote the interests of the Italian workers—as Nenni himself acknowledged in his opening speech to the congress. Now the outcome of the Socialist Congress offers at last a concrete opportunity for a departure in Italian politics. The majority of the Socialists have reaffirmed their support for the political and economic integration of Europe. They now accept Italy's membership in NATO and the consequent obligations. But the Socialists show a marked distaste for the whole idea of a multi-lateral nuclear force for NATO.

"In domestic policy, the majority of the Socialists agree that the Communists must be excluded from the projected center-left government's majority. They have taken further steps to loosen their ties with the Communists in the local administration. But they still hesitate to go all the way in that direction.

"At the same time," I further reported, "the Socialists are pressing for speedy implementation of a broad economic and social reforms which, while more typical of a modern democracy than of a Socialist society, are opposed not only by the conservative groups but also by many moderate forces within the CD camp. Another question mark is represented by the faction led by Riccardo Lombardi."

As recently as last December, I wrote in the *Washington Post* (November 10), "Lombardi gave the Communist leaders, assembled in Rome for their party congress, a typical sample of his bent, bordering on coquetry, for voicing his views in terms most likely to arouse a maximum of controversy. Socialists and Communists, Lombardi said, 'now hold different and actually opposite views' on the major domestic and international problems. The main reason, he added, is the Socialists' conviction that the interests of the working masses must be promoted only by democratic means and can be promoted without taking Italy 'out of the Western system.' In recent months, however, and again at the Socialist Congress ten days ago, Lombardi went out of his way to shock just as violently his party's prospective partners in a center-left government as well as many of his fellow Socialists. To combat mounting inflationary pressures, he proposed measures that most orthodox economists can gladly endorse. But in pressing for far-reaching social reforms, he used a language suggesting that he wanted those reforms more to 'punish' Italian capitalists and private economic operators than to modernize the country's admittedly outdated structures and institutions. More-over, Lombardi, while going along with Nenni in accepting Italy's membership in the Atlantic Alliance, voiced outright opposition to the whole idea of a mul-tilateral nuclear force for NATO. No wonder that both Communists and con-servatives should now consider Lombardi as their main hope for wrecking the impending negotiations for a stable center-left regime.

"Lombardi told me a few days ago: 'Our goal is a Socialist society. But in the meantime our party and the progressive-minded bourgeois forces can and must work together for a generation to turn Italy into a modern democracy. That's why I am in favor of the center-left approach, despite all its limitations.' Lombardi feels that the party might refrain from 'slamming the door' on the multilateral force project, although the latter appears 'bound to promote, however indirectly, German atomic armament rather than to prevent it.' But in any case, Lombardi maintains that the Socialists cannot countenance that full and imme-diate Italian commitment on the matter which, according to newspaper reports here, is now solicited by Washington, the more so since the project in its present form is opposed by the British Laborites and by other European Social Democrats. Said Lombardi: 'If one of the first acts of a government in which we Socialists are represented should be the Italian participation in what would amount to a spreading of nuclear armaments, we would be confronted with an irrepressible and justified revolt by our rank and file.' "

In recent months, I had developed good contacts with Angelo Salizzoni and Tommaso Morlino, Moro's key assistants in the negotiations with the Socialists on the next government (Salizzoni became under secretary to the premiership in the Moro Cabinet and Morlino was given important posts in subsequent cabinets, notably the ministry of justice). In the early fall they told me that the CD Party was "absolutely firm" on two key issues: the Communists must be "kept outside the governmental majority" and "explicit reference must be made to Italy's role as a member of the Atlantic Alliance, thus reaffirming the 'continuity' of the nation's foreign policy." Morlino and Salizzoni explained that a formula, worked out by Moro during the negotiations with Nenni in June, spelled out, "without leaving room for doubts or ambiguities, ways and means to guarantee that the PCI would stay confined into the opposition." Said Morlino: "We fully realize that the Kennedy Administration's benevolent neutrality and actual sympathy for the coming to power of a full-fledged center-left government depend on the expectation that this not only will not have a negative influence on Italy's role in international affairs but can help our country to become a more effective supporter of key planks of American foreign policy. We cannot afford, either, to provide ammunition or even pretexts to those sectors of our own party which are opposed or lukewarm toward a governmental cooperation with the Socialists.''

Morlino and Salizzoni recalled that some commitments, in principle, on the MLF had been already made, notably by Fanfani during his visit to Washington early in the year. ''Would some doubts about Italy's loyalty to NATO be likely to emerge in Washington if the next government hesitates to reaffirm those commitments?'' My personal opinion, I replied, was that such would be the case. When we met again, in early November, Morlino went so far as to say that my answer had ''played a decisive role in crystallizing the CD party's stand.'' Accordingly, he had served notice to the Socialist representatives that the CD leadership would not tolerate any equivocations on the issue. The majority of the Socialists seemed ''now willing not only to refrain from questioning the commitments to MLF made by earlier Italian governments but to leave open subsequent developments. In the negotiations with the Socialists,'' Morlino added, ''we'll also point out that a solution of the MLF issue along the lines suggested by us is even more advisable because otherwise president Segni would be given an opportunity to interfere in the negotiations for the new government by resorting to his right to have a say on an issue directly pertaining to the politics of the Italian State.''

An agreement was eventually reached and included in the program of the new government: Italy would link her eventual acceptance of the MLF to the fulfillment of some conditions designed to take care, at least in part, of the reservations and misgivings shared by the Italian Socialists and by sizable political groups in other NATO countries.

The Leone Cabinet duly resigned and Moro was picked to form a center-left government with the direct participation of the Socialists. Negotiations on the program and the allocation of cabinet posts among the coalition partners seemed about to be concluded when on November 21 fresh reports were suddenly circulated that the United States requested an immediate and specific Italian commitment to join soon in the implementation of the MLF project. These reports reflected in part the pressures by some U.S. officials, known in Washington as ''the theologians'' of MLF but were mostly spread by those political and economic groups in Italy, in the United States, and elsewhere in the West, that still hoped that the accord for a Socialist role in the government would founder, possibly on the rock of a foreign policy issue.

Morlino and Salizzoni told me right away that, if those reports had some foundation, the Socialists would ''not be able to go ahead with the formation of the new government.'' Ranking Socialists, notably Senator Paolo Vittorelli, the top PSI expert on foreign policy, advised me that the pro-Communist wing of their party was on the warpath. Unless the MLF issue was settled on the basis that had been deemed acceptable by both CD and PSI negotiators or was at least set aside, their party would be confronted with a split of such dimensions as to jeopardize and probably block the accord for the new center-left government. To rescue the accord and give a real chance to the center-left coalition itself, both my CD and Socialist contacts insisted it was urgent to get a clear signal about Washington's stand on MLF and on the whole matter of a government role for the PSI.

I hastened to get in touch with Sullam and through him with Schlesinger. Within hours, word came back from the White House and reached quickly the leaders of the Italian parties involved: the president felt that MLF was important but it was even more important to have in Italy a center-left government with the direct participation of the Socialists. It was one of the very last decisions taken by John F. Kennedy before leaving for Dallas and his appointment with death.

7

Underdeveloped with Fifty Million Car-owners?

Time (November 8, 1963) stressed the seriousness of the crisis faced by Italian democracy and reported that, according to PLI leader Giovanni Malagodi, the collaboration with the Socialists, keynote of the next government to be led by Moro, meant "abandonment . . . of solidarity with the West . . . of a free economy and an open democratic society." U.S. policymakers, the weekly concluded "perceive no such perils."

The Reporter asserted that it was difficult to see how the platform adopted by the PSI National Congress "is different from that of the Communists—except that it is advanced by men who are not Communists. The case of Italy must be taken seriously, for it could become contagious" (November 21). The magazine's editor, Max Ascoli, further charged that, "while slandering an ally like de Gaulle . . . the [Kennedy] administration has shown benevolence toward the various types of positive or active neutralism, and has explicitly encouraged openings to the left in Italy, in other allied countries, and in Latin America."

Paul Hofmann, who had replaced Cortesi as chief of the *New York Times* Rome bureau, wrote on November 17 that the door that had been "slammed when De Gasperi ousted the Communists and the leftwing Socialists from the government and had been unlocked by Fanfani 15 years later," seemed about to "be pushed wide open again" to let the Socialists into the government and might be left ajar for the Communists to come in, too.

In Italy, rightist papers and journalists were furious over the prospects of a center-left government coming to power with the support of a U.S. administration: "If nothing happens to change Kennedy's policies and if, after the 1964 election, he'll be free to continue his dismantling of anti-Communist defenses," wrote Adolfo Coltano in *Il Borghese* (November 7), "the Italians will have to draw their conclusions. If we must end up the way [South Vietnamese leaders]

Diem and Nu have ended up in order to allow the U.S. to be on good terms with the Soviet Union, then we might as well start on our own down the road to neutralism . . . getting out of NATO and closing down U.S. bases in Leghorn, Vicenza, Naples and Sardinia.'' Augusto Guerriero, longtime foreign policy editorialist of *Corriere della Sera*, wrote in the weekly *Epoca*, where he ran a column under the pen name of Ricciardetto: ''I've almost come to the conclusion that Communism, a Westernized version of Communism, is better than the center-left. At least, Communism is not stupid, has its grammar right, and sends to their death those who steal public monies.''

When the first Moro government was formed, *Time* quoted again Malagodi to the effect that the new ruling coalition headed ''Italy 'directly toward Communist shores' '' (December 6). *Newsweek* stressed that ''with Nenni as deputy premier, Moro is likely to find it hard to avoid a slow erosion of Rome's traditional postwar attitude of automatic agreement with Washington on major foreign policy questions. The opening to the left which the great compromiser has effected could also open some doors that Moro, and the U.S., have long considered permanently locked'' (December 9).

Paul Hofmann reported in the *New York Times* (December 2) that the Nenni Socialists opposed the appointment as defense minister of Giulio Andreotti, a champion of close political and military collaboration with the West. A *New York Times* editorial pointed out, instead, that for the first time since the war, Italy's Communist party was isolated while there was a concrete prospect for the emerging of a large, Democratic Socialist party. In spite of the strains within both the CD and the Socialist parties, the editorial concluded, the center-left represented the country's ''best chance for progress'' (December 11).

''For the first time,'' I wrote in the *Washington Post* on November 24, ''the Socialists led by Pietro Nenni, formerly close allies of the Communists, have undertaken to participate in a government firmly pledged to pursue an active pro-Western policy.'' The main planks of the new government's program included, I further reported in the same paper (December 5), ''a foreign policy based on full loyalty to the Atlantic Alliance and related commitments. The domestic platform calls for a long-range program of economic expansion, social reform and institutional modernization.''

The right-wing CDs gave up plans for a walkout after the Vatican paper *Osservatore Romano* called on the party to stay united. The pro-Communist wing of the PSI, instead, split away and formed a new party (PSIUP).

In asking for the first vote of confidence, I reported in the *Washington Post* (December 13), ''Moro pledged that his country's foreign policy will continue to be based 'upon loyalty to the Atlantic alliance, with all the political and military obligations stemming from it.' When the [MLF] project takes final shape, Moro indicated, the Italian government will approve it if it conforms to the avowed aims of strengthening Italian security, insuring collective control of nuclear arms and preventing the risks of atomic proliferation.

''On the domestic scene, the first and most difficult task of the new government is checking the inflationary pressures that have recently developed in the wake of the Italian economic boom. The second step will be the implementation of a program to eliminate Italy's outdated administrative and economic structures. Moro said there will be no further nationalization measures. But the government will undertake a drive to expand educational facilities, promote [modern plans for] urban development [and curb real estate speculation], set up land development agencies, enact effective anti-trust legislation and modernize the tax and social security systems. The government will also strive to implement the 1947 Constitution by setting up semi-autonomous regional administrations throughout the country and by revising police regulations and other legislation pertaining to relations between the citizen and the state which in too many cases still go back to Fascist times.''

"Time will tell," I wrote in the *Washington Post* on December 30, "whether the center-left coalition can implement its program. But at hand is an opportunity for establishing the young Italian democracy and the country's allegiance to the West on a wider foundation of popular support. Strong opposition by both Communists and conservatives," I concluded, "has failed to block the center-left alliance but has managed to delay its consummation. As a result, the Moro government takes office at a time when the economic situation has become less favorable.''

About 1960, many U.S. and other Western observers suddenly discovered the Italian "miracle." They extolled indiscriminately the unexpected developments which seemed to enable Italy to join the leading group of the major industrial nations of the West and were given additional luster and appeal by a happy season of Italian creativity in such disparate fields as interior decoration, movies, shoes, architecture, and office equipment.

In articles and talks, in the United States as well as in Italy, I pointed out that "miracles" do not occur, in the economy, least of all. To label as a miracle Italy's performance represented not only a dangerously superficial reading of current events but was grossly unfair to many Italians. It was unfair to the politicians who had fought successfully to replace the protectionism traditionally prevailing in Italy with a wide-ranging liberalization of the country's foreign trade. It was unfair to the industrialists, technicians, and businessmen who had risen to the challenge by making many Italian products competitive on the international markets. It was most unfair to the millions of hard working and often poorly paid Italians who had played a decisive part in the "quality jump" achieved by key sectors of the national economy.

The use and abuse of the word miracle also made it harder to perceive the real nature of the economic expansion as well as the new problems and dangers bound to surface as soon as such a disorderly and uneven boom sapped some of the basic conditions which had helped to spark it—notably the low level of wages and mass consumption that reflected in turn a large and chronic unemployment and underemployment. Too many foreign (and Italian) observers, furthermore, forgot that any sudden speedup in economic growth involves and sharpens tensions, imbalances, and frustrations. In the case of Italy, the costs could but be very high because the benefits of the "forward jump" were mostly concentrated in the industrial sector (and did not affect all of it, either) and because the country's administrative, economic, and financial structures were far from adequate to the requirements of a modern democracy.

In 1963–1964 Italy was thus confronted with her first crisis as a nation that had achieved a fairly advanced stage of economic development but could not rely on modern tools to handle her new condition. The key task of braking an overheated economy, or of speeding it up again afterward, could not be performed by a fiscal system that was socially inequitable and technically backward. Timely and effective action to curb, or expand, public expenditures was made impossible by the cumbersome and inefficient bureaucratic apparatus. There was no alternative to resorting to money and credit controls, which only too often were used belatedly and heavy-handedly. Their impact, moreover, was bound to be distorted by the shortcomings of the banking system and of the stock exchanges which only too often operated as gambling tables for a few groups of speculators and were too narrow and hobbled by old-fashioned practices to perform as adequate conveyors of funds to finance truly productive activities.

"The labor situation in today's Italy," I reported in the *Washington Post* on July 3, 1962, "reflects in capsule form all the hopes and the strains, the problems and the opportunities of a country which, for the first time in its history, has come within grasping distance of the rungs reached years ago by the most advanced Western societies.

"The unrest among the metalworkers is basically rooted in a simple fact: Italy is the only Western country where, throughout the recent boom, industrial wages have risen much less than productivity. Moreover, the newly developed shortages of skilled manpower and the overall dynamism of the Italian economy have had a profound psychological impact upon many workers. Their interest is no longer confined to strictly bread and butter issues but begins to extend to many other matters affecting their life inside the factory or even outside its gates.

"That is why the latest metalworkers' strike has been successful even at the huge Fiat motorworks in Turin [which] over the last ten years had appeared to be effectively insulated from major labor troubles. This was the result of a generous wage policy and of the strength developed by a plant union independent from all the nationwide labor organizations. The successful strike at Fiat has had an interesting sequel. Fiat president Vittorio Valletta took this opportunity to spell out publicly his sympathy and support for the center-left government which many of his fellow industrialists and the whole conservative alignment in Italy have been blaming for everything under the sun, including specifically the current wave of strikes. Valletta blamed the strikes both on the 'violent and intimidatory' methods used by communist unionists and on some Italian industrialists."

Among government employees, the other large group involved in the current strikes, "the stiffest demands for salary increases and for an immediate reorganization of the whole bureaucratic apparatus come from an independent union that represents the top ranks of the civil service. It has the wholehearted support of the right of center press. Too many of the middle and high echelon civil servants have rightist sympathies as shown, among other things, by the large vote polled by the neofascist movement in Rome where most of those civil servants are concentrated.''

In the *Washington Post* of September 23, I wrote about another strike, organized in Milan ''by both democratic and Communist controlled unions to protest the continuing steep increase of rents, one of the major components of the mounting cost of living in Italy [which] in recent times has climbed by as much as 9 percent a year.'' In Milan, September 29 is the traditional deadline for renewing leases and ''during the past weeks tens of thousands of tenants have been notified by their landlords that they must accept rent increases ranging up to 30 percent or move out. But the situation is basically the same in all other major urban centers and it calls for measures much more far-reaching than the emergency bill which is now being rushed through Parliament and empowers the magistrate to block evictions and freeze rents at their current levels for up to two years.

''In the 1950–1960 decade, the Italian population increased by 2,718,000. Seventy-six percent of this was concentrated in the four largest cities: Milan, Rome, Turin, and Naples.'' Even in Milan's ''unfashionable outlying districts, new two- and three-room apartments are renting for the equivalent of about half the take-home pay of a skilled worker or a white collar employee. Rents of old homes and apartments are nearing the same level. The only exceptions are apartments whose rents were frozen after the war, but these comprise less than one-third of the total in cities like Milan.

''The steep rise in land values,'' I went on, ''has also curtailed the effectiveness of low-price housing programs undertaken or financed by government agencies and local authorities. At the same time, the expansion of most Italian cities has developed along lines dictated by the interests of powerful private groups. For many years, the enactment of remedial measures was blocked by the pressure of vested interests.'' Only in April 1962, ''Parliament finally empowered rapidly expanding towns to draft 10-year plans for urban development and to expropriate any areas those plans required for low-cost housing construction or public facilities. Another measure taxing real estate capital gains, retroactive for ten years, was enacted last March after being before Parliament since 1956. The implementation of both measures, however, is running into strong resistance on the ground that they encroach upon the independence of private property and involve 'unfair discriminations.' Still another bill, giving the national government and local authorities wider powers to control town development in the public interest, was the target of violent rightist attacks during the election campaign last April and the subject of much controversy within the CD party.''

''Italy is a country of 50 million underdeveloped car owners.'' This crack, attributed to representatives of the European Common Market,'' I wrote in the

Washington Post (November 17), "contains at least an ounce of truth. The concern currently voiced abroad over the Italian economy seems somewhat exaggerated, just as was the case for the indiscriminate praise heaped only a short time ago upon the Italian 'miracle.' Conservative groups [accuse] the Fanfani government of having encouraged an excessive rise in wages. Wages indeed have gone up sharply since 1961, but for too many years they had lagged far behind the remarkable rise in productivity. At the same time, hundreds of thousands of generally unskilled and mostly illiterate laborers are still unemployed or underemployed in the South. The stepped-up rise in imports can be largely traced to increased consumption, reflecting the more decent living standards achieved at last by the Italian masses. Weather conditions have been an occasional contributing factor. But a major role was played by the still largely backward conditions of Italian agriculture. And the rise in food prices has been magnified by a distribution system that makes for tremendous spreads between the prices paid to agricultural producers and the prices charged to consumers. But the vested interests have stoutly opposed all efforts to streamline the system.

"When the Fanfani government nationalized the electric power industry," I also recalled "The campaign of all-out opposition by the big private producers and by their friends in the press and in Parliament had the main result of scaring small stockholders into selling their shares at a loss, despite the government's pledge to fully protect their interests. A withholding tax on dividends was met by large-scale transfers of capital abroad, involving an estimated total of 3 billion dollars over the last 18 months. The alarm campaign and the capital transfers have seriously affected the Italian stock market and contributed to a negative trend of the balance of payments, while threatening to dry up domestic investments.

"The current Italian economic troubles," I concluded, "still appear to be the drawbacks of a too rapid and disorderly growth process, rather than symptoms of a basic illness. But political stability and a more balanced expansion of the economy depend upon gradual but steady social reforms and institutional modernizations."

In the *Washington Post* of June 15, 1964, I updated the description and assessment of a boom that threatened to turn more and more into a boomerang: "In Bari and other southern Italian cities, soccer fans have taken recently to throwing their shoes into the playing field to vent their disgust over the performance of the umpire. Ten years ago, many of them could not afford to wear shoes at all. Last month, 25,000 Milanese traveled to Vienna to cheer their favorite team which was playing Madrid for the European soccer championship. A Social Democratic member of Parliament deplored that several million dollars should be spent on such a trip while Italy is confronted with a serious inflation and a heavy balance-of-payments deficit. He was berated as a spoilsport by both conservative and Communist papers.

"The fact is that, sometime in 1961, many Italians acquired the sudden notion that theirs had become at last an affluent society. And too many of them have clung to that notion and behave accordingly, although recent economic and financial developments have made clear that for some years the country has been living beyond its means.

"This largely explains why banking and government authorities failed to take timely action in late 1962 when the Italian economy showed the first signs of overheating. It also illustrates one of the difficulties confronting the incumbent center-left government of premier Aldo Moro as it strives to proceed with the harsher measures that have become imperative. Its task is further complicated by the urgent need to modernize the country's economic, social and administrative structures. These reforms are bound to hurt many interests. Moreover, the expense involved, while spread over a period of years, will begin to increase the burden on the Treasury at a time when the country must fight inflation and maintain a high rate of capital investment.

"But concrete progress in implementing reform is imperative for political and economic reasons. It offers the only way to maintain the collaboration between the Socialists and their 'bourgeois' partners in the present government, and to isolate the Communist party and eventually cut down its electoral following. On the economic side, it is necessary in order to protect the country against disastrous swings of the business cycle and to promote more balanced development. Need for reform has been dramatized by the recent disorderly boom, which quickly backfired, leaving the country exposed to runaway inflation and/or economic depression.

"To a great extent," I recalled, "the Italian 'take-off' of the early 1950s was made possible by the existence of a pool of 2 million of unemployed and the related low level of wages. The boom uncovered acute shortages of trained manpower, a direct consequence of the long-standing failure to expand and modernize the education system. The belated rise in wages became even sharper as industrialists bid for technicians and skilled workers. The banking system continued to extend liberal loans and credits even after wages and consumption had begun to rise much faster than productivity and investments. Competitive capacity of the Italian economic plant was further weakened by wasteful operation of the Social Security system."

"Things have turned out to be much worse than we thought when the Moro government was formed," Nenni told me as early as February 1964. "This is the main obstacle to the implementation of the agreed-upon reforms on which the PSI must insist to prove that our participation in the government makes really a difference." The Socialist leader recalled that late in 1961 Moro had lined up with the moderate CDs rather than with Fanfani and had thus contributed to delay the setting up of regional governments and other reforms included in the government's own program. "I'm worried now by Moro's silence," Nenni added. "Fanfani talked too much, but Moro talks too little."

His recent, unhappy experience as budget minister in the Fanfani Cabinet unquestionably colored La Malfa's views. But his assessments of the behavior of the labor unions and its consequences were borne out by the role they played at the time and in subsequent years to the detriment of the national economy and eventually of their own prestige and influence. "If the unions do not take a more moderate and constructive approach," he told me in March, "they will knife in the back the center-left just as it seeks desperately to restore financial stability and to defeat the rightist attacks. 'If you insist on demanding further, sizable wage increases,' I told the labor leaders, 'it will be impossible to curb inflation and the government's austerity program, unpopular as much as it is necessary, will fail to produce positive results. Since Communism will then appear as the only alternative, the rightist forces will be able to ride to power the fear that the PCI will get into the government and will force upon the country their own policies and first of all a devaluation of the lira to be paid for, as usual, by the workers and by the fixed-income social groups.' "

Such prospects, La Malfa added, appeared to be "the more regrettable because on other counts the Moro government's performance is reassuring and even satisfactory." The Republican leader recalled that he had been "the first one to take a bold stand against de Gaulle's project for a 'European Europe' which would exclude Great Britain, adopt an authoritarian policy in domestic affairs and pursue, under the leadership of a Paris-Bonn axis, a policy of 'antagonistic independence' toward the U.S." His stand was now "widely shared by the center-left parties and Italy was becoming an important, perhaps decisive factor in blocking de Gaulle's plans. A downfall of the center-left government, which might be precipitated by domestic developments related to economic and financial issues, would change substantially the whole European picture to de Gaulle's benefit and to the detriment of all projects and hopes for an Atlantic partnership. Notably in Germany," La Malfa concluded, "the balance of power is still far from settled and the coming to power in Italy of a center-right coalition might well tip it in favor of the still strong 'French' party led by Adenauer and Strauss."

In two conversations late in February and early March, Moro was cautiously optimistic about domestic affairs: "The split in the Socialist ranks has cut down the majority margin of the center-left coalition and modified to a certain extent its internal balance of power." (This was a significant reference to the weakening of the PSI and to the related strengthening of the moderate wing of the ruling coalition.) "The PCI," the premier further told me, "can benefit from the split because its efficient party machine may rake in the votes of some Socialist defectors. On the other hand, the split has provided conclusive evidence, if any was still needed, of the sincerity of the commitments that Nenni and the majority of the Socialists have undertaken toward our party as well as toward the Social Democrats and Republicans. The split has also provided an opportunity to show that the government, while it still aims to broaden the democratic area, is quite firm in excluding from its majority the PCI and any other group which refuses to support loyally Italy's democratic institutions and her pro-Western foreign policy. All the coalition partners, and this goes, I am happy to say, for Nenni and most Socialists, are determined to keep working for a European Community which must be democratic, open to British participation and committed to a

close partnership with the U.S. in political, economic, and military affairs.''
During the recent visit to Paris by president Segni and foreign minister Saragat,
Moro went on, ''the latter told de Gaulle in plain terms about Italy's stand on
all these issues.'' Developments in Latin America, the Italian premier also told
me, ''are becoming more and more important for the U.S. and for the Western
alliance as a whole. Italy can play a significant and constructive role in that area,
putting to good use not only her long-standing cultural ties with Latin American
countries but the experience gained recently in dealing with the social and economic problems of her own underdeveloped areas.''

The conditions of the national economy represented the major concern for
Moro, too, although he sounded less pessimistic than La Malfa about the disposition of both the major labor unions and the most powerful groups of businessmen and other private economic operators.

Actually, ''the first batch of serious measures'' announced by the government
to ''check inflation, reduce the deficit of the payments balance and stimulate
savings and investments . . . immediately drew cross-fire from the right and from
the extreme left,'' I wrote in the *Washington Post*, of March 2. ''The rightwing
parties, as well as most of the economic groups making up the national associations of landowners and industrialists, claim that the government's measures
are inadequate to stem inflationary pressures and at the same time are bound to
hurt both consumers and producers. Even the revision of the withholding tax on
dividends, specifically intended to reassure large stockholders determined to keep
their portfolios secret from the tax collector, has failed to appease big business.
According to the rightwingers, financial stability can be restored only through
a freeze on wages, and the confidence of private savers and investors can be
won back only through a sharp cut in public expenditures and the scrapping of
the present government's reform program. On their side, the Communists charge
that the government 'is calling upon the working class to foot the bill of measures
intended to restore financial stability under conditions that favor only big interests.' The Communist leaders hasten to add . . . that the Red-controlled unions,
which account for about one-half of organized labor in Italy, could persuade
their members to 'sacrifice' and back the reform measures if there were 'a real
shift to the left in the political field.' In effect the Communists were bidding for
acceptance as partners in a new governmental majority.

''The bid was rejected by the top representatives of all the government parties.
[At the same time] Premier Moro, in a televised address to the nation last
Saturday, made a special appeal to both labor and management to cooperate.
Should they fail to take a constructive and responsible attitude, the premier
warned, the present 'crisis of growth' of the country's economic system would
turn into a political crisis.''

8

The Reform Drive Falters

A serious political crisis did develop in the early summer of 1964. It reflected the growing economic troubles and related strains within the center-left coalition but was further complicated by interferences from abroad and from some military and secret service groups in Italy herself.

As I reported in the *Washington Post* (June 27), "the age-old issue of state aid to private schools was the immediate cause of the Moro government's downfall. But it climaxed a long-smoldering squabble among the coalition parties over measures to curb mounting inflation and economic recession. The majority in each of them strove to promote financial stabilization while avoiding drastic measures that might trigger an economic recession and large-scale unemployment. At the same time, they tried to proceed gradually with reforms to prevent disastrous swings of the business cycle. But the success of such a double-barreled approach required both a truce in the factional squabbles within the coalition and the adoption of an overall 'income policy' which in turn would have required the collaboration of all groups of the population and first of all of the labor unions."

Such a collaboration was not forthcoming from CGIL, "Italy's biggest labor organization, which is largely dominated by the Communists and also includes workers politically affiliated with Nenni's Socialist party. The attitude of these Socialist unionists strengthened the hand of other groups within the party that were already impatient over the slow implementation of the government's reform program. Within the CD camp, the impending national congress of the party has led the moderate groups to step up their pressure for dropping or at least putting off the implementation of major reforms."

There were also strong international overtones and implications of the crisis, I noted, beginning with the enthusiastic reaction of Italy's "radical right" to the prospect that Senator Barry Goldwater would be the Republican nominee in the U.S. presidential election. "The daily *Secolo d'Italia*, mouthpiece of the Neo-Fascist movement [wrote recently]: 'John F. Kennedy and Republican party radicalism had placed the U.S. on the sliding platform of collectivism. Goldwater is fighting for the freedom of the individual.' *Il Borghese* likewise denounced as 'cowardly and inept demagogues' both the Democratic party leaders and the 'liberal and socialistic wing of the Republican party,' all the way to former President Eisenhower. Regular contributors to the weekly include survivors of the Nazi puppet regime, set up by Mussolini, and veteran Fascists and Monarchists some of whom now sit in the Italian Parliament as representatives of the conservative Liberal Party. A publishing house, also controlled by *Il Borghese*, recently put out an Italian edition of Goldwater's *The Conscience of a Conservative* with a blurb reading 'not all Americans are stupid.' A leading role in the pro-Goldwater campaign," I went on, "is played by *Lo Specchio*, another weekly popular among avowed Fascists as well as among Catholic arch-conservatives and rightwing CDs. Its editor, George Nelson Page, is the scion of a well-known American family who renounced his U.S. citizenship in the 1930s and served in Mussolini's foreign propaganda office during the war.

"Goldwater's approach appeals both to the resentments and to the hopes of the Italian radical rightists because it appears to them as a complete disavowal of the policies followed by the U.S. during most of the last 25 years. Giovanni Guareschi, the well-known author of the Don Camillo books and now a regular contributor to *Il Borghese*, charged last month that 'the paralytic in the White House [Roosevelt], . . . entered the war to let the Russians into our homes and above all to take Africa and African oil away from Italy and France.' To counteract the policies attributed to Washington, Italian Fascists and radical rightists want to promote a European continental alignment that would play the U.S. and Russia against each other. Some of them even look upon Red China as a potential ally against both the U.S. and the Soviet Union.

"The powerful political and economic groups that make up the backbone of the conservative alignment in Italy and elsewhere in continental Europe do not share such extreme views. However, those groups have become annoyed that in recent years Washington has no longer allowed the U.S. to be identified with a rigid approach to international affairs and above all with the economic and social *status quo* in domestic European affairs." (*Washington Post*, July 3).

In a subsequent article in the same paper (July 12), I dwelt on the "weird atmosphere of drama and international intrigue which has developed around the current government crisis in Italy, largely as a result of alarmist reports in many West European papers and statements by some ranking French and West German officials.

"The alarm appears exaggerated. But the attending circumstances suggest that the whole Atlantic alliance may be deeply affected by the present struggle between the proponents of another center-left Italian government, clearly oriented toward the U.S., and those who plump for a conservative regime favorable to joining a Guallist 'Europe of the Fatherlands.' On the eve of the government crisis, *Die Welt*, *Süd-deutsche Zeitung* and other West German papers described the Italian situation in the most pessimistic terms: 'People are talking about the devaluation of the lira, about revolutionary plans . . . and about impending coups by navy and air force officers,' said one report. Following the resignation of the Moro government, *Paris Presse* and *Le Figaro* likewise mentioned 'the danger of revolutionary developments' and reports 'of possible moves by high ranking representatives of the armed forces.' At the same time, the West German minister of economic affairs, Kurt Schmuecker, said in an interview with *Der Spiegel* magazine that 'the center-left experiment in Italy has definitely failed and the new government will have to use all its strength to curb inflation and save the lira. Schmuecker added that, in order to become eligible for German aid, Italy must give up her recent 'political vagaries.' ''

''These statements,'' I further reported, prompted an official protest by the Italian ambassador in Bonn. In France, *Le Monde* reported that de Gaulle had told a group of French members of Parliament, ''Italy has reached the point where France stood under the Fourth Republic.'' This comparison between the present Italian situation and France on the eve of de Gaulle's return to power, noted the influential Turin daily *La Stampa*, ''is the main argument of those who press for the coming to power of an authoritarian regime in our country, too.''

A few months earlier, I recalled, ''some members of the European Economic Commission also were reportedly miffed because Italy had turned to Washington rather than to her Common Market partners [for financial aid] and because the Moro government did not resort to stronger doses of deflationary medicine to cope with the country's economic and financial troubles. Now some conservative papers here are stating flatly that Italy cannot pursue the center-left approach without jeopardizing her membership in the Common Market. On their side, center-left papers here charge that Italian, French, and West German conservatives and Gaullists are working to sever Italian ties with the U.S. and to turn Italy into a subordinate member of a European grouping intended to operate as a third force in world affairs.''

Moro, Saragat, and Nenni told me afterwards about their sharp confrontations with opponents of the center-left policy, notably with president Segni, godfather of the CD groups most hostile to the alliance with the Socialists and most inclined to share the goals of Gaullist and conservative circles in the key nations of continental Europe.

In mid-July an agreement was reached to put together a new government which would reflect a weakening of the original center-left reform drive and at the same time a strong sense of continuity particularly in foreign affairs. The most significant change, I reported in the *Washington Post* (July 24), was the exclusion of the Socialist faction led by Riccardo Lombardi which ''joined openly with the party leftwingers in charging that the Nenni majority has made too many concessions to the CDs. Lombardi has resigned as editor of the Socialist daily *Avanti* and his friend Antonio Giolitti has given up the post of budget minister.

"On the domestic front the new government is committed to pursuing the three-fold approach: consolidate the progress achieved in recent months toward financial stabilization and a balancing of the country's foreign accounts, maintain a high rate of economic activity and employment by channeling into productive investments the resources made available by curbs on non-essential consumption and by a containment of further wage increases, and carry out the basic social reforms and institutional modernizations pledged by the previous Moro government. The reappointment of Saragat as foreign minister is a further guarantee that the new center-left government not only will pursue a pro-Atlantic course but will continue actively to support Washington's policies with special regard to the economic and political integration of Europe and the approach to East-West relations."

The solution of the government crisis in Italy, friends in Washington wrote me, was greeted with "great relief" in U.S. political circles. This bore out what Moro told me in the same days: "With the exception of a few die-hard opponents in the center-left, the Americans have concluded that the operation to bring the Socialists into the government has been carried out in a way that makes for an improvement rather than for a worsening of the situation, particularly with regard to foreign policy." Clear evidence of the climate prevailing in Washington had emerged already early in the year in connection with a visit by Segni and Saragat. When Segni made some noises reflecting his dislike for the center-left, he was cut short by a visibly annoyed Dean Rusk. Reliable sources further told me that top representatives of the Johnson administration had been most favorably impressed by Saragat's views. "For us, the visit to Washington," the Italian foreign minister had told me on the eve of the departure, "is first of all an opportunity to reaffirm once more the significance of the close ties between Italy and her number one ally as well as our steadfast commitment to the success of the 'great design' aimed at turning the alliance into a genuine Atlantic Community. Its American pillar is already in place; the problem is to build the other pillar, a united Europe which must be big and strong enough to become a full-fledged partner of the U.S. and must therefore include Great Britain."

During my stay in Washington in the spring of 1964, I met with Harriman and Bill Tyler at the State Department, with Bob Komer and Dave Klein of the White House staff (Schlesinger had left shortly after Johnson became president), with Vic Reuther and Augusto Bellanca, with Dick Gardner and Francis Meloy (who had been appointed minister-counselor in the Rome embassy), and with several members of Congress, notably Senators Humphrey, Fulbright, and Vance Hartke, and Representative Daddario. All of them praised warmly the foreign policy pursued by the Moro government. Several key officials in Washington, Harriman first of all, seemed fully aware that the hostility to the center-left coalition, apparent in many French and West German circles and due to emerge openly in connection with the subsequent government crisis in Italy, was largely actuated by more or less avowed anti-U.S. feelings and purposes. During that crisis, I was told later on, Harriman and Walt Rostow, then chairman of the State Department's Policy Planning Council and later on special assistant to the president for national security affairs, had sent word to Paris and Bonn that interferences in Italian domestic affairs to the detriment of the ruling center-left coalition were "far from welcome in Washington."

At the same time, U.S. political circles began to look with some concern at the conditions of the Italian economy and with growing disappointment at the failure of the center-left governments to carry out even modest improvements in the social and administrative fields.

Some uneasiness was also apparent in Washington about the behavior of Fanfani's followers who, after their leader was forced out of the premiership, did not conceal their dislike for the Moro government. The uneasiness emerged more clearly among the U.S. officials and politicians who had been the most outspoken supporters of Fanfani when he had promoted and headed the first governmental coalition backed by the Socialists. This apparent paradox reflected a steady inclination by Washington's ruling circles. All-too-ready to embrace and warmly praise the Italian political leader who at any given time seemed able to ensure governmental stability, they looked with concern and distrust upon any other leader who could be suspected of "rocking the boat." When the game of musical chairs, so often practiced in Italian politics, produced a change at the helm, it was the loser and his friends who were soon suspected of "rocking the boat."

The severe stroke suffered by president Segni in August made inevitable the early selection of a new chief of state. After Segni formally resigned, I reported that "a wide-open race" was on for the choice of his successor. "The president of the Republic," I explained in the *Washington Post* (December 9), "is elected by members of both Houses of Parliament meeting with the representatives of the semi-autonomous regions. On the first three ballots, a two-third majority is required for election, while the simple majority is sufficient in subsequent balloting."

A stalemate prevailed for more than 20 ballots, drawing derisive comments from many Western media and arousing some worries in Washington political circles. "The stalemate," I wrote in the *Washington Post* (December 25), "stemmed mainly from the fact that the CDs have been more divided than usual over the choice of their candidate. The moderate and conservative majority picked Leone without bothering to seek a previous understanding with their partners in the center-left coalition. Those parties in turn backed Saragat. About 100 CDs also refused to support Leone. Most of them gave their votes to Fanfani."

I was in touch with representatives of several parties and notably with politicians close to Moro and Nenni, the two leaders who managed to develop a parallel and largely concerted action to pilot the conclusive phase of the election's process. On December 20, I sent word to Moro, through his diplomatic adviser ambassador Gianfranco Pompei, that Nenni was determined to work for Saragat's election. Nenni needed some assurances about the government's reshuffle scheduled to take place after Saragat's election, in order to overcome the opposition of Lombardi's followers and of other Socialists. Moro let me know that he would provide the assurances required by Nenni. Friends of the Socialist leader also told me that the Communists were trying to rally behind Nenni much the same combination of leftist and rightist forces and of CD "dissidents" which had put across Gronchi's election in 1955. I replied that, in my opinion, the Socialists should not only turn down such a Communist bid but have Nenni himself announce his withdrawal from the race and his endorsement of Saragat at the right moment, that is as soon as Moro managed to persuade most CDs to do likewise.

An agreement was eventually hammered out whereby the Socialists would switch their votes to Saragat who would issue a statement calibrated to win Communist support and at the same time to allow the CDs not to withhold their votes from him. I was further told by ranking Socialists that, following Nenni's own instructions, they had rejected a last-minute bid to join the Communists in putting Fanfani back into the race.

"The many-sided stalemate," I reported in the *Washington Post* (December 29), "was finally broken by the patient efforts of Moro and Nenni. The premier persuaded the CD majority to swing behind Saragat. Nenni did the same with his party and informed the Communists that he was withdrawing in favor of Saragat. The factional and personal rivalries that were responsible for the long deadlock did not enhance the prestige of Italian democratic institutions or aid the stability of the incumbent government. But the final outcome brought to the presidency a figure noted for progressive sympathies and friendship for the U.S. It also held out hope that the embattled center-left coalition can continue to govern Italy. A report circulating in Rome tonight said an attempt may be made to heal the animosities of the recent days by getting Fanfani to join the government, possibly as foreign minister," the post vacated by Saragat following his election to the presidency.

Despite some hasty and worried reactions, related to the Communist role in Saragat's success, the election did not affect the positive assessment of the center-left approach that prevailed in Washington. Back from his visit to the United States, which took place in early 1965, Nenni told me about his "very satisfactory" meetings with Vice-President Humphrey, with Harriman and with Adlai Stevenson, then ambassador to the United Nations. "The representatives of the American administration," Nenni added, "have inquired about the implementation of the reforms pledged by the center-left and seem disappointed by the limited progress in this connection. A more adequate progress, I explained, is most difficult when the government is not only confronted with a strong and convergent opposition by the Communists and by the economic and political Right, but must cope with serious and urgent financial and social problems. I have reaffirmed, anyway, our government's determination to proceed with its reform program."

The Socialist leader voiced "understanding" for the U.S. stand on Vietnam. He was fully aware "of the difficulty to start negotiations under the present circumstances as well as of the necessity to resort to reprisals as the U.S. had to do a few weeks ago and may be forced to do again. The key point is to keep confining the [American] bombings of North Vietnam to military targets: should they be extended to Hanoi, the reactions of world opinion would be most serious, as I told the U.S. representatives I met recently."

Saragat voiced similar views when I saw him again shortly after his election to the presidency: "The bombings are also required to prepare the ground for a negotiated solution of the conflict by persuading the North Vietnamese and their Chinese backers that they cannot hope to force the Americans out of Vietnam." Moro's recent statements in the Italian Senate, Saragat added, had been "well balanced. The premier has taken into account both Italy's solidarity with the U.S. and the fact that we have no specific commitments in that area, but are interested in peace and progress toward international *detente*."

Saragat recalled having told recently the major Italian industrialists that "they must learn to operate within a political and social framework which has become similar to that prevailing in the modern democratic societies. They have modernized their factories. But they have not learned to accept a new relationship with political power. Angelo Costa (longtime president of Confindustria, the Italian Association of Private Industrialists) could go see De Gasperi whenever he wanted and expect that his organization's requests would at least receive a sympathetic hearing. At bottom, De Gasperi was a conservative. Moreover, the influence of our (Social Democratic) party was effectively counterbalanced by that of the Liberal party. Today, the conservative groups do not control the CD party any longer; the Liberals are out of the ruling coalition and the influence of our party is strongly bolstered by Socialist participation in the government. When the incumbent president of Confindustria gets to see Moro (something that does not happen frequently), he is confronted with a premier who is not a conservative, who wants to and must take into account the requirements and requests of many other forces, notably of our own party, of the Socialists, and of the labor unions. . . . Many industrialists do not like this at all. But I remind them of conditions in other democratic countries, first of all in the U.S. where a president can get the FBI to bring the leading steel industrialists to the White House for a dressing down if he feels that they are acting against the interests of the national community."

Reviewing the circumstances of his election to the presidency, Saragat said: "Contrary to reports by most Western media, the problem was rather simple: the new president, whatever his party affiliation, would be elected either by the Communists with the support of democratic groups, or by the democratic parties with Communist support (and this is what happened)."

Saragat took the opportunity for a wide-ranging indictment of the coverage of Italian affairs by U.S. and West European media: "With few exceptions, their Rome-based correspondents do not seem interested in developing good contacts with Italian leaders. During my 18 years as head of the Social Democratic party, I've been contacted only by half-a-dozen Western newsmen. The most important American and West European papers, moreover, rely often on columnists and 'traveling journalists' who spend a couple of days in Italy, talk only with a few people (who hardly reflect the wide range of opinions that exist in our country) and presume to have understood everything about Italy.'' For the Western media, Saragat went on, ''only Communism and the Catholic church matter in Italy. They also neglect or ignore Italy's role, her very existence on the international scene. It would be ridiculous to overrate Italy's weight and role; but there have been instances when her action has produced results of general significance. Not so long ago, for example, we've managed to convince de Gaulle that he could not expect us to support many aspects of his policies with regard to Europe and to relations with the U.S.''

There was more than a dash of exaggeration in Saragat's strictures on the Western media, but distorted and often contradictory readings of the Italian situation and prospects had become, if anything, more frequent in recent months. The 1964 summer crisis had been barely settled when *Time* predicted that ''new elections may be coming anyway'' (July 31).

''Surprisingly, the opening to the Left seems to be working out very well. . . . Despite the presence of the leftwing neutralist Socialists, Premier Aldo Moro's new coalition is behaving no less responsibly at home and a good deal more warmly toward the West than some of its predecessors,'' Claire Sterling conceded in *The Reporter* (February 13, 1964). She insisted, however, that ''survival [of Moro's government] depends essentially on Communist sufferance.'' Having committed the Socialists to an austerity program, ''Nenni is at Togliatti's mercy.'' With ''Italian workers spoiling for a fight—he can only hope that the Communist party will . . . turn the workers loose sufficiently to make life miserable but not impossible for the Socialists.''

In a subsequent article (September 24), Sterling maintained that Segni's illness had deprived Italy and the CD party in particular of a ''steadying presence. Without him, no one knows how much longer the CD party can go on with an experiment [the center-left] that at least half its leaders, for different reasons, dislike and distrust.'' It was a truly astonishing assessment, since it was well known, in Italy and abroad, that Segni's actions, both before and after his election to the presidency of the Republic, reflected a deep dislike for the collaboration with the Socialists.

The PSI was going through lean years. But its conditions and prospects did not warrant Sterling's catastrophic statements and predictions. By underwriting a government program of financial stabilization the Socialist leaders had alienated a large sector of their party. If the policy of austerity could be sustained for some time, she concluded, ''the threat of a depression might recede'' and ''the center-left coalition might be free to go ahead with some of the plans for social reform on which the Socialist party had set such store—providing, of course, that there is anything much left of the Socialist party by then.''

A *Washington Post* editorial noted on December 31: "It took 13 days and 21 ballots to elect the fifth president of Italy. . . . But . . . the important point is that a sturdy democrat, a champion of the Western alliance, and a friend of reform will serve as president of Italy during a critical moment. . . . That seems to us more important than the agony of the election or the presence of Communist ballots in the vote for this staunch democrat."

The AP, however, had hastened to proclaim that Saragat was "the country's first Socialist chief of state, winning with crucial Communist backing" and that his election had come after he had given the Nenni Socialists and the Communists "just what [they] had wanted—a blanket acceptance of leftist support" (*New York Herald Tribune*, December 29). In two editorials and in its Sunday supplement, the *New York Times* mixed praise for the new Italian president with sharp rebukes to the CDs for their factional divisions and overlong reluctance to swing behind Saragat, and with some pessimism over the "disarray" in the democratic camp which encouraged Communist hopes to promote "a Popular Front government" (December 28 and 30, January 3, 1965). In several columns (*New York Times*, January 18, 20, and 23, 1965), Sulzberger maintained, among other things, that if the stalemate over the election of the new chief of state had gone on for some more time, "the military would then take over." However, the Carabinieri commanding general, Di Lorenzo, was "loyal to the republican idea" (except, one may add, that he ended up as a member of Parliament elected on the Monarchist ticket).

Representatives of the church reacted angrily to Sulzberger's assertions, particularly to his report that high ranking Vatican officials were favorable to the efforts by CD leftwingers to develop a dialogue with the Communists: "Such allegations and speculations," I was told by Father Roberto Tucci, editor of the authoritative Jesuit magazine *Civiltà Cattolica*, "reflect the false reports circulated by a rightist alignment which ranges from conservatives like Luigi Barzini to Neo-Fascist publications like *Il Borghese*. If anything, the church seeks to use its influence to neutralize the leftwing factions in the CD camp."

Federico Alessandrini, assistant editor of the Vatican daily *Osservatore Romano*, told me: "The rightwing and 'independent' press in Italy, and the foreign newsmen who echo its arguments an attacks against the CDs, are taking upon themselves a serious responsibility because they give credit and aid to the PCI. They seem unaware that any further weakening of the CD party, whether to the benefit of the Right or of the Left, would reduce its margin over the Communists and eventually enable them to win a plurality of the votes in some future election."

On September 28, 1964, I wrote in the *Washington Post*: "The worst may be over in the economic troubles that hit Italy in the wake of the vigorous but disorderly boom of a few years ago. Barely three months ago, representatives of the EEC and high West German and French officials criticized the Moro government for its failure to take stronger inflation-curbing measures. They hinted broadly that Italy could hardly expect help from her Common Market partners unless she abandoned the social and economic reforms pledged by the center-left coalition. Some conservative Italian papers charged that the stabilization measures advocated by Western European authorities were opposed not only by the Communists and other Italian leftists but also by 'powerful American circles which favor further inflation in Italy and elsewhere in Europe because it would help the U.S. balance of payments.' This week, the vice-president of the EEC, Robert Marjolin, stated that 'the Italian government is doing all it can to restore economic stability.' The fight against inflation, he added, must be continued but should not lead to disregarding long overdue social and economic reforms. The position of the lira now appears quite solid and Italy has already repaid part of the loans that were made available to her in March when Washington took the lead in extending financial assistance to the Rome government.

"However," I continued, "a complete solution of the economic difficulties depends upon two main conditions. The political forces making up the center-left coalition must close ranks. Italian businessmen must cooperate wholeheartedly in the task of reviving the country's economy without conditioning their contribution on the abandonment of necessary social reforms or guarantee of a return to the swollen profit margins of the past."

In a two-part article published in the *Washington Post* on February 25 and 26, 1965, I recalled that "a year ago conservatives and Communists in Italy, as well as many Western observers, were forecasting financial disaster and economic collapse which in turn would have imperiled Italy's democratic institutions. Today, those dangers appear to have been averted. However, the economic situation and short-term prospects for an upturn in production and employment still look less encouraging than optimists had forecast late last summer when it became clear that the Italian authorities had won their battle against the immediate threats of runaway inflation and of a disastrous deficit in the country's foreign accounts.

"Inflationary forces" were still at work and could "largely be traced to the wasteful and cumbersome distribution system, to the ability of big corporations to 'administer' prices and to the pressure of Communist-dominated unions for further wage increases. More generally, structural deficiencies and bottlenecks, the attempts by both the Communists and by large sectors of the business community to exploit the economic difficulties for political purposes, and some mistakes by the monetary and government authorities, have combined to raise the cost of financial stabilization while opening the door to a slump in industrial production and employment. Most industrialists still contend that a revival of the economy requires not only restoration of profit margins squeezed by soaring labor costs, but 'a change in the psychological climate,' in effect the abandonment or considerable watering down of social and economic reforms. While using their hold upon large sectors of organized labor to block any effective incomes policy, the Communists broadly hint that the Red unions might collaborate if their party is given at least a back seat in the governmental alignment."

Economic and social problems were a main topic when I had another opportunity to talk with Moro in March, on the morrow of the government reshuffle featured by Fanfani's re-entry into the government as foreign minister. During the negotiations for the reshuffle, the premier said, "the Socialists have displayed once again a reasonable and constructive approach. They recognized that the number one task is still to give new impulse to the economy and sustain employment without jeopardizing the results recently achieved in curbing inflation and strengthening the lira." The CD party had provided "a reassuring show of unity" during those negotiations. Moro also termed "encouraging and significant" the progress made recently "in widening the democratic area at the local level, too, by forming center-left administrations in cities and provinces which for 20 years had been run by coalitions including Communists and Socialists."

The premier confirmed that he would visit the United States in a few weeks and spelled out his government's stand on major international issues: "Understanding and solidarity toward the American position in Southeast Asia and at the same time strong hope that the situation there would soon become a source of less worry"; lively interest for developments in Latin America (the government and the CD party had done "their utmost" to help Christian Democracy to win the elections in Chile); steady support for "the process of European economic and political integration . . . which must be broadened to include Great Britain and should be pursued in close accord and association with the U.S."

Moro was warmly received in Washington. President Johnson praised highly the Italian premier and gave him the privilege of attending a meeting of the U.S. Cabinet. "For almost a year and a half now," a *Washington Post* editorial pointed out on April 20, "Mr. Moro has headed a center-left coalition Cabinet which has served to liberalize the political instincts of his own CDs as much as to moderate the leftist instincts of his Socialists colleagues. . . . Both Mr. Moro and his accompanying foreign minister and predecessor as premier, Amintore Fanfani, showed that they know Italian politics best when they ignored the advice of the American embassy in 1962 and decided to get together with Pietro Nenni's left-leaning Socialists. Now deputy premier Nenni too has moved, to the extent of visiting that capitalist stronghold, New York, a few weeks ago and, even more recently, paying a call on the Pope. . . . Italy," the editorial concluded, "has been a stalwart NATO ally; she had been understanding of the U.S. position in Vietnam and has shown no panic over recent American moves to conserve the investment and tourist dollars here at home."

Even *Time*, in a report on the audience granted Nenni by Pope Paul VI, admitted: "[Nenni] is hardly a fellow traveler these days, having split with the Communists over the 1956 Hungarian revolt and finally joining the CDs as vice premier in the present government" (April 23).

Late in 1965, the events leading to Fanfani's resignation from the foreign ministry post received wide coverage in the United States because they were directly related to the Vietnam issue and also because Fanfani himself was at the time president of the United Nations General Assembly. It was in this capacity that he forwarded to the White House the information gathered in Hanoi by his old friend Giorgio La Pira which seemed to revive hopes of a negotiated settlement in Vietnam.

La Pira himself, whom I had known for many years, told me (and I reported in the *Washington Post*, December 19): "Both Ho Chi Minh and North Vietnamese premier Pham Van Dong are National Communists with a Western European cultural background. Both are inclined to seek a political solution of the Vietnamese crisis and are determined to steer their country on a course 'as independent as possible' from all foreign control, including Red China's. Their immediate objective is described as " 'a complete cease-fire" to be achieved on the basis of the *status quo*, although no specifications are apparently available at this stage about the exact meaning of this expression or about the guarantees for enforcement of the cease-fire. Following the cease-fire," I further reported, "the North Vietnamese would be willing to enter negotiations without asking for such pre-conditions as an American withdrawal from South Vietnam.

"La Pira," I noted, "is a law professor who proclaims that the law must give way before the gospel. He is a devout Catholic with the self-bestowed mission of building bridges between the Western and Communist worlds. Some of his many adversaries have dubbed La Pira 'a disarmed prophet, a 20th century Savonarola.' Others denounce him as a tool, or actually a willing stooge, of the Communists. But La Pira knows how to mobilize both popular and political support for the causes he champions, and while in recent years some of his initiatives met with a mixed reception in the Vatican, he is known to enjoy the confidence and the support of high-ranking representatives of the Catholic church."

While serving as mayor of Florence and in more recent years, La Pira organized in that city "a number of meetings which brought together representatives of Eastern and Western Europe, Cardinals and Russian ambassadors, delegates from Arab countries and from Israel. His latest undertaking was the establishment, some months ago, of a world political center with headquarters in Florence which includes among its directors well known spokesmen for the European and non-European Left. According to sources close to La Pira, the purpose of this group is to promote closer contacts between East and West—to be carried out by unofficial but respected and influential representatives on both sides and intended to further peaceful coexistence. A more specific objective is to explore the possibility of Red China's participation in arms control negotiations and eventually her admission to the United Nations under conditions favoring international security and world peace. As La Pira himself indicated to me yesterday, the establishment and projected activities of the World Political Center have been responsible for his being invited last month to visit Hanoi."

La Pira told me some time later that "the anticipations on the prospected negotiations," aired by "an American newspaper [*St. Louis Post–Dispatch*] compelled the Hanoi government to deny having initiated peace feelers, although the denial concerned only the label on the bottle rather than its contents," that is, the substance of what he had been told by the North Vietnamese leaders.

Shortly after his return to Italy, La Pira attended a party given by Mrs. Fanfani and was quoted by *Il Borghese* as having "voiced sharp criticism of [Secretary of State] Rusk and to a much lesser extent of President Johnson. Also according to *Il Borghese*," I further reported in the *Washington Post* (December 29), "La Pira attacked Moro and Nenni. He forecast that the present coalition government would soon be replaced by an all-Christian Democrat cabinet headed by Fanfani and supported by all parties, from the Communists to the Fascists. La Pira denied having given the interview to *Il Borghese* [and added that] whatever political statements he made during the conversation were purposely paradoxical and moreover were twisted and distorted by *Il Borghese*."

A bitter polemics, however, was on and Fanfani resigned as foreign minister. The resignation was rejected by premier Moro. Fanfani himself repudiated any connection with the anti-U.S. statements attributed to La Pira, but refused to withdraw his resignation.

Moro himself took over the post of foreign minister on a temporary basis, but the whole affair, I noted in the *Washington Post* (December 30), was "bound to increase pressure for other changes in the governmental lineup." A full-fledged government crisis "was precipitated by a fresh flareup over the issue of private versus state control of education," I further reported in the *Washington Post* (January 22, 1966).

From the outset of the crisis, Moro emerged again as the most likely candidate to form a new center-left government. This duly happened. Fanfani took over again the foreign ministry, while the defense post went to Roberto Tremelioni, "a right-wing Social Democrat and a long-time opponent of both Fascism and Communism. The outcome of the crisis has confirmed," I further wrote, "that in today's Italy there is no safe or workable alternative to the center-left coalition and that Moro is its most suitable leader" (*Washington Post*, January 26, February 5, 18 and 24).

9

Communist Gains: A "Revolt Against the System"?

In the next couple of years, the U.S. media paid scant attention to Italian events and at the same time looked at them through rose-tinted glasses. On the eve of the 1968 general election, *Newsweek* warmly praised premier Moro, who "since he took office in 1963 . . . has given Italy the most effective and stable government it has known since the death of . . . De Gasperi" (May 20, 1968). Back in the fall of 1966, *Newsweek* had already reported in glowing terms on the economic recovery in Italy and wondered whether it would amount to "a new miracle" (September 26, 1966). For *The Christian Science Monitor*, the prospects of the Italian economy were quite promising as evidenced also by an EEC report which forecast for the next four years an overall growth in a climate of revived confidence (September 10).

In the fall of 1966, a *New York Times* editorial spoke of "the decomposition of the Communist party" hit hard by the defection of Nenni's PSI. Communist losses in the municipal and provincial elections held in many parts of Italy were seen by the *Times* as a possible "watershed in Italian post-war history" (June 16). According to *Newsweek*, "the setback for the Communists—though technically a mere slip of 1.5 percent in the total vote—was clearly a matter of historic moment" (June 27).

Many U.S. media also failed to understand or badly underrated the significance of the student movement which in early 1968 was already surfacing as a new and important component of Italian society. Some AP and UPI dispatches (March 4 and 9) mentioned that the students' "revolt" did not only reflect "seething . . . resentment of an antiquated university system" but was "a challenge to the entire Italian establishment." Yet, even after the protest movement had spread to "veterans and civil servants," reports to the *New York Times* insisted that "the groups involved did not represent any significant percentage of the electorate" (February 12 and March 12).

Except for occasional references, moreover, there was no real effort to address the political and economic consequences of further delays in fulfilling the long-standing pledges to provide Italy with the structures and the tools required by a modern industrial society. There was no adequate perception that the impact of such failure was bound to be dramatic in a country which had become so open and exposed to the urgent pressures for change at work in the more "advanced" Western democracies and so vulnerable to the shocks of international economic and trade crises.

In my articles and in talks with friends in Washington and representatives of the administration and of Congress, I pointed out, beginning in 1965–1966, that "perpetuation rather than improvement" had become the prevailing trend in Italian politics. Therefore, the Communists "might well be enabled not only to overcome the troubles currently besetting their party but to make additional gains at the polls mostly at the expense of the PSI by pointing out that Socialist participation in the government has failed to produce a truly better deal for most Italians." Even the formation of center-left administrations in some areas traditionally governed by leftist alliances, could not by itself produce "a decline in the Communist voting strength. In fact, elections held over the last couple of years," I reported in the *Washington Post* on May 12, 1965, "indicate that an immediate result of the Socialist switch to collaboration with the 'bourgeois' parties could be an increase in the electoral following of the Communists as the latter become the only beneficiaries of the leftist protest vote. The current erosion of Communist positions of local power, while offering the center-left parties a great opportunity, also underlines the overall challenge that confronts them." In Perugia, which had been governed for almost 20 years by a coalition of Communists and Socialists, "the new democratic administration must now come to grips with the problems and strains of a city whose population has increased from 50,000 to 115,000 in 20 years. There is an acute shortage of low-rent housing. Motorized traffic clogs the old, narrow streets, and thousands of newcomers, mostly unskilled peasants from the countryside, must be fitted into urban life."

Toward the end of 1965, Nenni drew for me a telling picture of the difficulties which hampered "progress in implementing at least some of the planks of the government's program." The bureaucratic apparatus, he stressed once again, "has proved even more inefficient than we had thought before we entered the government. Moro's intentions are good and he is honest—and that's quite something nowadays. But he lacks the vigor and talent required to provide a strong leadership. . . . And yet who could take over the Premiership? Fanfani is in many ways Moro's opposite, but where would he lead us?"

Once again, the shortcomings of the democratic parties helped the Communists to overcome or bypass their own troubles and uncertainties. On the day following Togliatti's death, I noted in the *Washington Post* (August 22, 1964) that "for all [his] tactical skill and resourcefulness, the [Communist] party never succeeded in undermining Italy's loyalty to the Western alliance and in spite of the steady increase of its electoral following it did not manage to force its way into the governmental alignment.'' As a consequence of the Socialists' shift to ''a governmental alliance with the traditionally democratic and pro-Western Italian forces, the Communists have now a better chance of becoming the main beneficiaries of the dissatisfaction stemming from Italy's current financial and economic troubles. On the other hand, their sphere of influence has been materially reduced by the Socialist shift.''

A few days later (September 9), I noted in the same paper: ''The most significant fact about the memorandum on the problems of international Communism, written by Palmiro Togliatti just before his fatal stroke last month and released yesterday here in Rome, is that it has been published by the new Italian Red leadership so promptly and over the reported opposition of the Soviet chieftains. The case for a measure of 'autonomy' for the individual Communist parties, which is the keynote of the Togliatti memo, is but a reaffirmation of the 'polycentrist' approach that was originally proposed by the Italian Communist leader as far back as 1956. Since early this year, moreover, Togliatti and the other top Italian Reds had repeatedly urged Moscow to use caution and moderation in dealing with the Chinese challenge.''

Following Khrushchev's ouster from the top posts in the Soviet Union, the Italian Communist leaders (I wrote in the *Washington Post* on October 19), ''have sought to catch up with the process of 'de-Khrushchevization' now well under way in the Soviet Union.'' At the same time, ''they have striven to cope with widespread concern and disarray among their party's membership and electorate by insisting that the latest upheaval does not involve major departures from the dethroned Soviet Premier's policies of domestic 'liberalization' and peaceful coexistence.

''Two posters, plastered on the walls of Rome over the last couple of days,'' (*Washington Post* October 24), ''underline the nature of the troubles that beset the Italian Communists as a result of Khrushchev's ouster. The first carries a picture of Stalin and reads: 'Communists of Rome! Khrushchev has fallen. Stalin has been avenged.' It is signed: 'The Chinese Comrades.' The second poster, put out by the Rome Federation of the Socialist party charges that the Italian Communists have contributed to Khrushchev's downfall by criticizing his politics toward Peking.''

On November 8, I reported in the *Washington Post* that ''following the trip to Moscow by an Italian Communist delegation, the party's directorate approved a resolution which in effect accepts the official Soviet explanation of Khrushchev's removal.'' The PCI leaders also ''seek to minimize the negative impact that such a swinging in line with the latest shifts in the Soviet Union coming so soon after the ouster of Nikita Khrushchev'' might have ''upon their party's chances'' in forthcoming elections in Italy. In the next few years, I developed broader and more frequent personal contacts with ranking Italian Communists.

Since the mid–1960s, for instance, I met about once a month with Emanuele Macaluso who, after a stage as a local party leader in his native Sicily, was elected and constantly reelected to the Italian Parliament, became a member of the PCI national directorate and for several years editor of *l'Unità*. According to Macaluso, there was "a lot of exaggeration" in the reports about deep dissensions and possible splits within the PCI as a result of the divergencies and rivalry between the groups lined up behind Giorgio Amendola and Pietro Ingrao: "It is wholly inaccurate to say that Amendola looks exclusively to building unity among leftist parties while neglecting all opportunities for a dialogue with Catholics and possibly with the CD party itself. It is just as incorrect to say that Ingrao wants to bet everything on the approach to Catholics and spurns all efforts to revive good relations with the Socialists and possibly extend them to other left-of-center groups. All of us agree that the two approaches are at least in part complementary; for instance, a concrete relaunching of the collaboration with the Socialists would help our efforts to persuade or, to put it more correctly, to force the CDs to revise their attitude toward our party." Yet Macaluso conceded that "divergencies" did exist between Amendola and Ingrao and freely criticized both of them in terms apparently shared by party secretary general Luigi Longo and by the majority of the PCI: "Amendola's recent proposal to form a single party of the workers, stemming from his conviction that neither Communism nor Social Democracy have provided an effective answer to the problems confronting the workers in the capitalistic countries of Europe, has met with lively reactions within our party. Some consequences of this proposal such as the possibility of changing our party's own name," Macaluso spelled out summing up the opinions voiced by several other PCI representatives, "are rejected by 95 percent of the Italian Communists."

Macaluso and other leaders of the party's "centrist" majority emphasized the "two main motivations" of their disagreement with Ingrao: "First of all, his assessment of the situation and prospects in Italy is much too pessimistic. According to him, the center-left coalition, while failing to implement far-reaching reforms, has been successful at least in the sense that it has 'split the workers' movement' by separating the bulk of the Socialists from the Communists. Therefore we should give up hope of developing a cooperation with other parties and political groups and concentrate on promoting 'the mobilization of the masses' as the only effective means to change political conditions in Italy. The majority of our party," Macaluso went on, "feels instead that, by accepting the 'moderate' line of the center-left coalition, the bulk of the Socialists has provided us with valid arguments for winning votes among the PSI followers." Other PCI representatives, such as Senator Franco Calamandrei, joined Macaluso in pointing out that another major source of disagreement with Ingrao was "his persistent request for more freedom of debate and even of dissent within the party."

At the PCI National Congress, I reported in the *Washington Post* (February 2, 1966), "Ingrao, who is the Communist floor leader in the Chamber of Deputies, was directly and violently attacked by two top lieutenants of PCI Secretary

General Pietro Longo who condemned not only any attempt to organize dissent but also the right to hold permanent doubts about the party line. While backtracking on many of his demands and criticisms, Ingrao has refused to recant completely. Several of his followers have now been excluded from the new Communist Central Committee." On his side, "Amendola admitted that his idea of a single workers' party was faulty and has rallied in effect to Longo's more cautious and vague proposal for building up a new majority as an alternative to the center-left government."

Some talks I had with Amendola and Ingrao during the following summer shed more light on the divergencies within the PCI leadership. "Our party is going through some hard times," Ingrao said. "My opinions about the best ways to overcome such difficulties are not fully shared by many other PCI representatives. We must revise, I'm convinced, some of the main assumptions on which we have based our efforts since 1947. We felt that an already strong leftist alignment, led by our party and supported by most Socialists, could win a plurality and eventually a majority of the votes. We admit now that such a 'Popular Front' strategy cannot represent any more the decisive tool for coming to power in Italy, at least in the foreseeable future. The main responsibility for this changed outlook lies with Nenni who has played a key role in drawing his party away from collaboration with us." According to Ingrao, the center-left coalition had managed "to stick together even during the period when economic difficulties were greatest. As a result, more and more of our people feel not only that the struggle to defeat the center-left coalition will be longer than anticipated but that a 'quality jump' is required if we are to broaden our electoral appeal. This means that we must work out and offer to the voters a model of our own for the growth of Italian society. It will also provide an excellent platform for achieving the threefold cooperation (Communists, Socialists and Catholics) which represents the only way to steer Italian politics on a truly new and promising course."

In a subsequent talk, Ingrao emphasized that the sharpening tension between Moscow and Peking was "a bitter blow" for the Italian Communists. "Our people," he said, "were persuaded that the coming to power of Socialist regimes would contribute decisively to reduce and eventually eliminate armed conflicts. There are also mounting worries about the impact of that tension on the overall capabilities of the Communist international movement and notably on developments in Vietnam."

Ingrao confirmed that the PCI had agreed to participate in the Conference of Communist parties willed by the Soviets as a reply to the Chinese challenge. Although the PCI leadership still insisted that the Conference must seek to preserve "the highest possible degree of unity within the Communist international movement," Ingrao went on, "the official party approach to the issue continues to arouse worries and misgivings among Italian Communists mostly because they fear that it will contribute to isolate the Chinese and to sharpen tensions" among Communist parties and regimes.

According to Amendola, instead, "we Italian Communists have made it clear that we side with the Soviets in the quarrel between Moscow and Peking." Amendola praised the "tolerance" shown by the Soviet leaders toward the Chinese regime and their efforts "to keep alive the process of *detente* despite the conflict in Vietnam."

In recent years, Amendola pointed out, "ties and contacts" within the Communist international movement had begun to develop "on a multilateral basis, too. This is in line with the approach advocated by Togliatti who was always against 'too much national individualism' and maintained that closer multilateral links must be cultivated among Communist parties and governments especially on a regional basis. Accordingly," Amendola went on, "we have been most active and made some concrete progress in promoting coordinated action by the Communist parties operating in the capitalist countries of Europe. One of the major problems we must face is the approach to the Social Democratic parties which play such an important role in so many parts of Western Europe. The article I wrote a year and a half ago was interpreted, incorrectly, as if it referred only to conditions in Italy and as if it advocated the formation of a single party neither Communist nor Social Democrat. Its real meaning and purpose was to stress the need to review the performance and the future role of both the Communist and Social Democratic parties of Western Europe in order to promote at least some degree of collaboration among them."

Togliatti, Amendola recalled, "said time and again that we are 'a government party,' which feels entitled to play an ever more important leadership role in national politics. We have exerted a significant influence even in the last 19 years when we have been excluded from the government and from the parliamentary majority. It is obvious, however, that a party like ours with its large electoral following and a well defined program of its own, must aim to get into the government as the only truly effective way of implementing its program and fulfill the aspirations of its electorate. Togliatti made it quite clear as well that our program calls for a radical but gradual transformation of Italian society to be pursued through far-reaching reforms carried out with democratic methods and with the collaboration of all the non-Communist forces willing to work with us to that end. That is still my own approach, Longo's approach, our party's approach."

In reply to a direct question, Amendola said: "Unquestionably, there are among us divergencies or at least different shades of opinion about relations and eventual alliances with other parties. I'm giving top priority to the connection with the Socialist forces, even though the reunification between PSI and PSDI is taking place on a platform which positions the reunified party to the right of most West European Social Democrats. We do not intend to neglect any opportunity, either, to develop joint or parallel actions with groups of Catholic leftwingers. But here, too, we cannot expect to make significant progress unless we manage to establish some new kind of relationship with the leading CD groups, even if this will become possible only after they are taught some lessons at the polls.''

The quickening prospects of the merger between PSI and PSDI were greeted with exaggerated expectations by many U.S. media. On December 2, the *New York Herald Tribune* ran an article by Godfrey Blakeley which emphasized that, as a result of the forthcoming Socialist reunification, ''for the first time, a real alternative to the ruling CD party is coming into being, as is the beginning of a two-party system.'' The *New York Times* editorialized about a new chapter in Italian history featuring a return of Socialism to its ''liberal, reformist origins.'' The CDs were ''in a process of breaking up'' (January 15, 1966). *Time* stressed (January 21) that following the Socialist merger, the CDs ''at last seem likely to face a responsible and united opposition.'' According to a *New York Times* editorial (October 31, 1966), ''credit for the reunification'' belonged not only to Saragat and Nenni but to Fanfani, Moro, and the other CDs who had realized that the best way to defeat the Italian Communists was to separate the Nenni Socialists from the PCI. This was the purpose of the ''opening to the left'' policy ''so often misunderstood and distorted by Americans.''

With the Johnson administration firmly committed to backing the center-left coalition, some U.S. officials, both in the Rome Embassy and in Washington, probably felt it advisable to try to live down their reputation for coolness or even hostility to a government role for the Socialists. Word began to circulate in Italian political circles that ''the Americans'' looked upon the CDs as a declining force and were shifting their bets to the reunified Socialist party credited with good chances of widening quickly its electoral following at the expense of both CDs and Communists.

I was not surprised, therefore, when in September 1966 Mariano Rumor, secretary general of the CD party, told me: ''It would be a big and dangerous mistake to think that after the break between Socialists and Communists and the merger between Socialists and Social Democrats, our party's role as Italy's number one political force is coming to an end and that such a role can be played henceforth by the reunified Socialists.''

''Do you feel then,'' I asked Rumor, ''that your party has a God-given mission to be forever the dominant force in Italy?'' ''Of course not,'' he retorted: ''But I think that for a long time to come we'll keep a primary role in Italian political affairs, a role that no other party is in a position to play. But unfortunately even among officials of the American embassy here and of the State Department, it seems to have become fashionable to underrate and disparage our role.''

Rumor branded as ''wholly unfounded the suspicions, apparently shared by some American circles, that CD leaders seek to undermine the Moro government and to hinder Socialist reunification. I've tried time and again to clear up any possible misunderstandings and more generally to establish good communications, at the proper level, with American officials. But the reaction suggested a lack of real interest. . . . I had a similar experience,'' he went on, ''with the project to visit Washington on the way back from my recent trip to Latin America. Eventually, I gave up the project because I was unable to ascertain whether I could expect to meet with leading representatives of the Johnson Administration and possibly with the President himself.''

I told Rumor that the ''fashion'' might have involved some U.S. officials. It would be a mistake, however, to think that such inclinations and assessments were prevailing; in Washington: ''American political circles do feel that a strong Socialist and democratic party can play an important and highly positive role in Italy. It can provide an attractive alternative for those voters who have backed the PCI because the center and right-of-center coalitions faced belatedly and inadequately the urgent need to modernize the structure of the Italian state and of Italian society. A significant erosion of the PCI's electoral following, however, will take several years, at best. The reunified Socialists can hardly be expected to gain quickly much ground at the expense of the CD party either; if they should give priority to such a goal, moreover, they would precipitate an early collapse of the center-left coalition, or condemn it to paralysis.''

In my talks in Washington and with U.S. officials in Rome, as well as in my articles, I elaborated on these considerations. ''Some electoral losses for the CDs coupled with more votes for the reunified Socialists could actually mark a significant progress toward endowing Italy with a modern set of political parties,'' I pointed out in the *Washington Post* on January 13, 1966. But on one condition: the cutting down to size of the CD party must come after the voting strength and the political weight of the PCI have been cut down at least as much.

It was also advisable, I added, to take into account that Rumor could well become premier in the not-too-distant future, possibly soon after the 1968 general election. Early in 1967, I was informed by friends in Washington that a ''more serene assessment'' of the CD party's conditions and projects as well as of the role of its general secretary was emerging in Washington, thanks in part to Wells Stabler, country director for Italy, Austria, and Switzerland, whom I had met when he was political officer in Rome about ten years before. On his side, Rumor kept assuring the embassy (as he told me himself) that ''the majority of the CD party is now determined to help Moro retain the premiership until after the 1968 election.'' Rumor's trip to Washington could then be organized under circumstances guaranteeing that it would be a success. ''He has been received as if he were a premier,'' my sources in Washington told me afterwards, and the attention given to his visit had been the more remarkable because ''the Administration tends to forget everything that has not to do with southeast Asia.'' Upon his return to Rome, Rumor told me that he was most pleased with the reception he had been given, notably with his 45-minute talk with the President and meetings with Vice-President Humphrey as well as with several officials directly interested in Italian affairs.

According to Mario Tanassi, secretary of the Social Democratic party, I reported in the *Washington Post* (January 13, 1966), ''the merger with the Socialists would allow the reunified party to face the 1968 election as 'the third force' in

Italian politics, right behind the CDs and the Communists. Looking farther into the future, Tanassi actually envisages a Socialist party that will 'outvote the CDs [and] cut down the Communist strength by winning over the majority of the Italian workers'. Those are, at best, long-term projections,'' I noted. ''By now, the political differences between the two parties have been substantially narrowed down, mostly as a result of the 'new course' pursued in recent years by the majority of the Nenni Socialists.'' In the PSI, however, ''opposition to the merger continues to be voiced by left-wing groups, representing less than 20 percent of the party. Some trouble may also arise over the posts and roles to be allotted individuals in the reunified party.''

When a constituent assembly including representatives of both PSI and PSDI ratified the merger, I noted (*Washington Post*, October 31, 1966): ''As yet, the reunified Socialists command the support of less than 20 percent of the electorate, while the CDs and Communists respectively poll 38 and 26 percent of the votes. Accordingly, Nenni and most other leaders of the reunified Socialist party envisage a fairly long period of 'competitive collaboration' with the CDs. They reject firmly any political deal with the Communists and intend to speed up the break of the remaining local alliances between Socialists and Communists. As regards labor unions, the members of the party will be free to belong either to CGIL, largely run by the Communists, or to UIL which includes Social Democratic, Republican and independent workers.''

By early 1967, it was clear that very little if any further progress would be made in implementing ''the center-left's program agreed upon back in 1962–1963. Some of the planks of that program,'' I pointed out in the *Washington Post* on February 11, ''were quickly carried out. But then the paramount need to avoid an economic slump, following the disorderly boom of earlier years, led to the delaying or watering down of the other social reforms originally pledged by the alliance. This has suited most CDs, who seek to gain votes from the fading parties of the Right. But most Socialists, fearful of losing ground on their left, are pressing again for more vigorous action.''

A month later, I reported that ''recent strikes and continuing unrest among university students underline the challenge to the political establishment. Unprecedented protests and rebellion by student activists represent the most significant symptom of the problems besetting a country which has become one of the eight leading industrial and trading nations but retains many institutions and administrative practices which have undergone little change since the turn of the century. The student population, which was less than 60,000 in 1935, has now reached almost 450,000. Despite some recent progress, physical facilities have expanded at a much slower pace and the number of professors has risen only to 8,000 against 2.700 in 1935. Many, moreover, are too busy in politics or business to show up for classes, let alone to devote sufficient attention to their students. University power is concentrated in a small and self-perpetuating group of deans and full professors. Students demand a complete revision of the present system and want their representatives, as well as those of junior lecturers, to have a voice in running university affairs. Under the leadership of a small group of activists, sometimes self-labeled as 'Maoists,' 'Castroites' or 'anarchists,' this has turned recently into a vague but loud and even violent revolt against society. Such a development has taken place just when the center-left governmental coalition had finally presented a reform bill intended to correct at least the most outdated features of the university system—which was inaugurated in 1865 and made more authoritarian by the Fascist regime in 1923. This belated effort, while failing to pacify student militants, has been thwarted in Parliament by conservative forces, which felt that the government bill went too far, and by the Communists, bent on proving that no meaningful measures can be put across by a government that does not enjoy or curry their favor.

"A similar situation underlies recent industrial and civil servants' strikes and recurrent unrest over such issues as reorganization of the bureaucratic apparatus, modernization of the social security system and hospital reforms. In those and other fields, the center-left coalition has achieved more than previous governments but less than it had pledged" (*Washington Post*, March 12).

"A truly startling change had taken place in the Italians' approach to such issues as divorce and birth control," I further reported (*Washington Post*, May 11): "In the latest and largest public opinion survey, 58.6 percent of 12,645 Italians interviewed have come in favor of introducing divorce. A similar survey, conducted as recently as 1962, still showed that almost seven Italians out of ten were against the introduction of divorce. Last winter, a divorce bill made some headway, for the first time, in the Italian Parliament. The bill would provide for dissolution of marriage under specific conditions including insanity, a lengthy criminal sentence or *de facto* separation for at least five years. Despite strong opposition from the Catholic Church and from the CD party, the key sections of the bill were approved by the Justice Committee of the Chamber of Deputies [with the support] of a broad alignment of forces ranging from the Socialists and Republicans, who are allied with the CDs in the center-left governmental coalition, to the Communists and to the right of center Liberals. However, the CDs managed to prevent any further action on the bill before the dissolution of Parliament early in March" (*Washington Post*, May 1). "Three out of four Italians," I reported November 18, "favor birth control and two out of three say their views or behavior on the subject have not been affected by Pope Paul's recent pronouncement reaffirming the Catholic church's rigid ban on contraception."

Against this background, well placed observers felt that the electoral outlook was mixed for the center-left coalition as a whole and uncertain, at best, for the newly reunified Socialists. Rumor was hopeful that the CDs would score some gains, possibly edging up toward a 40 percent share of the popular vote. Nenni told me shortly before the 1968 general election: "When I hear some of our people talk freely about getting 7 or 8 million votes, or 20 percent and perhaps more of the total, I get the shivers. Of course, I hope that we'll gain some ground but before talking about the additional votes we might get, we must think about keeping the votes we have."

10

The *Washington Post* Joins the Media Panic over Italy

The outcome of the Italian election of May 19–20 1968 was a bitter disappointment for U.S. political and journalistic circles: "The sizable gains scored by the Communists have not been a pleasant surprise" for Washington, AP reported, quoting private statements by U.S. officials. A *New York Times* editorial stressed that the younger generations and particularly the students had given many of their votes to the PCI. But this did not mean that they wanted a Communist government. They voiced their protest and disappointment over the performance of the center-left coalition, all too slow in implementing its pledges of social, educational, and administrative reforms. Yet, the editorial concluded, there was no other combination that could command a majority in Parliament.

The day following the election, I reported in the *Washington Post* (May 21–22): "The center-left coalition has increased slightly its share of the popular vote and parliamentary representation. But the Communists and the extreme left Socialist splinter group also increased their vote, jolting the governing coalition." The Christian Democrats "continued to gain some ground at the expense of the far right. They also won back some of their conservative-minded followers who in 1963 had defected to the right-of-center Liberals. The CDs seem to have benefitted also from the stability and recovery following the 1964–65 economic slump." The reunified Socialists lost ground because their followers "have become increasingly disappointed as their presence in the government appeared to make little difference in terms of social change and modernization of institutions. This explains why the Communists increased their share of the lower-house popular vote to 26.9 from 25.3 in 1963. The Socialist Party of Proletarian Unity, which split away from the Nenni Socialists when they became full coalition partners four years ago, polled 4.5 percent of the vote."

The recently reunified Socialists "received 14.5 percent of the vote" and lost four seats in the Chamber of Deputies, while the more reasonable expectations had credited them with 16 percent. In the Senate, they kept 46 seats. "Left-wingers in the United Socialist Party," I further noted, "will demand a pullout from the coalition, with any decision on the party's future to be remanded to its national congress next fall. Some CD chieftains may feel that the time is ripe to unseat premier Aldo Moro and make their own bid to head either a revamped center-left coalition or an all-Christian Democratic government. For practical purposes," I concluded, "these are the only available alternatives. The CDs will reject any Communist bid to join the government alignment. And most of them are likewise opposed to forming a center-right government which could command a majority in Parliament only by accepting the votes not only of the Liberals but of the Monarchists and Neo-Fascists."

A *Washington Post* editorial added some rather optimistic interpretations and comments: "The two center parties in the governing coalition won, giving the coalition another five years in power. . . . Overall, the elections showed that Italy continues its post-war drift to the left. This is generally a healthy move. It allows the government to stay in touch with rising mass expectations. . . . Communist strength spreads but at a rate which, if maintained, would not bring the party to power until the 21st century. Meanwhile the Communists, tamed, provide a useful stimulus to reform. The emergence of the radical Proletarian Socialists affords a taste of what lies ahead if Italy does not adequately tend to its various ills. But, encouragingly, most young people are willing to play politics. Some of the 3–1/2 million youths taking part in their first national poll voted in hope, for government parties; others voted in protest, for the left. But they voted. The tensions which in France were suppressed until recent days are in Italy finding a political outlet" (May 22).

Ten days later, I reported that a majority of the United Socialist party's Central Committee had decided "to withdraw from the center-left coalition." The move was the result of a temporary alliance between Francesco De Martino, a Socialist leader who had advocated the withdrawal for some time, and Mario Tanassi, a top representative of the Social Democratic component of the reunified party. This peculiar alliance had defeated Nenni and his followers who had "warned that the Socialists should not take responsibility for plunging Italy into a political crisis."

At the same time, the Socialist Central Committee "rejected political collaboration with the Community party and confirmed that the Socialists are prepared to support a minority CD government pledged to swift implementation of social and institutional reforms" (*Washington Post*, June 2). Giovanni Leone was called upon to form a "minority CD government, expected to take care of urgent economic and administrative matters while the CDs, the United Socialists, and the Republicans try to work out terms for forming another center-left coalition government. Leone "headed a similar caretaker government under nearly identical circumstances from June to November 1963," I further noted (*Washington Post*, June 25) "and has come to be called the 'baby-sitter of Italian politics.' "

After the summer recess, the Leone government approved "a new bill to reform Italian universities," I reported in the *Washington Post* (September 19). The bill ran immediately "into criticism from most of the student groups who occupied schools and paralyzed higher education in a boisterous uprising last Spring. Conservative politicians and professors, on the other hand, accuse the government of having made too many concessions to 'the small minority of students bent on violence and subversion.'

"If the bill is passed by Parliament," I continued, "students, assistant professors, and instructors will gain a voice in the arrangement of the curriculum and in university administration. Universities and departments will be granted a larger measure of self-government and latitude to 'experiment with new forms of research, organization, teaching, and exams.' Professors will have to give up their university posts when they become members of Parliament or accept other important posts. All members of the teaching staff will be required to show up for a minimum number of lectures and generally to make themselves available to students on a regular basis.

"But the main thrust of militant student protest has broadened beyond the issue of university reform. Many students have concluded that the whole establishment has let them down. This widespread feeling plays into the hands of the small but most active groups which want to exploit university unrest to spark a wholesale revolt against society" which in turn was the breeding ground for terrorism.

"The Communists do not want student extremists to 'contaminate' the workers or plunge the country into chaos under circumstances likely to benefit reactionary drives from the right. But it would suit the Communists perfectly if a new wave of unrest in the universities should force the Leone government to resort to police action to bring the students to heel. In that event, it would become very hard for the Socialist National Congress scheduled for late October to endorse the early resumption of governmental partnership with the CD."

The outcome of the local assemblies held to choose the delegates to the Socialist National Congress, I wrote (*Washington Post*, October 24), made it clear that a large majority of the party was ready to heed Nenni's call "for joining again with the CDs and with the Republicans in a center-left government." CD secretary general, Mariano Rumor, I reported (*Washington Post*, November 20), "has the inside track for the Premiership." Rumor won his party's support but "former Premier Aldo Moro, who lost his post after last May's election, broke a six-month silence to disassociate himself from the majority backing Rumor" (*Washington Post*, November 27).

The new center-left government was "slightly more leftist in makeup and domestic policy than the three-party coalition that stepped down after last spring's general election," I noted (*Washington Post*, December 13). "A left-of-center Socialist faction headed by Francesco De Martino has four Cabinet posts, with De Martino as Vice-Premier. Party chairman Pietro Nenni, who was Vice-Premier in the last coalition, becomes Foreign Minister and is expected to give new impetus to Italy's championship of European integration and to work closely along these lines with Britain's Labor government and West Germany's Social Democratic foreign minister, Willy Brandt. Nenni is also known to be more favorable to Israel and less pro-Arab than former premier Amintore Fanfani, who served as foreign minister from March 1965 to last June. At the same time, premier Rumor's government can be expected to pay more attention to Italy's left-wing politicians and to those private and government-controlled industrial firms that have been pressing for the establishment of diplomatic relations with Communist China.

"Formation of the Rumor government," I concluded, "reflects the resiliency of the center-left coalition and the determination of Italy's major parties to restore stability and work for the enactment of the reforms needed to modernize Italian society and placate mounting labor and student unrest. The largest question mark regarding the new government's tenure and effectiveness revolves around the factional and personal strife within the CD and Unified Socialist parties."

The solution of the governmental crisis in Italy was greeted with relief and hope by Italian "experts" in Washington. Some sectors of the media, however, indulged in the traditional inclination to swing suddenly from one extreme to the other, to look for "sensational" angles or for more or less superficial "color notes," and generally to provide a confused mix of old and new delusions and pessimistic interpretations. *Time* pointed at an Italy racked not only by large scale strikes and student protests but by a "crisis of confidence . . . *Siamo pronti per i colonnelli* [We are ready for the colonels], cried a young Roman in disgust at the nation's squabbling politicians" (November 29). According to a dispatch from Rome to the *London Observer*, picked up by the *Washington Post* (December 26), "Italy sports a new brand of Fascism under a skimpy disguise. . . . Among the young, the movement has a surprisingly large following. . . . The neo-fascist Italian Social movement (MSI) . . . took 4.6 percent of the total vote in this year's general election." But it "must be considered in the spectrum of Italy's numerous far right parties." Without offering any facts to substantiate his surprising estimates, the *Observer*'s correspondent, Charles Foley, went on to state that these parties "collectively . . . hold 15 percent of the electorate—enough to sway the balance of power in a setup where the majority CD party must find allies to stave off the threat from the Italian Communist party, Western Europe's largest."

The correspondent of the *Los Angeles Times*, Louis Fleming, argued instead that the divisions within the United Socialist party and among the ruling CDs improved "the prospects for an accommodation between the Communists and the left-wing Catholics. If such a government should be created, the certain result would be Italian neutrality at a time of growing Soviet influence in the Mediterranean" (November 19).

Some sectors of the U.S. media went overboard when the PCI and other Western Communist parties criticized the Soviet invasion of Czechoslovakia. In the fall of 1968, Victor Zorza, an "expert" on Communist affairs whose columns appeared in the *Washington Post* and several other U.S. dailies, asserted that "the growing bitterness of the arguments between the French and Italian parties on the one hand, and the Soviet-bloc parties on the other, is rapidly approaching the point of no return." The leaders of the PCI "have made it known that if the Soviet troops are not speedily withdrawn [from Czechoslovakia] a Western European Communist conference might have to be called." Moreover, PCI leader Luigi Longo had "declared that . . . if the troops were not withdrawn, he could see no point in holding the world Communist conference in Moscow in November" (September 18).

"By voicing disapproval of the invasion of Czechoslovakia," I wrote in the *Washington Post* (September 11), "the Italian Communist party has departed for the first time from its basic allegiance to the Moscow line. At the same time, it has reaffirmed its 'brotherly' relationship with the USSR and with the Soviet Communist Party. Even within those limits, the party's criticism of Moscow has aroused widespread disagreement among the rank and file of the Italian Communists. On the basis of letters to the editor printed recently by *Unità*, more than 25 percent of the Communist membership appear to feel that 'the USSR must have had its good reasons for sending troops into Czechoslovakia.' Many militants say openly that the party leaders 'hastened to condemn the Soviet move because they have become bourgeois-minded and yearn to collaborate with the bourgeois parties.'

"Italian Communist leaders," I continued, "have indeed become increasingly convinced that their party can gain national power only as partner in a coalition reaching into the very center of the political alignment. To promote such a coalition, they have sought to project their party as rather moderate in domestic affairs and, above all, autonomous and 'national-minded' in foreign affairs. This image would have been thoroughly shattered if the Italian Reds had failed to dissociate themselves from the Soviet attack on Czechoslovakia. At the same time, the Red leaders are fully aware of the dangers of leaving their left flank exposed, particularly in view of the fact that the radical Socialist party of Proletarian Unity has refrained from condemning the Soviet invasion. Accordingly, many Communist spokesmen tend now to soft-pedal their own criticism of the invasion while stepping up their appeals to 'all revolutionary and progressive forces to join the fight against imperialism' and their attacks against Italy's membership in NATO."

After the PCI National Congress held in Bologna in February 1969, I reported: "The party showed at last a tendency to break out of its totalitarian mold, but the movement in that direction is still proceeding with the pace of a glacier. The movement, such as it is, stems mainly from two recent developments: the Soviet invasion of Czechoslovakia and the upsurge in Italy of radical groups, mostly among students, which in their militancy against society extend their attacks to the Communist 'establishment' itself. . . . When Soviet bloc troops crossed into Czechoslovakia last August, the Italian Red leaders voiced 'dissent and disapproval.' This stand was reaffirmed at Bologna by Secretary General Luigi Longo and other party spokesmen. At the same time, Longo reasserted the party's loyalty to the Soviet Union and also made clear that the Italian Reds are no longer reluctant to participate in the summit conference of Communist parties long sought by Moscow and now expected to take place in the late spring. The same line was taken by Enrico Berlinguer, the party's new vice-secretary and likely successor to Longo, who is 69 and suffers from a circulatory ailment.

"Giorgio Amendola and Pietro Ingrao now appear to have neutralized each other in the race for Longo's job. A dissenting minority charges that the international Communist movement is not sufficiently 'revolutionary' anymore and that the Italian party is likewise unable or unwilling to meet the demands of the militant left-wing dissidents. Spokesmen for the majority retorted that 'the Italian crisis cannot be overcome solely through an alliance between workers and students,' and called for a much broader alignment, including the 'more advanced' CD and Socialist forces. To promote such a broad alignment, the Communist leaders are ready not only to ignore the demands of the party left-wingers, but to endorse a most moderate and gradual program of social and economic reforms. This flexibility, however, does not extend to foreign policy. At the Bologna Congress, all Communist chieftains insisted that the party will support only a government pledged to take Italy out of NATO" (*Washington Post*, February 21).

On the eve of the international conference of Communist parties, I wrote: "The Italian delegation will voice strong criticism of the basic documents sponsored by the Soviets and will probably refuse to support some of them. At the same time, the Italian party will endorse once again the Soviet Union's 'decisive role in the worldwide struggle against imperialism.' The Italian Communist leaders are willing to be counted on Moscow's side in the dispute with Peking, but they continue to oppose any attempt to excommunicate the Chinese and insist that the whole matter, like the Czechoslovak question, must be handled on the basis of the 'the twin principles of the solidarity among Communist countries and parties and of the autonomy of each of them,' to quote an intimate of party secretary Longo" (*Washington Post*, June 2, 1969).

New developments threatened to further weaken the center-left alignment and thus to make easier the task of the PCI leaders who felt that their party's evolution should proceed to the extent required to enable it to enter into the government but stop short of endangering its cohesion and its substantial loyalty to the domestic and international goals of Communism.

Another split was impending in the Socialist camp: "What would you do if your wife should betray you?" Saragat asked me in mid-June. "You get a divorce," the president of the Republic went on, answering his own questions. "And I believe in divorce, in politics, too. In this instance, it will take place because several representatives of the United Socialist party want to get together with the Communists and I'm not willing to consort with people who want to join the Communists." Saragat accused De Martino, among other things, of anti-U.S. feelings (conveniently forgetting that a year earlier he had worked hand in hand with De Martino to pull the party out of the governmental coalition).

When I said that a split in the Socialist ranks would precipitate another government crisis, Saragat shot back: "True enough, but a crisis can be solved." "And how?" "By putting together an all-Christian Democrat government which would be supported by both Socialist parties for six or eight months." "And what next?" "A general election and we Social Democrats get 60 seats in the Chamber of Deputies."

The president of the Republic's forecasts proved correct with two significant exceptions: a general election took place only three years later, and once again the Social Democrats' performance at the polls represented a bitter disappointment for Saragat's hopes to make the PSDI the strongest party in the Socialist area.

On July 2, I reported in the *Washington Post*: "A [serious] political crisis appeared to be in the making in Italy today." At the National CD Congress, "the moderate faction, led by premier Mariano Rumor and party secretary Flaminio Piccoli, retained the allegiance of the plurality (38 percent) of the rank and file. It also can hope to command a two-thirds majority in the new executive bodies of the party, thanks to the support of the groups headed by former Premier Amintore Fanfani and by Minister for the South Paolo Emilio Taviani. But the moderates have come under increasingly sharp attacks from a confederation of left-wing forces that control one third of the party and have recently found a prestigious leader in Aldo Moro. The left-wingers demand a more dynamic approach to the problems and requirements of a growing and changing Italian society. Such an approach, they add, calls for a 'democratic confrontation' and even a 'dialogue' with the Communist opposition. The immediate goal of Moro and his allies is to change the power balance in the party by reaching an agreement with Fanfani's followers, many of whom are unhappy over the alliance with the moderates, and securing an adequate number of posts in the new CD directorate to be chosen within three weeks. If they fail, they plan to pull [their representatives] out [of government]."

"The crisis may be precipitated even earlier," I further reported; "A new polarization of forces has developed among the Socialists as a result of a shift to the left in the party's balance of power. The former Social Democrats and a few old-line Socialists charge that the other factions, the largest of which is headed by De Martino, have violated the principles of the reunification charter by pressing for an 'opening' to the Communists. De Martino and his friends want the government to pursue a more advanced social and economic policy and would accept Communist votes in Parliament if needed to implement such a policy over the opposition of conservative and moderate CDs." When the new Socialist schism materialized, the Rumor government resigned, I reported in the *Washington Post*, July 6. As recently underlined by Nenni, I went on, the danger now was that "one Socialist splinter" would fall "into the orbit of moderation and the other into the orbit of Communism."

A few days later, I pointed out that Italy's political crisis had taken "a possibly more hopeful turn as the dominant CDs closed ranks to work for the formation of a center-left government very similar to the outgoing cabinet headed by Rumor. The newly reconstituted Social Democratic party, however, has already served notice that it would not take part in a government alongside the old-line Socialists" (*Washington Post*, July 11).

The new split in the Socialist camp and the government crisis produced disarray and nervousness in U.S. political circles. Continuation in office of the center-left coalition and Socialist reunification, viewed as the foundation of a new electoral and political force of major proportions, had become a sort of personal achievement and commitment for several U.S. officials, notably in the State Department. Their frustrations were aggravated when the new President, Richard Nixon, appointed Henry Kissinger as his National Security assistant, a choice that clearly signalled the White House determination to confine the traditional foreign policy operators to a relatively secondary role.

The appointment of Graham Martin as ambassador to Rome was likewise a personal decision by Nixon. It was reportedly influenced by the warm and respectful reception that Martin, then ambassador to Thailand, had been smart or lucky enough to give the former vice-president at a time when very few people thought that Nixon would again be a candidate, let alone a successful candidate to the White House. Martin was a far from engaging personality, very poorly suited to represent the United States in a country like Italy, apparently uninterested in learning anything about the Italians and at the same time quite confident in his ability to know how and when to bring U.S. influence to bear on Italian affairs. Thanks to his good relations with Nixon, the ambassador's views, usually reflecting far right sympathies and prejudices, usually prevailed over the opposition of old Italian hands in the State Department and other agencies. U.S. and Italian media referred time and again to the financial assistance given by Martin to ranking officials of the Italian secret services who later on were identified as politically associated with extreme right-wing groups. As a personal note, I can add that Graham Martin was the only U.S. ambassador to Italy in almost 40 years with whom I never had the opportunity to talk at any length— an opportunity that I don't regret having been denied.

On July 7, 1969, the *New York Times* correspondent Robert Doty described in appalling terms the "wreckage" of Italy's political structure. According to a subsequent editorial in the same daily (July 8), the ongoing political crisis might well represent "the greatest threat to democracy in the life of the Italian Republic." Both the newly dominant left-wingers in the Socialist camp and the CD left now led by Moro looked forward to some sort of collaboration with the Communists or at least wanted to develop a "dialogue" with them. Even more alarming, prominent CDs, like treasury minister Emilio Colombo, had felt it necessary to deny persistent reports of an impending right-wing coup. Barely a week later, another *New York Times* editorial drew a different picture: the CDs had agreed to put together again the center-left coalition and Nenni had drawn away from the Socialist majority bent on opening the door to the Communists (July 15).

Columnist Joseph Kraft concluded a report from Rome by writing: "The probability is that there will be a new center-left government built around the CDs and the two Socialist parties. But if the immediate future in Italy seems not grave, the long-run outlook is less certain. For it remains a serious question whether politics Italian style can be reformed in the grace period of, say, five years. Economic progress has assured this period in which government and administration in this country can be brought into harmony with the vast social changes that have taken place." (*International Herald Tribune*, July 15).

A *Washington Post* editorial stated: "It would be comforting to think that Italy is now undergoing simply another 'crisis' of [the] familiar remediable sort. There is mounting evidence, however, that something far more ominous is happening. Italy may be disintegrating. Its unresolved social tensions may finally have jammed the gears of its antiquated political machinery. Chaos, civil war, a coup—these calamities are real threats, many Italians believe. . . . Party and personal narrowness did the center-left in. The Communist party has steadily grown, as a vehicle for protest as well as a contender for power and now—with the center of the Italian political spectrum in tatters—the far right and the far left confront each other directly across an abyss of deep distrust and class hate" (July 10).

The editorial was criticized by wide sectors of the Italian middle-of-the-road media and severely deplored by democratic politicians, including president Saragat. On my side, I conveyed to the paper's editors my dissent from such catastrophic assessments. Some of my arguments were apparently accepted and in the next few months I had the opportunity to point out again that, while the situation in Italy was indeed a matter of deep concern, it did not call for apocalyptic sensationalism. The new government headed by Rumor included only members of his own CD party, but won a vote of confidence in Parliament thanks to the votes of the Socialist and Republican parties. The immediate purpose of the new Cabinet was to provide a breathing spell during which the wounds of the Socialist split might heal to the point of allowing the center-left parties to join together in a more durable government coalition. Contrary to the predictions of many observers in Italy and abroad, the Cabinet crisis was brought under control before it could force the holding of new elections under circumstances bound to involve serious dangers for the country's democratic institutions.

That summer's confrontation with the *Washington Post*'s foreign desk, however, foreshadowed the end of my 16-year connection with the paper. Early in 1970 another editorial portrayed Italy as a country "caught up in a swirl of violence and civic distrust that some feel could lead to a Communist take-over, a coup from the right, or a civil war." Quoting Luigi Barzini and his gloomy assessments, the editorial spoke of "a situation quite possibly beyond remedy, barring good fortune of a sort and a duration not commonly available to nations or men" (January 19).

Two weeks later, the same concepts were repeated, in somewhat sharper terms, in a letter sent me by Philip Foisie who had been in charge for some years of the paper's Foreign Desk and recently appointed assistant managing editor: "Every specialist on Italy in Washington, including—you should know—Italy's official representatives here," Foisie wrote, "describe the events in Italy in very serious terms, and there is much talk among the above-mentioned sources of a crisis that may be irreversible. We do not get this picture from you." I replied that the gist of my recent articles for the *Washington Post* was "substantially similar" to the approach taken by other stories in U.S. papers, notably the *New York Times* and the *Los Angeles Times*. "What you say about the most gloomy views of the Italian crisis being held by 'every specialist on Italy in Washington, including Italy's official representatives here,' " I continued, "just does not check with my information. Furthermore, I strongly suspect that some of the sources you refer to are not 'specialists on Italy in Washington' but rather Italian visitors of very conservative views who play the usual game of discrediting and belittling the possibilities of the democratic forces that seek to bring about long overdue reforms in Italy. As to your own views on Italian political affairs or on the way of covering them, the most charitable thing that may be said is that you never had a real interest in the matter."

I further recalled that "over the years the *Post*, thanks to my articles, was one of the very few papers to give a correct reading of Italian political events and prospects not only in connection with the coming to power of the center-left but in 1954 and 1964 (just to mention two other controversial phases of Italian politics which likewise were the object of alarmist, sensational and quite unfounded reportings and interpretations by large sectors of the foreign press)."

"The *Post*," I concluded, "is one of the most influential papers in the land. In order to maintain this standing, it must, I believe, steer clear of the cheap sensationalism of those who see a Communist or a colonel under every bed or think that only reports of revolutions and civil wars in the offing make good copy."

Since Foisie had also referred to my nonpolitical stories that "just did not come off," I reminded him that I had never received any word of criticism about them from anybody on the *Post* and added: "One of those stories pleased you so much that you had it published under your own byline rather than under mine. I have a letter of apology from you on this." (The story covered the restoration of the Sistine Chapel ceiling.)

The network of foreign bureaus, developed under the guidance of Al Friendly, had enabled the *Washington Post* to compete on equal terms with the *New York Times* in covering international affairs. In the mid–1960s, Friendly was eased out of his longtime job of managing editor as a result of friction and maneuvers which involved the paper's owners as well. His removal gave Foisie the opportunity to give free rein to his inferiority complex toward the foreign correspondents who had been hired by Friendly before Foisie himself joined the paper. They were pushed out one way or the other: It happened to Waverley Root, the *Post*'s longtime man in Paris and to several others. In my case, there was the additional fact that Foisie, as pointed out in my last letter to him, never had a real interest or understanding for things Italian. Nor was it by chance that the articles filed from Rome to the *Post*, which had reached up to two a week in the late 1950s and well into the 1960s, dropped quickly afterwards to less than half that many and further dwindled to less than one a month on average in later years (and very few of them included some sort of insight or analysis of Italy's political, economic, or social conditions and prospects).

11

Communists or Colonels for a Country That "Has No Future"?

A major factor in precipitating the break with the *Washington Post* was their refusal to print an article of mine filed at the end of January 1970. According to Foisie, this article, like earlier ones, failed to convey an appropriately gloom-and-doom picture of Italian events and prospects. The article duly appeared on January 30 in the *International Herald Tribune*, published jointly by the *Washington Post* and by the *New York Times*.

"In recent weeks," I wrote, "developments combined to reduce the impact of the Socialist schism and to favor a revival of the [center-left] coalition holding the promise of political stability after six months of minority rule and of strikes, unrest and the upsurge of violence culminating in the bank explosion that killed 16 persons in Milan on Dec. 12."

A few days after that bombing, several U.S. media reported that the Italian democratic system had "withstood the test." Rumor's proposal for reconstituting a center-left government was warmly praised in a *New York Times* editorial (December 20). According to Louis Fleming of the *Los Angeles Times*, there were "better than even odds that Italy will get another majority center-left government in the next fortnight" (*International Herald Tribune*, January 26, 1970).

Claire Sterling in *Harper's* proclaimed instead: "The center-left is finished." The prospect of the Communists "joining a government coalition . . . is not so remote any more," as both "big business and the Vatican . . . are not the implacable opponents they used to be." Otherwise, "a frightened and exasperated middle class might come up with an alternative coalition: 'The colonels' solution,' Italians call it."

Roy Meachum, a contributor to U.S. dailies and magazines, stated flatly that the Italian generals were ready to take over the government during the Christmas holidays (*Washington Star*, December 14, 1969). Although the takeover did not materialize on schedule, Meachum insisted that "there could be Communists in the government—or a military coup as in Greece—before elections" (*The New Republic*, January 10, 1970). "With the death of the Socialists as a political reality, the only choice is between the CDs and the PCI," Meachum further noted. "The impact on the national economy of ousting NATO would be minimal," he continued. "Only the military could be expected to fight the removal of NATO; they would be the only real losers in Italy. With something like only 300 slots for generals, the army has over 500 officers of that rank. Getting rid of NATO would eliminate some, but not all the excess jobs for high-ranking officers. The generals know this." Meachum played up again "reports of Italian general officers meeting in Lausanne, Switzerland [and] getting advice from the Greek officers running the junta in Athens. If they are planning a coup, the Italian military may hold back until Premier Rumor takes his first step to bring the Communists into the cabinet. . . . There is another road this unhappy country could take," Meachum concluded: "One Italian said: 'Our problem is Rumor is weak. And so are the other politicians. What we need is a strong man to straighten out the mess.' Another Duce? 'Not like that,' the man said, throwing up his hands to push away the question. 'But someone strong enough to come up and bump heads to get this country back in order.' "

In some articles published in the *New York Times* in late January and early February, Cyrus L. Sulzberger borrowed as usual from his friend Barzini: the CD party, he wrote, was "dissolving like a dead whale stranded upon a beach." The Socialists had "rotted," and a Communist victory was getting nearer while the United States seemed no longer ready to help block it. Since, however, many Italians were still anti-Communist, a prolonged crisis would encourage "right-wing adventurers." The *New York Times* columnist added some platitudes, echoed a few weeks later by Claire Sterling in the *Washington Post* (April 19, 1970) about "Italy's unique contribution to political life . . . the art of governing without a government" thanks largely to a "patient . . . stable . . . expert bureaucracy" which "manages to keep national services running" (a description bound to surprise most Italians and foreign observers). For many years, Sulzberger had denounced Nenni as a main promoter of the "opening to the left" which would be the anteroom to Communist participation in the government and to Italy's switching to a neutralist and even pro-Soviet policy. Now, the *New York Times* columnist suddenly discovered quite a different Nenni and recognized the special importance of the Socialist leader's stand against cooperation with the Communists.

Time quoted Barzini to the effect that in Italy "the unsolved problems pile up and inevitably produce catastrophes at regular intervals." The weekly went on to assert that the new center-left government formed by Rumor, "was running one step ahead of catastrophe" (April 6, 1970).

"The best informed circles in Washington," I wrote in *La Stampa* of Turin shortly after returning from a visit to the United States, "do not share at all the alarm reflected in the reports from Italy and in the editorials that have appeared recently in too many dailies and periodicals in the United States (and not only in the United States). 'When reading these reports and editorials,' says a ranking official who has followed for several years Italian affairs, 'one feels that on the even days of the week Italy is about to go Communist and on the odd days that a rightist coup is impending, while on Sundays the reader can have his pick.' This did not mean, of course, that officials and other observers ignore or look with indifference on the increased political instability and on the sharpened social tensions which have become more apparent following the Socialist split last July. But such developments have never been read as the symptoms that Italian democracy is facing an irreversible crisis.'' I quoted the opinions voiced by a well placed Congressman: ''Even during the long and occasionally confused events that have preceded the formation of the incumbent Rumor Cabinet, we've continued to hope and expect that a solution could and should be found within the framework of the center-left alignment'' (June 3).

The outcome of the regional elections held on June 7 was ''better than expected,'' as the headline of a *New York Times* editorial put it. The government coalition actually made modest gains compared with the 1968 parliamentary election. The Communists did not advance and their ally, the left-wing Socialist splinter party, lost ground. Despite the many strikes and the turmoil in Italian cities, the Neo-Fascists made only limited gains at the expense of the other right-of-center parties, the Liberals, and the Monarchists (June 10). On the same day, Claire Sterling noted in the *Washington Post* that, contrary to the predictions of editorials at home and abroad, Italy was certainly not on the brink of calamities such as a spectacular Communist advance or a takeover by rightist military groups.

Once again, I wrote in *La Stampa* of June 26, many foreign newsmen had swung all way from the direst forecasts about Italy to warm praise of the Italians' good sense which had spared the country so many disasters and possibly opened a better future for it. The main explanation, I felt, lay in the ''complex nature not only of the political game [in Italy] but of the substance of the national facts of life. Hence the strong temptation to file alarmed and alarmistic stories so much easier to write and so much more impressive than analyses in depth of a condition of affairs that is multifaceted and full of shadings. Hence, too, the delusion to have fathomed and understood such a condition while actually failing to go beyond the first of its many skins. And when events belie hasty and superficial readings, the way out is to blame 'this unpredictable country,' as it has been done, time and again.

''Just as a sizable share of the Italian GNP escapes the statisticians (and the tax collector),'' I concluded, ''the country has capacity reserves and safety valves sufficient to allow it to overcome crises and troubles apparently so serious as to foreshadow impending disasters. Italian politicians themselves display a remarkable knack for staving off, often at the last minute, the worst consequences of their own mistakes.''

Over the next few years, Americans interested in Italian affairs continued to be taken by most of their media on a roller coaster ride of comments and forecasts. By and large, the emphasis was still on gloom and doom: "Italy: bent for chaos," was *Newsweek*'s headline on August 10, 1970, after the downfall of the Rumor government and Andreotti's failure to put together again a center-left coalition.

Under the heading "Spaghetti with Chile sauce," (*New York Times*, January 12, 1971), Sulzberger wrote that the Italian Communists were moving closer to seize power by the ballot just as their comrades had done in Chile. Should they succeed, NATO would be destroyed, the European Common Market undermined and the Soviets would gain the upper hand in the Mediterranean.

At the same time, the U.S. press discovered once again "The Fascist phenomenon," to quote *Newsweek*'s headline (March 1, 1971): "Until recently, Fascists were regarded by most Italians as the nostalgic remnants of a regime that was totally discredited by the disaster of World War II. But with right-wing violence on the rise throughout the country, Italians are beginning to think more and more about the unthinkable."

Somewhat less gloomy assessments began to surface when CD Emilio Colombo managed to stay on as premier for more than six months and got ready for a visit to Washington. *Time* dug up an outworn stereotype: "Some Italians are already saying, perhaps prematurely, that [Colombo] may be the best man in the job since the late Alcide De Gasperi, Italy's premier Premier" (February 22). According to U.S. officials, I reported in the weekly *Oggi* (May 24), Italy was not "on the critical list." They did not "minimize the political instability, the social tensions and the challenges to public order which are the earmarks of the current, delicate phase of transition in Italy." But they felt that "any confusion with developments in Chile [was] absurd even more than just superficial."

The gains scored by the MSI in the local elections held in mid-June 1971 unleashed a new wave of alarm in the U.S. media. "Il Duce's shadow," headlined *Newsweek*, emphasizing the "discomfortable parallels between the social conditions that spurred Mussolini's rise to power and the chaotic state of present-day Italy" (June 28). Several reports pointed out that the balloting had involved less than one-fifth of the electorate and most of it had taken place in the South where right-wing parties were traditionally stronger. Yet even those reports stressed that both CDs and Communists were in for "an agonizing reappraisal" since their mutual "courting" had been based "on the assumption that the electorate was drifting leftward," while it now appeared "to be drifting the other way" (Claire Sterling in the *Washington Post*, June 15). The *U.S. News and World Report* described Italy as a country on its way to disintegration where Communist and Fascist extremists were waiting for the opportunity to seize power.

Sulzberger had no doubts (and proved wrong once again): "The tide turned politically last month when regional elections marked a major victory for the MSI, called Neo-Fascist by its adversaries," and a loss for the Communists (*New York Times*, July 21).

According to Claire Sterling (*Washington Post*, October 11), Italy was "sliding down the slippery slope into what may be its worst post-war recession" (but just about at that time the country's economy was emerging from stagnation and gaining a momentum that was to develop further in the next year or two). In early December, Graham Hovey wondered in the *New York Times* whether Italy had become the "sick man" of Europe. He emphasized the serious rifts in most democratic parties, the sharp dissensions over the divorce issue and "the worst recession since Italy's post-war recovery."

Claire Sterling stressed the likelihood that in the election of Giovanni Leone to the presidency, the drawn-out balloting would "change Italy's political system" (as the headline of her article read). The parties that had governed Italy for "nearly a decade" were "in shambles," she wrote. "The CDs . . . have evidently been shattered by their shameful impotence in this election. . . . There is a strong presentiment here that what had started as a tactical alliance between Socialists and Communists [during the presidential balloting] may prove more enduring. The same could happen to an originally temporary alignment of the other three center-left parties with the conservative Liberals" (*Washington Post*, December 27).

The failure to stitch together once again the center-left coalition, the formation of a minority government headed by Andreotti, and its defeat in Parliament made it inevitable to resort to a general election a full year ahead of schedule.

In a dispatch from Rome front-paged in the *New York Times* of March 29, Paul Hofmann quoted "an internationally known writer [presumably Barzini] who, when asked for an article on Italy's future . . . guffaws and says: 'Italy has no future.' " According to this writer, Hofmann further reported, there would be "a civil war" if after the elections the CDs formed an alliance with either the Neo-Fascists or the Communists.

I was in the United States when this article appeared and I reported in the *Daily American*, Rome's English language paper, that the reactions of officials in Washington were fairly uniform: "Poppycock," "Nonsense," and "other shorter but less printable words" (April 16).

"Predictions of civil war, impending Communist takeover and/or rightist coups are old stuff indeed for Italian experts in the State Department, in the intelligence community and in other agencies of the U.S. government," I went on. "One high official told me that he was still studying for his Foreign Service admission when the first such reports were circulated following the general election of 1953. Other specialists recall similar 'scares' back in 1960, in the summer of 1964 and again in late 1969 and early 1970."

According to U.S. experts, "there is less factionalism among the CDs, the party which, whatever its shortcomings, is bound to remain, in the words of one analyst, 'the fulcrum of every reasonably conceivable government in Italy.' . . . For the time being, they add, the party can only benefit, in terms of votes and prestige, from the fact that it no longer looks like a 'can of worms,' as ambassador Zellerbach used to say back in the late 1950s.

"Italy watchers in Washington," I further reported, "are fully confident that the CDs will stick to their determination not to ally themselves either with the Communists or with the Neo-Fascists." The prevailing view in Washington was that, while the CDs would "suffer some losses to the benefit of the Neo-Fascists, such losses are likely to be offset by the gains of the Socialists, Social Democrats, and Republicans; so, on balance, the center-left alignment should retain a comfortable majority.

"Some U.S. experts are convinced that the size of the shift to the extreme right will be cut down to the point of leaving a numerical margin, however small, for a 'democratic alternative' to the center-left, that is, for a revival of the center alliance of CDs, Liberals, Social Democrats, and Republicans. Other specialists feel that a government from which the Socialists were excluded would 'lack built-in brakes against a slide to the right, notably in its approach to labor relations, and might well provoke a strong reaction from the left leading to an ominous polarization of the political struggle.'

"To sum it up, Washington experts do not believe that the forthcoming election will usher in dramatic changes, but they worry over its being followed by a protracted period of suspended animation and petty infighting for power among and within the democratic parties." According to the U.S. specialists, on the other hand, there was no "real danger that Italy will go down the Red drain or will be swept away by a tide of anarchy and civil war."

In earlier articles in the same daily, I recalled that the Communists had scored their major gains at the polls during the years when *per capita* income had registered an unprecedented increase: "The key to this apparent paradox was the all too great discrepancy between the rates of material and civic progress." Confronted with "the urgent task of restoring financial stability while warding off a major recession," the center-left governments had made "little progress in implementing their pledges to introduce long overdue social reforms or in attacking the bottlenecks and structural weaknesses which had been largely responsible for putting an end to the 'Italian miracle.'

"The performance of the center-left governments, which looks more disappointing when measured against pent-up expectations, has driven additional protest voters into the Communist fold and has increased the militancy of the labor unions. Chronic industrial strife has ushered in economic stagnation. On top of the strikes, outbreaks of violence in the streets, plants and universities have produced a sizable backlash, especially in the more volatile South and among the petty bourgeoisie, to the benefit of the Neo-Fascists. Last but not least, an open conflict between the lay forces and Catholics could split the country down the middle if a referendum on repealing the year-old divorce law is held in late spring.

"Yet," I concluded, "things are not so bad as they are described by many foreign papers in their recurrent bouts of alarmism about Italy. There is reason for concern over Italy's future. But through the years, the country has proved to have a degree of resiliency and reserves of strength that escape most foreign observers'' (January 23).

In a subsequent article, I noted that despite the differences and strains among and within the parties making up the center-left alignment, ''reports of a final collapse of the coalition may well prove premature, as has happened so many times in past years'' (*Daily American*, January 30).

On the eve of the PCI National Congress, I pointed out that the party's electoral following and political influence had grown steadily not only thanks to ''an efficient party machine, staffed by a large number of dedicated and well-trained cadres,'' but because ''as the main opposition force'' the Communists ''have often seemed to be more attuned to the mood of the country than the center or center-left coalitions. These coalitions are held responsible'' for the frustration and contradictions that have ''become more apparent and more galling as the country has acquired many of the features of modern mass civilization.'' Some recent signals, however, ''have suggested that, just as they seemed closer to winning a share of national power, the Communists have begun to find it harder to hold together the vast confederation of protest groups that make up the bulk of their electorata.'' For instance, if the party failed ''to disavow the more radical groups of workers and students [it] runs the risk of alienating some and perhaps many of the Italians who vote Communist not because they want to 'wreck the system' but because they want to improve their economic and social conditions or to impress upon the powers that be the need for a more honest and efficient management of public moneys.

''The coming to the fore of a Neo-Fascist movement,'' I further noted, ''may actually help the Communists by promoting a radicalization of the political struggle. The Italian Communists could then secure the leading role in an anti-Fascist 'front' which would reach into the center of the political alignment and face an equally broad and composite alliance made up of moderate, conservative and extreme rightist forces. The Communists have not lost, either, their chances of gaining power through some slower and less dramatic process. For instance, if the conservative and moderate groups within the democratic camp continue to block long overdue reforms, more and more Socialists and progressive-minded CDs may conclude that Communist participation in a new parliamentary majority and eventually in the government is the only way to implement the pledges of social progress and institutional modernization made by the center-left coalitions. But things could take quite a different turn,'' I concluded, ''if the center-left parties emerge from the [forthcoming] elections with the strength and the determination to give the country some political stability and at least some of the reforms required to meet the needs and demands of the protest voters. The pressure would then be on the Communist party and most strongly on those of its members who after waiting for over 20 years outside the halls of governmental power are already eager to come in from the cold'' (*Daily American*, March 11 and 12).

On the eve of the elections, I interviewed Giorgio Amendola, a leading proponent of a policy aimed "at gaining a share of national power by extending [the PCI's] alliances toward the center and the number one Communist representative in the European Parliament" (*Daily American*, May 7). Amendola said: "Together with the popular forces, which follow Socialist and Catholic principles, we want to play a role of political guide of the country. We believe that Italy needs a government with authority founded on popular consensus, able to smash all reactionary attempts and implement an earnest reform."

Amendola answered "yes" when asked "whether the Italian Communists' platform, calling for gaining power through democratic methods, commits them also to relinquishing the government if such a shift should reflect the will of the voters. Said Amendola: "Apart from subversive attempts by domestic and international reactionary groups, against which we would naturally defend ourselves with all available means, we see an advance led by a plurality of forces and opposed by other political forces operating within the Constitution and enjoying the guarantee of freedom."

The role of the Italian Communists in the European Parliament, Amendola stressed, "is one aspect of our overall effort to eventually overcome the hegemony of the big monopolistic groups in Western Europe as well as defeat any attempt to block contacts with Eastern Europe. . . . Western Europe is now facing the problem of freeing itself from the traditional subservience to the economic, political, and military interests of the U.S.

"The question of NATO," Amendola went on, "cannot be answered with a 'yes' or a 'no.' . . . A policy intended to keep Italy out of either bloc is for us a valid prospect not only over the short term but for the most remote future because it coincides with the interests of our country. We have also said that if Italy were to get out of NATO now, this would help, irrespective of what others may contend, the overall effort to overcome the confrontation between the blocs in Europe and in the world. But we have stated and we reaffirm that we are concretely interested in prospects and proposals that might place Italy's withdrawal from NATO within a broader context intended to bring about a downgrading of the blocs on our continent."

Amendola concluded: "We are looking forward to Italian neutrality as part of our determination to fight the division of Europe into two political and military blocs. It is equally evident that, as partners in a national government, we would express this determination in terms that would not only be agreed upon with the other forces represented in such a government but would be in line with the international situation existing at the time."

In private conservations, both CD leader Rumor, who had become interior minister in the Andreotti Cabinet, and premier Andreotti himself, told me that their party was "recouping most of the ground yielded to the MSI in recent years." Both Andreotti and Rumor hoped that the lineup in the new Parliament would make it possible to form a center majority providing at least "a numerical alternative" to the center-left and thus enabling the CDs to negotiate with the

Socialists from a position of strength. Andreotti hinted that in such an event he would prefer to put together a centrist government while attempts to revive the center-left coalition could better be undertaken later on. Rumor, instead, was clearly inclined to open negotiations with the Socialists right after the election: "Our primary goal," he told me, "remains the formation of a center-left government."

In an interview which appeared in the *Daily American* on April 30, Andreotti stressed that since the end of World War II and up to this day, the Italian democratic system has been quite stable. The Italian situation differs substantially from the conditions in other democratic countries. The largest opposition party, the Communist party, has been unquestionably actuated and is still actuated, because of its nature, by ideologies quite remote from political concepts that call for different parties, all loyal to the four basic freedoms, to alternate peacefully at the helm of the government. And what I just said about the PCI applies as well to the opposition represented by the extreme right.

"We are not an underdeveloped country," Andreotti further told me. "Following a revival of confidence and thanks to an earnest and austere administration—and this must be the next government's task and pledge—I trust that Italy will be able to play a most concrete role in the construction of Europe."

Good relations with the United States, Andreotti said in reply to another question, "have always represented an essential and steadfast component of our foreign policy. I am certain that those relations will continue to be ever more fruitful even while both the Italian society and the American society undergo rapid changes. . . . While the impact of progress in the construction of Europe cannot be exactly foreseen right now, I think that it will give further breadth and a more marked character of interdependence to the relationship between our country and the U.S. It is a matter of joint interest to make sure that social and economic progress in Europe and in America be accompanied by a widening of their collaboration. This should involve an ever growing readiness to operate concretely in favor of those countries where the consequences of underdevelopment are still most painful."

On the eve of the election, Claire Sterling seemed to have outgrown her alarms about Italy's future. "The sense of imminent political collapse spreading through the country when Parliament was dissolved," she wrote in the *Washington Post* of May 7, "has plainly subsided. . . . It is widely believed here that the combined vote for all moderate parties should be at least enough to contain the Communists and the neo-Fascists both. . . . In any case, the returns are expected to show that, contrary to Communist and Fascist claims in this campaign, Italy is still governable."

A *New York Times* editorial (May 7) maintained that if the neo-Fascist Italian Social Movement made big gains and the Communists kept over 25 percent of the total vote, the CDs would be unable to form a government relying only on the democratic forces. In that event, Socialist party leaders would press the CDs into forming a government dependent on the Communists, while right-wing

Catholics would urge a parliamentary alliance with Fascists and Monarchists. In either case, there would be serious "risks of civil war."

On the same day, I wrote in the *Daily American* that the election would not "bring about major shifts in the political balance," the same forecast I had made in the same paper as far back as February 27: "The CDs will retain their traditional role as the largest political force in the country and the mainstay of government." The four parties that had been allied in the center-left coalition were "expected to win a combined total of 55 to 60 percent of the votes. The size of the inroads that the neo-Fascists will make into the CD and Liberal electorate" would determine whether there would also be a working majority for a center coalition government. In sum, "the returns should show that almost two Italians out of three continue to support the parties—from the Liberals on the right to the Socialists on the left—that have governed Italy during the last 25 years. This would not mean at all that most Italians are happy about the performance of those parties. But it would confirm that a large majority of Italians reject firmly a slide toward an authoritarian regime, whether of the right or of the left, as well as a departure from the international approach based on loyalty to the Atlantic alliance and support of European integration."

12

The 1972 Elections and the Revival of the Center Left

The first comments by U.S. media on the 1972 electoral returns reflected surprise and relief. A *New York Times* editorial (May 10) stressed the unexpected show of strength by the Christian Democrats. Claire Sterling likewise conceded that the CD performance (38.8 percent of the votes) had been a surprise for most political observers (*Washington Post*, May 10). Both papers paid tribute to the "maturity and stability" of the Italian electorate. The major weeklies indulged in the usual cliches: "More of the same in Rome" (*Newsweek*, May 22) and "Forward to the past" (*Time*).

There was no alternative to recreating a center-left coalition, most observers agreed, including those who in a more or less recent past had rushed to proclaim that it could not and should not be revived. When Andreotti managed, instead, to form a center government, the prevailing consensus was that it would have "a short life" (Don M. Larrimore in the *Washington Post*, June 27). A *New York Times* editorial noted that the new cabinet faced serious trouble within the CD party itself, where dissatisfaction was widespread "because of the Socialist exclusion." Moreover, rising economic and social difficulties could precipitate a new wave of devastating strikes. Barely five months later, a *New York Times Magazine* article by William Murray, a newsman living in Italy, extolled Andreotti's performance as head of an efficient government and the most interesting and possibly most gifted democratic leader to come to power after Alcide De Gasperi (November 22). It was another example of the apparently irresistible inclination of the major U.S. media (and of sizable political circles in Washington) to praise indiscriminately any Italian premier who managed to hold on to the job for a few months and, in the meantime, had not publicly denounced the Atlantic Alliance or brought about civil war or the collapse of the national

economy. Given the average life of Italian governments, such tributes had the
nasty habit of turning into only slightly premature obituaries.

The returns, I wrote (*Daily American*, May 10), "exposed as baseless or
exaggerated reports that Italian democracy was fighting on the 'last beach.'
Rightwing inroads into the CD electorate were not large enough to affect substantially the political balance of power. Neo-Fascists and Monarchists fell far
short of their performance in the 1953 election when they polled a total of 13
percent. Altogether, the Communists, their PSIUP ally and the new radical group
('Il Manifesto') that was read out of the PCI in 1969, received 30.5 percent of
the popular vote, or 1 percent less than the Communists and the PSIUP had
polled in the 1968 election." The CDs "still have an option" between reviving
the center-left alliance and forming a center coalition which, despite the losses
suffered by "the conservative-minded Liberal Party, mostly to the neo-Fascists,"
would still "command a slim majority in both branches of Parliament."

The general election provided further evidence, I noted (*Daily American*, May
21), that "the roots of Italian democracy are less fragile than many people, at
home and abroad, are inclined to think." But the new government, "whatever
its makeup," would be confronted with many problems that were not new but
both "serious and urgent. The Italian man-in-the-street must be given concrete
evidence that the recent crackdowns on crime and political violence were not
occasional gestures dictated by electoral expediency. A far-reaching modernization of social, economic, and administrative structures appears imperative to
meet the demands and requirements of the protest voters as well as to protect
the country from disastrous swings of the business cycle and to promote its
further and more balanced growth. The tax system is not only inadequate and
inequitable but so unwieldy that it cannot provide the tools for timely action
either to curb inflation or to stimulate economic expansion. The government's
ability to undertake a policy of deficit spending and emergency public works
programs is further and most seriously impaired by a cumbersome, top heavy
and generally inefficient bureaucratic apparatus. It takes three and a half years
on average from the time the money is allocated for a construction project and
the time the construction is carried out. The many controls and authorizations
(up to 42 of them in some cases) require a seemingly endless shunting of papers
from one department to another but only too often do not even offer sufficient
guarantees against abuses of power or graft."

Reviewing the history of the trade union movement in Italy, I pointed out that
for a long time its power had been "severely limited by chronic unemployment
and underemployment." Only in the early 1960s, the unions' hand had been
strengthened as a result of far-reaching changes in the economic and social
conditions, of the new makeup of the governmental coalitions and of the progress
toward a reunification of the labor organizations themselves. During the "hot
autumn" of 1968, a "long and bitter confrontation which involved labor, management, and the politicians as well, the unions won sizable wage increases, a
few improvements in working conditions and some say in production planning

and fresh promises of more concrete progress in making available decent low cost housing, schools, hospitals, and public transportation. But much additional bitterness and strife developed when the national labor contracts concluded at the end of 1969 had to be implemented at the local plant level. The major labor organizations found it increasingly difficult to deal with the wildcat strikes and the sabotage of production lines carried out by small numbers of workers inspired by radical leftwing groups. The traditional political differences between the unions were again brought to the fore during the campaign for last May's general election. Republicans and Social Democrats within UIL, as well as large sectors of the predominantly CD CISL, voiced the renewed vigor their worry that the new united labor organization would be controlled in effect by the Communists. [The latter] would not represent a majority in the joint union but would certainly make up its biggest and best organized minority" (*Daily American*, July 11).

In the early fall, I devoted two articles to highlighting the main factors that had influenced Italy's international posture in the last century and were to retain much of their significance over the following decades (*Daily American*, September 24, October 1). The peg was provided by French president Georges Pompidou's proposal for closer collaboration between the two countries. The main purpose was apparently to promote France's position as the leader of a "Latin alignment" within the EEC, an alignment which "would offset the influence of Great Britain and of the other Northern countries scheduled to join the Community on January 1; it would also become the spearhead of a European policy in the Mediterranean that would strongly reflect France's drive for close collaboration with the Arab countries and for 'autonomy' from the U.S. On the economic side, President Pompidou was said to have offered several concessions, notably with regard to Italian farm exports and to Common Market support for the development of the Italian South, and have asked in return that Italy opt for the French SECAM system of color TV rather than for the German PAL (Italy's choice is expected to influence the decision of several Mediterranean nations, such as Spain, Libya, Tunisia, Greece, and Turkey, as well as of some Latin American countries)."

Shortly afterwards, "the Italian government announced that 'experimental' color TV broadcasts would begin at the opening of the Olympic Games using alternatively SECAM and PAL transmissions." La Malfa "promptly reaffirmed his party's opposition to early introduction of color TV. In any case, he added, the PAL system should be chosen because it would forge closer ties between Italy and Western Europe as a whole (most West European countries have taken up the German system, while the French have sold theirs to some Arab and East European countries, and the USSR itself uses a modified version of SECAM). Saragat charged that adoption of SECAM was intended to loosen Italy's ties with the U.S. and with Western Europe and to lure the country into following, especially in the Mediterranean and in the Middle East, a course dictated by 'the French-Soviet policy of Gaullist inspiration.' "

By putting off any decision about color TV, I continued, "premier Andreotti managed both to stave off a government crisis and to set aside the specific issue that had sparked the latest outbreak of polemics over Italy's role in Europe and in the Mediterranean.'' Yet, the episode had spotlighted once again the ''debate as to whether Italy should be considered (and behave) as the most Mediterranean of the European countries or rather as the most European of the Mediterranean countries. Actually, both definitions are correct, but the emphasis on one or the other has determined or greatly influenced most of the shifts of the Italian foreign policy.

''Back in the 1880s,'' I recalled, ''resentment over the establishment of a French protectorate in Tunisia played a decisive role in persuading the Italian government to join with Germany and Austria-Hungary in a Triple Alliance and thus in effect give priority to expansion in the Mediterranean and in Africa rather than to 'redeeming' the Italian populated areas (Trento and Trieste) which were still part of the Hapsburg Empire. In the early 20th century, the pendulum swung in the opposite direction and Italy entered World War I primarily to win control of those areas, as well as to prevent German domination of continental Europe. After the Fascist takeover, the dream of turning the Mediterranean into an Italian lake and of establishing an Italian empire in Northeast Africa became more and more the guiding star of Italian foreign policy. The result was Italy's disastrous participation in World War II as a camp follower of Nazi Germany.

''Reconstruction of the domestic economic and refurbishing the country's international image were the absorbing preoccupations of Italy's first postwar democratic governments. The very progress achieved on both counts soon encouraged some Italians to envisage a less modest role for their country.'' I recalled the efforts by Enrico Mattei, Giovanni Gronchi, and Amintore Fanfani and ''the strong opposition'' they met ''in Italy herself.''

Since 1956, I continued, ''the U.S. has become the main provider of military and economic assistance to Israel. The Soviet Union has emerged as a major factor in the new strategic and political balance of power in the Mediterranean and in the Middle East. Gaullist France has switched from active friendship for Israel to a clearly pro-Arab policy. In Italy, however, much the same people are still quarreling, and using much the same arguments, about the approach to be followed with regard to Mediterranean and Middle East problems.

''Italy's international posture,'' I concluded, ''will remain keyed to two fundamentals: membership in the Atlantic alliance and championship of European integration. What may be getting under way is a reappraisal of the role that Italy can and should play within the Western alliance and within the expanding European Community.''

Foreign policy themes and prospects were the main topics covered in several talks I had with president Giovanni Leone in the next few months. ''Leone does not view the emergence of a European identity and personality,'' I reported (*Daily American*, March 21, 1973), ''as an opportunity, let alone a tool, to 'make the Atlantic wider.' On the contrary, he sees it as a condition for facing up, with closer solidarity and increased efficiency, to the problems confronting the West in its relations within the Eastern countries and within its own camp. It would be less difficult to reach a reasonable compromise on the sharpening differences between the U.S. and the EEC on trade matters if negotiations with the Americans were conducted within the broader and more balanced context provided by an adequate progress toward European integration in other sectors, notably foreign policy and defense. At the same time, such progress, pursued within the framework of Atlantic solidarity, would enable Europe to play an active role in promoting detente with the East while avoiding the risks that would confront the West European countries if they were to develop the dialogue with the Soviet Union after drawing away from the U.S. and while still divided among themselves. Within the Europe to be unified, balance means no hegemony, directorate, or other privileged combination of two or more members of the Community to the detriment of the others.''

As "a Neapolitan by birth," I continued, president Leone "is fully aware that ties with the countries of the great Mediterranean arc—from the Iberian peninsula to the northern shores of Africa and Asia and to the Balkans—have a truly major importance for Italy and particularly for her southern regions. At the same time, the President knows well that 'Italy has her feet in the Mediterranean and her head in continental Europe.'

"Authoritative observers, both in Italy and abroad," I further recalled, had "recently voiced the opinion that Italy, as a result of her economic troubles, persistent social gaps, political and administrative inefficiency, 'is sliding away from the West and toward the Near Eastern world.' " President Leone "does not ignore, nor minimize, those negative factors and circumstances. But he feels that their significance should be realistically cut down to size. Above all, 'a new and most encouraging development' must be entered on the other side of the ledger: 'the aspiration to European unity, which until a few years ago, was confined to an elite of Italians, is now becoming, in fact has already become to a large extent, a popular feeling, an essential fact confirmed by my daily contacts with representatives of a wide variety of social groups and sectors.' ''

On the domestic side, Leone told me time and again that it was "necessary to bring the Socialists back into the government coalition. Otherwise, we would be confronted with the consolidation of a leftist grouping backed by 40 percent of the voters," that is stronger than the CDs.

Former premier Rumor told me as early as June 1972: "If the centrist government headed by Andreotti should manage to remain in office beyond the National Congress of our party, scheduled for next Fall but likely to be put off until the spring of 1973, the Socialists would be sucked back into a leftist alliance."

By the end of the summer, it was clear that powerful groups, especially among the CDs and among the Social Democrats, I reported (*Daily American*, September 10), looked forward to "an early revival of the center-left alliance." A key condition for such a revival was about to be fulfilled, thanks to a shift in the balance of power within the Socialist camp, which was to dislodge Giacomo

Mancini from the PSI secretaryship and replace him with Francesco De Martino. "The political alignment which supports the Andreotti government," De Martino told me in an interview (*Daily American*, October 25), "is dangerously unbalanced. It leaves out on the right only the neo-Fascist *Movimento Sociale*, which represents less than 10 percent of the electorate and in many cases gives its votes or a benevolent neutrality to the present cabinet. On the left, that alignment leaves out our party, with its 10 percent, as well as the Communists who poll 28 percent of the popular vote." It was necessary and urgent, therefore, to exclude from the government "the Liberal party, right wing of the ruling coalition" and to revive "our own collaboration with the CDs. Following such a revival, the center-left approach must be given a stronger thrust with regard both to its program and its efficiency. The experience of the earlier center-left governments, which was not negative but disappointing under certain aspects, has taught us that, while it is not easy to enact the reforms, it is even more difficult but all important to implement them."

A revived center-left coalition, De Martino pointed out, "should affirm the self-sufficiency of its majority, but should not lock itself in like a besieged citadel. . . . The conservative and moderate forces, operating within the CD camp and within other coalition partners, must not seek to block reforms already agreed upon, as they have done time and again in the past, thus giving ammunition to those who maintain that Communist support is necessary to enact any meaningful reform. At the same time, Communist votes in Parliament should not be rejected out of hand when they might swell the majority backing specific measures advocated by the center-left coalition or help to introduce amendments acceptable to the government parties." The Communists would then be confronted with a concrete test of their proclaimed determination not to pursue the policy of 'the worse the better.' . . .

"We must not forget that the PCI is the standard bearer of the aspirations of large popular masses, even though it often seeks to promote them in a way that we cannot approve, just as we cannot share the strongly bureaucratic and centralized concept of democracy that marks the international organization of the PCI." In any case, De Martino went on, "the main reason why the participation of the PCI in a governmental majority does not appear possible, today and for a long time to come, stems from the party's positions in foreign affairs and specifically from its ties with the Soviet Union. . . . The PCI despite some progress in that direction, has not really tackled the main issue, namely its autonomy in international matters." "The Italian Communists," De Martino concluded, "should move into positions similar to those we adopted before the center-left coalition was formed, when we accepted the Atlantic Alliance as an accomplished fact of Italian life, even though we were not enthusiastic about it, and insisted that the related commitments be given a strictly defensive and geographically well-defined interpretation."

A PSI National Congress sanctioned the victory of the factions led by De Martino and their alliance with Nenni's followers. In the CD camp, there were still widespread doubts and hesitations about an early revival of the center-left approach. In an interview (*Daily American*, December 23), party secretary general Arnaldo Forlani told me: "We have not closed the door to the left and we have not opened it to the right." The CDs were interested in resuming "a constructive dialogue" with the Socialists who, however, "should give more conclusive proof of their determination to work with the other democratic parties, rather than with the Communists, in running municipal, provincial and regional administrations. We realize that there may be special cases and exceptions, but the basic tendency should emerge clearly: Otherwise, even the proclaimed Socialist readiness to collaborate with us in the national government takes on a rather ambiguous coloration." Forlani did not anticipate serious trouble in the foreign policy area: "This was definitely not the main weakness of the center-left alliance."

At the same time, Forlani defended the Andreotti government: "While our main concern is still to widen the democratic area to the left, it is also important to keep up a dam against threats from the right and therefore to maintain a working relationship with the Liberal Party." The CD leader further argued that it was "inadvisable to tie up Italy's democratic prospects to a single government formula, namely the center-left alliance."

At the end of February 1973, Rumor told me that it would soon become both necessary and possible to form a government including the PSI." Otherwise "the position of the Socialist leaders would become untenable and their party would be compelled to seek again closer relations with the Communists. We would be forced, on our side, to accept the support of the rightist parties and the country would be impelled toward a polarization that would split it down the middle."

While using more cautious language in an interview he gave me for *Corriere della Sera* (March 3), Rumor spelled out that a resumption of center-left approach remained "a prospect which is not only still valid but has an essential importance for the future of Italian democracy." It is hard to say whether or to what extent this interview had a role in cutting short my contributions to *Corriere*. The daily's editors, who had recently praised and encouraged those contributions, did not dare to justify or explain the decision to end them. A major, possibly decisive factor was represented by the anti-American (and pro-Communist) inclinations increasingly apparent among the owners, the editors, and the union organizers at *Corriere* and in other Italian media (see Chapter 14). Much in the same way, it might be added, I had been given no explanation when in the early 1960s an end was similarly put to my earlier relationship with the same daily. Alfio Russo, who at the same time had just been appointed editor-in-chief of *Corriere*, was known for his narrow-minded conservative views. These views, as I found out personally when he was editor of the Florence daily, *La Nazione*, made Russo feel that my sympathies for the center-left approach reflected dangerous, possibly "subversive" inclinations.

In the *Daily American* of April 29, 1973, I wrote: "It would be unfair to say that on the whole the Andreotti Cabinet has performed worse than most of its predecessors. But the replacement of the Socialists with the Liberals in the governing coalition has not produced the major changes for the better anticipated by moderate and conservative groups." Many CD experts, notably the minister for state participations, Mario Ferrari-Aggradi, told me privately that they had strong misgivings about the approach followed by treasury minister Giovanni Malagodi, the top Liberal representative in the Andreotti Cabinet. "The policy of deficit spending pursued by the treasury," I wrote in the *Daily American*, "does not reflect a coherent effort to solve basic problems (such as the development of the South, the modernization of agriculture, or the improvement of key social services); it rather follows much the same pattern of piecemeal and wasteful concessions to local and sectorial pressures for which the Liberals, when in the opposition, used to blame the center-left coalition. The government, moreover, has countenanced a floating of the lira which amounts to a sizeable devaluation with respect to most foreign currencies. Under the circumstances, this seems bound to produce all the negative and few of the positive consequences that are usually associated with a devaluation carried out officially and at a single stroke."

In an interview given the *Daily American* on the eve of a trip to the United States (April 15), premier Andreotti branded as exaggerations recent reports that Italy was drifting away from Europe. Referring to "the decision to let the lira float independently . . . while the currencies of the other six Common Market countries float jointly, Andreotti said: 'Temporary difficulties may place special emphasis on Italian measures that do not coincide automatically with those adopted by most other nations of the European Community. But of what use to Europe would be an Italy ravaged and bled white?' "

The Italian premier, who had visited the Soviet Union in the fall of 1972, told me that "the increasingly good relations between the U.S. and the USSR sustain and promote detente in Europe and throughout the world. The task of the forthcoming conference on security and cooperation in Europe is to help consolidate this trend to the point where it may prove stronger than all reasons for polemics and political differences.'

"In reply to another question, Andreotti said: 'Friendship with the U.S. within the framework of an efficient Western solidarity, continues to be the guiding star of Italian foreign policy.' In this context, Italian efforts 'should now be directed at improving overall relations between the U.S. and Europe.'

"Turning to domestic affairs, the Premier conceded that 'the government's majority is so slim that it becomes hard to get action in Parliament. But a majority cannot be put together by just looking at its numerical size.' In any case, Andreotti stated flatly, 'Up to now, no alternatives are in sight.' "

Within the next few weeks, however, Social Democrats and Republicans, both key partners in the governmental coalition, made it clear that they no longer backed the Andreotti cabinet. Their stand precipitated the crystallization of a new CD majority committed to supporting a return to the center-left coalition. "Italy's largest party," I wrote (*Daily American*, June 12), "is now ready to shift again the government's axis to the left-of-center, by dropping the conservative-minded Liberals and reviving the alliance with the Socialists. The shift was reflected in a document worked out by Fanfani, Moro, and Rumor, all former premiers and former secretaries of the CD Party, and endorsed by the [party] Congress. It is reliably reported that Fanfani will become CD secretary, replacing Arnaldo Forlani who was one of the main supporters of the Andreotti government. Rumor is expected to be entrusted with the task of forming the new center-left government. Moro may be offered the foreign ministry, a post he held from mid–1969 to early 1972."

In the same daily I noted (June 24): "Quite a few foreign observers (and some Italians as well) seem quite puzzled by the quickening prospects of the return to the helm of a governmental combination which collapsed just 18 months ago after ruling for a decade marked by some accomplishments but also by growing controversy and disappointment. Their puzzlement appears to reflect scant knowledge and/or understanding of some basic facts of Italian political life which have emerged clearly over the last twenty years. The center-left alliance is the only combination of democratic forces that can enjoy a fairly large majority in Parliament and in the country; it is the only combination that can be supported or tolerated by most CDs. It is the only combination of democratic forces that can at least hold out a promise to carry out the social reforms and institutional modernizations which appear more necessary than ever to achieve both political stability and a steady and more balanced expansion of the national economy.

"This will involve," I continued, "some understanding with the workers' organizations and therefore is bound to bring to the fore the delicate issue of the role of the PCI. The Communists say that their opposition to a revived center-left government will not prevent them from giving 'a constructive and necessary contribution to the solution of the country's serious and urgent problems.' Most Socialists and CD leftwingers feel that the Communist offers should be put to a concrete test. But many other CDs, as well as quite a few Social Democrats and Republicans, fear that any such opening would enable the Communists to infiltrate and divide the governmental majority and thus win a share in running national affairs.

"Some observers," I concluded, "have referred to the next government as 'the last beach.' Things are not that bad. But the collapse of the current efforts to restore political stability and administrative efficiency would mean, at the very least, losing another opportunity, probably the last one in the foreseeable future, to consolidate and modernize the still fragile foundations of Italian democracy."

The downfall of the Andreotti Cabinet and the prospects of the center-left's comeback were greeted rather coldly by many U.S. media. The *New York Times* emphasized the responsibilities now placed on the Socialists and even more heavily on the CDs (June 15). "It has been known for months—indeed ever since Andreotti took office a little over a year ago—that his government would not last," *The Christian Science Monitor* said two weeks later. "The pity of the Italian government change is that it will likely achieve little."

Up to the last minute, the prevailing view at the White House favored the continuation in office of the Andreotti cabinet, although not so much so as the Italian premier's spokesmen sought to convey. One of them told me right after Andreotti's return from the United States: "Whatever progress may have been made in promoting a relaxation of international tensions, the Nixon Administration looks with scant sympathy on the 'Liberal' forces in any Western country. ... Nixon personally has not only voiced great satisfaction about the politics pursued by the Andreotti government but was very pleased when told by our premier that an eventual return to the center-left coalition must take place under conditions to be laid down by the CDs rather than by the Socialists."

U.S. officials more directly involved in keeping track of Italian events had foreseen for quite some time that the Andreotti cabinet would be replaced fairly soon by a center-left coalition, and were far from displeased by such a prospect, I was informed by friends in Washington. Graham Martin, moreover, had left Rome and was succeeded by John A. Volpe, the first American of Italian origin to be appointed ambassador to Italy. Volpe was no "liberal" but was a man of good sense, warmly interested in the welfare of his parents' country, who tried to understand and convey to his government the Italians' aspirations and requirements.

In the interview he gave me, his first since taking over the embassy's top post in Rome, Volpe said: "European integration has been a cornerstone of U.S. policy through four previous presidential administrations and continues to be fully supported by President Nixon." The ambassador emphasized Nixon's determination not to withdraw U.S. troops unilaterally from Europe and added: "I am optimistic that a resolution (or bill) in favor of such a pullback could not get enough votes in Congress ... to override a presidential veto." Volpe further underlined that the recent proposal by presidential adviser Henry A. Kissinger for a reexamination of the Atlantic alliance was intended to produce a plan, jointly developed by the Europeans and by the U.S., which would give the Europeans a sense of participation and partnership, "and this is as it should be." The ambassador went on to say that "despite what some people have suggested, Italy is not about to leave her moorings in Western Europe. At the same time, she does not want to follow blindly what one or two other members of the European Community may want to impose on the rest. ... Italy has a tremendous potential for leadership in the European Community." The United States does "recognize the importance of the Mediterranean for the Italian nation because of its geographic and historical tradition." But if Italy is to play her full role, "Italians must have more confidence in their own abilities; this applies especially to the young people of Italy" (*Daily American*, July 14, 1973).

From subsequent talks with the ambassador's closest assistants, notably Tom Trimarco, I gained the distinct impression that in their view there were no promising alternatives to the center-left approach in Italy. In fact, they felt that it might be desirable for a "special relationship" to develop between CDs and Socialists as the keystone of the ruling coalition. As I stressed during those talks, it could only be hoped that U.S. diplomacy would not miss the opportunity to show its appreciation for such a relationship. Otherwise, Washington's approach to Italian events might well be blamed once again for "being late by an idea, by an army, by a year," as Napoleon used to say about Hapsburg Austria.

Actually, the long quarrel over the introduction of divorce and the large Communist gains in the 1975–1976 elections made it appear that the chances for such a "special relationship" had been overtaken by events. But the matter was to surface again and take on new features and significance in the 1980s, following the collapse of the "historic compromise" between CDs and Communists.

13

PCI Leaders Bid for a Deal with the Christian Democrats and Probe U.S. Reactions

"How would the United States react if the PCI should enter the government?" Several high ranking representatives of the party began to ask me this question in early 1973. Most of them felt that the PCI was now likely to win a government role "within the next five or ten years." They also agreed that "the key to secure such a role [was] a new relationship with the CDs."

Both Macaluso and Ingrao felt that such a governmental accord would produce a split in the CD camp. Wouldn't it run into opposition among the Communists, too? Yes, they agreed, but it would hardly bring about an actual split which, in any case, "would come after the split in the CD Party and would be definitely smaller in size."

Macaluso and Calamandrei stressed that while "in the past our party's policy aimed not only at blocking the process of European integration but at dismantling whatever had been achieved in that connection, now we recognize that the European Common Market and the integration process in general are here to stay. Accordingly, we want to participate actively in their development while working to weaken the all-too-strong influence enjoyed by the major industrial groups and the all-too-close ties with the U.S. which distort Western Europe's growth to the benefit of America." Both Macaluso and Calamandrei referred time and again to the prospects of East-West detente as "one of the main factors that should help our party gain a government role in the not-too-distant future."

Luigi Granelli, a leading CD left-winger, told me in February 1973: "The PCI wants to play a role in building up a Europe more or less equidistant between the U.S. and the USSR. It is still a rather vague approach which must be clarified on many counts before it can become as acceptable as the Communists would like it to be." The Italian Communist leaders, he added, "are well aware that better relations between Washington and Moscow would help their party to gain more autonomy and room for maneuver in Europe and first of all in Italian politics; on the contrary, they could only side with Moscow in the event of new, sharp tensions in East-West relations.''

I told Macaluso, Calamandrei, and Granelli that any concrete and significant signals of a new PCI approach to major international issues would be noticed with interest in the United States. In my opinion, however, such signals would not be sufficient, by themselves, to alter substantially the negative attitude of U.S. political circles, both Republican and Democrat, and of U.S. public opinion toward a government role for the PCI. The developments advocated by the Italian Communists with regard to Europe would still involve a decisive shift in the international balance of power to the benefit of the Soviet Union: according to the PCI leaders, for instance, Western Europe, currently made up mostly of countries allied with the United States, would have to move on positions which, at best, would be equidistant between Moscow and Washington.

In the fall of 1973 the PCI leadership made it official: the Italian Communists would seek to enter the government through the door of a broad agreement with the CD party, the so-called ''historic compromise.'' Close collaborators of Berlinguer began to tell me about the motivations and features of the new departure several months before he announced it in a lengthy essay published in the party weekly *Rinascita*. Macaluso told me in September, shortly after the downfall of the Allende government: ''The differences between Italy and Chile should not be minimized, but the recent events over there have spotlighted the silliness of those who keep contending that an alliance between Communists and Socialists is enough to allow the leftist forces to gain control in our country. Such an alliance is necessary but not sufficient. Since the early postwar elections, the combined Communist and Socialist vote has been around 40 percent of the total (even though our share of this 40 percent has steadily grown while the Socialists' has been gradually cut down to one half of what it was back in 1946). But the CDs have managed to retain the support of another 40 percent of the electorate and have been able to rely, more or less constantly, on an additional ten percent at least represented by the Social Democrats, Republicans, and Liberals.'' Other PCI representatives emphasized likewise that ''we would make a tremendous mistake if we should forget or underrate the need to reach a working understanding with Christian Democracy *as a party*. We must keep pushing the CDs to change their policies. But we must be ready to collaborate with them even though in the foreseeable future they are bound to remain a basically moderate party.''

Following the publication of Berlinguer's essay, the same Communist sources sought to present his proposals as ''an updated edition of a strategy that goes back to Togliatti and even to the basic lines laid down by [Antonio] Gramsci in the 1920s.'' They admitted, at the same time, that Luigi Longo, a former secretary general and now president of the PCI, was ''quite skeptical about the chances of working out with the CDs an understanding that will allow our party to develop a reasonably effective government collaboration with them . . . and this skepticism is shared by sizable sectors of our party, including notably Amendola and Ingrao. Both of them, however, have missed their opportunity to take over the party's helm which is now held firmly by a 'third generation' of Communists led by Berlinguer. . . . These are people," I was further told, "who have no personal experience or recollection of the time of the 'cold war' and of the 'frontal' clashes with the CDs. On the other hand, they have lived, from the inside so to speak, the great changes that have taken place recently in the schools, in the factories, and elsewhere in our country, and are much better equipped to understand the new generations."

PCI leaders close to Berlinguer, I gathered, realized that a governmental accord with the CDs could hardly be achieved "overnight" and would "meet with strong opposition from Fanfani and other CD chieftains." Yet, they insisted, "it offers the only concrete opportunity to prove that this country of ours can be governed." Circumstances and prospects would be much better than they were or turned out to be in the case of the Christian Democratic-Socialist alliance: "We are much stronger than the Socialists and a coalition including our party and the CDs would command a much bigger majority in the country and in Parliament than the center-left coalition could hope to rely on. Such a majority would not only allow and sustain a more rapid and effective government action, but would provide a numerical and psychological 'buffer' wide enough to soften the impact of the electoral losses that some of the measures taken by the new ruling coalition might at first produce for its main partners."

The PCI representatives most favorable to the "historic compromise" stressed that "the remarkable growth of the middle classes' size and political clout was a major factor in persuading us that the approach traditionally followed by the Italian left ('the country can and must be governed by an alliance of industrial workers and peasants') does not reflect anymore Italy's conditions and requirements. It must be replaced by a more comprehensive outlook taking in large sectors of the middle class and the party which represents many of them, that is Christian Democracy. On the other hand, some middle class groups (many businessmen and quite a few members of the bureaucracy) have acquired or consolidated privileged positions and incomes which represent a social and economic burden for the national community and must be sharply curtailed if Italy is to be governed with more justice and efficiency. These groups can be expected to fight vigorously against any attempt to curtail their privileges." As a result, the CDs might lose "as much as two million votes," PCI spokesmen spelled out, "but it will be better for the country and in a sense for their own party too if it were able to help give Italy a good government while polling eleven million votes than keep giving her a bad government while receiving thirteen million. . . . Our own party has already accepted some electoral sacrifices in order to pave the way for our participation in the government: we have come out strongly against the most 'radical grouplets' although we well knew that we would alienate some fringes of the extreme left. We also realize that in order to implement the 'historic compromise' we'll have to pay some additional price at the polls. But even a drop from 9.5 to 9 million votes would not be too high a price to enable our party to make a more direct and substantial contribution to governing Italy in the interest of the workers and of the national community as a whole.

"Where would the 'historic compromise' leave the Socialist party?" The standard answer I got from PCI spokesmen close to the party top leadership ran as follows: "We have never aimed at excluding the PSI from an agreement between us and the CDs. Nor is it true that the result of such an agreement would be to squeeze the Socialists out. To be sure, if we become partners in the ruling coalition, the Socialists could no longer play or pretend to play a role greater than warranted by their 10 percent of the popular vote on the ground that they can participate in the government while we are still excluded."

"The latest, dramatic turn of events in Chile," I wrote (*Daily American*, September 23, 1973) "has sharply underlined the basic fallacy of the reading of Italian conditions and trends which in recent years has been epitomized by the slogan, "spaghetti in Chile sauce.' " The slogan "reflects a disconcerting ignorance, or a willful disregard, of the far-reaching differences between the two countries. To begin with, an Italian chief of state not only wields much less power than a Chilean president but could not take over the office on the strength of having received just a plurality of the popular vote as was the case with Salvador Allende. Likewise, a parliamentary majority is required both to confirm in office a new government and to give legal validity to its subsequent actions. Equally important, Italy is a country which whatever its weaknesses, is more developed and less unbalanced, socially and economically, than Chile. The Italian CDs have proved much more adept than their Chilean namesakes in maintaining a dominant position in the government and among the voters. They have avoided being trapped and squeezed between a very strong leftist alignment and an equally strong rightist movement. Many members of the Italian middle and petty bourgeoisie prefer to support a lackluster, often inefficient and occasionally populist party like the CDs rather than favor the formation of a large rightist movement or yield once again to the lure of an authoritarian, nationalistic regime bent on 'putting the workers back where they belong.' A majority of Italy's big industrialists and businessmen have learned some lessons from the experience of the Fascist dictatorship that so many of their fathers or predecessors powerfully helped to usher in 50 years ago.

"To be sure," I continued, "the CDs' basically moderate approach to urgent social problems, coupled with administrative inefficiency and widespread graft, was bound to arouse strong dissatisfaction among the unprivileged sectors of the population; and the consequent protest vote, largely monopolized by the efficient apparatus of the PCI, has enabled the latter to gradually increase its following to 28 percent of the electorate and to emerge not only as the biggest leftist force but as the major alternative to the CD 'regime.' The impact of those developments, however, was partly neutralized as many Socialists drew away from the Communist alliance [and] joined with the CDs, the Social Democrats and the Republicans in a governmental partnership." The center-left coalition, I further recalled, had not only governed Italy for more than 10 years but had been "patched up and returned to power last July. This persistent readiness of the Socialists to work together with the CDs is another key difference between the Italian and Chilean makeups." A collapse of the center-left coalition" would unleash a polarization process. The Socialists would be driven closer again to the Communists while conservative and even moderate CDs would be tempted to ride the tiger of an alliance with the Fascist right and so would quite a few big industrialists and businessmen. At that stage, many generals and colonels would be likewise eager or available to put down, or forestall, a Communist coup.

"No one can rule out completely the possibility that things might eventually develop along those lines," I concluded, "just as it is not unconceivable that, sometime in the future, CDs and Communists may agree to deal out all other parties and share power among themselves. But as long as most CDs continue to oppose an understanding with either the Neo-Fascists or the Communists, and most Socialists stick to the policy of collaboration with the CDs on a platform of social reforms and institutional modernizations, there will be no real danger that the Italian spaghetti will be cooked in Chile sauce or in black squid juice."

Recent developments in Italy and abroad, notably in Chile, I further wrote (*Daily American*, November 11), had persuaded the Italian Communist leaders: "(1) that in the foreseeable future they will not succeed in putting together a coalition able to command the support of 51 percent of the voters; (2) that even such a majority would not guarantee the survival and operation of a leftist government. This means, as Berlinguer has spelled out, that to gain a share of national power the Communists must reach 'a compromise' with the CD party as a whole rather than try to split it and then form an alliance with its leftwing splinter."

The official CD reply, I went on, was "expected to be substantially negative but so couched as not to bar continuation of the 'dialogue' that the major government party and the main opposition force have been carrying out for years, notably in Parliament. The CDs do not want to weaken, let alone discard, the recently revived center-left coalition." Yet, they "know only too well" that a determined hostility by the PCI (and by the powerful leftist unions) would "seriously jeopardize" the success of the efforts "to curb inflation and sustain economic growth. The other partners in the governing coalition, the Socialists first of all, are equally aware of this danger, while they are also deadly afraid to be crushed or squeezed out by 'an embrace between the two giants' (CDs and Communists).

"Most important," I further noted, "even the latest proposals by the Communists fail to reflect a reassuring readiness to clear away the many obstacles that have traditionally made them ineligible for participation in a democratic government. They have softpedalled their opposition to integration of Western Europe and their demands for an immediate Italian withdrawal from NATO. But their international approach is still closely tied to the Soviet Union's as again evidenced by the latest crisis in the Middle East. They have been stressing more and more that their aim is to reform rather than subvert Italy's economic and social structures. But they have refrained from outlining the concrete shape of the new society they want to bring about.''

Furthermore, "quite a few members of the Communist Central Committee have warned against rushing into a collaboration with the CDs to be reached through 'deals' negotiated between the two parties' top leaders. Such warnings underscore once again the basic flaw in the strategy of the Italian Communist chieftains: the more they strive to close the credibility gap that prevents the PCI from being accepted as a partner in a democratic government, the more they risk losing credibility and support among the most militant sectors of their own party.''

An important signal of the changes under way in Italian society was the mounting significance of an issue like the introduction of divorce. Back in late 1970, I recalled (*Daily American*, October 7, 1973), "Parliament enacted a bill making it possible to obtain a divorce in cases involving extraordinary hardship or a long established breakup of marriage. The vote cut across the boundaries between majority and opposition: the CDs and the neo-Fascists voted against the bill, which was supported by all other parties from the Communists to the right-of-center Liberals. Pope Paul VI reaffirmed the Catholic Church's intransigent defense of 'indissoluble marriage.' The introduction of divorce, the Pope further charged, represented an unilateral breach of the 1929 Concordat whereby the Fascist regime granted civil effects to marriages performed by priests in Italy and made the Catholic church supreme in most matrimonial matters.

"Militant Catholic groups quickly gathered over 1.3 million signatures (as against the 500,000 required) on a petition to hold a national referendum on repeal of the law.'' The PCI had come out for divorce but "improved relations with the CDs (and with the Vatican),'' I wrote (*Daily American*, February 3, 1974), "have long been regarded by the Communist leadership as the key for gaining access to government power. The lay and democratic groups (Socialists, Social Democrats, Republicans, Liberals), know that the referendum will make it more difficult, at best, to continue or resume their governmental alliance with the CDs. The CDs themselves are united only in opposing divorce. The party leftwingers have come out against the referendum and other powerful factions are also afraid that it will strain to the breaking point relations with the lay democratic forces. Within the Vatican, too, there are strong doubts about the wisdom of a test that can be expected to produce, at most, a narrow victory for the anti-divorce forces in a nominally 99 percent Catholic country.'' Yet repeated rounds of negotiations "failed to produce agreement on a revision of the present law that might prove acceptable to most pro-divorce forces as well as to the Church and to a large majority of the CDs.''

Eventually the referendum took place on May 12, 1974, and 59 percent of the voters upheld the 1970 law. "This pronouncement,'' I noted in the *Daily American*, "was widely held, at home and abroad, as evidence that Italy has come of age as a modern nation. The most lavish praise came from influential sectors of the foreign press which had indulged in the most somber forecasts about the Italians' ability to outgrow the tutelage of the Catholic church and their own 'rural and feudalistic heritage.'

"The outcome of the referendum," I continued, "unquestionably represented a setback for the CD party but did not foreshadow an early end of its political supremacy. The referendum's returns helped to improve the credit and image of the Communists, the largest single force in the alignment that successfully opposed repeal of divorce." Communist participation in the government, however, continued to be opposed by "the majority of the CDs" as well as by most representatives of the other democratic parties. All in all, the vote on divorce "cannot be construed as reflecting an urge to shatter or radically recast the political framework. On the contrary, it strongly suggests widespread support for a rational, progressive-minded approach involving gradual reform and modernization" (May 15 and 26).

Pretty soon, however, highly pessimistic reports about prospects in Italy were filed again by journalists like Claire Sterling and Cyrun L. Sulzberger, despite their recent public admissions that their forecasts of impending doom had been belied in a country where "a catastrophe is always looming but never comes to pass" (*La Stampa*, December 17, 1971 and June 15, 1973; *Europeo*, November 1973). Sterling mixed warm praise for the Italian voters' performance in the referendum on divorce with new, dark predictions about a country which "continued to inch inexorably toward economic ruin" (*Washington Post*, May 16). According to Sulzberger, even the attempt to work out a compromise between Communists and Catholics had come to an end as a result of the Pope's stand on divorce. Italy, he concluded, seemed, "headed once more toward the only remaining opening—chaos and despair" (*New York Times*, June 22).

Columnist Victor Zorza saw the Communists "on the march across Southern Europe, not to the revolutionary barricades but into government coalitions that could give them a share of power in a wide Mediterranean belt stretching from Greece through Italy, France, and Spain into Portugal. . . . In Italy, the Communists are beginning to talk as if they were willing to make a deal with Washington, to assure it that they would do no harm to the cohesion of NATO, in exchange for U.S. acquiescence to the Communist party's participation in the coalition. . . . .But until the Italian Communists find a way to express themselves more clearly, . . . no one is going to take them very seriously. This is a pity, because the Italian Communists' implied promise to work for the restoration of political stability could be very important for Europe in the difficult times that lie ahead." (*International Herald Tribune*, September 17, 1974)

According to Claire Sterling, economic and political conditions in Italy continued to be so bad that "the nagging question in everybody's mind is still whether this or any other democratic government in Italy can go on much longer without calling in the Communists." Sterling's conclusion, soon to be disproved by facts, was that the Communists "would in fact accept nothing less than a full partnership with the CD Party. . . . Even assuming that such invitation would be forthcoming, they are by no means certain to accept. Running this country . . . these days would be one of the world's most ungrateful jobs." And here Sterling trotted out a statement attributed to Mussolini which had become one of the favorite cliches of Western journalism: "to govern Italy . . . is not hard, but it is useless" (*Washington Post*, September 16).

Newsweek (October 28) had its figures wrong. The PCI's influence, it said, had "become so great that it would likely win as much as 25 percent of the vote were new national elections held." (The party's share of the popular vote had already topped 27 percent in the 1972 general election.)

From talks with ranking PCI representatives and from other contacts, I gathered that even for those party chieftains who bet more openly on an agreement with the CDs, a full-fledged government role was still a "medium term" goal requiring "three to five years" and involving "a gradual process" marked by "ups and downs" (as Macaluso told me in the summer of 1974). During the early phases of the process, Communist leaders would be willing to accept a more or less direct participation in the governmental majority. They were aware that implementation of the "historic compromise" required significant "revisions" of the PCI's positions not only in the domestic but in the international field. At the same time, even the most outspoken champions of these revisions did not feel it possible to push them to the point of an actual "break" with Moscow and with sizable sectors of the PCI's own rank and file. They further confirmed that the party would not give up its efforts to contribute to an overall shift in the international balance of power to the benefit of the USSR and to the detriment of the United States. The much-touted PCI championship of an European "equidistance" between Washington and Moscow, for instance, concerned only *Western* Europe and even in this connection the "equidistance" was bound in effect to "lean" toward the East and anyway to make the Atlantic much broader and deeper.

Macaluso, for one, told me time and again: "For us, it is both possible and necessary to work within the framework of the existing European institutions. At the same time, our purpose is to change their basic approach which is intended to build a Europe dominated by the major capitalistic and monopolistic interests as well as closely associated with the United States. . . . A process of internal liberalization in the Eastern European countries," he added when I raised the issue, "is highly desirable but should develop without affecting their ties with the Soviet Union."

Sergio Segre, head of the PCI's foreign affairs department, maintained that his party "was doing or trying to do many things to help promote changes and improvements in Eastern Europe. . . . Sometimes, the local governments themselves ask us to dissuade the Italian government from pressing too hard in this connection because it is bound to backfire. During recent meetings of the Conference on Security and Cooperation in Europe, for instance," Segre went on, "Eastern Europe's representatives pointed out to us that their governments would be unable to be as forthcoming as they would like on matters relating to the 'third basket' [human rights, contacts and exchanges] if Italian [and Dutch] representatives kept harping so much on the need to secure concessions on that score.''

All the PCI leaders whom I was meeting at the time were clearly pleased about the climate of detente that appeared to prevail between Washington and Moscow. At the same time, they made it clear that there were limits to their party's championship of detente (as well as of European integration). In February 1974, for instance, I reminded Macaluso that Gromyko had gone all out in praising the French stand at the Energy Conference in Washington which could hardly be regarded as constructive either by the Americans or by other West Europeans. The answer I got was: "The Soviets want sincerely an agreement with the U.S. on major international issues, but you can't expect them to overlook or fail to exploit any opportunity to strengthen their hand in view of such deals with the Americans.''

Both Macaluso and Segre condemned as "a fruit of vanity, stupidity, and anyway of a wholly wrong assessment of the situation and of its prospects,'' the behavior of other PCI representatives who, notably in interviews to the weekly *L'Espresso*, had outlined specific foreign and domestic policy planks of a platform for Communist participation in a government or at least in a governmental majority: "Some of them,'' Segre noted scathingly, had "spoken as if they expected to become cabinet members within a few months! We can well afford to wait and pick the right moment for taking over direct responsibilities in governing the country. It remains to be seen,'' Segre concluded, "for how long the country itself can afford to wait, to tolerate the harmful consequences of the way it has been governed or rather misgoverned for so many years.''

In the late fall of 1974, Macaluso voiced similar views: "Our party's entry into the government must and will come after several intermediate steps. The first might be the recognition of the positive role we can play in matters of national relevance even while we remain in the opposition. Another could be our participation in running local administrations even where such a participation is not required from a numerical viewpoint but is necessary to achieve concrete results to the benefit of the population. A further, important step would be represented by our giving support to the government from the outside, something that would obviously call for a formal acceptance of our party as a component of a new majority in Parliament. Our rank and file would react negatively,'' he went on, "if the party leadership should appear ready to enter into a governmental alliance with the CDs without securing clear and concrete guarantees that such an alliance would bring about truly significant changes in the methods and results of governing the country.''

A few weeks later, Segre told me: "The most serious issue, much more serious than the 'NATO issue,' concerns the relations with the CDs. Some of us favor a compromise with the CD party *as it is*, feeling that opening negotiations with us will be enough to produce significant changes in the CD camp. Others maintain that a pre-condition for a compromise is a change in the CD Party so deep as to bring about a split in its ranks and that this must be in effect our main goal. An important psychological factor,'' Segre continued, ''is what happened to the Socialist party. It started down the road to participation in the government claiming that it wanted to and could 'force' the CDs to accept basic changes and far-reaching reforms; and it has ended up in a way that no one of us wants our party to end up.''

President Leone told me in September 1974: ''The so-called 'historic compromise' will not materialize. The CDs would be crazy if they did take seriously into consideration a development which would split their party or cost it anyway one half of its votes. They would lose the support of all Italians who spit on the CD symbol but then vote for the party because they know that for 30 years it has represented the main obstacle to a Communist takeover, and they hope that it will continue to play such a role.'' Francesco Principe, a member of Parliament then very close to PSI secretary general De Martino, told me in the same days: ''Seventy percent of the Socialists are against a government role for the PCI and any kind of 'historic compromise.' We're fully aware that an immediate consequence would be a serious weakening of our party and that pretty soon we would be eliminated as a political force able to play a significant role.'' While moving from quite different positions and considerations, the leader of the PSI left wing, Riccardo Lombardi, likewise told me: ''I have strong misgivings about the 'historic compromise'' and I doubt that it would prove a workable, let alone an advisable political course for Italy.''

Drawing on those talks, I spotlighted ''both the mounting pressures for an early Communist participation in the government and the still strong opposition to it by sizable political and economic forces'' (*Daily American*, September 15, 1974). ''Last month . . . some high ranking CD leftwingers stated that collaboration with Communists might be necessary to cope with the country's serious economic and political troubles.'' But ''party secretary general Fanfani replied that an alliance with the Communists would cause a loss of votes for the party and produce serious changes in the Italian situation 'without assurances of appreciable compensations.' It would also bring about a 'change in Italy's international position, with harmful effects on the European, Mediterranean and world balance.'' Such a viewpoint, I continued, was shared by ''most other CDs [as well as by] Social Democrats and Republicans. The President of FIAT, Gianni Agnelli, speaking in his capacity as head of Confindustria (the Italian National Association of Manufacturers), said that Communist participation in the government would 'substantially alter the nature of Italy's economic and social system, and quickly lead Italy away from the Western world.' The Vatican paper *L'Osservatore Romano* made a similar assessment of the impact upon Italy's international position.

''The Socialists are usually careful to steer away from collision courses with the Communists. A major reason is the Socialists' desire to bolster their bargaining power within the center-left coalition by claiming to represent the bulk of Italian labor including the many workers politically affiliated with the PCI. Most Socialists, however, are keenly aware that if the CDs and the Communists actually enter into an alliance, their party would not only lose leverage in dealing with either of the two giants of Italian politics but would soon be crushed by their embrace.''

The Communists themselves, I added, ''point out that 'by now, people are no longer wondering whether we'll get a share in the government but when, how, and to what purpose.' It is an open secret that many government bills can be enacted only because they have been 'cleared' with the major opposition party, the PCI. Communist spokesmen now say that their party will not press for 'unilateral Italian withdrawal from the Atlantic Alliance' but rather for 'a balanced dismantling of the military blocs.' They are strongly opposed, however, to granting NATO additional facilities in Italy (to replace those that may have to be vacated in Greece). The Communists insist that their help is necessary both to rescue Italy from the current economic crisis and to achieve social reforms and political stability. But they seem unable or unwilling to produce a recipe of their own for Italy's economic ills or to spell out a program for modernizing the country's social and administrative structures that differs substantially from the measures pledged so often and implemented to such an inadequate extent by the center-left governments.''

All this, I concluded, ''may turn out to matter very little if the Communists become partners in the government in the rather early future, that is, following a collapse of the center-left coalition (and perhaps new general elections next year) or as a result of some truly dramatic emergency such as economic chaos and political anarchy. In that event, the PCI would enjoy from the outset an all-too-strong position in dealing with its partners in the government. If the center-left parties, however, manage to stick together and make some progress with regard to the economy and to reforms, the PCI would be caught off balance just when poised to jump with both feet into the governmental area.''

On the eve of the PCI National Congress, I reported (*Daily American*, March 15, 1975): ''Segre told me that the PCI 'wants to help maintain and stabilize the international military and strategic balance of power, not to upset this balance whose essential hinge is the relationship between the U.S. and the Soviet Union. . . . That's why we do not press for unilateral steps to take Italy out of the Atlantic alliance.' [Our main approach] 'is to help promote a parallel and gradual fading away of the two blocs [by coupling] political detente, already under way in Europe, with a military detente.' The latter should involve agreements 'for the thinning out, to be pursued up to actual elimination, of foreign forces and bases in each European country. . . . This means,' Segre stressed, that 'Italy stays in the Atlantic alliance and the allied bases stay in Italy until agreements are reached to get underway, both on the NATO side and on the side of the Warsaw Pact, a concrete and balanced process of gradual de-escalation of the confrontation between the two blocs. . . . Of course,' the Italian Communist spokesman added, 'foreign bases in Italy must not be used for purposes running contrary to the interests of detente and to Italy's national interests.' Such a basic approach, Segre stated, 'is valid whether our party remains in the opposition or becomes a partner in a new governmental majority.'

"Segre emphasized at the same time that the foreign policy advocated by his party calls 'for upholding the autonomy of Italian domestic policy, that is, the Italians' right to seek, within the framework of the Republican Constitution and without interference from abroad, all the political, economic, and social solutions required to ensure the country's democratic development. . . . Our stand on the Atlantic alliance,' Segre further said, 'is not a passport to get us into the government, but the outcome of an analysis of the international situation.' "

"By following the preparation of your National Congress," I told Segre, "one gets the impression that three main positions exist within the party with regard to Italy's membership in the Atlantic alliance: Those who accept in effect the *status quo*, that is, Italian membership in the alliance and the American bases that exist on Italian soil; those who ask for starting right away to cut down the alliance's commitments and the American bases; and those who refuse to underwrite in any way Italy's membership in NATO."

Said Segre: "During the debate preparatory to our Congress, there have been differences in emphasis of the kind you mention: quite a natural thing to happen, I think, and a mark of democratic mentality. It is possible, however, to note right now that the party line calls for a foreign policy which would not pursue a unilateral change in the strategic and military balance of power."

In drawing a balance sheet of the Communist National Congress, I wrote (*Daily American*, March 27): "Some hasty foreign observers had talked about a 'historic' event, presumably fated to mark a major step in the PCI's long march toward the 'governmental area.' But the Congress and the attending developments have done little more than highlight, once again, the facts and circumstances that still unleash a broad negative response whenever the largest Communist party in the West seems to get actually closer to regaining a government role (the PCI has been in the opposition since 1947)."

It was unfortunate for the PCI, I noted, "that its Congress happened to take place just when public attention was riveted upon events in Portugal. The Portuguese Communists have been working hand in hand with radical members of the armed forces to ban the local Christian Democrats from the forthcoming elections and to confine to secondary roles the Socialists—that is, to squeeze out the same forces with which the Italian Communists seek to form a governmental partnership."

Leading Italian Communists, notably Macaluso and Segre, emphasized that in his closing address to the Congress Berlinguer had "taken his distances from the current situation and prospects in Portugal." More generally, they strove to project an image of the party quite different from the parties' ruling in the Eastern European countries included in the Soviet sphere. When I mentioned that, according to many Italian and non-Italian observers, the PCI would exploit its eventual role in the government to push Italy toward neutralism and possibly into the Soviet orbit, Macaluso retorted: "Buy why should we want to put Italy into the position of a Czechoslovakia?" Both Macaluso and Segre maintained that "if we should disagree from the Soviets on issues concerning Italy's foreign (or domestic) policies, we would behave like the Yugoslavs have done so many times since 1948. It would actually be easier for us to tell frankly the Soviets about such disagreements because our party would not be alone in running a Socialist country like Yugoslavia but would share in the government with sizable non-Communist and non-Socialist forces."

"To be sure," other PCI representatives likewise told me, "we'll never take the initiative of precipitating a crisis in our relations with the Soviets. But we'll continue to stick to the policies that we believe to be right for our party even if they should be condemned by Moscow."

All these PCI leaders made a point of criticizing and even ridiculing the comments appearing in "the bourgeois and radical media" in Italy and elsewhere in Western Europe to the effect that the windup of the war in Vietnam marked "the beginning of America's decline and withdrawal from the world." In their opinion, "the U.S. has suffered a defeat of a local nature and significance, but it remains a great power with worldwide interests which does not intend at all to take refuge in isolationism."

The same PCI sources took pains to stress again that "the main obstacles to be still overcome on the road to the 'historic compromise' [were] the anti-Communism that is still so strong in large sectors of the CD camp and the widespread reluctance within our own party to enter into a governmental alliance with the CDs. We are confident that the CDs, or many of them, will be compelled or persuaded to change their behavior. Yet, we must say frankly that if such a change does not occur, the 'historic compromise' will not take place."

Over and above the latest developments in Portugal and their repercussions in Italy, I stressed (*Daily American*, March 27): "There are more significant and durable factors, rooted in the political and social conditions in Italy, which explain why quickening prospects of a Communist participation in the government keep producing a proliferation of antibodies in large sectors of Italian public opinion including the PCI itself. Such a boomerang effect" was reflected not only in a stiffening stand by most CDs and by many Socialists, as well as by the minor democratic parties and by powerful economic groups, but "in the surfacing of significant differences among the Communists themselves. These differences, which have again emerged at the PCI Congress, bear upon the timing, the terms and the advisability itself of the 'historic compromise.' "

In foreign affairs, I went on, "the party line does not call anymore for "taking Italy out of NATO and NATO out of Italy.' It envisages a loosening of the country's Atlantic ties to be carried out within the framework of a balanced reduction of foreign troops and bases on the Warsaw Pact's side as well. Some sectors of the party, however, call for an immediate cutting down of the country's Atlantic commitments or refuse outright to underwrite in any way Italy's membership in NATO.

"On the core itself of the 'historic compromise' the party line was keyed to a steady drive for an early accommodation and then for a broader and firmer deal with the CDs. This process would allow the PCI to join a 'new majority' and then the government itself even while the CD party would become more and more amenable to Communist demands as a result of some electoral losses, especially on its right, and of a shift to the left in its internal balance of power. [But] prominent Communists, including old-timers like Umberto Terracini and middle-aged 'leftists' like Pietro Ingrao have come out openly or warned against collaboration with the CD Party before it has been shorn of its conservative and reactionary wings and in any case before it has been 'forced to undergo a radical change through the dismantling of its political and economic system of power and privilege.' The PCI's ability to reabsorb or muffle dissent,'' I went on, ''was again demonstrated when the party Congress passed unanimously a final resolution which reiterated the pledge not to take Italy out of NATO and the call for 'a political alliance among the Communists, the Socialists, the CDs and other popular and anti-Fascist forces.' The resolution made it clear that the PCI can expect to share in the government only as a result of a long and hard battle. In his closing remarks to the Congress, Berlinguer emphasized that the party's 'essential objective today [must be] to defeat the policies advocated by the incumbent CD leadership.' By stepping up his attacks against the drive by the Socialists to secure a 'preferential relationship' with the CDs within the ruling center-left coalition, Berlinguer also confirmed that the Communists oppose such a 'preferential relationship' because they see it as an alternative to the 'historic compromise' rather than as an anteroom leading to it.''

Pointing at the potential impact of the forthcoming regional elections, I concluded: "If the center-left forces perform fairly well at the polls and the governmental coalition manages to do something better than just muddling through, the pressure will shift on the Communists. But if the PCI scores sizable gains, while the CDs lose heavily and the Socialists fail to make significant progress, the Communists will recoup many of their chances of pushing through the 'historic compromise' over the medium term.''

14

The Oil Crunch and Communist Gains at the Polls

The downfall of the fifth Rumor Cabinet (October 3, 1974) and the subsequent, prolonged government crisis unleashed another wave of alarmism and wild predictions by the major U.S. media.

The *New York Times* ran an editorial headlined "Italian roulette" and a few days later asserted that if Fanfani failed in the attempt to put together a new Cabinet, the next government would almost certainly include some Communists (October 16). A similar forecast was made in a dispatch from Rome by Dusko Doder to the *Washington Post* (October 21): "An apparently collapsing economy, recurring social conflict and now a new government crisis," he also wrote, "have led to a resigned acceptance that the quality of life throughout the country will continue to show a downhill slide." For *Newsweek* (October 21), "Italy's gravest government crisis in a generation unfolded . . . with all the predictability of a Sicilian puppet show." To add another color note, the weekly wrote that the politicians consulted by president Leone rode to the Quirinale Palace "in small black Fiat sedans." (At that time, official cars in Italy were fairly large, blue Alfa Romeos and Lancias.) *Time* ran a cover story under the headline "Italy in Agony" (November 18): "The question is whether postwar Italian democracy can survive the unprecedented strains now placed upon it." The Communists were "standing in the wings" while "the idea of a historic compromise continues to gain adherents . . . "

It was at that time that mid-echelon embassy officials were authorized to develop fairly regular contacts with PCI representatives (notably Sergio Segre). This did not portend an "opening" to the PCI. But it provided additional evidence that U.S. official circles were aware of the growing relevance of the "Communist question" in Italy and felt it advisable to establish some direct channels of information.

On his return from a trip to the United States in the early fall, president Leone told me: "In Washington, there is a widespread conviction that the center-left coalition represents, today and in the foreseeable future, the only combination capable of rallying an adequate majority in Parliament and in the country as well as to produce a program which, if properly carried out, can hold out the promise of a better future for Italy." *Time* itself included in its cover story on "Italy in Agony" a report on the "vote of confidence" given the country by "U.S. government experts." They felt that a Communist takeover was "not . . . in-evitable, although a severe epidemic of unemployment could well strengthen Communist power." Despite this and other concerns, there was in Washington "a surprising lack of doomsday thinking about Italy's future."

During the June 1974 government crisis, I pointed out that "on the political side the trouble with Italy has not been instability but rather stability turned into stagnation. It is true, of course, that Italian governments are short-lived: there have been 36 since the country became a republic in 1946. But it is equally true that during those 28 years Italy has had more political stability than any other Western democratic nation."

While stressing that there were no palatable alternatives to the center-left coalition, I concluded that "the big question remains whether it can be reshaped as to fulfill at least in part its original promise of brining Italy a New Deal." (*Daily American*, June 16 and 23, 1974).

When a new government was finally patched together under Moro's leadership, I noted (*Daily American*, November 24) "This time only the CDs and the small Republican party [held cabinet posts, while] the feuding Socialists and Social democrats will provide the additional votes in Parliament required for a com-fortable majority. Communists close to the top part leadership," I continued, "Speak privately of their chances of becoming partners in a governmental co-alition as 'a medium term proposition' which in Italian politics means anywhere from five to ten years. They know that it will take at least that long to overcome not only CD opposition but the strong aversion by sizable sectors of their own rank and file to anything smacking of 'a compromise with parties dominated by bourgeois and priests.' "

On the economic side, too, conditions and prospects did not appear so bleak as most U.S. media made them out to be or predicted they would prove. "The energy crunch," I wrote (*Daily American*, January 27, 1974), "has hit Italy [when] after three years of stagnation, industrial output had begun to rise again." Inflation has been checked and the lira had regained almost one-half of the ground lost following "the devaluation of over 20 percent against the major currencies" which had been the result of the "float" adopted in February 1973. "A 3 percent growth in GNP and of 6 percent in the rate of investments look quite possible in 1974." At the same time, the energy crunch itself and its ramifications had "dramatically borne out the views of those Italians and foreign observers who have long maintained that implementation of overdue reforms concerning housing, schools, transportation, health care, public administration, and the development of the still depressed South represents not only the best investment for achieving social progress and political stability but a primary condition for steady and balanced growth through a more efficient management of available resources. A major drive to promote a modern and specialized agriculture would go a long way not only toward improving living standards in the Italian South but toward cutting down to more manageable proportions the import bill for farm products. An updated urban legislation and a large-scale program of housing construction, subsidized and controlled by national and local authorities, would not only provide desperately needed low-cost dwellings but open up many new jobs in the building industry which depends very little on imported materials and in recent years has concentrated too much of its activity on expensive apartments in big towns and 'second homes' on the seashore and in mountain resorts. A crash effort to improve public transportation (bus lines, subways, commuter trains) would not only relieve congestion in the major metropolitan areas but provide additional orders and jobs in an economic sector hit by restrictions on the use of private care.''

When GNP registered a 3.4 percent growth in 1976, I pointed out (*Daily American*, April 20, 1975): "Once again the resiliency of the Italian economy and the good sense of most Italians have confounded the prophets of doom. Only a few months ago, many foreign observers described Italy as a country on the verge of bankruptcy and as 'the sick man of the West.' Now some of the same observers seem to be going overboard in the opposite direction and to view the Italian economic situation and prospects through rose-tinted rather than through all-too-dark glasses.''

In fact, "the country is still not out of the woods. The impact of negative international factors upon the Italian economy,'' in this case of the energy crunch, had been "magnified by the long-standing shortcomings and imbalances of the country's social and administrative structures. The skyrocketing costs of oil and other imported raw materials [fueled] a tremendous rise'' of the deficit in Italy's foreign accounts which was made worse as "the weakness of the lira contributed to swell illegal exports of capital. To reverse such trends, severe credit and import restrictions were introduced in the spring of 1974 [and were followed by] hikes in direct and indirect taxation as well as in the price of gasoline and utility rates. The turnaround was spectacular. The payments balance has moved into the black, while the rising rate in the cost of living has dropped by one half in comparison with a year ago.'' But the cost was high "in terms of a slowdown of the country's economic engine.

"The overwhelming majority of the Italian people,'' I further noted, "has kept its cool in the face of continuing bomb outrages and other acts of political violence. The political framework is holding up, although the outcome of the nationwide regional and administrative elections, due June 15, may cast some heavy shadows on future developments.''

By late April both the *New York Times* and the *Wall Street Journal* had reversed the catastrophic opinions and forecasts voiced only a few months earlier. David

Rockefeller, chairman of Chase Manhattan and brother of the then vice president of the United States, was quoted by *Corriere della Sera* (April 25) as being "tempted to use the word 'miracle' " about the performance of the Italian economy, and declaring his "admiration for Italy's achievements which could be an example for some other countries."

Paul Hofmann reported in the *New York Times* that, according to quite a few Italians, Communist participation in the central government was "inevitable and only a matter of time" (February 14). The same paper gave for the first time a big play to a long piece by a leading PCI representative, Giancarlo Pajetta. Pajetta argued that the only logical and effective alternative to the rising threat of a rightist, authoritarian regime was the Communist proposal for a "historical compromise" with the CDs (March 13). Clair Sterling noted (*Washington Post*, March 18) that Pajetta had failed to mention, among other things, that "Italy might still have some democrats who are not yet prepared to settle for either one" of these two alternatives. Sterling deplored that Pajetta's piece "appeared in the world's most influential paper just four days before the Italian Communist party was to make its pitch for a partnership with the democrats, at its 14th National Congress. . . . Pajetta's sudden appearance as a distinguished contributor to *The New York Times* has rocked a good many Italian democrats on their heels: [the Americans' feelings] could make an immense difference either way" with regard to the prospects of a governmental collaboration between the Communists and the democratic parties in Italy.

When President Ford visited Rome, the *Washington Post* correspondent reported, he was not the target of the hostility the Italian Communists had displayed against his predecessors on similar occasions. The PCI leaders knew that "one of the few remaining deterrents" to the coming to power of "a Communist-Catholic coalition in fairly short order" was that such a development "might incur Washington's grave displeasure. There oughtn't to be much doubt about it, Henry Kissinger having expressed himself plainly to that effect in at least three high-level encounters with the Italians during the last year. Nevertheless, Italian Communist leaders keep hinting that Kissinger doesn't really mean it." Sterling added that the image of the PCI as "a modern, sophisticated, flexible, reasonable, independent and even democratic party is so widely accepted by now that it simply cannot be fought, in 1975, with the same cold-war cliches of 1948 . . . nor by joining forces with the ultra-conservative right, military and/ or fascist." This was the peg for an attack on ambassador Volpe who, the *Washington Post* correspondent charged, had "persistently kept the wrong company and scandalized Italian democrats by broadcasting his unfortunate personal views." Sterling mentioned among the ambassador's "intimates" the editors of *Il Tempo*, "a Roman daily distinguished mostly, if not solely, for its pro-fascist leanings. Three months ago, ambassador Volpe paid a formal visit to the office of *Il Tempo*, the only Italian newspaper he has so honored" (June 4). The U.S. Embassy issued a detailed rebuttal spelling out, among other things, that Volpe "neither meets nor consorts with fascists or their sympathizers, as a matter of policy and conviction'' and that he had visited the offices of some 20 newspapers throughout Italy. Right after Ford's visit, president Leone told me that ''top U.S. representatives'' shared his own view that ''a PCI participation in the government is far from inevitable, despite its further, likely advance at the polls. The main obstacles that can bar a Communist role in the government, are time and the Socialists.''

In several articles (*Daily American*, February 16 and 23; May 11 and 18; June 13, 1975), I emphasized that the forthcoming regional and local elections could ''well affect the entire course of Italian politics because they come at a critical juncture for each of the three major parties: The CDs, the Socialists, and the Communists.

''A red thread,'' I wrote, ''runs through the returns of all major elections held in Italy over the last quarter of a century. It signals a gradual but steady swing from the right and center to the left of the political alignment, with the Communists as the end beneficiaries.'' Back in 1948, the parties of the center and of the right (CDs, Liberals, Monarchists, and Neo-Fascists) ''received the support of 58 percent of the voters compared with 31 percent'' for the leftist alignment (Communists and Socialists). The gap between the two groups of parties had gradually narrowed down to the point that they were generally expected to ''run neck to neck'' in the forthcoming elections.

''Within the short span of a generation [Italy] has undergone more economic, social and psychological changes than any other Western democratic society.'' In the mid-to-late 1960s and early 1970s, I further wrote, ''the country has acquired some of the features of a modern industrial society, such as divorce, fairly liberal family laws, and labor unions strong enough to deal with government and management on a power to power basis. But centrifugal pulls, factional rifts, and personal rivalries within the ruling coalition prevented any major progress in implementing the center-left governments' own pledges to overhaul the social, economic, and administrative framework. Under the impact of spreading criminal activities and political violence, as well as of the continuing high rate of strikes, even some moderate and conservative voters are beginning to feel that participation in the government by the strong and disciplined Communist party might prove, after all, the best way to 'restrain' the labor unions and restore 'law and order.' ''

As a result of the massive emigration ''from the southern countryside to the major cities of northern and central Italy,'' I continued, ''farmer and peasant associations, which traditionally backed the CDs, have not only suffered sizable drops in their membership but are less able and willing to continue to give their wholehearted support. Catholic labor organizations have become increasingly critical of the policies followed by the CD-dominated governments in the social and economic field. Since the death of Pope Pius XII in 1958, the Vatican itself has become wary of getting into the front lines of Italian politics. Many bishops and parish priests keep supporting the CD ticket but their determination and even more their ability to 'deliver' the Catholic vote have been gradually weakened even when it comes to issues of direct interest to the Church, as witnessed by the outcome of the referendum on divorce. The CDs have gained support among some expanding sectors of the middle class, notably among officials and employees in the national and local bureaucracy and in other instruments of patronage, as well as among groups of economic operators and middlemen (real estate speculators, importers and wholesalers of key commodities, construction firms specialized in government contracts). But in order to keep those groups happy and loyal, the CD leaders have not only blocked or watered down social and economic reforms but have promoted or countenanced gross mismanagement of available resources. This in turn has antagonized other sectors, all the way from some groups of industrial workers to representatives of big business, which had traditionally backed the CDs.

"Against such background, it is not surprising that most observers expect next month's elections to mark a further increase in the leftist vote [while the CDs] suffer fairly sizable losses. If those forecasts prove correct, it would mean that the tides flowing leftward have become strong enough to knock out or shake some key props of the traditional balance of power. The CDs could no longer outpoll any combination of two other parties, but would be easily outpolled by an alliance of Communists and Socialists. The old equilibrium is tottering under the accumulated pressure of the trends and shifts of the last twenty-odd years, while the foundations and features of a new political framework have not yet taken definite shape.

"On the face of it, the PCI appears to be in the best position to deal with the challenges and opportunities that loom down the road. But the Communists are likely to find out that the going gets hardest just as they seem to be nearing the end of their lengthy and patient drive to win a share of national power. How long, for instance, can the PCI leaders keep up the balancing act whereby they strive to overcome the opposition and distrust of still strong sectors of public opinion by presenting their party as a credible partner in a democratic and reform-minded government, while seeking, on the other hand, to control and muffle the revulsion of the more militant groups of the Communist rank and file against 'any compromise with the bourgeois and pro-Western forces'? The Socialists have misplayed their hand time and again but continue to hold some good cards. The CDs are in deep trouble but can still expect to remain, over the short term at least, the single largest party in Italy."

On the day following the June 1975 elections, I wrote (*Daily American*, June 18): "For the first time in postwar Italy, there is no longer a single dominant political force. Two parties, the CDs and the Communists, are batting in the same league polling respectively over 35 and 33 percent of the votes. The Socialists scored some gains, and represent more than ever the needle of the balance although their 12 percent of the votes is not quite enough to form a working majority either with the CDs or with the Communists."

In a subsequent column in the same daily (June 29), I pointed out that the CDs remained the largest party in the country and retained a substantial plurality in Parliament. "The 'moderate' and cautious line currently adopted by the Communist leaders reflects their awareness that the party needs time and quiet to 'assimilate' the two million additional votes it has received."

On this score, Macaluso was quite frank and added: "The CD party has still the capability and inner strength to rebuild itself from top to bottom." (*Rifondazione* was becoming the fashionable word in this connection.) The PCI, Macaluso continued, "does not intend to raise right away the issue of its participation in the government but will concentrate its efforts on translating into effective measures the indications that have emerged from the polls concerning ways and means to improve the management of public affairs, beginning with the local and regional administrations."

In the same column, I noted that "the latest expansion of the Communist electoral area, while increasing the party's influence at the local and national levels, sharpens the unprecedented challenge facing the Italian Reds: how to define and successfully implement the role of a Communist party strong enough to bid for national leadership in a country which, despite serious shortcomings, belongs socially, economically, and culturally to the democratic and industrialized world?

"Last week, Communist general secretary Enrico Berlinguer reaffirmed his party's opposition to a unilateral Italian withdrawal from NATO which would 'upset the whole process of detente.' On the same day, Giorgio Amendola wrote in the party's daily *l'Unità* that Italy's membership in NATO represents 'a danger for peace and national security.' It is too early to conclude that such conflicting statements reflect actual divergencies within the PCI rather than 'an allocation of roles' as between Berlinguer and Amendola. Yet the episode bears out the feeling, shared privately by many prominent Communists, that just as the party gets closer to sharing national power, it will face serious trouble within its own ranks as well as in relations with its prospective partners in the government."

Conversations with prominent CDs who, like left-winger Luigi Granelli, could hardly be suspected of preconceived hostility to agreements with the Communists, confirmed that the CD leaders could be "expected to put off any major decision at least until they had 'tested the water' once again in a general election" (*Daily American*, June 18).

The reaction of the major U.S. media to the outcome of the June 1975 elections mirrored the widespread expectation of an early government role for the PCI and of a further, possibly terminal decline of the CDs.

Claire Sterling noted in the *Washington Post*, (June 18): "It is evidently not true that Italy's democratic leaders have done little or nothing in the last 10 or 15 years: They have built a terrific Communist party. . . . The chances can no longer be ruled out of [the Communists] overtaking the CDs to become the largest single party in Italy by the time the next Parliament is elected two years from now." On the same day, a *Washington Post* editorial branded the "geriatric incompetence [of] the present Italian government. It is the misfortune of the Italians, and their friends, that the choice now seems to lie between a paralyzed but democratic right and a Communist left whose commitment to democracy is highly conditional.''

The *Los Angeles Times* worried about the problems that the steady slide to the left and away from the CDs would produce for NATO and more directly for the Southern flank of the alliance. *Time* quoted Berlinguer as saying: ''We do not propose that Italy give up membership in any international organization to which it belongs. . . . We ask only that America not interfere in Italian internal affairs.'' Yet, *Time* concluded: ''Berlinguer leaves no doubts as to his ultimate loyalties: 'Whoever expects us to break with the Soviet Union . . . and the international workers' movement,' he says, 'always will be disillusioned' '' (June 30).

Cyrus L. Sulzberger had long and strongly opposed a government role for the Socialists. Now, he played up Berlinguer's reported purpose to install in Italy ''a socialism based on true democracy.'' Sulzberger also insinuated once again that the U.S. was no longer setting as the first priority of its ambassador in Rome ''to keep Italy from going Communist'' (July 28). Sulzberger's approach appeared to reflect a peculiar similarity to the campaign undertaken by sizable sectors of the Italian media to undermine U.S. influence and prestige in Italy and at the same time to spread the feeling that Washington was giving up at last its opposition to a PCI role in the government.

The origins and main features of this campaign were reviewed and documented in an essay which appeared in the May–June 1979 issue of *Freedom at Issue*, the magazine published by Freedom House, but was based on material in earlier years beginning in the mid–1970s. ''Operating in the red,'' I pointed out in the essay headlined ''GETTING A BAD PRESS IN ITALY,'' had been ''an established tradition for the Italian press, with the exception of quite a few news magazines and some dailies, mostly local. Newspapers openly identified with political parties have their own ways of balancing their budgets. But most dailies, including almost all the big ones, have long piled up sizable deficits year after year. Overall circulation has remained quite low (less than a copy a day for every ten Italians). . . . The government controls newsstand prices, and the advertising base still represents a very small percentage of GNP (0.33 percent in 1977 compared with 0.65 in France, 0.90 in West Germany, 1.27 in Great Britain, and 2.07 percent in the United States).

''Yet this state of affairs has never troubled unduly the newspaper owners: whether businessmen or other wealthy individuals, corporations or economic groups and associations, they do not look upon their journalistic holdings as money-making ventures. Rather, they regard them as tools to protect and promote other and bigger interests of their own through a complex combination and interplay of pressures and counterpressures, favors and concessions involving the government and the political forces which share, or are expected to share soon, in running national or local affairs. In recent years, this web has further widened and thickened as government aid to the press, badly hurt by skyrocketing labor and newsprint costs, has come to include not only indirect subsidies but direct allocations running into the tens of millions of dollars a year.

"Following the 1948 elections," I continued, "most of the private groups which had built up powerful economic positions during or before the fascist years, were allowed, or actually helped, to retain or regain control of key enterprises, including Italy's major 'independent' dailies. This was notably the case of *Corriere della Sera* of Milan and *La Stampa* of Turin controlled, respectively, by the Crespi family (with textile and other industrial interests) and by the Agnelli's (of the Fiat empire), as well as of *Il Messaggero*, Rome's largest daily, owned by the Perrone family (which had made a fortune in steel and other industries). It was hardly surprising that the media thus controlled or influenced by the political and economic establishment should project an image of America which reflected the basically conservative bent [of that establishment]. The real meaning and motivations of the 'pro-American' stand of most independent Italian papers (and of their financial backers) were crudely exposed when the Kennedy administration made clear its sympathy for Socialist participation in a center-left government committed to a strongly pro-Western policy and a New Dealish program of social and institutional reform. For most of the right-of-center journalists, Americans are 'fools' when it comes to foreign affairs and, at the same time, are so convinced of their world-wide 'mission' that they are likely (to quote Luigi Barzini) to embark 'on risky adventures which jeopardize international peace.' Other right-wingers wonder whether Americans waited so long before entering two world wars 'which they could have nipped in the bud,' because they wanted a Europe so enfeebled as to be forced 'to entrust its survival to U.S. protection.'

"Spokesmen for right-of-center circles like to dwell both on the American 'habit of deserting their friends, leaving them to cope with the troubles created by the U.S. itself,' and on the mixture of 'Quaker moralism and hypocrisy' in U.S. private and public life."

Even some of the most traditionally pro-U.S. business groups and the media they control "have begun to attack sharply 'American protectionism,' an approach which reflects their emphasis (or overemphasis) on exports as the main engine of the Italian economy, and the sharpening differences between the U.S. and the EEC on trade matters.

"For the Neo-fascists, the U.S. continues to be basically the nation most directly responsible for the collapse of Mussolini's regime and, together with the Soviet Union, for the defeat of Nazi Germany. The trends and slant of the Neo-fascist and right-of-center press in Italy," I noted, "are documented by dozens of clippings in this writer's files. Many more, running into the hundreds just over the last few years, evidence the bias of the media influenced or controlled by a wide array of leftist forces. Anti-American propaganda gained wider audience and greater impact as the U.S. armed intervention in Southeast Asia proved less and less able to achieve its proclaimed goals. Watergate [provided] additional encouragement and ammunition to all those bent on portraying the U.S. as a decadent and bumbling imperial power—one that was racist, corrupt, racked by domestic crises, and increasingly unable to face up to its adversaries and reward its allies in the international arena, but still seeking greedily to promote its selfish interests at the expense of friend and foe.

"In the Italy of the mid–1970s, this image was peddled by a widening and increasingly active coalition. It included, in addition to Communists and radicals, restless Catholic left wingers, traditionally antagonistic toward 'Protestant and capitalistic America' and carried away by all-out solidarity with the most militant 'movements of liberation' in the Third World; quite a few intellectuals who felt free at last to vent their basic anti-American bias; and many others who simply concluded that the winds were blowing against the U.S. and that Italy's future was red-colored. Communist gains at the polls brought to full fruition the PCI's patient and skillful efforts to 'colonize' large sections of the Italian cultural establishment. Soon, what was perceived as the new mainstream engulfed many key dailies, news magazines, and movie-producing organizations, as well as a significant sector of the State-owned radio and TV networks.

"Control of *Corriere della Sera* passed into the hands of people who apparently regarded as both unrewarding and unfashionable to retain the paper's traditional line of bourgeois moderation. The thrust of many other dailies and magazines shifted in the same general direction, whether by decision of the publisher, pressure from unionized printers and/or journalists, or such other factors as accommodating financial backers and big advertisers. A leading role was played by some weeklies, notably *Espresso* (published by a group including some Agnelli relatives and several radicals and Socialist left wingers), and *Panorama* (owned by Mondadori, Italy's biggest book publisher). Mondadori teamed up with the *Espresso* group to publish a new daily, *La Repubblica*, which at once moved into the forefront of the anti-American campaign and of the drive to bring the Communist party into the government, preferably at the head of a leftist coalition that would consign the CDs to the opposition.

"As most traditional landmarks, from religion and family to long-entrenched social and moral codes, seemed to be engulfed by an unprecedented and apparently irresistible surge of protest and permissiveness, especially among the young," I further noted, "media operators began to feel that in Italy, too, they could and should play not only an independent but an aggressive role in national affairs. They would do this by challenging openly the 'established authorities' (which seemed ready to give up, anyway) and by resorting boldly to 'investigative journalism.' Like other sectors of Italian society, however, quite a few newsmen and publishers lacked a deeply rooted democratic tradition; they did not have, either, the cultural background required for a mature and balanced approach to their new role. The Italian press has become less stuffy and much more enterprising; there has been a long overdue debunking of stale ideas and antiquated institutions; graft, abuses, and other illegal activities in high places have been exposed. But independence has quickly degenerated into arrogance; boldness into irresponsibility; 'investigative' reporting into sensationalism, scandal-mongering and a search for scoops unrestrained by respect for facts and the rights of those involved. In an obsessive competition to uncover 'plots,' space and consideration in widely circulated and (formerly) authoritative papers have been given to 'purple tales,' worth at most of pulp magazines (although the Moro affair and other still mysterious events have provided a strong inducement and some material for spinning such tales).

"At the same time, a new conformism began to prevail. Leftist forces expanded their area of control from newsmen's unions to key management posts; and individuals, groups and 'grouplets' fitting into the fashionable 'progressive' and 'permissive' mold were publicized and lionized out of all proportion to their actual significance."

Directly or indirectly, "the PCI was the main beneficiary of the new trends and circumstances. Radicals and other non-Communist leftists continue to criticize the Italian Communists for failing to take a stronger stand on such issues as the treatment of dissidents in the USSR and, above all, for trying to reach an accommodation with the CDs rather than turn them out of power. On the whole, however, the Communist party has been portrayed by a widening band of Italian media as a political force strongly committed to democracy and social progress—in fact, as the only force able and determined to give the country an effective and just government. At the same time, the fire has been concentrated on the 'American party' in Italy: that is, the groups that are singled out for attack as bent on furthering, by hook or by crook, the influence and wicked designs of the U.S., as well as their own selfish interests and privileges.

"A determined and sustained effort has been and is still being made to associate the U.S. (and more specifically, the CIA or some other 'American secret service') with the recent terrorist actions by the Red Brigades and/or extreme rightist groups, including the kidnapping and murder last year of former premier and CD leader Aldo Moro.

"*Europeo* printed last October several excerpts from a 1970 'Manual of the Secret Services of the U.S. Army, which had been already published in other countries and branded as counterfeit by the American authorities. The weekly presented the excerpts in such a way as to suggest a marked similarity between some aspects of the Moro affair and the plans and techniques outlined in the alleged Manual to 'infiltrate subversive groups' and 'destabilize countries threatened by the Communist peril.' Many leftist papers played up rumors of bad feelings between U.S. ambassador to Rome, Richard N. Gardner, and Moro, because of the latter's alleged intentions to bring the Communists into the government. Such rumors were used to convey the impression that the U.S. being opposed to the plans attributed to Moro, might be among the instigators and, in any case, had been one of the main beneficiaries of his kidnap-murder. But the same papers paid little, if any, attention to some statements which were made by Moro during the "trial" he was subjected to by his kidnappers and were found by the police after his death, which give the lie to those rumors and pay tribute to Gardner's approach and behavior during their meetings. The Ambassador has also been quoted as having told some Italian labor leaders that 'the U.S. would give no help to fight terrorism in Italy' as long as the Communist party continued to have a major influence in the political life of the country (*La Repubblica*, March 28, 1978). This report drew immediate denials from both the U.S. embassy and the Italian unionists who had met with Gardner.

"Another weekly (*Il Mondo*) carried, some time ago, a column, signed with a pseudonym used by a Communist member of Parliament [Davide Lajolo, known under the pen name of Ulisse], which stated flatly that since the late 1960s many terrorist activities in Italy had been fueled by the 'Greek fascist colonels' under the overall guidance of the CIA.

"While much less space and attention have been devoted to speculation on a KGB role," I further reported, "a frequently used approach was echoed recently by *La Repubblica* (January 25, 1979): 'There is no point in drawing here a distinction between the initiatives originating with the Soviet military-police complex or with its American opposite-accomplice.' The same apparently 'equidistant' approach is often taken on most other issues involving the U.S. and the USSR (a top official of the national newsmen guild was reported recently to have branded 'the experiences' of the U.S. and Soviet press as 'equally repressive'). According to *Europeo*, if the Soviets have played a role in destabilizing Iran, they would have had a right to do so, since the U.S. does not tolerate Soviet missiles in Cuba, but feels entitled to place its own in Turkey and Iran, next door to the USSR.' After the invasion of Cambodia by the Vietnamese, some radicals and other left-wingers in Italy have admitted, more or less grudgingly, that some of their 'evaluations and prophecies' (about the nature and behavior of Communist regimes) have turned out to be wrong. In the next breath, however, they have used much more violent terms to denounce again 'the bombings . . . the massacres . . . the corruption' which in their opinion must be blamed on the Americans in Vietnam, Latin America, the Middle East, Greece, and elsewhere (see, notably, an editorial by Eugenio Scalfari in *La Repubblica* and a column in *La Stampa* by Andrea Barbato, head of the News Section of the Second Channel of the State TV). A reference to the Soviet Gulag calls for an allusion to the U.S. use of napalm in Vietnam (*Corriere della Sera*), and a reference to Brezhnev's recent letter warning the Italians against selling arms to China calls for a reminder that, during the cold war, Washington opposed the sale of Fiat buses to Poland (from a column by Vittorio Gorresio, a long-time staffer of *La Stampa*, published in *Epoca*, one of the weeklies owned by Mondadori).

"The anti-American slant," I went on, "is even more apparent in other statements and comments freely bandied around or mentioned almost casually as established facts: 'The Yom Kippur war was unleashed by Sadat with Washington's assent' (*Europeo*); 'The Bolivian and U.S. governments decided to kill Guevara' (*Espresso*); 'Anti-Americanism, which is generally the fruit of a higher political education of the peoples' (*Corriere della Sera*); 'The U.S. lets the lira sink' (*Europeo*); 'A poet in the American hell' (headline in *Corriere della Sera* referring to the death of Robert Lowell); 'The American people . . . have very little dignity and often no dignity at all. . . . The average American has undergone a sort of historical and political lobotomization and is not aware of his political identity, of the tremendous social and racial differentiations and discriminations that exist in the country. . . . Poverty in the U.S. is the blackest in the world' (from a series of articles by writer Goffredo Parise published not long ago in *Corriere della Sera*).

"Film reviewers miss no opportunity to blame the troubles of the Italian movie industry on 'American colonization' of the Italian market, and movie directors do likewise when their works get a bad reception (the latest case in point is Lina Wertmuller).

"The Second Channel of the state-controlled TV network featured recently a five-part program which stressed that the American view of Italy was shaped by 'old prejudices and cliches as well as by recent alarms [over a Communist takeover],' as a columnist of *Il Corriere della Sera* noted approvingly. The program emphasized the pro-fascist bias of leading U.S. circles (especially, but not only, during Mussolini's heyday), the importance of gangsterism and of the Mafia in U.S. society, and the harsh and discriminatory treatment given Italian immigrants, while down-playing the recent rise in the economic and social status of Italian-Americans. Two prime-time hours were devoted to an opus, by a far-out leftist showman (Dario Fo), called *The Lady Is Fit to be Thrown Away*— the lady being America, portrayed, to quote the gleeful review by the Communist daily *l'Unità*, as 'an air-conditioned nightmare where Presidents are made and unmade (the sneering parody of Kennedy's assassination is one of the high points of the show), infamous wars are unleashed, and monstrous machinations are organized for the glorification of a system dominated by an obsessive cult of money, and by the overwhelming power of capital.' Another program provided evidence, always according to *l'Unità*, of the 'destabilization of the Italian democratic regime pursued in recent years by the CIA and by the State Department in cahoots with the World Bank.' These programs received favorable notices not only by the leftist press but by leftist reviewers of 'independent' papers like *La Stampa*.

"Many of the same media," I also pointed out, "have consistently opposed any substantial strengthening of Italy's contribution to NATO defenses and have carried out a persistent campaign against U.S. bases in Italy. More generally, radical and other leftist journalists and 'experts' have sought to 'sell' the idea that Italy has been and still is 'a province,' a most compliant and exploited province, of 'the American Empire.'

"Several books issued by leading publishers (and favorably reviewed in the press owned by them), deal with the events of the last decades in such a way as to convey the feeling that the U.S. has resorted to mostly foul means to back conservative and reactionary forces in Italy and in other nations, while exploiting its 'dominant influence' in these countries to gain privileges for itself.''

I also pointed at some recent indications of a changing trend, notably a shift at *Corriere della Sera*, where, following a reported inflow of West German money and a change of editor, "some of the most militantly anti-American contributors have left, while others (and many staffers) have trimmed their sails to the new trade winds. By and large, however, a sizable sector of the Italian media continues to wage a campaign whose overall thrust and accumulated impact, whatever the feelings and motivations of the individual journalists and publishers involved, can only contribute to pushing Italy down a neutralistic path and thus to shifting substantially, and perhaps decisively, the balance of power in Europe and in the Mediterranean to the benefit of the USSR. Nor does it appear to be just a coincidence that the same media should display a marked bias in favor of Arab leftists, coupled with an anti-Israeli slant often bordering on outright anti-Semitism.

"All this should not suggest," I cautioned, "that most Italians, or even a majority of them, have become anti-American. The reservoir of good will, respect, and admiration for America, which in a recent past was still the biggest of any European nation, has dwindled, but remains fairly large and deep. And so does the feeling that, after all, Italy's security and welfare continue to depend, to a great and probably decisive extent, upon her relationship with America.

"TV Channel One of the state-owned network, which reaches the great majority of the national audience, is still largely controlled by the CDs and leans toward the U.S. side. It is much less aggressive and biased than is Channel Two on the opposite side. One of the two major radio networks follows a militantly pro-Christian Democrat, anti-Communist, anti-Soviet and basically pro-American line, while the other is controlled by leftists. Private TV and radio stations have proliferated in the last few years, following changes in the legislation which sanctioned state monopoly. Many of these stations reflect the views of center and center-right groups and can be rated as basically pro-American; quite a few radio stations are controlled by far-out leftists and radical 'grouplets.'

"Newspapers identified officially with political parties have little influence and limited circulation, with the notable exception of *l'Unità*. A basically pro-Western approach is still followed by several 'independent' papers which take a center or right-of-center approach in domestic affairs. The most important among them are *Il Tempo* of Rome, *La Nazione* of Florence, and *Il Resto del Carlino* of Bologna.

"On the political level," I concluded, "the pro-Communist wave also seems to have crested, as a result of the party's failure to translate quickly its gains at the polls into a full-fledged role in the central government and of its disappointing performance in the regions, provinces, and municipalities where leftist administrations have taken over in recent years. The consequent erosion of the Communist image appears to affect the party's appeal to the intellectual community as well."

This, however, was far from being the case as yet when, in the wake of the great Communist advance in the June 1975 elections, the media influenced by the PCI or anyway favorable to its participation in the government, launched a campaign to persuade the Italians that wide sectors of U.S. public opinion, including representatives of the establishment, both Republican and Democrat, were becoming inclined or at least resigned to accept Communist role in running national affairs.

The pegs were flimsy, to say the least. Eugenio Peggio, a Communist member of Parliament, was given a visa to attend, as a journalist, a meeting of the International Monetary Fund. Sergio Segre was invited to take part in a debate slated for late October by the New York Council on Foreign Relations. When an official of the Council, Zygmunt Nagorski, met in Italy with Segre and other PCI representatives, some of his statements were given great prominence as confirmations of a changed approach by authoritative U.S. circles to the "Communist issue" in Italy. Actually, Nagorski had been rather cautious both in talking with Italian newspapermen and in an article published in the *New York Times* (July 24). He argued that, in view of the changes apparently under way within Italian Communism, the United States should open a dialogue with the PCI or at least show more flexibility toward it. Nagorski stressed, however, that Americans could not be sure that a Communist government would actually let Italy stay in NATO and in the EEC or accept the rules of a democratic pluralistic society (*Panorama*, August 21). Some months later Nagorski himself wondered whether Italian papers had distorted his statements out of ignorance, bad faith, or desire to engineer a political maneuver (interview printed in the book *Gli USA e il PCI* by Rodolfo Brancoli, published by Garzanti in January 1976).

Yet, the weekly *Il Mondo*, generously quoted by *Corriere della Sera* (August 8), hastened to speak of a big "turnaround" by the Americans and of "secret negotiations" (between Segre and Nagorski) in view of an early trip by Berlinguer to the United States. According to *Il Mondo*, the turnaround had been foreshadowed by the *New York Times* decision to replace his long-time Rome correspondent, Paul Hofmann ("a cold war warrior"); in the meantime, coverage of Italian affairs had been entrusted to Sulzberger whose recent columns on Berlinguer and on "Leninism Italian style" were amply quoted. *Il Mondo*, whose editor was Antonio Ghirelli, later on press secretary to president Sandro Pertini and to premier Bettino Craxi, and editor of the PSI daily, *Avanti*, further announced the early return home of ambassador Volpe, a man "too far to the right" to fit in with the new U.S. course in Italy. A few days later, *Panorama* noted that there had "been no denials" of the reports of an impending trip by Berlinguer to the United States. *Espresso* headlined "Dear Jerry, dearest Enrico," although it added that "things have not yet reached this stage between Berlinguer and Ford." In his column in *Espresso*, Antonio Gambino wrote that the PCI would soon "overtake the CDs as the plurality party" while before long the CDs themselves would split and their leftist splinter would collaborate with a leftist government. Gambino concluded by warning the U.S. administration against "trying to strangle a political and social evolution which is now felt to be necessary by the absolute majority'' of the Italians. *Europeo*, too, played up the favorable prospects for an early ''mission of goodwill'' by Berlinguer in the United States. A major role in seeking to improve relations between the United States and the PCI was attributed to Gianni Agnelli whose preferences were said to go now to ''an embrace between technocracy and Communism,'' to ''an enlightened totalitarianism'' backed by a PCI which was offering itself as a party committed to ''order.''

The campaign had some impact in Italian political quarters. In early September, representatives of several parties, ranging from the CDs to the Socialists, asked me whether Washington was really inclined to ''open to the PCI,'' abandoning or at least shoving into the background ''the political forces which for so many years have operated to give strength and cohesion to the alliance and cooperation between Italy and the U.S.'' (as I reported in the *Daily American*, September 21).

In an interview to *Epoca* (September 13), Volpe not only denied flatly the alleged shifts in Washington's approach to the PCI but explained the basic motivations of the U.S. opposition to a Communist role in the governments of Western Europe and did so in terms that were to be substantially endorsed by the subsequent U.S. administrations. ''As pointed out explicitly by President Ford, by Secretary of State Kissinger, and by other U.S. officials,'' Volpe emphasized, ''a basic contradiction arises if Communists share or come to power in national governments which are members of NATO,'' an alliance ''created to protect its members against potential aggressions from the Soviet Union and its allies in the Warsaw Pact. . . . In view, moreover, of the political, historical, cultural, and social bonds that solidly unite the U.S. and Italy, we could not favor the coming to power of a governmental system alien to the Western democratic tradition.

''Of course, Volpe went on, ''Italy's domestic affairs are a matter solely for the Italians to decide. In this sense, we are an interested onlooker, not a direct participant. But we and our allies obviously favor those forces which wish to remain allied with us in a progressive democratic system which avoids extremism of either left or right.''

The interview sparked fresh charges of U.S. interference in Italian domestic affairs which came also from papers not tied to the political left (notably *La Stampa*, September 11). Further claims that the U.S. administration did not agree with Volpe's stand elicited this statement from the State Department's spokesman Robert Funseth: ''The ambassador's comments were an accurate and complete reflection of . . . how the U.S. would feel about Communists in governments of NATO countries.''

Over the next few months, this policy was reaffirmed at the highest levels. In an electoral speech in Keene, New Hampshire (February 19, 1976), President Ford said that he ''would vigorously oppose any Communist participation in the Italian government. . . . I don't think you can have a Communist government or Communist officials in a government and have that nation a viable partner in

NATO.'' Kissinger told the House International Relations Committee on Security Assistance (November 6, 1975): ''We were of course disturbed by the dramatic gains made by the Communists in the recent regional elections in Italy. Basically, the U.S. cannot determine the domestic structure of Italy by its own decision. . . . However, the U.S. hopes very much that the Christian Democrat Party will revitalize itself so that it can gain the necessary public support and that coalitions can be put together among the democratic parties that will prevent the entry into government of the Communist party of Italy, since the impact on NATO of having one of the major countries with a major Communist participation in its government would be very severe.''

A month later, the secretary of state devoted to the issue many of his remarks to a meeting of U.S. ambassadors held in London (a summary appeared in the *New York Times* on April 7, 1976). The dominance of Communist parties in the West was unacceptable, Kissinger maintained, irrespective of their reasonableness or of the degree of their independence from the USSR. If one or the other of these parties gained control of a Western government, it would hardly take the risk of being removed from office as a result of a free election. A major Communist participation in Western governments would ''erode'' the foundation of Atlantic security because under such circumstances the United States could not permit ''the setting of a precedent in which by our inaction we have facilitated the success of a Communist party. The Soviet leaders themselves would probably prefer not to see Communist [parties] taking over Western Europe. But in the final analysis their ideology requires them to assist in those efforts. . . . As for Socialists,'' the secretary of state concluded, ''we will continue to support them. We do so in Portugal. We must do so in Italy, although the Italian Socialist party will be unreliable until the CDs can organize themselves.''

Speaking at the meeting of the American Society of Newspapers Editors in Washington (April 13 and 14), Kissinger said: ''The advent of Communism in major European countries is likely to produce a sequence of events in which other European countries will also be tempted to move in the same direction. The U.S. must not create the impression that it could be indifferent to such developments.''

On the same occasion, the issue was discussed by leading Democratic experts such as George Ball, under secretary of state in the Johnson administration, Zbigniew Brzezinski, who was to become President Carter's assistant for national security, and Paul Warnke, a former assistant secretary of defense who was to be in charge of the SALT II negotiations during Carter's presidency. As reported by the *New York Times* and the *Washington Post*, their speeches appeared to reflect a conviction that a Communist role in governing Italy was ''likely'' and that it should not be regarded as ''fatal to NATO'' (to quote Leslie Gelb in the *New York Times*, April 15). In fact their views were rather different as stressed in a letter to the editor by George Ball printed in the *Washington Post* on April 22. Ball charged that his statements before the ASNE had been ''grotesquely misinterpreted'' by *Post* staffer Stephen Rosenfeld (April 16). ''Far from regarding Communist participation in the Italian government with equanimity,'' Ball wrote, ''I fully share Secretary Kissinger's concern that the advent of Communists in the Italian government would gravely complicate existing security arrangements within the Western alliance and weaken the structure of European unity, although I do not share his dour prediction that it would produce a domino effect with other European States. Where I disagree with the Secretary is on the tactics to avert such a disaster and the way to deal with it should [it] occur in spite of our efforts. To mutter that it would bring about the dissolution of NATO or force the withdrawal of American troops from Europe is to spur the Communists to more determined activity, since that is exactly what they have long been seeking to achieve. To announce that it would be 'unacceptable' to Americans sounds like Queen Victoria at her prissiest. If it should occur, we will have no other course but to accept it, unless we propose to send in the Marines.

''In my view,'' Ball concluded, ''our diplomatic efforts should be concentrated on trying to push the Common Market nations front and center in the effort to deter the Italians from bringing the Communists into the government.''

Ball further explained his views in the *Washington Post* of May 30: ''To argue, as some do, that Communist participation holds no peril because the Italian Communist voters are not 'real Communists' quite misses the point. For the party's representatives in the government would not be a cross section of the Communist electorate but disciplined professionals, rigidly committed to a party line and party tactics. [Berlinguer] and his colleagues have left little doubt that they would support the Soviet proposal to trade off the liquidation of the Warsaw Pact for the liquidation of NATO. They would almost certainly oppose the continuing outlays necessary to maintain adequate NATO defenses and would make increasingly difficult the maintenance of American bases and installations in Italy (13,000 of our own fighting forces with 45,000 civilians are now stationed there).''

According to Ball, there was little or no substance to the hopes of some Italian industrialists that the coming to power of the Communists would produce at least ''a respite from industrial strife. . . . If Communist leaders within the Italian government acted to salvage the rapidly disintegrating Italian economy . . . Moscow itself might undertake to finance and incite a more radical Communist faction, since it dares not risk a Western Communist party moving toward 'bourgeois collaborationism' for fear of creating deep disquiet among the uneasy Communist regimes in Eastern Europe. Still, even without the fear of their own leftwing or of mischief from Moscow, Berlinguer and his company would not play the role of moderation very long. They are by no means mere 'agrarian reformers' and the party has made its long-term objectives very clear. . . . All the fine talk of 'the many roads to socialism' and of 'humanist Marxism' . . . [is] clearly a tactic by which power is to be gained; once it is achieved, [it] would be jettisoned.''

While ''tough warnings based on threats to Europe's security probably did more harm than good,'' Bell went on, ''the Italian people should still be put on notice that Communist entry into government would jeopardize their *economic* well-being. To be effective, such a warning should come from Italy's European neighbors rather than the U.S., though it should be part of a coordinated strategy.'' With the United States ''contenting itself, for once, with a silent supporting role,'' Ball concluded, the EEC could and should take the initiative in conveying to the Italians the consequences of a Communist role in running their national affairs. In order ''to prevent the destruction of democracy'' in one of its member nations, the community should point at and eventually make use of its ''capability of reducing the level of economic activity in Italy seriously by a whole range of devices—from imposing sanctions on agricultural imports to stopping the flow of regional assistance funds. As the ultimate sanction, the other members could expel Italy from the community.''

Brzezinski had already noted, in an interview to *Il Giornale* of Milan (February 7): ''It is not enough for the Communist parties of Western Europe, which for decades have supported one of the most atrocious tyrannies in history and maintained that its experiences could be applied usefully and creatively elsewhere, to come out one fine day and say that they have changed their mind and now believe in pluralism and have become democratic. It is necessary that they take stands much more explicit and involving clearer commitments. . . . Do these parties repudiate in toto the Stalinist experience or not? . . . Do they reject the Leninist experience or not? . . . Is there a genuine democratic process at work within those parties? If the answers to such questions do not satisfy us, we'll be wholly entitled to say that there is no foundation to these parties' pretence to be democratic. . . . On the contrary, if their answers should be satisfactory, this would be a magnificent step toward the inclusion of the Communists into the system.''

According to Brzezinski, it was in the interest of the United States to ''maintain contacts, both official and unofficial, with all the sectors and shades of the political spectrum in the various countries . . . The problem is to develop such contacts without letting them be exploited by the Communists in the sense of making them appear as an American support.'' The U.S., Brzezinski concluded, should not take ''explicit stands'' with regard to ''internal matters. Obviously, we have our own preferences concerning more the outcome of these European internal processes than the processes themselves in the sense that we're interested in maintaining and strengthening the democratic system. And surely we should not hesitate to say so.''

Similar considerations and assessments were part of an analysis by Columbia University's Research Institute on International Change. Yet, *Corriere della Sera* referred to this analysis on May 10 under a headline which said in quotation marks: ''The PCI in the government would not threaten private capital or NATO.'' The article's content, moreover, was such as to prompt Brzezinski, as director of the Institute, to send *Corriere della Sera* a note which was published a few days later and read: ''I want to make it clear that according to the report [by the Institute] a Communist participation in coalition governments in Western

Europe is a factor which would in fact introduce in the situation a number of uncertainties of the first magnitude. The article published in *Corriere della Sera* created the impression that the report would look with favor on such participation. This is not true.''

In *The Wall Street Journal* of April 2, Arthur Schlesinger Jr., denounced as ''self-defeating'' the kind of ''hectoring intervention'' carried out by the Ford administration against a Communist participation in the government of West European nations. Schlesinger noted that he was ready to believe that Berlinguer was sincere ''in his declaration in favor of an independent foreign policy and a pluralistic political order [and] that the Italian Communist party has become in an important sense a national party, though still with an unconquerable inner predilection toward the Soviet Union and against the U.S. But I cannot believe that it has become a democratic party. . . . If I were an Italian, I would oppose Communist entry into the government. If I were a Frenchman, I would emphatically do so.''

Quite different not to say opposite opinions and interpretations came from professors and researchers who made up a minority in the academic circles themselves but had gained access to some rather prestigious publications. Peter Lange, a young researcher at Harvard, became the fair-headed boy of the Communist and radical-socialist press in Italy. Lange made the following main points in the winter 1975–1976 issue of *Foreign Policy* and voiced them in bolder terms in his statements in Italian dailies and magazines:

1. The PCI will keep gaining votes and the CDs will keep losing ground.

2. The PCI ''has been able to convince large numbers of people and political elites that there is an 'Italian road to Socialism' that will be paved, on the one hand, with democratic institutions and civil liberties and, on the other hand, with independence from the Soviet Union and a rejection of the Soviet Socialist model.''

3. A Communist role in the national government was practically inevitable ''within the not-too-distant future [and] barring direct intervention of an overt or covert nature, there is little that the U.S. can do to prevent the Communist party from assuming'' such a role.

4. Maintaining ''a posture of intransigence'' on the issue ''would require the U.S. to support the most anti-Communist elements with the CD. But those leaders and factions are, for the most part, the same ones which want to block reform of the corrupt, clientelistic, and inefficient practices which have so greatly contributed to the party's current crisis and to the rise of the Communists.''

Furthermore, the U.S. ''would impair its ability to influence the PCI's behavior once it became a partner in the government and would ''weaken the party's ability to maintain . . . the considerable autonomy from the Soviet Union [it had] developed . . . in recent years.''

Lange concluded his plea by asserting that a Communist participation in the government must not be expected to bring about ''great changes'' in Italian foreign policy since "the PCI will want to show that it is contributing to a more active pursuit of Italian interests internationally, but that its chief concerns will be domestic." In any case, none of these changes "would be fundamentally damaging to U.S. strategic interests, though they might disturb the *status quo*. It is safe to say that these changes in Italy's policy are greatly to be preferred to the major and damaging changes that could take place if the U.S. persists in futile railings against the PCI or moves to direct intervention to block the Communists' access to national power."

15

The U.S. Traffic Light Stays on Red for the PCI

"As an American journalist who has covered Italian affairs for more years than I care to remember," I wrote (*Daily American*, October 12, 1975), "I have developed many good contacts and made quite a few friends among those who, at different times and in different capacities, in Washington and in Rome, have had and still have a role in shaping and carrying out U.S. policies toward Italy. A cross-section of their views [shows] general agreement with the opinion, voiced by a key official in Washington, that 'it would be sheer folly if we were to undercut, let alone turn our backs on, true and proven friends in Italy by embracing other people and groups which actually represent worse than unknown quantities.' To be sure, says an old Italian hand in the State Department, 'we have been telling leading CDs from way back in the 1950s that their party was moving too slowly and reluctantly in implementing social reforms and institutional modernizations. More recently, we have emphasized the mounting danger that, by countenancing more maladministration of public affairs and failing to uphold law and justice, the party would lose credibility even among moderate voters.'

"Yet, in the executive branch as well as on Capitol Hill, the prevailing consensus is that the CDs can still play a major role 'by keeping or winning back the support of a wide central band of the electoral spectrum,' to quote a diplomat who was stationed for several years in Rome. A Congressman of Italian origin chimes in and adds: 'Provided, of course, and I know it is a tall order, that the CDs manage to project a vigorous and refurbished image as a party that stands for orderly change.'

"To a question about the Socialists, a veteran Italy-watcher says: 'Frustrating but indispensable.' Other U.S. officials note regretfully that the PSI is 'split prone' and inclined to swing 'from all-too-ready acceptance of some crumbs of power and patronage as the price of its collaboration with the CDs to ultimative demands for immediate enactment of every conceivable reform.' ''

Quite recently, I further recalled, ''a trip to Washington by Giorgio Almirante, leader of the Neo-fascist *Movimento Sociale Italiano* (MSI), and his meetings with some members of Congress and of the National Security Council were played up [by Italian media critical of the United States] as evidence that the U.S. was now backing the extreme right in Italy. Last Wednesday, the U.S. embassy in Rome stressed that Almirante had not been invited by the U.S. government and that his meetings in Washington should not be 'interpreted as an American endorsement of the MSI or its policies.' '' On the MSI, I added, ''the comments of Italian old hands, in Washington and in Rome, are short and to the point: 'Whatever our faults, we should be given credit for two things: we have rather good memories and we know how to count. Less experienced people in the executive branch and some people on Capitol Hill may not know or remember that most MSI leaders, from Almirante down, held posts in the puppet regime set up by Mussolini in the last years of World War II to serve the Nazis up to their final defeat. We also remember, ' say the old Italian hands, 'that the MSI, which now claims to be the sole true champion of NATO in Italy, was far from enthusiastic, to put it mildly, about Italy joining the Atlantic alliance.' Pointing out that the Neo-fascists polled less than 7 percent of the votes in the latest elections and are shunned by all other Italian parties, the U.S. officials add: 'If you tried to include the MSI in a center-right combination, the latter would suffer so much disruption and so many defections to precipitate the polarization of a broad left-of-center majority dominated by the Communists.'

''U.S. opposition to a PCI participation in the government,'' I further noted, ''rests on a more complex mix of motivations and assessments. For quite a few American officials it is still mainly a matter of principle. Others emphasize that, should the Communists win a share of [national] power in Italy, the key Mediterranean country in NATO, the balance of power would be shattered throughout Southern Europe.' Still other Italy-watchers, in and out of the U.S. government, agree that the attempts by the Italian Communists to develop 'their own way to Socialism' deserve attention. But, to quote a key official in Washington, 'no one in this town, no one in a position of authority, takes seriously the reports that the PCI is about to turn into a Social Democratic party or to take a neutral stand as between the U.S. and the USSR.' ... Another key U.S. official sums it up this way: 'While there are some indications that the present Communist leaders are trying to free their party from the Kremlin's apron strings, the PCI's batting average in support of the Soviet line has dropped only minimally, say from 1,000 to 900.' ''

With specific reference to the statements attributed to Nagorski, Macaluso told me in early September: ''It is absurd to talk about us as if we had all become Social-Democrats and were ready to castigate with equal sternness the behavior of either superpower, notably of the U.S. in Vietnam and of the Soviet Union in Czechoslovakia.'' A trip to the U.S. by Berlinguer, Macaluso went on, ''is a matter that we have not discussed even as a distant possibility. We're certainly interested in cultivating contacts and achieving a better, mutual understanding with the Americans and with U.S. government representatives. But it must and can only be a cautious, gradual, and selective process.''

In early December I met for the first time Enrico Berlinguer. In reply to his questions, I said that, in my opinion, quite a few Italian Communists had entertained recently many ''illusions'' about a ''softening'' of U.S. opposition to a government role for the PCI. If the PCI leadership was actually determined to bring about a less negative U.S. approach to their party's role, it would be advisable, to begin with, for the mass media controlled or influenced by the Communists ''to give a less unfavorable and less distorted image of the U.S., of its foreign policy, and also of its domestic conditions and developments.'' More ''attention and concern'' should be paid to events and prospects in the East European countries, with the natural consequence of taking a more critical approach to Soviet policies in the region.''

Berlinguer conveyed some of my remarks to Communist newsmen, as Alberto Jacoviello (then a ranking staffer of *l'Unità*) told me shortly afterway, but no significant results were apparent.

''The PCI,'' Berlinguer said time and again during our conversation, ''does not only accept Italy's membership in NATO, of course on the assumption that it is and will remain a defensive and geographically circumscribed alliance, but has no intention to influence Italian foreign policy in such a way as to alter the international balance of power. This approach is valid both while our party remains in the opposition and after it wins a role in the government. I know,'' the PCI leader went on, ''that in the U.S. the sincerity of this intention of ours is being questioned. I can only hope that such an American stand will be revised without waiting as long as it has happened on other very important issues with such bad consequences for the U.S. itself. How much did it cost the U.S. in terms of prestige, credibility and influence to have failed for so long to understand what was actually going on in China after World War II? How much did the U.S. pay, in blood too, for its failure to realize for so long that the Vietnamese brand of Communism is quite different from the Soviet or Chinese brand? And what about Spain or Greece? In Greece, the U.S. administrations have behaved as if they felt that the continuation in power of a fascist regime was in their interest. They would compound their mistake and run worse risks if their approach to Spanish affairs should be dictated by the conviction that their interests would not be served by a speedy process of democratization, notably by participation in the government of all the political forces, including the Communist party, which represent Spanish public opinion. . . . Much in the same way, the U.S. must decide whether its interests in Italy (and generally in Europe and in the Mediterranean) can best be served by a continuing deterioration of the Italian political, economic, and social conditions, or rather by the coming to power of a new government which would include our party and would give the nation political stability, speed up economic recovery and social reforms, while underwriting Italy's continued participation in the Atlantic alliance.''

The PCI, Berlinguer stressed, was not ''in a hurry'' to enter the government or join a governmental majority: ''We have steadily increased our electoral strength while staying in the opposition and we are fully confident that it will continue to be so. But any combination of forces which excludes our party is not only unable to solve the country's basic problems but makes them more serious and dangerous.''

''Are you thinking about a rightist coup, political anarchy, or a collapse of the Italian economy?''

''We can deal successfully with anything that may be attempted by rightist forces,'' Berlinguer replied. ''But the deterioration, which has gone on for so long, might actually produce political anarchy or a collapse of the national economy. . . . In either case, we would have to step in on our own or we would be asked by other political forces to join them in the government as the only way of saving the country from total disaster. . . . But we do not want to gain national power under such circumstances, we do not want Italy to go through so many further crises and misfortunes before we are given the opportunity to rescue her by joining in a governmental majority.''

''What's preventing you from giving this contribution right now?''

Berlinguer smiled and answered, ''To put it bluntly, the CDs and the Socialists, or at least very powerful groups within both parties, do not want us as partners in running national affairs. Under the circumstances, our party can serve the country's interests only by sticking, insofar as it is up to it, to a gradual, cautious policy aimed at making as little traumatic as possible the transition from the opposition to a government role.''

''You mean 'as little traumatic as possible' for your own party too?''

''Yes,'' Berlinguer shot back. ''We realize that the implementation of our plans involves some costs for our own party too, because not every aspect of our strategy for securing a governmental role can win the approval of every PCI member and voter. We're ready to pay the price, however, because we are convinced that our policy serves the national interest.''

To a question about the ''national road to Socialism,'' Berlinguer replied, ''Our party is not only determined but compelled to follow this road because it cannot afford to change a basic approach which has been developed over many years with the consent and support of the overwhelming majority of its members and voters. This 'Italian road to Socialism' is quite different from the roads followed by the PCUS and other Communist parties in Eastern Europe as well as by the Chinese Communists. At the same time, our ideas and policies are broadly shared by an increasing number of Communist parties in capitalistic countries and notably in the nations that are partners in the Common Market. Our approach is the only one suitable for Communist parties operating in this area, and therefore is irreversible, as shown also by the experience of the Portuguese Communist party. It is now in deep trouble because it has stuck to a policy which does not take into account the conditions prevailing in Western Europe.''

When queried about the situation and prospects in Eastern Europe, the PCI secretary replied rather testily: "Our party's primary tasks and commitments have to do with Italy and Western Europe. As a consequence of Yalta, moreover, the Eastern European countries must have a special relationship with the Soviet Union.'' When reminded that "respect for democracy and human rights cannot be said to be practiced in those countries,'' Berlinguer said: "The principles of democracy and pluralism, which we fully endorse and support, do not necessarily require to be implemented everywhere in the same forms or by identical methods. You may have a pluralistic system without a full-fledged democratic setup, as in quite a few Third World countries, or you may have a democratic system without a multiparty setup, as portended by developments in Czechoslovakia during the 1968 Spring . . . Of course,'' he added quickly, "Czechoslovakia is a country which before 1938 and in the early postwar years, enjoyed a truly democratic, multiparty system as well as a remarkable degree of economic and social progress. That's why we have voiced and will continue to voice our outspoken dissent from what happened there in the summer of 1968 and afterwards.''

The PCI secretary conceded, rather reluctantly, that "some mistakes and some delusions'' had possibly marked the interpretation given by some of his party's representatives of the alleged disposition not only of the United States but of the Vatican concerning a Communist role in governing Italy. Macaluso told me shortly afterwards that he had been "surprised and rather disconcerted'' by the statement issued recently by the Permanent Committee of the Italian Episcopal Conference which reaffirmed explicitly "the incompatibility between Catholicism and Marxism.''

From my talks with Archbishop Giovanni Benelli, substitute secretary of state, with Archbishop Agostino Casaroli, at the time secretary of the Council for Public Affairs and later on secretary of state, and with Cardinal Ugo Poletti, the Pope's vicar in Rome, I had already concluded that concern over the Communist advance and the weakness of the CD party had become so strong as to persuade top representatives of the church to take an open and resolute stand.

"We have felt for many years,'' Benelli told me, "that the church's position on Communism has been spelled out most authoritatively so many times and in such explicit terms that it would continue to have its impact even if it was not repeated again and again. Nevertheless, we have been compelled to realize, especially in view of the major electoral gains made by the PCI, that it is necessary to dispel any doubts and ambiguities which may have emerged and would increase if the church keeps silent any longer. On this need there is a general agreement that goes far beyond the prelates who are considered, rightly or wrongly, as holding 'conservative' views.' ''

Benelli carefully added that the Vatican would continue "to refrain from direct involvement in Italian politics.'' But exhortations and public pronouncements would come from "individual bishops" and "at some most serious junctures" the Episcopal Conference would "speak up."

"And the Christian Democrats?"

"In spite of all its faults, shortcomings, and mistakes," Benelli replied, "the Christian Democrat Party still appears as the best available 'chosen instrument' for giving Italian Catholics a political organization." The church did not contemplate "promoting or underwriting 'a second Catholic party.' '' Such an approach found no sympathy or support "in any influential quarter even twenty or thirty years ago when the threat to CD supremacy was much less strong. Right now, any split in the ranks of the Catholic electorate would be tantamount to handing over to the PCI, on a silver platter, a plurality of the votes and making it much harder, not to say impossible, to prevent the Communists from gaining a prominent role in governing Italy. On its side, Christian Democracy must undergo far-reaching changes and a thorough 'renovation' if it is to retain or win back the allegiance of large sectors of the electorate."

Archbishop Casaroli told me: "There is a solid front of us all on the need to reaffirm publicly the church's stand with regard to Communism. . . . The statements made recently or about to be made by top representatives of the Catholic hierarchy reflect special concerns over electoral developments and prospects in Rome and in Italy, but they are related to and are strengthened by the more general worries aroused by the phenomenon which, under different names and forms ('Christians for Socialism,' 'Marxist Christians'), is taking shape in many countries, from Belgium to France and West Germany."

Making it clear that he shared the recent pronouncements by CD secretary general Benigno Zaccagnini about his party's continued opposition to a Communist-controlled government, Casaroli added: "For us, too, matters of principle are most important. But even on grounds of practical politics how can anyone ignore or minimize the fact that the Communists have never yielded power peacefully?"

"What about the 'Italian road to Socialism,' touted by the PCI leaders?"

"I don't want to question," Casaroli replied, "the sincerity of Berlinguer or of other top representatives of the PCI when they voice their determination to follow an approach that must reflect the peculiarities of the Italian condition and therefore must differ in important ways from the approach adopted by other Communist parties. I do not rule out, either, that they may intend to stick to such a 'national' road even after gaining a government role. The key point, however, is whether they will be able to do so. Should they behave in a manner truly independent from Moscow, the Soviets would not lack the means to make their dissatisfaction clear and effective. Moscow's hold on sizable sectors of the PCI is sufficiently strong to force Berlinguer and his backers to bow to its requests or to replace them at the head of the party."

On November 30, 1975, I published in the *Daily American* and in *Il Tempo* an interview with Cardinal Poletti and reported at the same time the gist of my recent talks with other top representatives of the Catholic church.

Poletti told me right away: "The prospect that Italy, whose culture is so deeply steeped in Catholicism, should pin her hopes for the future to an atheistic doctrine, is a source of deep sorrow and concern for all of us, from the Holy Father down." This concern "is based on matters of doctrine and is sustained by experience showing that wherever Communism wins control the church is in trouble. Here in Italy, too, where the Communists have been long in charge of local administrations (such as in Emilia-Romagna and in Tuscany) the social welfare agencies set up by religious institutions have been gradually pushed aside and deprived even of the contributions that according to the law should accrue to all such agencies."

Asked about the recent electoral defeats suffered by the CDs, the cardinal said, "unquestionably this political force has been worn out by thirty years of running national affairs. Conditions in Italy, so different from those in the U.S., do not allow for diverse parties to alternate in governing the country and thus for the recurrent changes and almost automatic rejuvenation that this involves for them. The CD party needs to renew itself, to renew its program as well as its leaders and cadres. . . . If the party manages to convince again the voters of its commitment to serve concretely the people, it can recoup ground, especially on the left, the most exposed and truly decisive front of the struggle now under way in Italy."

The cardinal was asked whether the CD party was the only one that could be backed by voters opposed to Communism: "I'm not sharing the views which in the Italian political jargon are termed 'integralistic,' " Poletti replied: "There are other parties which are sincerely devoted to democratic principles and respectful of all human values. Yet, those who look for inspiration and guidance to the Christian doctrine are convinced that it can provide a full and adequate answer to all the problems of mankind."

In other articles (*Daily American*, September 21, October 19, November 23, 1975), I sought to produce an analysis in depth of the substance and of the more significant aspects of the "Communist issue" at a crucial juncture in Italian politics.

In my opinion, Italy was not "about to be engulfed by 'a red tide,' which would shake the country loose from its NATO moorings and open up prospects bound to 'send shivers down the spines of all democrats,' " as argued by many Western observers. The PCI leaders would undoubtedly "seek to capitalize" on their party's recent gains at the polls "not only to widen and consolidate its area of local control but to increase its influence and leverage at the national level. They would "continue to push a 'creeping compromise' with the CDs (and the Socialists)," as well as to couple the party's "long standing championship of social and economic reforms with a mounting stress on the urgent need for an 'efficient, honest and orderly administration of public affairs.' " They would seek to "keep up the very profitable balancing act whereby they have managed to present their party as a credible partner in a democratic and reform-minded government and to retain at the same time the loyalty of the Communist hardliners for whom any collaboration with 'bourgeois and pro-Western forces' is still anathema."

Of course, the success of such a balancing act would depend "not only on the PCI's own capabilities but on the performance of the other Italian parties, notably the CDs and the Socialists, as well as on the policies of the U.S. and of the USSR . . . and of the Vatican." The younger members of the PCI leadership, I went on, "may be sincerely determined to pursue 'a national road to Socialism,' but when some key turning point looms down that road they are still held back by a combination of persistent ideological commitment to Moscow, of awe before Soviet power and of fear of losing control over their own party and/or sparking a split in its ranks. Time and again, PCI spokesmen have criticized the treatment of dissidents in the Soviet Union and reaffirmed their determination to 'build Socialism in Italy according to a national model reflecting the country's own conditions and traditions' and therefore 'autonomous and quite different' from the pattern prevailing in the USSR and in other Communist-ruled countries. Together with the Yugoslavs, Romanians, and Spaniards, the Italian Communists have stoutly opposed Soviet efforts to turn a conference of European Communist parties into a tool for upholding Moscow's claim for supremacy over World Communism and the Brezhnev doctrine of 'limited sovereignty' " (intended to validate Soviet intervention in other 'Socialist' countries).

"PCI spokesmen, [however], have coupled their criticism of the treatment meted out to Soviet dissenters with strong attacks against the award of the Nobel Peace Prize to dissident physicist Andrei Sakharov and against Sakharov himself. More generally," I further pointed out, "the PCI leaders continue to react angrily whenever they detect what they call 'a revival of anti-Sovietism in Italy.' They also get very angry but fail to give a straight answer whenever the Italian Socialists point at the basic contradiction that features the current position of the PCI: it proclaims that the construction of Socialism in Italy and throughout Western Europe must be based on a multiparty system and on full respect of human liberties, but it continues to give solidarity and support to the Soviet Union and to the other Communist-dominated countries where a single party rules and human rights are so frequently and grievously violated. The PCI leaders further say that a policy of friendship toward both the USSR and the U.S. 'is in the interest of the Italian working class and of the nation as a whole.' But the main thrust of the Communist and Communist-influenced media continues to be slanted 90 percent in favor of the USSR and 90 percent against the U.S."

"We know very well," Macaluso told me as early as November 1975, "that no CD holding an important post in the party can afford to raise the issue of a PCI role, however indirect, in a governmental majority, at least until the next general election's returns are in." Luigi Granelli, then undersecretary for foreign affairs and a leading representative of the CD left-wingers, was equally explicit: "No turning point will be reached in the relations between our party and the PCI before the next general election. Most of us are opposed to any such early move; the Communist leaders don't want it either, while most Socialists do not know what they want but do not want either the 'historic compromise' or a Popular Front alliance with the PCI.''

When the PSI leadership brought about the collapse of the Moro government, which had been in office since the fall of 1974, I wrote (*Daily American*, January 20, 1976): ''Contrary to speculation by some foreign papers, the Communists will not be invited to join or to back officially the next government.''

''The PSI leaders,'' I further reported, ''charge that in recent months the outgoing Moro Cabinet ignored more and more their party's demands, while seeking 'under the table' accommodations with the Communists and favoring in effect the latter's 'creeping' progress toward a governmental alliance with the CDs to be achieved over the heads and at the expense of the Socialists. The CDs, in turn, have become increasingly impatient with their restless and demanding Socialist partners. Within the CD camp, moreover, there is growing confidence that the party would do well in a snap election.''

The speech delivered by Berlinguer at the 25th Congress of the Soviet Communist party in Moscow (February 27, 1976) was hailed by sizable sectors of the media in the United States (and in Western Europe) as evidence of the ''deeper break'' between the PCI and Moscow (*Washington Post*, February 28). For some ''experts'' on Soviet affairs like Victor Zorza, ''[The] dispute bids fair to produce an historic shift in the world's alignment of political forces, just as Moscow's quarrel with Peking did'' (*International Herald Tribune*, March 4). Thereupon, Italian correspondents claimed that ''even the sectors of American public opinion . . . more moderate and more sensitive to the official arguments of the White House'' felt that the stand taken by Berlinguer was ''more than a mere tactical maneuver but contains 'the seed of a schism' '' (Vittorio Zucconi in *La Stampa* of March 2, reporting on an editorial by *The Christian Science Monitor*).

Such comments, I wrote (*Daily American*, March 7), confirmed ''once again the tendency [of] substantial sectors of the U.S. and Western European press . . . to go overboard, one way or the other, where Italian affairs are concerned. . . . PCI leaders are the first to scoff at the notions of a break between their party and Moscow or of a broader 'schism' between a 'white Communism' allegedly emerging in Western Europe and a 'red Communism' still prevailing in the East.'

''According to prominent Italian Communists,'' I further reported, '' 'Berlinguer has not said anything that represents a substantial departure from the positions that our party has been taking publicly for quite some time. What's significant is that it was at a Soviet party congress that he said certain things and did not say other things.' When asked to elaborate, PCI spokesmen put it this way: 'Our views and those of the Soviet leaders continue to coincide only in foreign affairs, with special regard to the policy of international detente which the USSR pursues and which we heartily endorse and support. We disagree on ideology, or more exactly we disagree from the way the Soviets profess Marxism-Leninism; and we disagree when it comes to the kind of regime that's best for our respective countries. Our stand has been clearly outlined by Berlinguer's insistence upon our party's commitment to the construction of Socialism within a democratic and pluralistic framework as well as by the fact that he has pointedly refrained from endorsing the kind of regime they have in the Soviet Union.' ''

In two columns published in *Il Tempo* (February 20 and March 23, 1976), I recalled how the facts had ''demolished the maneuvers and ambiguities engineered last summer by some sectors of the Italian media with regard to the alleged 'openings' by Washington to the PCI. . . . Italian Communist representatives,'' I went on, ''are now telling me about their hopes that the American stand will be 'softened' if the Democrats gain control of the White House in the November elections. Actually there are not substantial differences in the attitude of the two great American parties concerning the prospect of a PCI entry into the government,'' I pointed out, quoting recent statements by Arthur Schlesinger and Zbigniew Brzezinski. ''If no definite guarantees are forthcoming that a government role for the Communists will not involve significant changes in Italian foreign policy nor departures from the democratic process nor a loosening of the economic ties with the West,'' I concluded, ''it is not foreseeable that for the PCI the American traffic light may shift from red to amber, let alone to green.''

16

U.S. Media Expect the PCI to Overtake the Christian Democrats

The unusual attention devoted to Italy by the major U.S. media in 1975–1976 reflected not only their interest for the PCI's growing electoral strength and prospects but their approach to domestic affairs in the wake of Watergate and in connection with the campaign for the White House.

Early in 1976, there were widespread reports about CIA plans to provide financial assistance to Italian political parties that opposed the Communist advance. The issue was given great prominence as part of the attacks against Republican groups and individuals still in power. In Italy, some dailies and quite a few magazines seized the opportunity to attribute to U.S. administrations, or at least to some of their "operative agencies," a heavy share of responsibility for the plots and other dramatic events featuring "the murky years from 1969 to 1974," so full of "massacres and attempted coups" (*Panorama*, February 18, 1976). *Stampa* and its evening edition *Stampa Sera* led the pack in playing up the information that emerged from congressional inquiries about U.S. subsidies provided in 1970 to prominent Italian politicians (notably Andreotti and Saragat, who promptly denied such reports) and about large sums handed over by ambassador Martin to general Vito Miceli, then head of the Military Intelligence Service (SID: Servizio Informazioni Difesa) and later elected to Parliament on the MSI ticket.

In the fall of 1975, two stories in the *New York Times* by Tom Wicker and Robert Kleinman pointed at an early and almost inevitable Communist participation in the national government. According to a *Washington Post* editorial, "it appears very possible that the Communists will get a bigger vote than the CDs (in the next parliamentary election" (January 11, 1976). Two weeks later, another *Washington Post* editorial stressed that the Communists had persuaded one-third of the Italians that they were "a legitimate and credible political group" when they claimed to believe in "democracy, pluralism and independence from the Soviet Union," but had not yet "persuaded the U.S. and so long as they will not succeed, instability will continue to rule in Italy."

Both *The Washington Star* and *Newsweek* voiced skepticism about the prospects of a "revitalization" of the CDs along the lines advocated by Kissinger. The weekly added that the risks involved in a continuation of the prevailing instability were no less serious than the risks of a PCI role in the government so insistently underscored by the secretary of state. For Joseph Harsch of *The Christian Science Monitor*, Washington's warnings, far from weakening the Communists' chances of success in Italy, had probably increased the likelihood that the CDs would ask the PCI to share in the burdens of governing the country. The coming to power of the Communists would not prove "necessarily fatal" for the West's interests. The PCI leaders were not all on the same positions; historic experience seemed to show that nationalism was currently a stronger force than ideology in Europe; furthermore, the fact that Communism had proved to be a tool of Soviet imperialism was "an accident of history" rather than the essential consequence of Communist doctrine.

In the latter part of March, the *New York Times* carried an interview with Berlinguer and several articles on the PCI that voiced opinions ranging from strong distrust to cautious favor with regard to recent statements by leaders of the Italian (and Spanish) Communist parties. In an editorial published on March 22, the paper sharply criticized the Ford administration's approach to the "Communist issue" in Italy and elsewhere in Western Europe as bound to backfire. A *Washington Post* editorial likewise stated: "Kissinger has been talking about Italy in extrordinary terms that may well give this country less influence than ever as time goes on" (April 14).

Five days later, another WP editorial said under the significant headline "Two elections": "This Summer, as the election campaign gathers momentum here, the Communists may well emerge as the dominant party in the Italian government. For the first time in a generation, the presidential candidates in this country will be confronted by a fundamentally new challenge to American policy toward Western Europe. It is the kind of large question that voters can reasonably use as a litmus test of candidates' good sense and their grasp of the job ahead. The rise of Communists to office in a major nation of Western Europe is obviously unwelcome. How ought the U.S. respond?"

The *Washington Post* editorial recalled that Ball, Warnke, and Brzezinski "generally agreed that the U.S. could not do much about events in Italy over the short term. Rather than squandering American influence on foredoomed attempts to tamper with internal Italian politics now, they suggested, it would be wise to reserve judgment and conserve influence until later. Mr. Kissinger, for his part, was unrepentant for his earlier characterization of a government including Communist as 'unacceptable.' He is addressing three quite different audiences. One audience is the American public. The inclination in this country at the moment is to leave the Italians' troubles to the Italians. But it would be highly uncautious to assume that this air of cool detachment would necessarily survive a dramatic surge to the left in Europe. A second audience is the Italian voters. A great many of them are genuinely reluctant to cast off their longstanding ties to the U.S. If Mr. Kissinger were now to soften his language regarding Communists in office, it might be interpreted in Italy as a sign that he was reconciled to them. That, in turn, would strengthen the Communists and make more likely the outcome that the administration must wish to avoid.

"Mr. Kissinger also has a third audience in mind: the other Western Europeans. . . . But with the notable exception of the West Germans, the Europeans do not seem to be taking any very active interest in Italian events. Perhaps it is the result of a long tradition of leaving these things to the Americans. Mr. Kissinger is trying to stir them into considering at least their own immediate interests."

Jim Hoagland, one of the *Washington Post* staffers assigned to other areas but occasionally dispatched to Rome to "discover Italy," contrasted the "slow motion collapse" of the incumbent Moro government and the widespread "gloom" about the economic conditions and prospects, with the Italian Communists' purposeful dynamism: "Working to establish their legitimacy as a political force domestically and abroad, the Communists have taken long strides in recent weeks out of the political ghetto in which pro-Western Italian politicians and the Ford administration have tried to confine them" (April 15 and 19).

In mid-June, Leslie Gelb of the *New York Times* quoted administration officials to the effect that Kissinger's stand and statements on Italy reflected the need to dispel any doubts about U.S. policy after leading CDs had called attention to press stories suggesting that Washington was reassessing its position on a government role for the PCI. In a special report on Italy (*International Herald Tribune*, May 3), British journalist Ninetta Jucker, longtime Rome correspondent of *The Economist*, wrote: "There is reason to expect that [in the forthcoming election] the Communists will outstrip the CDs as the biggest party in the country and that together the parties of the left—Communists, Socialist, and the neo-Trotskyist PDUP—will overshoot the dreaded 50 percent mark."

The cover story in *Time* of June 14 carried the headline, "Italy: The Red Threat" and Berlinguer's picture. In an interview, the PCI leader reasserted his program to forge a working cooperation with the CDs once they had lost votes to the left parties. Berlinguer insisted that what had happened in Czechoslovakia to Dubcek's Communism with a human face could not happen to the PCI: "In Italy, who would prevent us from following our own path? The frontiers are what they are." *Time* also listed the persistent doubts about the way the PCI would go after coming to power and specifically about its ability to withstand direct and indirect pressures from the Soviets.

According to Jim Hoagland (*Washington Post*, June 16), the historic compromise had "become a casualty in the strident Italian electoral campaign." Hoagland asserted that "senior [PCI] official Giorgio Napolitano confirmed (in an interview) that the decision to abandon the historic compromise plan had resulted partly from doubts within Communist ranks about the idea and partly from the sharp anti-Communist campaign that right-wing CDs have launched.'' These and other aspects of Hoagland dispatch turned out to be wholly off-the-mark (and it seems most unlikely that Napolitano, although known to favor a leftist alliance with the Socialists rather than a working collaboration with the CDs, would rule out the latter alternative especially before the electoral returns were in). Hoagland further quoted Napolitano as asserting that a Socialist party leader, later identified in the article as former budget minister Antonio Giolitti had ''relayed,'' following a recent visit to Washington, ''signals that the Ford administration could accept an important Communist role in determining government policy as long as it was kept informal and discreet.'' However, Napolitano ''said that the role reportedly suggested by Washington was no longer possible and that Communist participation either in the Cabinet or in a formal governing majority 'are the only necessary and correct possible results of the election.' ''

Sari Gilbert wrote in the same daily that ''Italian politicians seem to agree on only one point: 'After the vote, no government will be possible without the participation of the Socialist party.' '' Meg Greenfield, a columnist for the *Washington Post* and *Newsweek*, went to the other extreme. Whatever the election's outcome and its aftermath, ''it is beyond conception that anything like a vital non-Communist left will be seen in Italy in the near future,'' Greenfield wrote, thus joining the long list of U.S. observers whose predictions about Italy have been quickly and thoroughly disproved.

On June 19, a *Washington Post* editorial projected a patronizing insight into the subtleties of Italian politics: ''Perhaps, sitting innocently here in Washington you have had the impression that the Communists are trying to fight their way into office, and all the other parties are fighting to keep them out. But a closer look suggests that the truth might be precisely the opposite. . . . The country is still living substantially above its means, and it will have to go through a drop in its standard of living that will make its government of the moment very unpopular. That is why all the other parties are increasingly eager to have the Communists share the blame for whatever happens next. . . . But the Communists are wondering, with good reason, what benefit that arrangement offers to them.''

On the eve of the election, a *New York Times* editorial ruled out Communist gains so large as to allow them to leave the CDs far behind. Accordingly, the government most likely to emerge from the polls would be another edition of the center-left coalition or a minority CD administration; either, however, would be too weak to carry out the programs urgently required to curb inflation and promote economic recovery.

Before leaving Rome for one of my trips to the States, I touched home base, as usual, with leading representatives of the major parties. De Martino, Principe and other ranking Socialists confirmed that, as I had reported in the *Daily American* on January 9 and April 28, they had taken a ''calculated risk'' by precipitating the downfall of the Moro government early in the year. Their purpose was ''to 'smoke out' the PCI from the all-too-comfortable position where it can reap most of the benefits of staying in the opposition while worming its way into the governmental area; by contrast, the Socialists suffered "most of the disadvantages of being in the governmental majority and in the opposition."

In an interview to the *Daily American* (May 9), Giorgio Napolitano stressed the PCI's determination to keep Italy's international commitments: "We do not hold back in a drawer a ready made plan for a revision of NATO to be pulled out as soon as our party becomes a partner in a coalition government." The PCI expected to be "one component, however important, of a governmental alignment that should be possibly very broad." Accordingly, "the position of our party . . . may differ from the position of the government in which we would share. . . . For us, Italy's membership in NATO is, under present conditions . . . part of a political and military equilibrium in Europe that could not be broken unilaterally without endangering international detente. Even if the present division into two blocks should come to an end, the political, economic and cultural collaboration between Europe and the U.S., between Italy and the U.S., would continue to be an essential requirement. Obviously, the climate of such collaboration would depend, among other things, upon the attitude that the U.S. would take towards our participation in the government.

"We strongly criticize," Napolitano further told me, "some of the policies of the EEC, first of all the agricultural policies. In keeping with Italian obligations toward the Community, however, our economy must be open and it must be part, moreover, of a broader system of exchanges particularly with other capitalistic countries, first of all with the U.S. We can and want to give foreign capital industries the guarantee that they will be able to operate under the same rules in effect for Italian industries with regard to both freedom of initiative, which must be recognized, and to the compliance by private enterprise . . . with a programmed framework of development. When we talk about programming," the PCI leader spelled out, "we are not referring to binding guidelines of a bureaucratic nature intended to compel private enterprises to make specific decisions . . . but to a clear and correct use of the tools that are already available to the State for channeling the flow of investments—that is, incentives and easy term loans."

Napolitano hoped, of course, that as a result of the forthcoming general election the PCI would secure "a role in a governmental majority capable of coping on a new basis with the serious and urgent problems besetting Italy." This new majority should "include the major political forces in the country (the CDs, the Communists and the Socialists), but should not exclude other parties such as the Republicans who can play a significant role." Depending on circumstances, the PCI "may give outside support or participate in the government. . . . We do not make or forsake in advance any claim concerning the specific Cabinet posts that we might or might not get in the event that our entry into the government becomes possible."

Macaluso ruled out "significant changes in the political balance of power that had emerged from the 1975 vote," and therefore felt rather unlikely that "over the short term the PCI" could "become part of the government or even of a governmental majority."

In separate conversations Zaccagnini and Forlani told me that their party would do better than in 1975. Answering to a direct question, Zaccagnini stated flatly that, whatever the balance of power after the vote might be, his party would "refuse to conclude governmental agreements with the PCI." The CD secretary general authorized me to make this position known to administration and congressional circles in the United States.

During the meetings I had in Washington and in New York, I maintained that the PCI would not overtake the CDs at the polls and that the gap between the two parties, which had narrowed down to two percentage points in the 1975 elections, would widen again to about four percentage points, as it happened. But I expected the share of both CDs and Communists to be one or two points lower than it turned out to be. The leftist forces (PCI, PSI, and minor groups), I further felt and said, would not gather enough votes to reach a numerical majority. I also ruled out the possibility that the PCI would join the government in the relatively near future, that is before another general election took place, while it seemed possible, perhaps likely that the CDs would be forced to conclude with the Communists some sort of more or less formal or wide ranging accord. In my opinion, the PSI could still play an important and perhaps decisive role between CDs and Communists provided it freed itself from the "suicidal complex" reflected in the recently announced commitment not to participate in any government that would not enjoy at least the support of the PCI.

In my column in *Il Tempo* I reported on June 15, just a few days before the election took place, that such assessments and forecasts were increasingly shared by the best informed observers in the United States. At the State Department, the officials more directly involved in Italian affairs, such as Bronson McKinley and Jim Swihart, felt pretty confident that the CDs would maintain and probably strengthen their position as the number one party and that no combination of leftist forces could win a majority of the seats in the new Parliament. Less clear-cut views were expressed by the Italian "experts" of other government agencies and of such private institutions as the Carnegie Endowment for International Peace and the Council on Foreign Relations.

Shortly before I interviewed him in Washington, Senator Edward W. Brooke (R-Massachusetts) had introduced a resolution on U.S.–Italian relations which was approved unanimously by both the Senate and the House of Representatives. The resolution spelled out the continued "friendly interest" of the American people and government "for democracy and the democratic institutions in Italy" and called on Italy's European friends to join in extending to her economic and financial assistance and thus help the Italian people and government to regain confidence and attain full prosperity.

The resolution was warmly received by President Ford who seized the opportunity to confirm his "serious concern" about the dangers that the prospect of Communist participation in the government of a NATO country would involve for "the whole system of Western cooperation."

In the interview (*Il Tempo*, June 16, 1976), Senator Brooke voiced his "sincere hope" that in the impending election "Italian voters will continue to give their support to those parties which, while not devoid of major faults, continue to exhibit a firm commitment to the principles characteristic of open societies." The United States, he went on, "has a vital stake in the preservation of a strong democratic Italy able to operate as an effective member of the Atlantic alliance. Communist participation in the Italian government would seriously erode Italy's capacity to so function within the alliance structure."

Like other Americans who followed developments in Italy closely, I further reported, Brooke attributed the increase of the Communist vote largely to "the protest and the frustrations of the Italian electorate over the disunity of the democratic parties, the constant reminders of mismanagement of the economy, and evidence of widespread corruption." But to give the Communists a role in the national government would be "to use an Italian expression, a medicine worse than the illness."

Brooke listed item by item the reasons for questioning both "the will and the ability" of the PCI to translate into facts its "proclaimed policy of independence from Moscow," of loyal acceptance of the Atlantic Alliance and of "commitment to Western-style democracy."

Senator Brooke, "like all the other representatives of U.S. political circles I have talked with recently in Washington and elsewhere," I concluded, "emphasizes that 'decisions on the historic compromise and any other political shift in Italy are, of course, the perogative of the Italian people.' Yet, the Senator is convinced that, since such decisions will have a dramatic impact upon the policies and actions of Italy's friends and allies, expressions of deep concern and anxiety by them are fully justified."

Senator Edward M. Kennedy's positions and ideas had been described and would continue to be described by some sectors of the Italian media in a way calculated to suggest that he was favorable to some sort of "opening" to the PCI. But in an interview (*Il Tempo*, June 3), he voiced his "hopeful confidence" that the Italians would "keep displaying concretely their attachment to the values and methods of democracy" and would "strive to consolidate its foundations by undertaking needed and timely reforms in the economic and social fields and in the relations between the state and the citizen." Interest in and vigorous support for such reforms, Kennedy pointed out, "is a tradition in our family."

The next U.S. administration ("and it will be a Democratic Administration"), Kennedy went on, "will upgrade again the ties with our European allies as well as with Japan." The senator concluded: "The U.S. can and must help the Italians and other Western Europeans through economic support and by showing a basic confidence in their good sense and deep devotion to democratic values."

As it was to happen on similar occasions in the next several years, the interview was followed by a private chat. The senator peppered me with questions about Italian conditions and prospects. He recalled that his brothers John and Robert had looked with warm sympathy to the coming to power in Italy of a coalition committed to economic and social reforms. The senator made specific reference to the "battle" that, as Robert Kennedy had told me eight years before, was fought in Washington itself between those who favored and those who opposed the formation of a center-left government in Rome.

An interview with Jimmy Carter, who was about to clinch the Democratic nomination, was organized by Dick Gardner. He had been one of the first "eggheads" to realize that Carter could make it to the White House and by early 1976, he had joined his friend Brzezinski as one of the future president's closest foreign policy advisers. It was agreed that Dick would communicate to me Carter's final OK on the interview in time for it to appear before the Italian general election scheduled for June 20–21.

On June 7, Dick called me on the phone from New York. Carter had okayed the text and suggested including, "possibly right at the beginning," a statement branding as "totally false" the reports that he would look favorably on a Communist participation in the Italian government.

The presidential candidate stressed his "strong" conviction that "every people should be free to decide its future without foreign interference." He recalled, at the same time, that, speaking in November 1975 to the National Democratic Issues Conference in Louisville, Kentucky, he had said: "I would certainly hate to see Italy go Communist."

In reply to another question, Carter told me, "I have noted with interest that the leaders of the Italian Communist party have publicly pledged themselves to autonomy from Moscow, friendship with the U.S., constructive participation in NATO and the European community, and respect for Italy's democratic political process. In my opinion, the attitude of the U.S. government toward the Italian Communist party, whether in or out of power, should be influenced by the degree to which their pledges are translated into concrete action."

Like other leading U.S. politicians whom I interviewed through the years, Carter answered questions about aspects and prospects of broad international significance: "The commitments of the U.S. to the security of Western Europe," he said, "are an integral part of our own security." He rejected "emphatically" the notion that "the U.S. should pursue bilateral relations with one or two European powers in place of partnership with a uniting European community." The Democratic presidential candidate further said: "We should make it clear that detente requires that the Soviets, as well as the U.S., refrain from irresponsible intervention in other countries. Russians and Cubans have no more business in Angola than we have. The core of detente is the reduction in arms. We should negotiate to reduce the present SALT ceilings on offensive weapons before both sides start a new arms race. . . . The policy of East-West detente is under attack today because of the way it was sold to the American people and because of the way it has been exploited by the Soviet Union."

Mr. Carter concluded: "We must repeat and make the Soviets understand that detente, if it is to last, cannot ignore the legitimate aspirations of other people nor the human rights of the citizens of every country, be they the blacks in Rhodesia, the Asians in Uganda or the Jews in the Soviet Union. The benefits of detente must accrue to both sides or they are worthless. The mutual advantage must be evident, or the American people will not support the policy."

The Carter interview appeared in *Il Tempo* on June 10. The next day another Rome daily, *Paese Sera*, referred to it in terms typical of the techniques of manipulation used so freely and so often with regard to the U.S. stand on the "Communist question." *Paese Sera* refrained from mentioning Carter's flat denial of the reports that attributed to him an inclination to favor a government role for the PCI. Other statements by Carter were distorted by adding to them, in quotes, words that he had not uttered but were clearly aimed at conveying the impression that the Democratic presidential candidate was well disposed toward, or at least less opposed than was actually the case, to the Italian Communists' aspirations. To crown it all, *Paese Sera's* headline ("The Americans do not believe in the Communist danger") sought to suggest just the opposite of what actually emerged from my interviews with Mr. Carter and other U.S. political leaders.

My interview with Carter was evidently called to Berlinguer's attention and in late June he sent word that he would like to see me again. In reply to his questions, I told the PCI leader that Carter's election was "quite likely" and gave my reasons for believing that it would not alter the substance of the U.S. approach to the "Communist question" in Italy or elsewhere in Western Europe. "There will probably be changes of methods and style, such as a liberalization' of visas for Communist representatives who want to visit the U.S." (Gardner had hinted that much in one of our conversations back in May.) "But you delude yourselves and will be in for big disappointments if you expect substantial shifts in the fundamental assessment of your party's stance and policies and therefore in the negative attitude of the U.S. toward your participation in the Italian government."

Berlinguer said that his party's approach to foreign issues had undergone several changes, with special reference to the issues mentioned by Carter in the interview to *Il Tempo*. The PCI leader recalled what he had told *Corriere della Sera* on the eve of the June 20 elections, namely after that interview had been published, and in particular his statement that it would be impossible for the Soviet Union to hinder or condition the development of "a national road to Socialism" in a country which, like Italy, belonged to NATO and not to the Warsaw Pact.

Such statements, I answered, must have been duly noted by Carter and by his advisers, "but had not been sufficient to make them change their minds." As soon as the electoral returns in Italy had been known, Carter had voiced "relief" because the PCI had not won a plurality of the votes (the statement was made on June 23, after a speech to the Foreign Policy Association in New York).

"This does not mean," I told Berlinguer, "that there are prejudices strong enough to prevent Carter and his advisers from viewing and assessing objectively any evidence of an effective and substantial revision of the PCI's traditional positions. Such evidence, however, must include not only statements but concrete actions, as Carter has emphasized in the interview he gave me."

Berlinguer listened with interest. I had the impression, however, that the interest was coupled with a strong dose of skepticism. It was a reflection, I felt, of his inclination to trust more other reports, from Italian and possibly from some American sources which, as already pointed out, gave a reading of Carter's views and purposes much more in line with the PCI leader's wishful thinking. Both before and after Carter's election to the presidency and following Gardner's appointment as ambassador to Rome, talks with ranking Italian Communists produced additional evidence that the delusions about Carter's policies toward the PCI (and Eurocommunism in general) were indeed widespread and persistent among the party leaders.

Such delusions were fed by those Italian media which kept trying to sell the "myth" of a Carter administration that, at the very least, would not be hostile to a government role for the PCI. The purpose to disinform the Italians was only too apparent in the cuts made in an interview with Carter broadcast on July 14 by TG–2, the news program of the Second Channel of the state-owned radio and television network. After saying that a PCI role in the government would not necessarily be a catastrophe, Carter added: "This would not be my preference," a sentence that was deleted. When asked whether a European Communist party would actually wish its country to remain in NATO, Carter answered: "I think that it has been good electoral tactics to maintain this kind of thing. But I'm not sure that, if the Communists should gain power in one of the major West European countries, they will want to stay in NATO *other than perhaps to disrupt some of its objectives*" (emphasis supplied on the words that were likewise deleted from the broadcast of the interview). The original text of the interview was rebroadcast in its entirety three months later after these cuts were called to public attention by the U.S. correspondent of *Corriere della Sera*, Ugo Stille.

On the basis of the first information received from friends in Washington, I reported in *Il Tempo* as early as June 25 that the outcome of the Italian general election had been in line with the forecasts prevailing in the best informed U.S. political circles "on two key points:" Not only had the PCI not overtaken the CDs but the gap between the two parties had widened again, and the polls had not produced "a majority for a leftist alignment. "Observers in Washington," I went on, "had not expected, on the other hand, that both CDs and Communists would gain so many votes . . . to bring about a heavy shift of the overall balance of power to the detriment of the intermediate parties. . . . The sizable gains scored by Christian Democracy at the expense of the minor center parties . . . have allowed it to bring back up to a reassuring dimension its lead over the PCI, but have also narrowed its margin for maneuver . . . substantial weakening of the lay alignment'' had come about just when its ability to play a significant role ''appeared the more . . . desirable following the shift, however belated, in the stand of the Liberal party'' (in February Malagodi had been replaced by Valerio Zanone at the helm of the PLI, thus signaling the end of the party's long-standing opposition to the center-left approach). The PSI had paid heavily at the polls for failing to underline its main differences from the PCI, namely ''a basic independence from Moscow and an undeniable experience and daily practice of the democratic method within the party as well as in its relations with the other political groups. Obviously these differences tend to disappear or fade away when the PSI conditions its policies and specifically its participation in the government to Communist support'' (for that government). It is rather natural that, under such circumstances, quite a few potential Socialist voters should feel that they might just as well cast their ballots for the PCI as it actually happened.''

In summing up my assessment of the electoral returns, I quoted the old U.S. saying about ''not throwing away the baby together with the (more or less) dirty bathwater. . . . The majority of the Italian voters, however dissatisfied with the long CD tenure of power, had realized that a drastic 'downgrading' of the party would produce the coming to power of the PCI under conditions making for its hegemony.''

In my talks with representatives of the U.S. Embassy and of several Italian parties, I voiced the conviction that a PCI entry into the government would have to wait ''at least for the outcome of another general election.'' I also recalled in *Il Tempo* (July 12) some of my earlier columns in the same daily in which I had argued, on the strength of a documented survey of the most significant elections held in postwar Italy, that the behavior of the Italian voter ''deserved positive rather than negative marks especially in view of the many and deep traumas he had been exposed to.'' For instance, it was incorrect and unhelpful to brand, as some well-known journalists did, most ''Communist voters as underdeveloped people who voted that way because the husband or the wife had cuckholded them or a traffic policeman had given them a ticket,'' instead of recognizing that ''the PCI does exploit problems but does not invent them.'' (The specific reference was to an article by Indro Montanelli in *Corriere della Sera*, a paper he quit some time later because it had turned to the left.)

After the June election, I further noted, ''the contemptuous comments'' about Italian voters had ''mostly come from leftwingers who had predicted most arrogantly that the CDs would . . . be overtaken by the Communists, and that the leftist alignment would win at least 50 percent of the votes.'' When the returns disavowed their forecasts, ''the spokesmen and political 'experts' of the libertarian left have promptly unloaded their disappointment and frustration on the voters (just as their colleagues on the center-right had done on earlier occasions). The Italians have been accused of being 'dogmatic and totalitarian' and Italy has been branded as 'a crazy nation, anomalous and perverse where two parties can win, at the same time, the election.' . . . Those who cast ballots for the CD party have been labeled, at best, as conservatives . . . concerned only about keeping intact their own specific interests . . . or more often as tax evaders, parasites . . . all of them people who vote to sustain the mismanagement of public affairs' and to incite 'thieves and swindlers' to steal more and more.''

17

A Secret Memo: The Carter Administration's Policy toward Italy

In an interview to the West German daily, *Die Zeit*, released by the State Department on June 30, 1976, Kissinger stated: "[In Italy] there is now almost exactly the situation that produced the election except that now most of the opposition forces have moved toward the Communists and the anti-Communist forces have moved to slightly lesser extent toward the Christian Democrats. . . . I think the dilemma remains exactly the same. Major reforms are necessary in Italy. If they are carried forward with the Communists, will it set a precedent for many other situations? On the other hand, can the non-Communist forces create sufficient cohesion to carry out the necessary reform programs? We of course hope that the democratic forces will form a government without Communist participation to carry out the necessary reforms."

Referring to reports on the summit held in Puerto Rico by the major industrial democracies, President Ford said on July 19, that the United States did not intend to "dictate" any [government] formula to the Italians. At the same time, he recalled having stated on various occasions that his administration would be "much troubled" by a Communist participation in the Italian government because, among other reasons, it would have a regrettable impact on NATO.

Leslie H. Gelb reported in the *New York Times* that West German Chancellor Helmut Schmidt had "disclosed" that his country, the United States, France, and Britain had agreed "to bar further loans to Italy if Communists held Cabinet posts in a new government" (*International Herald Tribune*, July 19). Other U.S. newsmen played up the issue not only to denounce any such understanding but to exploit it within the framework of the ongoing presidential campaign. For instance, *New York Times* columnist Anthony Lewis wrote that, while Kissinger had tried to minimize his differences from Carter in foreign affairs, the approach to Communist presence in West European governments was an issue on which a Carter presidency might make a clear-cut difference. Lewis quoted the recent interview that the Democratic nominee had given to the Italian TG–2, of course in the . . . strongly edited version which had been broadcast on July 14. U.S. newspapers also gave unusual prominence to the negative reactions by Italian media to reports of the decision to bar aid to Italy in the event the PCI gained a government role (a comment by Michele Tito printed on the front page of *Corriere della Sera* denounced "the Puerto Rico blackmail" (July 20).

During the second TV debate between Ford and Carter (October 6), the president was asked what he would do if "the Communists threatened to come to power by peaceful means" in a country like Italy. Ford charged that the Democratic nominee had "indicated he would look with sympathy to a Communist government in NATO" and added: "I think that would destroy the integrity and strength of NATO, and I am totally opposed to it." Carter shot back that Ford's statement was "not true. I have never advocated a Communist government for Italy. That would obviously be a ridiculous thing to do for anyone who wanted to be president of this country."

During an interview published in the November issue of *Playboy*, Carter was asked: "What if the Communists actually become a key part of the Italian government?"

"I think," Carter answered, "it would be a mechanism for subversion of the strength of NATO and the cohesiveness that ought to bind European countries together. The proper posture was the one taken by Helmut Schmidt, who said that German aid to Italy would be endangered."

To the next question, "Don't you think that constitutes a form of intervention in the democratic processes of another nation?", the Democratic nominee replied: "No, I don't. I think that when the democratic nations of the world express themselves frankly and forcefully, and openly, that's a proper exertion of influence. We did the same thing in Portugal."

At the same time, Carter pointed out: "In my speeches, I've made it clear that as far as Communist leaders in such countries as Italy, France, and Portugal are concerned, I would not want to close the doors of communication, consultation, and friendship to them. That could be an almost automatic forcing of the Communist leaders into the Soviet sphere of influence. . . . I think the best way to minimize totalitarian influence within the governments of Europe is to make sure the democratic forces perform properly. The major shift toward the Communists in Italy was in the local elections, when the Christian Democrats destroyed their reputation by graft and corruption."

Right after his election, Carter told the Italian weekly magazine *Gioia*: "We expect great things from the Italian government. . . . We are allies and in the past thirty years the United States has assisted Italy with some 7 billion dollars. Now the time has come to ask something from Italy. What? The political loyalty that keeps together two allied countries. . . . Italians cannot expect continuing aid from the United States toward their development, and at the same time turn the peninsula's political boat to the left." The new U.S. president was also quoted as saying that the United States should maintain "an open relationship" with Italy even if the Rome government were to turn Communist: "We cannot and do not want to tell Italians," he went on, "how they should vote and what party they should bring into government. But we can remind Italians that alliance means also related views both in the field of international politics and in what concerns the future of our two nations" (November 15).

Brzezinski, slated to become national security adviser to the new president, told the French newspaper *Quotidien de Paris* that, while the new U.S. administration would not favor the participation of Communists in West European governments, "it has been perfectly ridiculous to agree to talk to Brezhnev and refuse any contact with Berlinguer." Communist participation in West European governments would at least have the virtue of "linking them to the democratic system, separating them from their Stalinist and Leninist roots" (November 4).

In early January, Carter was asked during an interview with *Time* reporters: "How much does it matter to the United States [if the Communists should] join the Italian government in 1977 and the French government in 1978?"

"It concerns me very much," the new president replied, "depending on the degree of Communist participation and the loss of the respect and confidence of the citizens of those nations in the democratic processes that we prefer over Communism." Another factor would be "the degree of allegiance shown by Communist leaders toward the Soviet Union and away from our own nation and from NATO."

In the fall 1976 issue of *Dissent*, a member of the magazine's editorial board, Erazim Kohak, noted that "in practice, a grand coalition of Italy's two big parties is deeply problematic. The potential senior partner, the *Democrazia Cristiana*, emerged from the elections with some requisite gains. Those gains, however, were won at the expense of the splinter parties of the center, caused less by the CD's intrinsic appeal than by the repugnance that most Italians feel for the Communist alternative." However, "the obvious partners, the various democratic socialist parties, cannot provide" the support that "even a thoroughly rejuvenated *Democrazia Cristiana* would still need [to govern:] Today Italy's Socialist parties simply are not a significant political force and, barring a concerted effort on the part of other European Social Democratic parties, analogous to that mounted in Portugal, are unlikely to become so." While favorably impressed by Berlinguer's recent statements, Kohak maintained that "unfortunately, the party he heads is far from democratic and . . . would lose much of its relevance if it were." Kohak recalled that in the interview to *Corriere della Sera*, published on the eve of the Italian elections of June 1976, Berlinguer "even admitted the need for the NATO shield to protect his democratic Communism against the fate of Dubcek"; but the editor of his own party's daily, *l'Unità*, censored out that statement when reprinting the interview."

In the Winter 1977 issue of the same magazine, Sidney Tarrow, professor at Cornell, argued instead that "whatever the short-range prospects, the long-range ones are for the PCI to build up its current control of local and regional governments into sufficient national power to join a coalition government within five years. . . . The Italian Communist party,'' Tarrow concluded with a remarkable lack of academic restraint, ''has now reached so great a level of both internal and programmatic evolution (not to mention its increasingly distant relations with the Soviet Union) that advocates of its further democratization are either foolish or hypocritical to argue for its continued isolation.''

Richard Pipes, professor at Harvard and later a White House consultant during the Reagan presidency, wondered whether Italian, French, and other Western Communist leaders would be ''willing and able . . . having joined their countries' administrations . . . to conduct (or support) a democratic internal policy . . . and a foreign policy that does not simply execute Moscow's instructions'' (Fall 1976 issue of *Orbis*). According to Pipes, ''even with the best intentions,'' the Communists would hardly ''find it possible to combine the centralization (nationalization) of the economy with democratic practices,'' as proved by ''the longterm experience of all countries with centralized, state-run economies . . . should the Western communists miraculously succeed,'' Pipes went on, ''in constructing 'socialism with a human face' . . . the Soviet Union would [be] . . . most likely [to] conspire with hard-line, Moscow-oriented elements in the Western Communist parties to remove their rivals.'' And Pipes recalled that ''from the Soviet point of view any country with a Communist government (or even a coalition government in which the Communist party plays a prominent part) may come within the purview of the Brezhnev Doctrine.''

Writing in the November 1976 issue of *Commentary*, Michael Ledeen, formerly Rome correspondent for *The New Republic* and a consultant of the State Department and of the National Security Council during the Reagan administration, stated that ''far too much'' had been made ''of European Communism, particularly the . . . PCI, as if it were a major schism in the world Communist movement and consequently a threat to the hegemony of the Soviet Union.'' Ledeen quoted from the PCI press and from talks with its leaders to bolster the contention that the party was still wedded to ''opposition to American interests and support for Soviet ones'' even in ''areas where one would expect a Socialist party 'with a human face' to be explicitly anti-Soviet.'' According to Ledeen, ''those who are deeply concerned with the future of Italy and the rationality of American foreign policy have an obligation to call the PCI to task, and to continue to challenge it. *The New York Times*, for instance, recently suggested that the Italians should be left alone to settle their own affairs, without the warnings of foreign leaders. . . . Are the Europeans (and the Americans) whose interests would in fact be threatened by PCI entry into the Italian government not permitted to voice their concern? And if they have decided not to send aid to such a government, should the Italians not be so informed, so that their electoral decision will be based on a thorough understanding of the consequences? . . . If the PCI wishes to function within the context of the Atlantic alliance and a more united Europe,'' Ledeen concluded, ''let it spell out for itself and its supporters the reasons for its allegiance.''

In some statements to *La Repubblica* (November 28), James Reston pointed out "Not even Carter could afford to tell the Americans, look, the Italian Communists with Togliatti and Berlinguer have learned the lesson and have become good boys. He could never persuade the Congress. . . . You cannot expect American public opinion to learn that in Italy there is a government with the Communists able to exert their own authority in NATO affairs, and expect that the ties with the West remain the same."

Republican Jacob Javits of New York, an influential member of the Senate Foreign Relations Committee, told me in an interview (*Il Tempo*, December 9, 1976): "The presence of Communists in the government of a NATO country would pose the problem of their access to the military secrets of the Alliance. If such a presence takes on a significant importance, we should not share military secrets with the country involved because our own security might be endangered."

"What would be the attitude of the Congress on giving economic aid to Italy, if it should be confronted with a PCI participation in the government?"

"The Congress," Javits replied, "would reach a decision on the basis of a combination of considerations: humanitarian considerations, friendship for the Italian people, political considerations (such as the behavior of the Italian Communists) and considerations of a historic nature, related to developments in the other countries where Communist parties have come to power." To a question about "Eurocommunism," Javits replied: "The peoples of Western Europe have seen at work the parties which call themselves Eurocommunists; they know what they are and know how they are viewed in the U.S."

The gist of a *New York Times* editorial on the Italian election was summed up in its headline: "Reprieve in Italy" (June 22).

A *Washington Post* editorial conceded that the Communist "presence in a government poses certain dangers to both Italian democracy and the vitality of European economic and defense institutions of which Italy is a part." But "the central feature of the Italian political scene . . . is that . . . unless the Communists are given some degree of responsibility and—yes—authority, the Italian political and economic scene is likely to become even more chaotic than it is now. . . . In fact, it is sometimes said that the so-called 'historic compromise' between the Communists and the government has already been made—but by telephone. . . . The Christian Democrats . . . have been tacitly working for months with the (equally tacit) cooperation of the Communists. . . . The question now is one of forms."

In Italy, *Corriere della Sera* summarized these and other comments by foreign media under the headline: "Is it still possible to govern Italy without the PCI?" (June 24).

On the same day, Joseph Kraft's column in the *Washington Post* (and in many other papers) minimized the "celebrated comeback of the CDs" and played up the "size of the Communist victory" at the polls which made the PCI "virtually sure to enter the government, sooner or later." The Communists had readied a program to redress the Italian economy which was "appealing and sensible. If the CDs accept it, the Communists will almost surely enter power to help in the execution. If it is refused, the Communists will be in position to win the next election."

In the early fall, some dispatches from Rome to the major U.S. dailies spotlighted the "disputes" and "divisions" within the PCI over the support given the ruling CDs by abstaining on crucial votes in Parliament (Alvin Shuster in the *New York Times* and Sari Gilbert in the *Washington Post*, October 20). But other reports and comments in the same papers, quoted much more generously by Communist and pro-Communist media in Italy, played up both the growing influence of the PCI on the policies and decisions of the Andreotti Cabinet and the moderation displayed by the party leaders in making use of that influence and advancing toward a full-fledged government role. In early November, Shuster stressed that the Communists were consulted more and more frequently by the CD government not only on economic matters but on appointments of police and military personnel.

J. W. Anderson, a member of the *Washington Post* editorial page staff, quoted at length Giorgio Napolitano to underline that the Communists were sincerely backing a policy of austerity and that their views were remarkably similar to those of the CDs (and of many businessmen) "about what went wrong with the economy. . . . Neither of the big parties sees much hope for a stable coalition with the frustrated and quarrelsome minor parties and have decided that they are going to have to work with each other." It was "quite possible" that their cooperation would become closer and that in the next elections "both of the big parties will gain support simultaneously—at the expense of the little ones."

Anderson also reported that Guido Carli, former governor of the Bank of Italy and currently president of Confindustria, "Italy's highly influential chamber of commerce and industry . . . thinks that it's necessary now to bring the Communists into greater participation in running Italy.

"Americans—particularly Secretary of State Henry Kissinger," Anderson concluded, "see the Communists' rising power as a sign of dangerous instability in Italy. But . . . a great many Italians—including the country's most eminent business spokesman—think that the reality is exactly the opposite. According to Carli, stability for Italy now requires a larger role for the Communist party" (October 25 and November 5).

Again in the *Washington Post* Jim Hoagland reported from Rome that the views of some Communist and Catholic spokesmen "point to a kind of inevitability in the [PCI] headquarters' becoming the Vatican of Eurocommunism, which in its simplest terms might be described as a decision to seduce and surround the 'working class enemies' Marx and Lenin wanted to destroy outright." Like other U.S. newsmen and "experts," Hoagland mentioned "the beginning of serious debate within the Eurocommunist movement about a European schism with the Kremlin that would be the most important since the split between Moscow and Peking" (September 20).

In *l'Unità* newsmen and other "intellectuals," returning from visits to the United States, conveyed the feeling that not only U.S. "experts" of Italian affairs favored broad "openings" to the PCI, but several officials in many branches and agencies of the U.S. administration saw a Communist participation in the government as a "way out" of the crisis besetting Italy. According to those reports, moreover, "nobody but a few fools believed anymore that bombings and *golpes* could come from the Communists, because everybody knows that in the last few years the American government and the CIA have been behind the *coups d'Etat* in all countries" (articles by Siegmund Ginzberg and Alberto Monroy, October 25 and June 21).

A survey prepared by the CIA in view of the June elections in Italy was played up by *Panorama*, *Europeo* and *La Repubblica* several months later as maintaining that Communist participation in the Italian government was not only "likely" but "desirable" in order to give more "credibility" and "stability" to the government itself. Other "secret" documents reportedly prepared by the State Department and by a congressional committee were likewise used by the same Italian papers to claim that "almost certainly" the new Carter administration would "not close the door to the PCI" and that actually Washington was "thinking about the 'historic compromise.' "

According to *l'Unità*, Peter Lange said during a visit to Italy shortly after Carter's election that the new president's stand on the "Communist question" was *"possibilista"* and that a U.S. policy of "closure to the PCI" would have disastrous consequences in any case: if pursued before the Communist entry into the government, it would contribute to "a rapid disgregation of Italian society," and if adopted after such an entry "it would involve the risk of *coups* very dangerous for the Atlantic alliance itself" (November 28).

In several columns in *Il Tempo* (January 26, August 23, September 13 and 17, 1976) I outlined the potential significance and likely prospects of an "historic compromise" viewed against the background of traditional features and major developments of Italian politics.

One of these features had long been known as *"trasformismo"* and was in effect a technique to entice, pressure, or bribe "individual members of Parliament or groups of them" into "transforming" themselves from opponents into supporters of the government. "Co-optation" was another and more significant phenomenon rooted in a basic fact that I had spotlighted in a 1962 article in *The New Republic*: "In Italy, the government and its majority have been always and clearly to the right of the electorate" and therefore were frequently impelled to widen or to reconstruct and "stabilize" their majority in Parliament by calling in political groups representing left-of-center sectors of the electorate. Back in 1852, several years prior to Italian unification, Count Camillo Benso di Cavour, prime minister of the Kingdom of Sardinia, persuaded some progressive-minded forces in Parliament to join the governmental alignment, isolating the conservative groups. Longtime premier Giovanni Giolitti had sought, before World War I, to "constitutionalize" and "include into the system" sizable forces

belonging to the opposition and notably to the Socialist party. This party was
already the main political representative of those "popular classes on the up-
swing" which Giolitti referred to in February 1901 when he said: "The friends
of our institutions have a foremost duty—to persuade these classes and to persuade them by deeds, that they can hope [to obtain] much more from the present
institutions than from dreams of the future."

Despite the "concurring mistakes of the most short-sighted conservatives and
of maximalist Socialists, and Giolitti himself," I continued, "the next few years
represented, to the extent that implementation of social reforms prevailed upon
the lures of 'trasformismo,' a time of economic growth and political evolution."

In the early 1960s, when the prospects of a governmental role for the Socialists
were quickening, CD leader Aldo Moro "was quoted as saying: 'If we can't get
them one by one, we must get them by the package.' What was envisaged by
Moro was an updated co-optation, a deal whereby opposition leaders (Socialist
in the specific case) would take sizable sectors of their party's electorate into
the governmental fold in return for some Cabinet posts and the pledge to carry
out social, economic, and administrative reforms which would meet at least some
of the requests and assuage the protests of that electorate." The coming to power
of a center-left alignment, I stressed, was "a typical operation of co-optation"
intended to correct at least in part "the deepening gap between the governmental
lineup and the electoral lineup. It involved only a partial correction because,
even after the inclusion of the PSI and the exclusion of the Liberal party, the
ruling coalition shut out 25 percent of the voters on the left and less than 15
percent on the right. The gap, moreover, quickly widened again as a result of
the Socialist split on the left (which gave birth to the PSIUP, closely allied with
the Communists), while the CDs were mostly intent on recouping ground on the
right." As a result, the center-left ended up by being mostly "the centrism of
the Sixties." The PSI not only failed to gain ground at the expense of the
Communists but suffered further losses to their benefit.

Yet, I went on, the latest developments had not borne out, either, the forecasts
of those observers who had decreed that "the last bus for the Socialists would
go by" with the 1976 general election: "While the returns have represented a
defeat for the PSI, [it] still maintains not only its prerogatives as the only middle-
sized party in Italy, but its ability to influence to a decisive extent the developments of national politics." The key in that connection was a concrete reaffirmation of the "Socialist autonomy . . . which must be displayed and underlined above all with regard to the PCI. . . . Hence, the positive significance of
recent statements by the new PSI secretary general, Bettino Craxi, who said,
'The Communists talk about a united Europe which should be neither anti-
American nor anti-Soviet. For us, a united Europe must be an ally of the United
States and a friend of the Soviet Union.' "

At the same time, the projected "historic compromise" could not be viewed
as "an updated edition of the co-optations and even less of *trasformismo*." To
begin with, I pointed out, "the group which was a candidate for co-optation

(namely the PCI) was almost as strong as the biggest government force (the CDs) and presumably more solid thanks to its 'centralized discipline.' The result, moreover, would not be to correct the traditional imbalance represented by governmental majorities located to the right of the electorate, but rather to create an imbalance in the opposite direction: a governmental coalition based on an accord between Communists and CDs would leave out only some radical fringes on the left while excluding on the right much larger forces likely to be further strengthened by the defections and/or splits that would take place within the CD camp much sooner and to a more significant degree than within the Communist ranks." Last but not least, the PCI's ideology and goals in domestic and foreign affairs "put it much farther away from the traditional government forces than was the case for other opposition groups at the time they were co-opted by those forces."

Right after Carter's election to the presidency, I noted that his statements about the Communist parties of Western Europe had been distorted, mutilated, or misinterpreted: "Yet, their basic inspiration was quite clear . . . a definite opposition to the coming to power of the Communists in Italy (or elsewhere). This opposition is reinforced, if need be, by the clearly anti-Communist feelings that prevail among Americans of Italian origin as well as among the leaders of the major labor unions." At the same time, "there is the conviction that it would be unwise and counter-productive to keep up an 'iron curtain' blocking any communication, any contact between Washington and the PCI. This said, however, it will be up to the Communists to persuade the administration and public opinion in America that they intend to pursue a policy of genuine independence from Moscow and to contribute both to the rehabilitation of the Italian economy and to the strengthening of the country's international commitments and democratic institutions. This has been the suggestion made in a very recent interview by Brzezinski when he referred to the possibility that the Communist parties of Western Europe 'detach themselves from their Stalinist and Leninist roots.' But if those parties (or substantial parts of them) should move that far, would it be still possible to call them Communists, in the effective and traditional sense?" (*Il Tempo*, November 8).

When I told archbishop Benelli, early in 1977, why the Carter administration's approach to the PCI was not and could not be substantially different from its predecessors,' he was apparently surprised to the point of exclaiming: "But then it is not true that Carter intends to 'open' to the Communists!" The archbishop labeled Eurocommunism a "purely tactical" affair. He further compared Berlinguer to "an ambassador who has a certain degree of autonomy in assessing local conditions and the tactical moves most appropriate to them, but always within an overall framework which remains basically the same." According to the archbishop, Andreotti was performing "a miracle by managing to remain standing on a tightrope." Benelli added, however, a perceptive comment on the relationship between the premier and the PCI: "If you wear a dress for too long, you won't be able to discard it easily whenever you might want to."

The appointment of Richard Gardner as ambassador to Italy was greeted by *La Repubblica* with a typically misleading headline: "Carter's ambassador: the PCI might be okay with us" (January 9, 1977). In some statements made to the newscast of the Italian TV's Second Channel, the new ambassador had reaffirmed, instead, that the aims of U.S. policy toward Italy would "remain the same" under the Carter administration, that is, "a democratic Italy able to provide freedom, social justice, and prosperity," even though "our methods in pursuing such aims might change." Paraphrasing the interview that Carter had given me seven months earlier, Gardner said that the U.S. approach to West European Communist parties "should be determined by the degree of actual commitment displayed by them with regard to their independence from the Soviet Union, to democracy as well as to cooperation with the European community and with the Atlantic alliance." The new ambassador told *La Stampa* on the same day: "The term 'Eurocommunism' is far from precise. There is in Europe a variety of Communist parties operating in different countries and each of them has its own characteristics which differ from each other in ways sometimes quite significant." The U.S. government would "take into account not only the words but the actions of the leaders of these different parties." When asked specifically about the yardsticks whereby "independence" from Moscow would be gauged, the new ambassador made a point that had been mentioned frequently in our talks: "If the paper of one of those Communist parties repeats parrot-like the arguments used by *Pravda* the day before . . . if you see that 'the line' is faithfully toed on the most significant [international] questions, it is not hard to conclude that the party involved is not autonomous." After reaffirming his "absolute" confidence in the Italians' ability to "outlive the crisis," Gardner said that "the Carter administration intends to help Italy:" (1) "by giving new impulse to the U.S. economy and thus communicate to the Italian economy the benefits of "our restored health"; (2) "by extending financial assistance in various forms" and by avoiding "unilateral decisions about NATO, such as withdrawals of forces . . . " (3) by refraining from "interfering in Italian domestic affairs."

While Gardner's appointment was processed all the way to its confirmation by the Senate, the prospects and guidelines of his "mission to Rome" were discussed in frequent meetings involving Brzezinski, Gardner himself, the assistant secretary for European Affairs, Arthur Hartman, and the head of the Italian desk, Bronson McKinley. The result was a memorandum dated March 16 and submitted to President Carter by Secretary of State Cyrus Vance and by Treasury Secretary W. Michael Blumenthal. I was the first outsider to have access to the document which bears the handwritten approval as well as some comments by President Carter. Its most significant parts read as follows: "We need an explicit policy framework within which to make a number of pending decisions of fundamental importance about Italy. We will soon need to comment publicly and privately on our policy toward Italian Communism. . . . With 34 percent of the vote, the PCI knows it can achieve power only if the CDs feel they have no alternative to coalition with the Communists. Aware that Western attitudes are one factor in the CDs' resistance, the Communists will try to exploit our position for their own purpose. Ambiguous signals from Washington would do much to discourage those struggling to revitalize the democratic parties, especially the Christian Democrats, bringing to the fore those who would seek refuge in an 'historic compromise' with the Communists.''

On the other hand, "previous policies" followed by Washington "have been criticized as anachronistic, as projecting a negative image of the United States, as failing to offer encouragement to democratic evolution of the PCI, and as depriving us of the insight into party trends and objectives that would be obtained through greater contact with them. Our attitudes toward the Italian Communists will be examined closely throughout Europe, and especially in France and Spain where the local Communist parties have sought with some success to benefit from the more moderate image projected by their Italian comrades. In neither country would the Socialists or other parties of the democratic left or center wish the inference to be drawn that we no longer regard the West European Communist parties as a serious problem, albeit one for the Europeans themselves to resolve. . . .

"Our policy should be aimed at preserving Italy's democratic system and its Western role. We need to approach this objective without, on one hand, appearing to interfere in Italy's domestic politics or, on the other, giving the impression that we favor accommodation with the Communists or are indifferent to Italy's political choices. . . . This would make any contradictions or incompatibility with Western interests the result of Communist action and not of attempts by us to thwart or punish them for being Communists.

"The principles of U.S. policy (which would apply as well to the issues addressed here) should be as follows:

1. The United States attaches great importance to Italy and intends to make every effort to strengthen our traditionally close ties.

2. We will not interfere in Italy's domestic affairs by such actions as dictating to Italians how they should vote, seeking to manipulate political events in Italy, or financing Italian political parties or personalities.

3. We prefer that our friends and allies be governed by political parties with strong democratic traditions, values, and practices. Naturally, we are concerned about the willingness and ability of Communist parties, which do not share these traditions, values, and practices, to cooperate with us and other members of the Western community on fundamental political, economic, and security issues. We would hope to work constructively with any Italian government that is truly independent of external dictation, that respects basic human rights, and that proves to be a constructive partner in the European and Atlantic communities.''

These specific moves were recommended:

Find an early opportunity to make public at a high level the three principles outlined above as a framework for future relations with Italy. In this regard, the U.S. ambassador should not be the first or principal proponent of a change in U.S. policies. To do so would complicate his role in Rome for the next four years;

[E]xpand slowly and carefully embassy Rome's contacts with Communist Party officials and relax remaining inhibitions on contacts with Communists who hold official governmental positions;

[P]ending general revision of our policy with regard to visa ineligibility of Communist Party members, liberalize our case-by-case handling of visa requests, while trying to make clear that greater flexibility does not imply approval.

A final paragraph read: "We believe our private views in exchanges with other governments should be consistent with those publicly expressed. We may, of course, wish to emphasize and elaborate our views on the risks of Communist participation in Italian or other Western governments more in private than in public. On visas, as long as our decisions are on a case-by-case basis we recognize that our decisions will unfortunately continue to imply political judgments and hence will carry undesirable signals to Italy."

The guidelines, the motivations, and in many cases the wording itself of this document were to be reflected in the actual policies pursued by the United States for a long time to come and specifically in the declaration issued by the State Department on January 12, 1978, as well as in the statements made by top U.S. political representatives during both the Carter and the Reagan administrations.

Gardner had suggested that a statement summarizing the key points of the memorandum be issued on the day he was scheduled to be sworn in as ambassador to Italy (March 18). A few days earlier, however, Vance told Gardner that changes in timing and procedures were required by circumstances related to France. In January, Socialist leader François Mitterrand had asked the Secretary of State to refrain from public statements which might be read as an interference in French domestic affairs intended to hinder the coming to power of the leftist parties. Any such interference would prevent him from placing his Communist allies in a condition of acute inferiority and thus maintaining and even improving the U.S. alliance relationship between France and the United States. Meanwhile, the time was getting close for the election of the mayor of Paris, a test that had taken on great political significance because of the duel between the candidate of the center-right, Jacques Chirac, and the candidate of the leftist coalition. Moreover, there was a growing expectation that the 1978 parliamentary elections would pave the way for a leftist government with the participation of the Communists but with a Socialist majority. Under the circumstances, Vance decided to refrain from airing publicly the guidelines adopted by the administration on Italy and to issue a statement taking into primary consideration the very different conditions and prospects prevailing in France. It is hard to say whether the Secretary of State was aware of the opposite danger, that is to say of the impact in Italy of such a statement which was issued on April 6 and read as follows: "We believe the position of a Communist party in a particular country is a matter to be decided by the people and the government of the country concerned. We do not propose to involve ourselves in the processes by which they reach their decisions on it. This does not mean that out attitude is one of indifference. We attach great importance to our ability to work with the countries of Western Europe on matters of vital interest. Our ability to do so could be impaired if these governments came to be dominated by political parties whose particular traditions, values, and practices are alien to the fundamental democratic principles and common interests on which our relations with Western Europe are based.''

In this document the concept of ''preference'' for governments made up of forces securely democratic and committed to an active solidarity with NATO, so clearly affirmed in the March 14 memo on Italy, was implicit rather than explicit. Most important, the reference to governments ''dominated'' by Communists (although substantially limited to the case of France, at least for anybody looking at the factual context in which the April 6 statement was issued) could lend itself to misleading readings by those who, in good or bad faith, might want to extend the document's scope and wording to different situations, like Italy's.

La Repubblica promptly headlined: ''The U.S. veto to a government with the Communists has collapsed'' (April 7) and ''Washington confirms the turn toward the Communists'' (April 8). The gist of the dispatches by correspondent Rodolfo Brancoli was less farfetched. Yet, Brancoli quoted Lange and Tarrow who read the April 6 statement as a favorable appraisal of the ''slow process of integration into the system on the part of the Communist parties.'' Similar readings were given by other journalists who likewise had already distinguished themselves for distorted interpretations of U.S. policies. Ricciardetto (a pen name of Augusto Guerriero, a former foreign policy editorialist for *Corriere della Sera*), wrote in his weekly column in *Epoca* that there was ''an abyss'' between the stand of the Ford-Kissinger administration and the position reflected in the April 6 statement by Carter's State Department. This statement meant that ''if the French or the Italian Communists were to become 'dominant' in the national government, the U.S. would not remain 'indifferent.' It emerges, therefore, that the attitude of the U.S. would be 'indifferent' if the PCI were to participate in the government but did not 'dominate' it.''

The major U.S. papers gave more cautious interpretations although they often ignored the differences between the Italian and the French situations. A dispatch from Washington to *The Los Angeles Times* (published in the *International Herald Tribune* on April 8) pointed at ''an apparent softening of U.S. hostility toward Communist parties in Italy and France. . . . Carter administration officials at first denied they were making a policy shift, asserting that U.S. opposition to any Communist participation in the West European Cabinet remains unchanged. But later that signal was switched, with officials suggesting that the intention instead was to leave the issue shrouded in artful ambiguity.''

According to a *New York Times* editorial (April 19) there might be some Communist Ministers in Italy or France ''within a year.'' In Italy, prospects were more worrisome because the troubles besetting the CDs might well bring about a split in their ranks and allow the PCI to become the strongest party. "The Americans have a right to assert their preferences" and to help European voters and politicians to "understand beforehand the strains that would inevitably develop in the Atlantic Alliance and in the EEC if they turned to the Communists for leadership."

A column by Evans and Novak, published in the *Washington Post* on March 31, denounced strongly "the Carter Administration's uncertainty about what to do about ever more powerful Communist parties in Western Europe," and the behavior attributed to ambassador Gardner. According to Evans and Novak, "eleventh-hour intervention by . . . Brzezinski blocked issuance of a Presidential statement . . . that would have been interpreted as breaking previous hard-line hostility to the Italian Communist party." Brzezinski's move, made with the agreement of Secretary of State Vance, "saved Italy's ruling CDs from embarrassment. But there has since been irritation in Rome over what the government there feels is oversolicitous treatment of the Communists and Italian left by ambassador Gardner." Quoting as their sources, "old line diplomats, including top hands in the [State Department] Bureau of European Affairs," the two columnists claimed that the presidential "draft" was an "amalgam" of two contrasting themes and viewpoints: "First (satisfying the old-timers) that the U.S. prefers democratically elected governments that govern democratically without foreign ideological alliances (meaning Moscow) and that the U.S. is concerned about the Italian Communist Party's upholding democratic values as promised. Second (satisfying the Carter new-comers), that the U.S. will never again intrude in Italy's internal political affairs (as in past CIA contributions to the CDs)."

After giving such a distorted and confused reconstruction of the March 14 memorandum, Evans and Novak asserted that, when word about the document "leaked in Rome, Prime Minister Giulio Andreotti's embattled CD government was distressed. The Italian government felt that any statement that does not put the U.S. squarely against the Italian Communist party would immediately be interpreted by Italian voters as a switch away from Henry Kissinger's hard line, raising Communist prestige."

It was a rather peculiar assertion about the reaction of a government largely dependent on the benevolent neutrality of the PCI and led by a Christian Democrat who was inclined, if anything, to develop the working agreement with the Communists into something more stable and far-reaching. Much the same may be said about the two columnists' assertion that the Andreotti government "soon found further cause for concern when Gardner . . . within hours of presenting his credentials to President Giovanni Leone, paid a call on Pietro Ingrao, a leading member of the Communist Party presidium who is president of the Chamber of Deputies."

About the call on Ingrao, which carried out the guidelines of the March 14 memo on relations with Communists holding official positions in Italy, Gardner told me on March 22, several days before the Evans and Novak column was printed: "I wanted to be done as quickly as possible with the visits required by protocol and to do so along the lines that had been discussed and agreed upon before I left Washington for Rome. And while I spent 50 minutes with the president of the Senate, Fanfani, I was careful to limit to 25 minutes my meeting with Ingrao." On the same occasion, the ambassador told me again that, for the time being at least, contacts between embassy officials and PCI representatives would be kept "at a low to medium level" and in any case could not and should not be read as "signals." The PCI was "changing but so far the changes have not gone far enough to reassure us about the party's nature and goals. From where we stand, therefore, a Communist participation in the government would not be helpful but actually harmful."

Despite the distortions and inaccuracies it contained (or because of them), the Evans and Novak column was widely quoted by Italian media. A front page headline in *Corriere della Sera* claimed that Washington had "censored" a speech by Gardner because it was "too pro-Communist." Premier Andreotti's office, on the other hand, denounced as baseless everything that Evans and Novak had attributed to the Italian government. Gardner called "false and wholly unfounded" the reports about his actions and intentions. Yet, some political circles in Rome, including quite a few CDs, continued to spread the word that Gardner's mission was to favor the entry of the "Eurocommunist" parties in the government of their countries and that the ambassador had been seen having dinner with ranking PCI representatives in this or that Rome restaurant. A few weeks later, the weekly *Panorama* devoted an article by its parliamentary correspondent Guido Quaranta to the "new attitude of the Democratic administration toward the PCI. . . . In the offices of the PCI Directorate they say that the new American President has made 'a happy choice' when he picked Gardner as his ambassador to Italy" (May 3).

The statement issued by the State Department on April 6 had come as an' unpleasant surprise for Gardner. In a dispatch addressed personally to Vance and Brzezinski, the ambassador stressed that the statement was "softer in two respects than the formulation agreed on in the presidential memorandum (of March 14): (1) Presidential memorandum explicitly expresses our concern about willingness and ability of Communist parties to cooperate with us on ground that they do not share our traditions, values, and practices. Last sentence in Department's Eurocommunism statement, by contrast, does not mention Communist parties explicitly so that PCI can argue they are not covered . . . (2) Presidential memorandum says we prefer that our allies 'be governed' by non-Communist democratic forces, while Department's Eurocommunism statement expresses concern only if their governments come to be 'dominated' by non-democratic parties. This is being interpreted by some here to suggest we would have no problem with governments in which PCI would participate but not dominate. Of course, I recognize that Department statement dealt with Euro-communism generally, while Presidential memorandum dealt only with Italy, and therefore some difference in wording was necessary." Gardner further pointed out that the Evans and Novak column, which was "widely quoted here," sought "to portray me as seeking to issue a 'soft line' statement on PCI—view repeated by Strobe Talbott in current international edition of *Time*—which as you know is exact opposite of truth."

In a subsequent phone conversation with Brzezinski, the ambassador, as he told me at the time, insisted that it was urgent for the U.S. administration to take a public stand, at the highest possible level, designed to clarify in unequivocal terms its position on the "Eurocommunist issue."

Shortly afterwards, Carter did so himself in an interview to four Western European dailies (*The Times*, *Le Monde*, *Die Welt* and *La Stampa*) which was recorded on April 25 and published on May 3. Said the president: "The first premise on which we function is that the European citizens are perfectly capable of making their own decisions about political matters through the free election process. . . . Secondly, we prefer that the governments involved continue to be democratic and that no totalitarian elements become either influential or dominant." Mr. Carter also noted: "Within my memory, this is the first time that all the NATO countries have been democracies. And I think this is a very good evolution that we have already witnessed.

"We certainly prefer," the president concluded, "that the democratic parties prevail in the future. And we can encourage that process, not by interfering in electoral procedures, but making the system work ourselves."

On the day of Gardner's arrival in Rome, I wrote in a column in *Il Tempo* (March 21) that the Foreign Relations Committee of the U.S. Senate had asked the ambassador to report, within two months from his arrival in Rome, on the most significant aspects of the Italian situation, including the "Communist issue." In this connection, I went on, special importance should be attributed to the remarks and recommendations by two ranking members of the Committee who had visited Italy recently.

Senator Javits concluded his report to the Committee by stating: "I believe that we should maintain our posture of unelaborated opposition to Communist participation in Italy's government. I think that such a posture is best calculated to keeping the threshold high in Italy of resistance to a Communist accession to power and is best suited also to require the Communists to come to terms with democratic forces if they do come to power."

Democratic Senator Claiborne Pell stressed the need to make clear that "we have no intention of interfering in Italy's internal affairs." At the same time, "we should not give the impression that the U.S. is indifferent to the prospect of Communist participation in the Italian government: that would help the Communists."

In my column I further recalled that Carter had stated time and again his clear-cut preference for an "Italy where the Communists did *not* share in the government. . . . American representatives continue to be fully aware of the need to avoid that political forces traditionally friendly toward the U.S. might feel abandoned or that the Communists might feel to have done already enough for Washington to deem advisable, or possibly even desirable, their participation in the government.

"Just because he is a sincere friend of Italy and fully convinced of the importance that a democratic and prosperous Italy has and will continue to have for the U.S.," I concluded, "the new ambassador would not fail to speak up in clear terms and to advise Washington to speak up as well when it should seem not only advisable to give a hand to the Italian friends but to point out to them the dangers involved in moving down a street bound to jeopardize Italy's relations with America and the future itself of the country."

18

What Is Eurocommunism?

The day after his arrival in Rome, my wife and I had dinner with Gardner who told her, "If today I'm here as ambassador, it is also your husband's fault!" It was a quip inspired by our long friendship and by the many talks that Dick and I had had over the years and were to become more frequent during his mission in Rome.

"The declaration issued by the State Department on April 6," I wrote in *Il Tempo* of April 27, 1977, "concerns not only the PCI but the other Eurocommunist parties, the French first of all. This explains why the document makes a particularly negative reference to the possibility that Communist parties take a 'dominant' role in Western Europe governments. The use of a more shaded term (such as 'significant') would have sounded like a heavy-handed warning about the consequences of a victory [in the forthcoming French elections] of a leftist coalition in which the Socialists are much stronger than the Communists.

"Three fundamental concepts or 'red threads,' " I went on, could be pin-pointed in the Carter administration's approach to the situation in Italy: (1) the importance of Italy for the U.S., and for the West as a whole, makes it a basic American interest to have Italian problems tackled and solved within a democratic, Atlantic, and European framework; (2) the U.S. does not want to force on others its will or its political economic and social system; it feels that it is up to the Italians to decide about their future without foreign interferences; (3) at the same time, the U.S. cannot give up and does not want to give up its right to "express its values and act accordingly," as Gardner has reaffirmed in his [recent] speech at the NATO War College in Rome.

Some weeks later I had in Washington several talks which bore out another remark made in the same column: "A very wide area of consensus has developed around the approach worked out by the Carter administration. It includes the best known 'eggheads' who have returned to government jobs, influential members of the Senate and of the House, leading career diplomats like the Undersecretary for European Affairs, Arthur Hartman, and Italian experts of the departments and agencies interested in the issue.'' The only ''marginal'' divergencies ''come on one hand from those who would have preferred an 'opening' to the PCI because they feel that the party is moving on positions acceptable from the American viewpoint or because they expect it to join soon the government anyway,'' and on the other from those ''who keep advocating a most rigid stand with regard to the Italian Communists and to the 'Eurocommunists' in general. The representatives of the first group can be found in some academic circles, and the second group mostly in some sectors of public opinion and of the Congress.''

This second group could be expected to exert a less marginal influence mainly because it included the top leadership of U.S. labor. In an interview (*Il Tempo*, June 13, 1977), Lane Kirkland, secretary-treasurer and later on president of AFL–CIO told me, ''We cannot trust professional Communists to move away from a world movement to which they have remained linked through all the experiences and traumas of recent decades.'' That's why ''the unions, the Congress, and American public opinion in general would react with the deepest concern to a Communist participation in the Italian government. We respect the right of other countries to make mistakes. But our concern and our reactions would stem from the very consequences that a PCI entry into the government would have for the future of the democratic process in Italy. The Communists have never shown any allegiance to that process. And even if they should be content to start with a few Cabinet posts, perhaps not very important, this would only be the beginning of the *salami* process, as it has happened in other countries.''

Senator Pell told me: ''The current concerns of many Americans over Italy's future are fed mostly by the PCI's electoral gains and by the dangers that may stem from them for the Italians' freedom and for our interests in Italy. . . . If Italy should leave NATO or ask, as France did in the 1960s, that American forces be withdrawn from her territory, the alliance might easily degenerate, for all practical purposes, into a series of bilateral accords based on West Germany, Great Britain and the Benelux countries.'' And if the PCI managed to secure a governmental role, ''this might bring about the crumbling of the resistance to a collaboration with the Communists in other Western European nations, such as France, Spain, and Portugal.''

In reply to another question, the senator said, ''The PCI is carrying out a well rounded campaign to show that its current policies meet with approval or at least do not arouse strong objections abroad. Therefore, any statement by politicians or other American personalities that convey the impression that the U.S. can cooperate with an Italian government including the Communists, or that the U.S. is indifferent to what happens in Italian politics, helps the PCI to increase its 'acceptability' as a full-fledged participant in the government. If the PCI is actually turning into a democratic party, this evolution must not be blocked by taking it into the government and thus signalling that such evolution has been already sufficiently completed. . . . If the Italian Communist party, on the other hand, has actually undergone a change in a democratic sense as a result of its long-standing confinement in the opposition, perhaps it will be possible to push it further in that direction while continuing to keep it into the opposition. . . . The U.S.,'' Pell went on "must refrain from engaging in a strident (and counter-productive) Communist rhetoric. In fact, wider and more frequent contacts between our officials in Rome and PCI representatives would be useful. These contacts, however, should develop only gradually and their rhythm should remain, if anything, a notch below rather than above those between the non-Communist Italian forces and the PCI.''

Pell outlined "there are two main scenarios" which might help the PCI to win a share of power at the national level: "The PCI might be invited in by a CD party pushed to desperation by its inability to cope with political violence and with a further deterioration of economic conditions. . . . Alternatively, the PCI might overtake the CDs in the next general election and make it numerically difficult, if not altogether impossible, to form a government without the Communists.'' Neither scenario, however, was "inevitable or even necessarily likely.'' In fact, "the strength and appeal of the PCI might have already peaked.'' A CD "revival'' could not be ruled out, either, although it would require far-reaching "reforms'' both of the party itself and of its methods of governing. Last but not least, the senator was still entertaining "some cautious hopes'' about a "renewed collaboration'' between the CDs and the Socialists "whose position might become stronger and more balanced if they could draw closer again to Social Democratic forces and policies'' (*Il Tempo*, June 20).

Republican senator Charles McMathias told me: "In recent years, the leaders of the 'EuroCommunist' parties have . . . begun to say that they want to keep their countries in NATO, retain private enterprise and be independent from Moscow. These changes are noted here in the U.S. but we also remember that in the past the same men and their parties were saying quite different things. It does not mean that we question their conversion but it is a fact that must not be forgotten.''

"What if the PCI participates in the government?''

"Such an event,'' the senator replied, "would raise many problems. The decisions must be made by the Italians themselves. However, to the extent that our country is associated with Italy in many ways, economic and military, serious difficulties would arise not only for the administration but for American public opinion which would be very reluctant to accept as an ordinary development such a change in a country that we feel so close. . . . Italy has been a very reliable ally in NATO. The facilities made available by the Italians are very useful not only to the U.S. but for the alliance as a whole. . . . Here in America there is also a strong interest in the future of democratic institutions as well as in the economic welfare of Italy'' (*Il Tempo*, June 27).

Democratic representative Robert Giaimo, one of the most respected congressmen of Italian origin, told me: "The Communist parties operating in Western Europe have undertaken an earnest attempt to disassociate themselves from the rigid structures of a monolithic, Soviet-dominated and strongly orthodox international Communist movement. But we must also ask ourselves how sincere this effort is. In a way, moreover, it poses a more formidable threat to Western democracy. It is easier to contest and fight against a rigid, Stalinist brand of Communism. . . . The threat is particularly serious in Italy, where the local brand of Communism is more innovator than elsewhere in Western Europe. . . . We must help the Italians, financially and trade-wise," Giaimo concluded, "in view of Italy's economic and strategic importance and of the strong ties between Italians and Americans" (*Il Tempo*, July 27).

In Washington I also met again with Averell Harriman, who displayed his usual lively interest in Italian affairs. I talked with Robert Hunter who had left his job as foreign adviser to senator Kennedy to join the National Security Council, with Tom Trimarco and with Ray Cline, a top fellow of Georgetown University's Center for Strategic and International Studies whom I had met several years earlier when he was director of the State Department's Office for Intelligence and Research.

Upon my return to Italy, I had an interview with Macaluso who had come back himself from a visit to Moscow as a member of a PCI delegation (*Il Tempo*, July 8).

Macaluso made clear that he agreed with the sharp attacks unleashed by Moscow against the Spanish Communist leader, Santiago Carrillo. Macaluso also stressed in more explicit terms than Berlinguer had done recently that for the PCI leaders Soviet society was, "despite some contradictions," a "Socialist society" whereas Carrillo had in practice denied it.

"We have always drawn a clear distinction," Macaluso recalled, "between the Soviet interventions in Hungary and in Czechoslovakia, among other things, because in 1956 the cold war was still on, while in 1968 detente was under way. . . . Our deep dissent [from the intervention in Czechoslovakia] stems from the fact that developments there took into account the actual framework in which Czechoslovakia operates [that is, the Warsaw Pact], while seeking at the same time to make the country's structures responsive to the real requirements of the national society."

I asked Macaluso whether his statements should be read as a confirmation that, in the event of a serious international crisis, the Italian Communist leaders would choose, as their natural side, to line up alongside the Soviet Union, in spite of their acceptance of Italy's membership in NATO. "We are convinced to begin with," he replied "that no act of aggression will come from Moscow. On the other hand, we respect the alliances concluded by our own country, provided, of course, that these are given a defensive meaning and thrust. In any case, and I am making this statement only within the framework of a purely theoretical hypothesis, we will oppose an aggression from whatever quarter it may come.''

"You maintain,'' I reminded Macaluso, "that you want Western Europe to be independent, a friend of the Soviet Union as much as of the U.S. This by itself would involve a major shift in the international balance of power to the benefit of the USSR since today most of the West European countries are allied with the U.S. But even such a shift does not seem to be enough for the Soviets who have denounced Carrillo, among other things, because he too has come out for a Western Europe that should be independent, a 'third force.' ''

"In our opinion,'' Macaluso retorted, "such a shift would not be possible nor justified in the interest of detente and peace. . . . Frankly, I do not understand why the Soviet leaders do not realize that the policy followed by us (and by other West European Communist parties) leads toward overcoming and liquidating the 'blocs' and requires a European initiative to that effect, leads therefore toward a goal that they themselves have claimed to be pursuing. In any case, we have told Moscow again and again that we'll keep promoting this policy of ours.''

According to Macaluso, the difference between the Carter administration and the Nixon-Kissinger administration on the "Communist issue'' in Western Europe were "not only a matter of style and tactics. We are convinced that Carter and his advisors will seek to avoid Communist participation in the governments of Italy or France. It seems to me, however, that they take this possibility into account more than their predecessors did. They do not like, for sure, but would tolerate, without traumatic reactions, to have Communists play a role in the government of those nations.''

This last sentence by Macaluso was reported, without mentioning how and where it had been said, in a front page article printed in *Corriere della Sera* over the byline of a well-known journalist, Gianfranco Piazzesi (July 12). In the article, Carter's approach to the "Communist issue'' in Western Europe was described as "more vague than ambiguous'' thanks to a manipulation of documents and statements which, as I noted in *Il Tempo* of July 19, recalled "the persistent efforts carried out by Italian media since the spring of 1976 to 'disinform' the Italians'' on the matter. Piazzesi ignored, I pointed out, "a concept that runs like a red thread'' through the statements made by the American President, that is, the resolute preference for governments made up of parties strongly democratic and proved friends of the U.S. . . . American experts feel that the westernization of the PCI has come to a halt and may be moving backwards. . . . They have noted, for instance, that the PCI leaders were inclined to 'take their distances' from Carrillo and to circumscribe the scope and significance of 'Eurocommunism' even before the recent clash between the Spanish Communist leader and the Soviet chieftains. . . . A recent survey of the media controlled or influenced by the PCI, moreover, highlighted how their attitude remains by and large sharply anti-American and substantially pro-Soviet.'' (The survey was carried out on instructions from Gardner and updated in the following years.) "The ambassador has experienced personally how and to what extent old prejudices and interpretations about the U.S. and its policies, are still alive and evident among the Communist representatives in local administrations with whom he had recent contacts dictated by protocol (the latest instance has been in Naples)." My source was Gardner himself and the episodes concerned mostly hints and references made, in line with the disinformation campaigns organized by the Soviets, "to the role of the CIA and other U.S. agencies in the murder of President Kennedy or in terrorist activities in Italy."

In the same article in *Il Tempo*, I also pointed out that the PCI daily *l'Unità* had accused Piazzesi of having left the door open to doubts about "the American readiness to accept Communist participation in the government not only as inevitable but indispensable for the future and effectiveness of democratic institutions in Italy!" (July 12). The writer, Carlo Maria Santoro (a historian and former diplomat who at the time was one of the PCI "experts" on the United States), gave a carefully purged version of Carter's interview to four West European dailies, and went on: "In Washington, they know well that no democratic government can be installed in Italy without the PCI's direct or indirect responsibility."

How did major U.S. media react when so many of the sensational developments they had so freely forecast, first of all the overtaking of the CDs by the Communists in the June 1976 election, failed to materialize, while others remained in a state of suspended animation (like the PCI's entry into the government), even after the party had given its abstention to the all Christian Democratic government headed by Andreotti?

Sulzberger continued to hail Berlinguer as "the Italian Communist boss who makes a fetish of turning his back on the Kremlin," while he "climbs the power ladder rung by rung." In some articles devoted to Italy in February 1977, the *New York Times* columnist quoted at length, without voicing doubts or reservations, statements by ranking Italian Communists which already sounded questionable at best and would soon prove wholly unfounded. According to Sergio Segre, for instance, the PCI was convinced that the Carter administration was about to take a different and much less unfavorable attitude toward Italian Communism.

A few weeks later, Claire Sterling wrote in the *Washington Post* (April 25): "There is a strong chance that before this month is out, the Italian Communists will end their nine-month trial run and start moving into the government. Talks have already started with the ruling CDs for a concerted program, formal inclusion of the Communists in a government majority and Communist-sponsored 'technicians' in the Cabinet."

According to Sterling, if anyone had "caused to think twice before getting in much deeper, it is the Communists."

Sari Gilbert quoted the well-known Italian political analyst Alberto Ronchey to bolster another contention that was likewise to be soon disproved by events:

" 'The Socialists will probably end up being absorbed by the Communists. The trend toward bipolarism is irreversible in an Italy that is, after all, a frontier country between East and West.' " (*Washington Post*, April 4).

In some columns written following a short visit to Italy, Evans and Novak ignored the latest statements by ambassador Gardner, and by Carter himself, which contradicted directly the criticism the two columnists had recently voiced concerning the administration's policies on Italy.

The illusion that "here is a Communist party with 'a human face,' " Evans and Novak noted on the other hand, "vanishes the instant Italian party operatives reveal their doctrine on life-and-death questions of world politics. . . . The party's real view of the U.S.–Soviet struggle, offered with refreshing candor, is chillingly anti-American.''

The two columnists quoted liberally from their conversations with Sergio Segre and Ugo Pecchioli, another prominent PCI spokesman. Pecchioli "came close to equating U.S. membership in NATO with imperialism. 'Certainly, the American pressure has conditioned the development of the countries of Western Europe,' he told us. 'The prevalence of American interests, American armaments— NATO uses American arms not European. And we have learned about the CIA operations from hearings in your Congress. . . . There is no element of Soviet imperialism in Eastern Europe,' Pecchioli further said.''

The drive by the PCI leadership toward a coalition government with the CDs was hampered, according to Evans and Novak, not only by the opposition from the party's "working class base" and from "university students (radicalized by the incredibly inept education policies of the CDs)," but by the change in the international climate featured by "the descent of detente into a twilight zone. . . . It would be a mistake," the two columnists warned, "to make too much of still slender evidence of trouble in Western Europe's most successful Communist party, but the agony of pleasing two souls at the same time could mark a turning point. One soul is rooted in Moscow, the other is striving for credibility within the free political traditions of the West . . . The PCI's future, however, may depend not so much on resolving its split personality, however debilitating, as on the economic and political chaos of Western Europe—particularly France and Italy herself" (*Washington Post*, May 7).

Evans and Novak continued: "To begin to set the Italian house in order" and "rejuvenating" their own party at the same time, "the center-right CDs" had "one year . . . until after the crucial French election . . . when the Italian Communists hope to be fortified by a Communist-Socialist victory putting the French party into the government in Paris. . . . No betting man," Evans and Novak concluded, "would wager much on the success of the CDs, despite promising infusion of young political talent now coming into the party." Should they fail, "the 'historic compromise' might become inevitable. . . . That would end the Western alliance in its present form or even, as some astute politicians believe and Communists hope, mark the beginning of the end of the present American role in Europe" (May 11).

19

Many Italians Ignore Washington's Preference for Exclusion of Communists from Government

One of the main topics of an interview with Giorgio Napolitano (*Il Tempo*, March 30, 1977), was Eurocommunism, a label, I pointed out, for several tendencies and ferments that appeared anyway to lose momentum and significance. In the meeting held earlier that month in Madrid, the top Italian, French, and Spanish Communist leaders had refrained from taking a stand on the burning issue of dissent in the USSR and in Eastern Europe, I reminded Napolitano, and added: "You keep affirming the indissoluble tie between Socialism and liberty, but you refuse to condemn as non-Socialist the regimes that do not respect fundamental human and civil liberties."

Retorted Napolitano: "Should we pronounce this or that country not to be Socialist, we would ignore a basic requirement, that is to understand and explore in depth both the specific features and the general positions that have led, from a Socialist-type transformation of relations in the field of production, to the construction of the kind of political regimes that exist today in the Soviet Union and in Eastern Europe and that we criticize because of their illiberal features."

I called to Napolitano's attention, as I had recently done with other ranking Italian Communists, the contradiction between their proclaimed wish to have Italy entertain relations of alliance with the United States and friendly ties with the USSR, and the line followed by the media controlled or influenced by the Communists: "The way they put it," I said, "it appears that the USSR is a very attractive lady with just some small warts here and there, while America is a bad woman, ugly and pockmarked, who from time to time may be granted a chance of redeeming herself."

Napolitano smiled, shook his head and said: "Our stand and our choices are clear and consistent when it comes to Italy's international position. Possibly, our reactions to specific events, as they emerge from our press, may not always reflect these choices with all the required consistency.''

In my next column in *Il Tempo* (April 4), I wrote, ''The 'Westernization' of the 'Eurocommunist' parties appears to be a process that is still far from reaching the point of no return. The PCI leaders state that they do not oppose Italy's membership in the Atlantic alliance and even that the 'NATO umbrella' helps their autonomy from Moscow. But the Communist press does not miss any opportunity to denounce 'the heavy military obligations forced by the U.S. upon its European allies,' even when the issue is the adoption of a modern system of air warning (AWACS), that is a clearly defensive measure. The determination of the Communist press to toe the Soviet 'line' . . . signals that the PCI leadership refuses or is quite reluctant to change or soft-pedal the indoctrination of the rank and file to make it less incompatible with a 'Westernized' tack of the party's policies. It also feeds doubts about the assertion by PCI leaders that, even after their party enters the government, the Italian economy would remain 'open and part of a large-scale system of exchanges with the more advanced capitalistic countries,' while in Italy herself private enterprise would operate freely within the framework of a 'democratic programming.' Furthermore, even those Communist representatives who appear most ready for change maintain that the party must continue to be run on the basis of 'democratic centralism.' . . . Now that it runs so many large cities and regions and has stepped into the [national] government area itself, the PCI . . . must deliver on the many and often conflicting I.O.U.'s that it has issued over the last 30 years. It must retain the support of the militants whose aim is still 'the revolution,' and consolidate the gains made among the moderate groups which hope to get from the PCI an orderly administration of public affairs; it must reassure those who still look upon the Soviet Union as their North Star, and it must 'not' disappoint those who believe in 'the national road to Socialism.'

''All this doesn't mean that by now the PCI can only do wrong whatever it may do, as one begins to hear from those same observers, Italian and foreign, for whom up to a few weeks ago the party could do no wrong. It means, however, that the PCI must begin to do some reckoning with a fluid and complex condition of affairs which has helped it to win many votes and substantial slices of power, but now makes it appear responsible for whatever happens or does not happen, even beyond the actual power it wields.

''It is understandable, ''I concluded, ''that the PCI leaders should want to avoid, or at least put off until after they win a government role, the further, decisive steps toward Westernization of the party which would have a serious impact both among the PCI's cadres and militants and upon its relations with Moscow. But extended delays and further coasting along, while possibly eschewing the risks of clear-cut choices, involve the danger of falling between two stools.''

Conditions were actually ripening for significant Communist setbacks at the polls. These setbacks played a key role in precipitating the collapse of the drive, so hopefully promoted by the PCI leadership, to reach national power through the door of the "historic compromise." The failure was also the produce of other factors which were likewise spotlighted at the time in my articles in the Italian and U.S. press, notably the strong opposition by many CDs to further Communist penetrations in the governmental area and the efforts by the Socialists and other intermediate groups to defend and possibly strengthen their own chances of survival and political influence. All those factors were already at work in 1977, well before the dramatic disappearance of Aldo Moro.

During one of his European tours, James Reston reported from Rome to the *New York Times* (June 11) that the Carter administration was not less concerned than Kissinger about the West European Communists' efforts to "sweet talk . . . their way to power." Its tactical approach, however, was different and apparently did not spark charges of interference. The emphasis placed by Carter on human rights, moreover, had induced the Italian Communists to proclaim their acceptance of the democratic system and of NATO. This may just be a tactical ploy, Reston noted, the more so since the Communist press generally refrained from criticizing Soviet policy or paying tribute to Carter's campaign for human rights. In a subsequent column from London (June 26), Reston stressed a very important and often neglected point: while in France and Italy a debate was going on over the approach that U.S. administrations did or would take to Communist successes in Western Europe, very little attention was given to the Congress and public opinion which "would react much more negatively and in the end be decisive."

Possibly because they were so balanced and realistic, Reston's columns were disregarded or dismissed contemptuously by those who, in Western Europe and elsewhere, insisted in giving distorted readings of Carter's policies or of the feelings of U.S. congressional circles and public opinion about the "Communist issue" in countries like Italy and France. Alberto Jacoviello wrote in *l'Unità* that Reston must "have very little esteem for the representatives of the American nation if he actually attributed to them a most backward vision of the world in which we live. . . . The time will come" when "even the U.S. Congress" would be compelled to "get accustomed to live with the reality we represent and the problems we pose . . . if Carter's America wants to win back part of the credibility it has lost since the time of the blind anti-Communist crusades carried out not only by words and paid for quite heavily."

A speech by Kissinger was the main event of the Conference on Italy and Eurocommunism held in Washington on June 7–9 and sponsored by the American Enterprise Institute for Public Policy Research and by the Hoover Institution on War, Revolution, and Peace. Kissinger said: "The ultimate decisions are for the voters of Europe to make. But they—and we—would be indulging in wishful thinking if we all did not acknowledge now: that the accession of power of Communists in an allied country would represent a massive change in European politics [and] would alter the prospects for security and progress for all free nations."

"Professions of the national road to Communism and of devotion to democratic principle" made recently by West European Communist leaders, Kissinger further noted, were in effect quite similar to pronouncements made by top representatives of East European Communist parties in the last years of World War II as well as early in the postwar period. "The key issue," he insisted, "is not how 'independent' the European Communists would be, but how Communist."

"If Communists participate in a significant way in the government of key European countries . . . the military strength and unity of NATO would be gravely weakened" and "NATO may turn by default into a largely German-American alliance. This specter could then be used in other West European countries to undermine what remains of Atlantic cohesion. . . . The French and Italian Communist parties . . . can be counted on to re-orient the Common Market towards close relations with the State economies of Eastern Europe and towards the more extreme of the Third World's demands for a 'new international economic order.' It can be assumed that they will not encourage European political unity to foster cooperation with the U.S.; rather they will urge it, if at all, to encourage third force tendencies. . . . The democratic forces of the West," Kissinger went on, "have it in their power to determine whether the Communist parties have opportunities to succeed. . . . Anti-Communism is not enough; there must be response to legitimate social and economic aspirations, and there must be reform of the inequities from which these anti-democratic forces derive much of their appeal.

"We do our friends in Europe no favor," Kissinger concluded, "if we encourage the notion that the advent of Communists and their allies into power will make little or no difference to our own attitudes and policies. . . . Some have argued . . . that a clear and unambiguous U.S. attitude [on the issue] would be counterproductive, that it would encourage Communist protest votes. I believe the opposite to be true. . . . Many voters in allied countries value the friendship of the U.S. and appreciate the security supplied by the Atlantic Alliance. We should not ignore them, or demoralize them, or undercut them. The gradual gains scored by the Communist parties over the past years occurred—by definition—at the margin, among voters who had not voted Communist before; who did not vote by anti-American reflex; who for one reason or another were persuaded that the Communists have now become acceptable or indispensable. If the U.S. has a responsibility to encourage political freedom throughout the world, we surely have a duty to leave no doubt about our convictions on an issue that is so central to the future of the Western Alliance and therefore to the future of democracy."

The purpose of the former secretary of state was clearly to influence the policies of the Carter administration by developing and seeking to motivate his own criticism of those policies. At the same time, he couched this criticism in terms that allowed the State Department's spokesman, Hodding Carter, to say: "We do not feel that there is substantial disagreement and we do not view former Secretary Kissinger's remarks as differing" from the views of the Carter administration (June 10).

In an interview to Marino De Medici, the Washington correspondent of *Il*

Tempo (June 18), Vance stated: "Insofar as Eurocommunism is concerned, we have tried to make clear from the outset that we believe it is not for us to tell any country whom they should elect in the way of their political leaders. That does not mean that we are indifferent to who is elected and who serves in the government of any country. As we have said on a number of occasions . . . we clearly prefer those who have a democratic backdrop." According to Vance, it would be inappropriate to make specific suggestions as to where to "erect a wall" to a gradual Communist participation in Western European governments: "That would be interfering with the internal affairs of the given country."

When asked whether the presence of Communists in some NATO governments "would erode the moral basis for the presence of American troops in Western Europe," Vance replied: "I think it could," thus coming close to the assessment voiced by Kissinger a few days before. De Medici further inquired whether Communist gains in Western Europe might help democratic nations by creating problems for the Soviet bloc that "would more than outweigh the damage that Eurocommunism could bring to the NATO structure." The secretary of state answered: "I think this is a possibility. I think it depends on how Eurocommunism develops . . . in the various countries of Western Europe." When De Medici asked again whether the West would "really be able to benefit in terms of a schism or a series of small schisms within the Soviet-Communist bloc," Vance replied: "I think this could have a meaningful effect, yes."

The last two questions and answers were not reported in *Il Tempo*. When these omissions were evidenced by publication of the full text of the interview by the State Department, De Medici sought to explain them away by maintaining that those questions and answers did not provide any new information and would take up too much space. But other Italian correspondents claimed that the statements by Vance "censored" by *Il Tempo* provided additional evidence of "a clear-cut difference of tone and substance from [those] of Vance's predecessor" (Jacoviello in *l''Unità*) and of "a political approach to Eurocommunism . . . substantially different from that followed by Kissinger" (Brancoli in *La Repubblica*, June 21).

Gardner cut down to size the actual significance of the whole episode when he told me: "If some newsman keeps asking whether Eurocommunism may have more of a destabilizing impact on the Soviet rather than on the Western system, we feel like guests who are asked by their hostess whether her little daughter will grow up into a handsome woman. The child may be cross-eyed and walk with a stoop, but how can the guests help saying, at the very least, that, yes, she may actually become a beautiful lady?"

In early July, a *Washington Post* editorial elaborated on the "dilemmas" that confronted both the Soviets and the Americans "in dealing with the Communists of Western Europe. . . . The U.S. is dismayed by the rise of the Communist parties, but there is very little that it can do. American threats of diminished support or of strategic dangers are merely counterproductive. . . . The advance of these Communist parties distresses Americans because they don't see enough evidence of real independence from the Soviets. It distresses the Soviets because they see too much evidence. . . . There's not much comfort in the thought, but the Russians' methods for dealing with Eurocommunism seem to be even less effective than the Americans'.''

The *New York Times* asserted in an editorial (July 1) that Eurocommunism was ''the greatest heresy in Soviet doctrine'' and a major threat to the Soviet regime, a threat even more serious for the Communist regimes in Eastern Europe. Yet, the coming to power by Eurocommunist parties would be far from an unmixed blessing for the West. Their uncertain evolution did not guarantee that they would not become again docile tools of Soviet policies. Their coming to power, moreover, might invite ''uprisings'' in Eastern Europe that the Soviet leaders would not tolerate and the West could not fully back without running ''unacceptable risks.'' The editorial concluded by stressing that the military and economic arrangements in effect among the democratic nations would be disrupted if the Communists gained a majority and control of government posts in West European countries.

As early as the spring of 1976, I recalled in a column in *Il Tempo* (October 10, 1977), I had said on Italian TV that Eurocommunism reminded me of a well known *couplet* by the eighteenth-century Italian poet Metastasio: ''The lovers' faith is like the Arabian phoenix. Everybody claims that it exists, but nobody knows where it is.'' The meeting held in Madrid in March (1977) by Berlinguer, Marchais, and Carrillo, which was hailed at the time ''as providing the launching pad for a further expansion of Eurocommunism, appears to have marked the onset of its downswing.'' When Moscow unleashed heavy attacks against Carrillo, ''who headed the weakest 'Eurocommunist' party and at the same time had pushed his criticism of the Soviet Union to the threshold of heresy,'' I pointed out, ''not only the French Communists but the Italians, looked upon as the standard bearers if not the inventors of 'Eurocommunism,' hastened to distance themselves from the Spanish comrades. Nor is it by chance . . . that top PCI representatives have not only . . . disclaimed any intention to give 'Eurocommunism' 'an organization center,' but recently stated that it actually 'does not exist' (to quote Amendola) or is 'a mere verbal expression' (Senator Gerardo Chiaromonte).''

It did not matter very much, I went on, whether and to what precise extent such behavior had been influenced ''by Moscow's calls to order, by the convictions (or uncertainties) of this or that representative of this or that sector of the PCI, or by loyalty to the Soviet 'myth' or to the Marxist-Leninist doctrines still strong and widespread among the militants. What matters is that there has been a temporary halt if not an actual step backwards in the PCI's Westernization process.

''On the key issue of the balance of power and security in Europe, the main concern of the Italian Communists, as well as of other 'Eurocommunists,' seems to be to prevent the West from counterbalancing the increased offensive capa-

bilities of . . . the Soviet military apparatus in the conventional field.'' On top
of their opposition to a modern system of air warning for NATO (AWACS),
''they have joined the campaign promoted by Moscow against the so-called 'N-
bomb' . . . which could effectively contribute to dissuade the USSR from using
its conventional superiority to unleash a conflict in Europe or to exert a growing
pressure and influence on the continent.

"A long time seems to have elapsed," I concluded, "since the days (which
actually go back only to the eve of the June 1976 election) when the top leaders
of the PCI referred to the shield represented by Italy's membership in NATO
as a factor that favored their party's autonomy from Moscow." This change
"reflects and feeds in turn the crises that stir up the smoky and multicolored
conglomerate of innovative ferments and ambiguities, of reform-minded inclinations and of persistent conformism, of autonomist impulses and of heavy
conditionings of a dogmatic and international nature, on which the label of
'Eurocommunism' has been forced."

In the U.S. media, the issues of terrorism and violence in Italy had meanwhile
begun to take more and more space. The dispatches spoke of *"la dolce vita*
having turned dangerous," of "violent crime, American-style," which "ter-
rorizes the streets of Rome," of "pitched battles between police and students
in Bologna, Rome, and other Italian cities," of Italian feminists "turning to
violence," of more and more frequent instances of wealthy people "held for
ransom" and of the increasing "boldness of kidnappers," as well as of the
violence breaking out "on the fringes of strike rallies in several Italian cities
. . . as millions stopped work to protest government austerity" policies. *Newsweek* reported that "politicians from both sides of the country's tacit coalition
of CDs and Communists have begun to wonder aloud whether the rising tide of
violence represents a coordinated conspiracy to undermine Italy's already shaky
governmental structure" (May 18). A *New York Times* editorial (June 27) pointed
at the conditions of the Italian economy as a major cause of the spreading violence
especially among the youth. Vigorous remedial action was made impossible by
the "virtual paralysis" prevailing in political affairs because the CDs depended
on Communist support but did not want to enter into a formal alliance with the
PCI. In fact, terrorism was "an even greater and more immediate danger" than
the Communists. And *La Repubblica* promptly headlined: "For *The New York
Times*, the terrorists, not the PCI, threaten Italy" (June 28).

Two weeks later, the *Washington Post* editorialized: "The terrorists are trying
to demonstrate, of course, that Italian society is falling apart. That's wrong so
far: Italian society is tough and remarkably shock-resistant. But a continued high
level of street violence carries sinister implications for the future. . . . Italy's
current wave of street violence and terrorism . . . is making the Communists look
increasingly like a party of law and order." On the other hand, the shootings
and kidnappings were viewed by "the great law-abiding majority of the Italians
. . . as further evidence of their government's inability to govern. The Com-

munists are now part of the government in every sense but the most narrowly legalistic, and the party's leaders are aware that this general condemnation of the national administration is rapidly coming to include them.''

Meanwhile, an agreement had been reached whereby a revamped governmental program would have the support of the PCI. ''Depending on how you look at it,'' Claire Sterling wrote in the *Washington Post* (July 6), ''this agreement does or does not mean formal acceptance of the Communists in a government majority. . . . The Communists say it does and the CDs said it does not. . . . What ordinary citizens . . . are inclined to care about is whether Italy's two biggest political formations . . . have actually decided to face the ugly facts of Italian life together, or have merely made another of the familiar power-sharing deals that have been post-war Italy's greatest affliction. Alas, the answer is hardly in doubt.'' The Italian economy was ''heading straight for the rocks,'' Sterling went on. The Communists, ''the only ones'' who could talk the workers into accepting the ''stunning sacrifices'' necessary to change course, ''demonstrably don't care to [do so]. Nothing remotely resembling such harsh sacrifices is mentioned in the concerted program. Should it in fact be carried out as written, it would send the country skidding off in the opposite direction.''

The conditions of a loan by the International Monetary Fund became a matter for long and complex negotiations revolving around the commitments by the Italians to curb inflation and notably the impact of the escalator wage clause tied to living costs. This clause, which was to prove so harmful to the Italian economy and was modified after a major political battle in 1983, was the key point of an accord reached early in 1975 between Communist labor leader Luciano Lema and Giovanni Agnelli, head of Fiat and at the time chairman of Confindustria.

Political and economic circles on both sides of the Atlantic were looking with mounting concern at the Italian crisis. Yet, on the eve of Andreotti's visit to the United States at the end of July, the correspondent of *L'Espresso*, Mauro Calamandrei, reported that U.S. financiers and economic experts were ready to praise ''the basic vigor of the Italian economy'' and the country's ''social and economic stability.'' In Washington, Andreotti would be welcomed as the man who had managed to ''domesticate'' the Communists and persuaded them to help avoid another government crisis and a further fall of the lira. Such exaggerated praise, however, was bound to make harder and more painful the return to reality when events soon tore away many of the ambiguities and delusions that contributed so much to the success of Andreotti's visit.

In interviews to the *Washington Post* and to *U.S. News and World Report*, Andreotti said time and again that the agreement with the PCI was not a prelude to the ''historic compromise.'' An alliance between his own CD party and the Communists would be ''a great mistake'' because it would virtually do away with the role that other parties must continue to play and would ''create such a political vacuum in the opposition camp as to produce a dangerous reaction by both the extreme left and the extreme right'' (July 26). Andreotti also made a point of assuring personally the leaders of the administration and of Congress that the new relationship with the PCI not only did not represent the anteroom of a Communist participation in the government, but would not go beyond the scope of the agreement on the governmental program without prior consultation with and approval by the Italian voters. Such assurances and commitments were regarded as necessary and possibly adequate in Washington because the administration leaders themselves did not see, for the time being, any workable alternative and therefore they felt, too, that the situation must be accepted for what it was rather than for what they might want it to be (as reported by Ugo Stille, the longtime U.S. correspondent of *Corriere della Sera*).

In connection with Andreotti's trip to the United States, Gardner told me once again about the administration's "clear-cut preference" for governments made up of parties securely democratic and pro-Western, and its consequent opposition to the PCI's gaining a government role or winning greater influence anyway. At the same time, the ambassador went on, Andreotti's visit to Washington provided the opportunity for voicing publicly the importance attached by the Carter administration to Italy's "vital role" within the Atlantic Alliance and its related commitment to develop through concrete agreements and initiatives the U.S. support to the Italian economy.

These were the mainstays of the talks between Andreotti and the U.S. leaders as well as of the joint communiqué issued at the end of the talks. The communiqué mentioned Carter's positive appraisal not only of Italy's steady contribution to Western cooperation and allied solidarity, but of her commitment "to democratic institutions."

On the eve of the Italian premier's arrival in Washington, the *New York Times* had already reported (July 26) that Carter and Vance were expected to voice their hope that Andreotti would continue to keep the PCI out of the government. They would also convey their understanding for his reasons for seeking Communist support. "The summit's goal," Stille wrote in *Corriere della Sera* (July 30), "was to strengthen as much as possible the position of Andreotti to whom the U.S. looks today both as the 'guarantor' of a political formula of stability that makes good use of PCI's support without letting it into the 'government area,' and a leader determined to carry out all the way a program of economic austerity involving remarkable sacrifices and therefore requiring a phase of substantial 'truce between social groups.' . . . Andreotti's pragmatism has been matched by Carter's pragmatism. . . . The present administration," Stille further noted, "shares with the earlier administration the opposition to any formula involving the Communist party's entry into the government in Italy and the determination to do everything possible to avoid such a development. But there is a clear difference over the strategy to be followed. Ford's and Kissinger's [strategy] was keyed to the concept of 'trench warfare': hammer away rigidly on American hostility to PCI's participation in the government by means of threatening warnings about its consequences in the international field. Carter's strategy, instead, is keyed to the concept of 'mobile warfare': avoid head-on clashes, resort to a more flexible and indirect method of an outflanking maneuver.'' Such was "the meaning," Stille concluded, "of the 'strategy of co-operation" launched by the Carter-Andreotti summit. It has a twin aim: to associate ever more closely Washington and Rome within a framework of Western interdependence on all political and economic problems both international and bilateral; and to guarantee the utmost support of the U.S. to the Andreotti government's program of economic rehabilitation whose success is indispensable for Italy's political stability in a democratic context.''

Vittorio Zucconi pointed out in *La Stampa* (July 29): "The fundamental result of Andreotti's trip to Washington . . . appears to be in having brought about, through an operation quite typical of Andreotti's, the apparent reconciliation of [two] opposed purposes. The Premier goes back to Rome after having won Washington's green light for a political formula that involves the Communists and after having persuaded the Americans that he and his party are intransigently anti-Communist.''

According to the official CD daily, *Il Popolo*, Andreotti had been given a cordial and friendly reception in the United States not as a consequence of the programmatic accord involving the Communists which had not "changed the political setup in Italy," but because foreign policy issues had been kept out of the accord and had remained under "the full responsibility of the all-Christian-Democratic government." Republicans and Socialists charged or hinted that the premier had drawn for the Americans an all-too-optimistic picture of economic conditions in Italy.

The Carter administration, moreover, had given Andreotti "a conditional confidence" pending a verification of the validity of his assurances concerning the spirit and limits of the collaboration with the PCI.

Andreotti replied in interviews to the weeklies *Oggi* and *Panorama*: "I have found out," he said notably, "that many apprehensions, sometimes emphasized . . . in Italy, do not exist in the U.S." Pessimistic assessments of the Italian government's performance, he added, might well hurt the nation by "weakening the Americans' readiness to help us, to favor investments in our country.''

Reporting from Washington to *l'Unità*, Jacoviello claimed that throughout the Italian premier's visit "no voice had been heard inviting Andreotti to exclude the Communists from the drafting of the governmental program. This marks a historic turning point in the American attitude. . . . The turn, however, stops right here. The Americans, Carter has said again, are hostile to a Communist participation in the government. And Andreotti has deemed it advisable to guarantee—it is not very clear on what grounds—that this will not take place. He has been forced to admit, at the same time, that today it is impossible to make do without them in outlining the government's program. And the Americans have acknowledged that it is so. . . . The Americans have seen Andreotti on one hand as the man who, in their view, manages to keep the Communists out of the government and, on the other, as the man who governs with the assent of the Communists. They bet, of course, on the former, but do not ignore the latter'' (July 29).

"Carter accepts the PCI," *La Repubblica*'s front page headline proclaimed, although the substance of the dispatch by correspondent Brancoli from Washington did not reflect such a heavily distorted reading of the U.S. administration's stand (July 28). A few days later, the same daily reported the gist of a paper prepared by the Research Service of the Library of Congress under these headlines: "The U.S. analyzes an hypothesis that is already seen as reality: that's how the Eurocommunists will govern" (July 31). The dispatch by Brancoli and even more so an article by Calamandrei in *L'Espresso* gave a very selective account of the paper and failed to mention, among other things, that it was dated June 1, 1976, or more than a year earlier, on the eve of the general election from which, according to some U.S. observers, the PCI was to emerge as the number one political force in Italy. Calamandrei attributed the paper to senator Brooke who held quite different views on the issue. Actually, Brooke had merely asked for a research on the matter and the paper was largely the handiwork of Stanley Sloan, an analyst on European affairs. Sloan gave prominence to a scenario which turned out to quite unrealistic. It envisaged an early Communist participation in the national government in Italy (and elsewhere in Western Europe) and downplayed its negative impact on relations between the countries involved and the United States. According to Calamandrei, the paper viewed such a participation as something that could be taken "practically for granted" although the PCI would have "a minority role." This would have a "favorable impact on the Italian economic situation" and would involve "minimal risks for NATO and Western security." Calamandrei further maintained that the paper readied by Sloan said in effect "what Carter had not wanted to voice explicitly." The correspondent of *L'Espresso* concluded that "although it remains unlikely that Carter will come out openly in favor of the historic compromise, the President of the U.S., having accepted Italy as she is and as Andreotti is changing her week after week, has actually bet on the Westernization of Italian Communism."

Distorted interpretations of U.S. policies toward Italy and more specifically toward the PCI were not a monopoly of the Communist and pro-Communist left. For instance, "the contradiction, the ambiguities and the silences" of the Carter approach were attacked as "extremely dangerous" by Achille Albonetti, an Italian who pursued simultaneously or alternatively political crusades and industrial interests and who was then seeking to carve for himself a role as an intimate of Kissinger and his spokesman in Italy. Those charges were aired by Albonetti in the introduction to a collection (edited in September 1977) of the "echoes" to the Conference on Italy and Eurocommunism held three months before in Washington. "The picture drawn by Albonetti," I wrote in *Il Tempo* (November 21), "is featured by . . . omissions and distortions similar to those marking the Communist and pro-Communist propaganda, even though he is pursuing quite different and actually opposite aims." The main thrust was in both cases to "neglect or dismiss" as "confused and equivocal" the expressions of the "determined preference" for governments made up of parties that were democratic and proven friends of the United States. Carter's interview to four West European newspapers, I pointed out, was not mentioned at all by Albonetti just as it had been "largely ignored . . . or deeply amputated by the Communists. Furthermore, Albonetti devoted only a few words to the statements made during the Washington Conference by senators Frank Church (D-Idaho) and John F. Chafee (R-Rhode Island), much as Carlo M. Santoro had given a "very partial version" of them in *l'Unità*. According to Santoro, the two senators had mostly concentrated on disavowing those Italian participants in the conference (like Albonetti himself, the right-wing CD Massino De Carolis, and the Liberal Enzo Bettiza) who "had openly called for a heavy-handed U.S. intervention in Italy."

Actually, I reported in *Il Tempo*, the statements by Church and Chafee "clearly reaffirmed that, far from being indifferent to what may happen in Italy, the U.S. should 'do everything [it] can to be supportive of the democratic forces in Italy' because 'we would have to regard a Communist victory in Italy as an extremely unfortunate event and one that would raise serious questions about the future of NATO and Italy's part in it.' . . . Church and Chafee have also stressed, as Carter did on several occasions and as ambassador Gardner has done quite recently in his interview to *Corriere della Sera*, that the basic factor remains the ability of the Italian democratic forces to resume the initiative so as to win broader popular support."

In the same article and in others related to the subsequent polemics with Albonetti, I wondered whether the inclination of several Italian right-wingers to attribute the PCI's growth mainly to the "diabolical ability of the Communists themselves" and/or to "the stupidity of the masses" was "a more or less conscious alibi for failing to look elsewhere for the causes and responsibilities for the PCI's political and electoral expansion." This could also explain "why those who insist obstinately in fighting Communism by clinging to old conservative positions," kept asking the U.S. government to "practice its anti-Communism through heavy-handed interference in Italian domestic affairs," and vented their "irritation and frustration when this does not happen." These same people, I concluded, did then "resort to techniques of disinformation and manipulation in order to project a distorted image of Carter's policies with regard to the 'Communist issue' in Italy and elsewhere. . . . These techniques . . . work wholly to the benefit of the PCI. The Italians who are anti-Communist and pro-American are exposed to doubts, unwarranted but insidious, about the attitude of the U.S. and more generally there is an increasing risk to fuel misunderstandings and resentments between the two countries." (*Il Tempo*, November 26, December 5 and 11, 1977).

20

The United States Speaks Up on the Communist Issue

In the latter part of 1977, several developments contributed to persuading President Carter and his collaborators that it had become not only advisable but urgently necessary to reaffirm the basic position of the United States on the "Communist issue" in Italy (and elsewhere in Western Europe) and to do so in such terms as to erase any lingering honest doubts and to discourage any further disinformation.

As early as July, Carter did not agree in advance to a meeting with Mitterrand (who therefore cancelled his plans for a visit to the United States). The episode was read by some observers as a signal that the administration had become "convinced that America, while continuing to avoid the brusque Kissinger methods, must make greater efforts to underline its 'preference' for political formulas keeping the Communists out of government in Western Europe" (Stille in *Corriere della Sera*, July 6).

Starting in early September, Ambassador Gardner told me time and again about his growing concern over the situation and prospects in Italy. This concern was gradually being shared in Washington and was fueled by the fact that "sizable sectors of the Italian media still do not understand or do not want to understand the actual position of the Administration." In its November 22 issue, for instance, *Panorama* asserted that "the very influential Trilateral Commission, after reviewing the possible Western reaction to a coming to power of the Eurocommunists, has concluded: resigned acceptance, with reservations." In fact Gardner told me, "several members of the Commission, including myself, opposed such a development." *La Repubblica* stated that "U.S. business winks at the PCI" (December 13). Again *Panorama* (December 20), asserted that a government including the PCI was "inevitable" and would be formed "next spring." Two weeks later, the same magazine claimed that Fanfani himself had stated that he was "available" for a government made up of CDs and Communists and "hinted that the U.S. too deemed that the situation was ripe" (January 3, 1978). In the early fall, Macaluso still felt that a Communist entry into the government might well have to wait until after the presidential election due at the end of 1978. The day after a huge antigovernment rally by industrial workers in Rome early in December, however, he told me: "The party has decided to demand that an 'emergency' government, in which we must be directly represented, be formed soonest." A few days later, the PCI's National Executive voiced the request in terms that made an early government crisis inevitable.

It was the end of the hopes and calculations that had played a key role in the warm welcome given Andreotti during his visit to Washington a few months earlier. U.S. political and diplomatic circles felt, I learned from some of their members in Washington and in Rome, that they could no longer expect that Andreotti and representatives of major economic groups traditionally considered pro-American, such as Carli and Agnelli, would be able or sufficiently determined anyway to block a deal giving the Communists a government role.

The behavior of the PCI leaders, moreover, hardly suggested that the "Westernization" of their party would register significant progress in the foreseeable future. On the eve of Carrillo's trip to the United States Berlinguer stated that, contrary to the Spanish Communist leader's recent contentions, Soviet society remained "Socialist" despite past mistakes and still "illiberal traits." During the Moscow celebrations of the sixtieth anniversary of the October Revolution, the PCI leader proclaimed his party's "diversity" from the Soviet model. The communiqué on his meeting with Brezhnev, however, emphasized the convergence of views and, in fact, the "solidarity" between the Italian and the Soviet Communist parties on international matters. This solidarity continued to be reflected in the approach that the media controlled or influenced by the PCI were taking to the major issues of the U.S.–Soviet confrontation.

Against this background, the Carter administration found more reasons for worry than for satisfaction in the resolution on foreign policy that was approved by the Italian Senate on October 19 and by the Chamber of Deputies on December 1, 1977. For the first time, the Communists joined the traditionally pro-Western parties in voting a parliamentary document which made an explicit and positive reference to "the framework of Italy's alliances and commitments in favor of the European community." The understanding among the parties which sustained the Andreotti government was thus broadened to foreign affairs. Moreover, Communist senator Franco Calamandrei, one of the main proponents of the resolution and vice-president of the Senate Foreign Affairs Committee, hastened to explain to *La Stampa* (October 25), that Italian foreign policy had become "much more progressive-minded . . . so much so that some observers call it 'an imperfect policy of non-alignment.' " Therefore, the interviewer noted, "the PCI's support of Italy's foreign policy must be attributed to the fact that it has changed (becoming 'more progressive-minded' and 'more inclined to take a third force' approach) and not to a change of course by the PCI."

During a long conversation summarized as an interview in *Il Tempo* (November 18), Calamandrei told me: "The evolution of the stand and watchwords of the PCI is in the direction of believing that, within the alliance itself, Italy and other European partners might manage to give greater significance to NATO's political role than to the traditionally prevailing military role. . . . Within this context, it becomes possible for Italy to develop a more autonomous foreign policy." Calamandrei denied that the thrust of his party's foreign policy was intended to lead Italy to assume a "third force" role: "Our country is an aligned country which belongs to the Atlantic bloc and has a Western European position. . . . As long as the international situation will require the continued existence of the blocs (and therefore our membership in NATO) as a condition for equilibrium, the Atlantic alliance can but have the U.S. as its primary partner. Should it be possible, however, to cut down the prevailing weight of the alliance's military role compared to its political and economic role, the relations between the U.S. and the European partners, Italy included, might develop beyond those unquestionably rigid and unilateral aspects that so far have given the U.S. its primary position."

Calamandrei also told me: "I was neither shocked nor surprised by the confirmation (given by Gardner a few days earlier in an interview to *Corriere della Sera*) that the U.S. does not want the Communist parties to have an influential or dominant role in the governments of Western Europe. At the same time, there is clear evidence that such a confirmation is coupled with the commitment not to interfere 'in the domestic affairs of any country.' "

It should be noted that Calamandrei's statement reflected the views of a small minority within the party's leading groups, as he himself made clear when he told me, only half jokingly, that among the members of those groups he was nicknamed "the American tank."

Both the label and the concept itself of "Eurocommunism" were substantially disavowed by Luigi Longo, former secretary-general and now chairman of the PCI, in an interview to *Corriere della Sera* (December 30). Longo sharply condemned Social democracy as a source of "negative influences which have nothing to do with Socialism." Social democracy, he went on, had "failed" even in Western Germany and in Scandinavia. Communism, instead, had produced great benefits "for the Soviet Union, for the so-called Eastern countries, for China," while similar benefits were "sprouting in so many emerging nations. Think about Vietnam, where a great revolution has been achieved, thanks also to Soviet military aid." Longo stated flatly that the PCI must preserve "its Leninist nature. The Russian revolution . . . represents, whatever people may say, a democratic and progressive-minded force not only for the Soviet country but for the world situation. Just think what this situation would be in the hypothetical event of a fading away of such a great force, ideological, economic, political, and military, yes military, too."

Franco Rodano, widely considered as one of Berlinguer's "intellectual mentors," took sharply to task and ridiculed the "illusions" and "pretensions" of some political observers who shared and attributed to the Carter administration the feeling that the "Eurocommunist" parties could be used to "create problems for the East." In the pro-Communist daily *Paese Sera* (November 9, 1977), Rodano quoted from an interview given *La Repubblica* by Norman Kogan, a specialist in Italian affairs and a professor at the University of Connecticut. While pointing at the fundamental "continuity" that since the Truman years had featured the U.S. approach to the Communist issue in Italy, Kogan said: "Vance himself has stated that over the long term Eurocommunism represents a bigger threat for the Soviets than for the Americans" (as already reported, Vance had used distinctly more cautious language in the interview published in *Il Tempo* on June 20). The key task of the Eurocommunists, Rodano stressed, was to promote changes that did not affect the policies of both superpowers but substantially and concretely only the policies of the United States. The acceptance of the Atlantic Pact represented in effect an instrument to "drain the 'blocs' of their substance" and the nations of Western Europe were called upon to "get out" of "advanced capitalism." The whole process, that the Eurocommunist parties were summoned to help implement, was outlined by Rodano in terms making all-too-clear that it was bound to lead in practice to the usual conclusion, that is extending to the entire European continent, at least, the ideological, political, and military supremacy of Soviet-style Communism.

In connection with a visit to Washington by French premier, Raymond Barre, and in an interview to the *Reader's Digest* which appeared in October, President Carter expressed not only "hope" but "confidence" that "the democratic forces" would "continue to prevail in Europe." He also spelled out his worries over the consequences that a Communist participation in West European governments would have for "NATO's defense system" because "there is reason to wonder whether some Communist leaders would stay loyal to their country or to the Soviet Union." Once again the spirit and the letter of such statements were distorted in *La Repubblica*'s headline: "Carter is not afraid of Eurocommunism in NATO" (October 19).

In a wide-ranging interview with Jonathan Power (*International Herald Tribune*, October 10, 1977), Brzezinski said: "First of all, we do not wish the Communist parties to come to power in Western Europe. Secondly, we have confidence that the West European electorates will use their best judgment to preserve democratic systems and will therefore opt for democratic parties. Thirdly, we have to deal with the world as it is. Fourthly, the existence of Eurocommunist parties, as of themselves, does encourage change in the nature of Communism, and it's unwise for the United States to engage in direct intervention in domestic affairs of other countries, of the sort that could make the Eurocommunist parties symbols of national independence. Lastly, Eurocommunism is a highly differentiated phenomenon. All it is really is a catchword for West European Communist parties. Some of these parties are still highly Stalinist, such as the Portuguese. Some of them have begun de-Stalinization, but they have only begun it, like the French. Some of them are relatively de-

Stalinized, but are still highly Leninist, like the Italians. Some are de-Stalinized and probably are de-Leninized, such as perhaps the Spanish.''

Ambassador Gardner replied with a flat ''no'' when he was asked by *Corriere della Sera* whether it was ''true that the Carter Administration had taken a new look at Europe and softened its attitude about participation by the PCI in the Italian government.'' The ambassador summed up the U.S. position in terms that, recalling recent statements by Carter, by Vance, and by Brzezinski, were in effect identical with those which were to be used in the official declaration issued by the State Department on January 12, 1978: ''First,'' Gardner told *Corriere della Sera*, ''our allies are sovereign countries, with the right to make their own choices about their political future. . . . Second, we are also a sovereign country, and have a right to express our view, and our view is that we do not wish Communist parties to be influential or dominant in Western European governments. Third, the best way to help to assure that Communist parties do not come to power in Western European countries is for democratic parties to meet the aspirations of their people for more effective, more just, and more compassionate government. International cooperation can help, but in the final analysis the outcome will be decided by the efforts the democratic parties make in the free political process'' (November 15).

In connection with Carrillo's visit to the United States, State Department officials told the *New York Times* and the *Washington Post* (November 22) that the Carter administration had shown its readiness to act in accordance with the Helsinki agreements and with the President's own statements on human rights, thus distancing itself from the ''rigid and hostile'' attitude taken ''during the Kissinger era.'' At the same time, the administration's refusal to have any political contact with Carrillo was intended to avoid sending to Europe ''the wrong signal,'' and to discredit any feeling that the United States was in any way inclined to underwrite Eurocommunism by giving its leaders publicity in the United States or more respectability. In this respect, the administration's position did ''not differ from Ford's.''

During a visit to Rome, Joseph A. Califano, U.S. secretary for Health, Education, and Welfare and the representative of the Americans of Italian origin in the Carter administration, told me: ''It is nonsense to say that these Americans are ignorant of today's Italy and/or wedded to a narrow, outdated, anti-Red approach'' (as maintained by leftist groups in Italy). ''The Americans of Italian origin,'' Califano went on in the interview (*Il Tempo*, November 25), ''are increasingly aware of the situation in Italy and overwhelmingly want Italy to be free, strong, and non-Communist. There is no question in my mind that at least 90 percent of the Italo-Americans would react unfavorably to a Communist participation in the Italian government.'' The U.S. secretary added: ''From our viewpoint, we don't want the PCI to win a role in governing the country. At the same time, Italy is an independent nation just as we are and so the Italians must make their own decisions on matters that concern them most directly.''

Shortly afterwards, I interviewed General Alexander M. Haig, supreme allied commander in Europe, at his headquarters in Belgium. When asked about the consequences of a Communist party sharing in the government of a NATO country, the general said: "This is a political question and it is for the political authorities to deal with. From a purely military point of view, I have the right to an opinion, and that is that it will have a deleterious effect on the ability of the Alliance mechanism to handle and process highly classified military information, planning material. . . . In a broader context but from a military point of view, I would be concerned because such a government, and of course upon the degree to which participation was manifested, and regardless of whether or not the particular party was affiliated with Moscow or not, it would by doctrinal conviction place the security requirement, with which I'm so concerned, at the lowest edge of national priority" (*Il Tempo*, December 3).

In a meeting with the press (December 20), Brzezinski emphasized that the United States must be "very, very cautious and skeptical" concerning the actual extent of the West European Communists' evolution "away from some of the worst excesses of their history in recent decades." He underlined the link between Western solidarity in defense matters and domestic political developments within individual NATO countries: "The commitment to collective security is a fundamental one. . . . It is a permanent structure for the political and military relationship with the Western European nations. As far as changes within these nations are concerned, our assessment, which has been voiced many times by the President and by the Secretary of State, is that the responsibility rests with the voters themselves. Having said that, however, we are wholly ready to state that we are not inclined to believe that Communist participation in Western Europe governments would be a positive step."

With very few exceptions, the U.S. (and Italian) media ignored or played down the increasingly frequent signals reflecting the Carter administration's growing attention to and concern over the "Eurocommunist question." Very little space was likewise given to the PCI's stepped up pressure for the formation of an "emergency" government with its direct participation.

Interest developed only in the wake of statements made by the President during his visit to Paris early in January 1978. "[Carter] warned Socialist leader François Mitterrand—and made the warning public—to stay at arm's length from the Communists," the *Washington Post* editorialized on January 9. "The Carter foray," the paper added, "suggested more the activism and alarm that marked Henry Kissinger's approach to 'Eurocommunism' than the rather relaxed pose the administration had struck earlier." On the same day, the *New York Times* praised the President's decision to publicize U.S. concern over the outcome of the French elections: "It would be a tragedy" if voters in West European nations went to the polls "under the delusion" that a Communist entry into the government would not have serious consequences for NATO and the EEC. Richard Burt reported to the same paper that administration officials were increasingly worried over the apparent likelihood that the PCI would gain a greater role in running national affairs. There was also skepticism about the chances that the

Andreotti government would heed the misgivings voiced by Washington about the prospect of closer ties between CDs and Communists. Within the Carter administration, Burt added, a debate was going on between those who advocated serving public notice of the consequences of letting the PCI secure a bigger role, and those who argued against such "a return to Kissinger's politics." Meanwhile, ambassador Gardner, Burt further reported, had been instructed to travel to Washington for consultations.

A few days before and again on the eve of his departure for Washington, Gardner asked me whether it would be advisable to issue soon an official statement spelling out, in strong and unmistakable terms, the U.S. administration's stand. "Under the circumstances," I replied, "the benefits produced by such a statement far outweigh the negative repercussions it would have in some sectors of public opinion in Italy (and elsewhere in Europe) and its exploitation by political and journalistic circles tied with or favorably inclined toward the PCI or generally anti-American." Of course, I added, "the terms of the statement should be carefully weighted in order to avoid providing ammunition to those who could or would look upon it as an interference in the domestic affairs of the Western European countries allied with the U.S., as well as in order to set forth clearly and cogently the grounds of American opposition to a Communist role in governing these countries."

The ambassador indicated that his mind was made up: a public statement was necessary. The latest pronouncements by Carter in Paris showed that such a conviction was now largely shared within the administration. "A government crisis is about to be opened formally in Italy," the ambassador pointed out, "following the massive efforts by the Communists to secure Cabinet posts for representatives of their party or for 'technicians' close to the PCI," Gardner stressed. "Some senior CD leaders are reportedly flirting with the idea of heading such a government. . . . The time has come when a move by us can tip the balance in favor of Italian democracy and of U.S. interests in Italy.

"A major aim of the statement under consideration," Gardner went on, was to convey an official expression of U.S. policy not only to political circles in Italy (and elsewhere in Western Europe) but above all to "those who do not belong to party organizations, and thus hearten again many people who may have been discouraged by an incorrect perception of the American position."

Gardner and I discussed also the differences between the French and the Italian situations: "In Italy," the ambassador noted, "the conditions do not exist for a strong reaction of a Gaullist-nationalistic type against an American initiative. . . . *La Repubblica* is not *Le Monde*." What about the PCI's reaction? Gardner and I agreed that it would be "obviously negative, but on the whole rather cautious" (as it turned out to be).

The ambassador concluded by summing up what he had apparently suggested in his dispatches to Washington: "We must emphasize that we are opposed not only to a government role for the Communists but to developments that would let them into the anteroom and give the impression that such a role is inevitable.

As I'll say again in Washington, the point is not to go back to Kissinger's approach but to voice our preferences in more explicit and more vigorous terms."

I was able, therefore, to anticipate in *Il Tempo* (January 11) the gist and the motivations of the declaration that the State Department was to issue the next day. The U.S. approach to the "Communist question" in Western Europe, I wrote, had been seriously distorted by those who had summed it up "in the bare formula of 'non-interference' and 'non-indifference.' " Such a summary ignored "a third, fundamental component . . . 'the clear-cut preference' for governments made up of parties that are democratic, well tested friends of the United States and *therefore non-communist* [emphasis supplied by authoritative American sources directly involved in the issue]. . . . The substance of the Carter Administration's reaction to the latest events and prospects in Italy," I continued, "is to call attention, in terms adequate to the requirements and the seriousness of the hour, to the strongly negative impact on Atlantic relations that would stem from a shift in the Italian governmental setup involving a government role for the PCI or portending such a role as inevitable in the politically foreseeable future." Such a move, I continued, "will rally and consolidate the broader consensus which in recent times has coalesced behind Carter's policies with regard to the 'Communist question' in the countries allied with the U.S. . . . The recent behavior of the French Communists and of the PCI itself has strengthened, even among those who look with interest and some hope at the evolution of the 'Eurocommunist' parties, the feeling that such an evolution can develop without jeopardizing the security of democratic institutions, if these parties continue to be kept out of the government."

In the concluding paragraphs of the article, I contrasted the military interventions of the Soviet Union in Eastern Europe with the policies of the United States which felt it had "the right and the duty to tell a friendly country: 'in our opinion you're about to get on the wrong track. The choice and the responsibility are yours; but before making dangerous and possibly fatal mistakes, please be sure to realize exactly what you're doing and how much it will hurt our friendship and your own future.' "

TEXT OF THE STATEMENT ISSUED BY THE STATE DEPARTMENT ON JANUARY 12, 1978

Ambassador Gardner's visit to Washington has provided an occasion for a general policy review with senior administration officials. There has been no change in the administration's attitude toward Western European Communist parties, including that of Italy, although recent developments in Italy have increased the level of our concern. As the President and other members of the administration have publicly stated on a number of occasions, our Western European allies are sovereign countries and, rightly and properly, the decision on how they are governed rests with their citizens alone. At the same time, we believe we have an obligation to our friends and allies to express our views clearly.

Administration leaders have repeatedly expressed our views on the issue of Communist participation in West European governments. Our position is clear: we do not favor such participation and would like to see Communist influence in any Western European country reduced. As we have said in the past, we believe the best way to achieve these goals rests with the efforts of democratic parties to meet the aspirations of their people for effective, just, and compassionate government.

The United States and Italy share profound democratic values and interests, and we do not believe that the Communists share these values and interests.

As the President said in Paris last week: 'It is precisely when democracy is up against difficult challenges that its leaders must show firmness in resisting the temptation of finding solutions in non-democratic forces.'] *end of paper*

When queried about the "evidence" supporting the belief that the PCI "does not share democratic values and interests," the State Department's spokesman noted: "There are many indications, among which are the party's undemocratic internal procedures, it belief that Soviet-style state Socialism is better than Western systems, and the behavior of other Communist parties once in power. If you want to see what the PCI believes in, you might consult the recent interview in *Corriere della Sera* by party President Luigi Longo, which reaffirmed the Leninist allegiance of the party."

A few hours after Gardner's return to Rome on January 13, 1978, we met as usual for drinks at the Villa Taverna, the ambassador's residence in the Italian capital. Summing up the circumstances and developments that had preceded and produced the drafting and publication of the document issued the day before by the State Department, Gardner told me: "In the first few months of my mission in Rome, a climate of some political stability appeared to prevail here. More recently, however, there have been increasingly strong signals that a storm was brewing, although the depth of the crisis and its possible outcome have not emerged clearly until a few days ago. Well before my latest trip to Washington, anyway, a consensus developed among the people involved on our side that we must take a clear and public stand. A draft was prepared at the embassy. On the evening of my arrival in Washington, I had dinner with Zbig (Brzezinski) who approved the key points of the draft. The next day I was received by the President. In the subsequent meetings in which I took part, at State and at the NSC, there have been no divergencies either on the substantial aspects of the statement. It does not represent at all a return to Kissinger's policies, but it reflects, possibly with some differences in style, the line followed ever since Truman's and Eisenhower's days. On this, there is broad consensus as well as an encouraging support in congressional circles, both Democrat and Republican, as confirmed during my meetings with influential members of both parties, including the chairman of the Senate Foreign Relations Committee, Frank Church, with representative Peter Rodino and members of the House Foreign Affairs Committee."

The only sentence in the document that aroused "some doubts in my mind," I told Gardner, was the reference to "our desire to see Communist influence reduced in Western Europe. I fully share such a desire," I went on, "and I'm confident that it will be borne out by facts in the not-too-distant future. Over the short term, however, the PCI, I feel, will move further ahead, rather than be forced to backtrack, in its march toward entering into the government. The outcome of the impending government crisis seems bound to involve some development in that direction. And I don't like the idea that our country may be cast, however temporarily, in the role of somebody ordering the waves to withdraw.''

Gardner readily conceded that my thoughts and reservations were not un-founded and went on to say: ''After assessing the various aspects of the situation and the possible repercussions of our statement, we concluded that it was nec-essary, first and foremost, to speak up most clearly, to do away with every possible doubt that our opposition may be limited to the event of a direct par-ticipation by the Communists in the government in Western European countries. On the other hand, we should not let ourselves be 'trapped' into a statement whose wording would specify which political or government formula would be acceptable and which would not. If we declared, for instance, our opposition even to a setup in which the Communists would not hold Cabinet posts but would be part of the governmental majority, we would expose ourselves to the charge of wanting to interfere even in specific aspects of Italian politics.

''By saying less,'' the ambassador concluded, ''we could have given the impression that we did not want to face up to our responsibilities; by saying more, we would have gone beyond what circumstances required and we would have risked adopting a stance that would appear provocative. . . . That's why we have avoided any word that might be interpreted as a threat or even as a reference to what we might say or do if certain changes take place in Italy. And that's why the State Department's declaration strongly reaffirms our determination to respect the sovereignty of Italy and of the other nations involved.

''It is the firm conviction of President Carter, in particular, that the United States must have no part whatsoever in giving financial support to parties or political groups in foreign countries or interfere in their domestic affairs by clandestine means or actions. And as long as I'll hold this post, I shall oppose any move that might run counter to these directives. It is evident, at the same time, that, in view of the multifaceted relationship between Italy and the United States, a change in the political orientation in Italy would affect the whole range of our relations.''

21

Italy Makes Progress at Home and Abroad

"Almost everything is noteworthy in Italy: Sicilian banditti, Florentine fashions, Gina Lollobrigida. . . . About the only exception is politics."

This was the lead of an article of mine which ran in the *Washington Post* on November 8, 1959. "A foreign correspondent," I went on, "has two choices, neither of them satisfactory. He can drive his home office crazy with long stories detailing the feuds between and within the many parties crowding the Italian political scene, whose differences are often measured in inches rather than yards. Result: a cable from the managing editor: 'who cares about those domestic intricacies?' Or, he can file a factual report after each general election (there have been four since the war), or after each government crisis (nine in the last ten years), which can usually be summed up in three words: 'Situation basically unchanged.'

"Only too often, in fact, Italian politics resembles one of those exquisite Oriental plays which run for hours on elaborate staging and a very thin plot. A large cast moves slowly in and out of the wings, but there is no drama. A few cognoscenti appear to enjoy a specific episode, but when they start explaining it to their neighbor, he gets bored long before he has been told the background which might enable him to share in the fun."

In the following sections of the article (as well as in many others among the several hundred published in U.S. papers in earlier or more recent times), I have sought to illustrate the deep and complex motivations, the genuine difficulties, the many real or apparent paradoxes, the often wearisome developments of Italian affairs, political and not only political, as well as the changes and achievements that have marked the nation's performance over the span of two generations.

Back in 1959 I underscored how and why "when the conversation turns to politics, the average Italian talks as a bystander rather than as an interested party.

To him, it is always 'they' and never 'we' when he speaks about the way his country's affairs are being run. . . . True, postwar Italy has all the trappings of democracy. It is also true that at election time Italians dutifully cast their ballots, with a turnout which usually totals 90 percent of the registered voters. But attendance at the polls has a ritual character, too, because it is accompanied by the widespread conviction that "there is nothing much that can be done about anything. The Italians may have been told that in a democracy the government should be their servant, never their master. In practice, they know that it doesn't work that way. . . . To put it bluntly, Italy is a country where most people have 'a vote without representation' and know it only too well.''

To support this contention, I described some of the many aspects of Italian daily life which brought out (and would continue to bring out, although in different ways and to a different extent) "the basic paradox of a country where economic and technical progress has not been matched by a comparable advance in civic consciousness and in the relations between the citizen and the state.''

Over many decades, I wrote, "there has been a jungle-like proliferation of laws and regulations compounded with a large measure of arbitrary administrative discretion in their implementation. No wonder the average Italian has a feeling of bewildered hopelessness when confronted with the machinery of the state, or that he looks with skeptical estrangement at the political game and its players. He knows that when the game takes a bad turn, he'll foot the bill; he is much less convinced that he'll benefit if things get better. . . . That's why Italians look for shortcuts instead of relying on their constitutional rights . . . and most of them seem to pin whatever hopes they have for the future on a lucky individual turn of the wheel. Evidence of this state of mind is the great number of people who 'invest' their meager earnings in the state lotteries and the soccer pools.

"Somewhat in the same vein, the average Italian is likely to refer, half jokingly but half in earnest, to 'lo stellone d'Italia' (Italy's lucky star) if reminded that, after all, his country is in a much better shape than might have been expected 15 years ago when two foreign armies and two Italian governments were fighting each other over its prostrate body. Now, this is both incorrect and unfair. It has taken more than luck for Italy to emerge from the wreckage of war and civil strife and achieve the economic expansion of the last ten years.''

It has taken much more than luck, it can and must be added today, for Italy to chalk up her record in the subsequent decades both in overcoming most serious dangers and troubles and in making substantial progress in domestic affairs as well as on the international scene.

A review of these achievements, which have been particularly significant in the 1980s, may well start with the events that followed the publication of the declaration issued by the State Department on January 12, 1978.

As reported in Chapter 20, the document not only reaffirmed U.S. opposition to a participation by Communist parties in the governments of Western Europe but its desire to see their influence reduced. The document came at a critical juncture in Italian affairs. Following the June 1976 general election, the long dominant CDs had been compelled to form a minority government that depended on the abstention and then on the support of the Communists in Parliament. This government was headed by Giulio Andreotti, a longtime representative of the Christian Democrat right wing who, in recent years, had pinned his ambitions to collaboration with the PCI.

For most Communist militants and party leaders, this was to be only a temporary way station on the road to a full and formal government role. By late 1977, they were pressing hard for Cabinet posts. Quite a few CDs seemed ready or resigned to accept the request, while representatives of the other democratic and pro-Western groups wondered helplessly whether their parties could avoid being crushed in the embrace between the two giants of Italian politics.

It is hard to gauge exactly the impact that the U.S. move had on the future course of events, but two things stand out. The State Department's declaration became a landmark and a key point of reference for U.S. officials and political circles during both Democratic and Republican administrations. To quote only one most important instance, Mr. Reagan himself told me in the summer of 1980 that the policy toward Italy and specifically that declaration were "about the only thing on which I can agree with the Carter administration." (The interview's most significant sections were published in *Il Tempo*, June 8, and in the newsmagazine *Oggi* on August 13.)

In Italy herself, the State Department's statement represented a bitter disappointment and a psychological blow for the PCI leaders and voters who, as shown in earlier chapters of this book, had deluded themselves that U.S. opposition to a government role for their party was relenting and would soon be dropped. The U.S. move was a shot in the arm for many CDs, Socialists, Social Democrats, Republicans, and Liberals who looked with dismay at a Communist participation in the national government, and gave pause to the political factions and individuals in the democratic camp as well as to the economic groups which favored or were ready to underwrite such a participation.

Yet, the drive for a broader and closer relationship between CDs and Communists had acquired such a momentum that it could hardly be stopped, let alone reversed, right away. A new arrangement worked out in early March 1978 provided for an emergency program to be implemented by a parliamentary alignment including the Communists and by a revamped all Christian Democratic government still headed by Andreotti. As this arrangement went into effect, Moro, who had again taken over the leadership of the CD confederacy as the main proponent of "a strategy of attention" toward the PCI, was kidnapped and later killed by the terrorist group calling itself the Red Brigades. This outrage had the temporary effect of pushing into the background the conflicting pulls within the ruling coalition. But the new CD–PCI relationship "had already begun to sour," I pointed out in the May–June 1980 issue of *Freedom at Issue*. Increasing opposition to Communist participation in the parliamentary majority, let alone in the government, surfaced more and more clearly in the CD camp. Moro himself had put his prestige at stake in support of the new arrangement but had won the backing of the CD parliamentary groups only after spelling out that he would personally object to closer cooperation with the Communists and that CD unity continued to be his paramount concern and commitment.

Over the next few months, Communist demands for Cabinet posts were rebuffed and the CDs made effective use of "their favorite tactics, rubber-walling" to block or water down most of the measures agreed upon with the PCI, I wrote in *The Commonweal* (August 1, 1980). PCI leaders became more and more painfully aware that their party was cast in a role involving "most of the burdens and very few of the benefits of sharing in a governmental coalition." Restlessness and discontent spread among Communist militants and voters "who had never stomached an association with the 'bourgeois' parties nor the cautious efforts by some top Communist chieftains to tone down the PCI's traditional identification with Soviet policies and its harsh strictures against the U.S." (*Freedom at Issue*, May–June 1980). The PCI leadership "gave strong support to antiterrorist measures and made some efforts to persuade the big labor unions to stem the sweeping tide of strikes and inflationary wage demands. This was enough to antagonize quite a few workers and drive many young people to join the libertarian Radical party or the far left grouplets or to abstain from voting altogether. Yet, the achievements were not sufficient to appeal to moderate voters. "Quite a few of them, who had looked with favor at the PCI when it seemed about to win national power, felt frustrated and turned away."

By the end of 1978, Communist leaders, including Berlinguer himself, the top advocate of the "historic compromise," decided "to cut their losses" by taking the party back into the opposition. This precipitated new general elections which were held in June 1979, two years ahead of schedule. The Communist share of the popular vote dropped from more than 34 percent to just over 30 percent. The myth of the PCI's inexorable, irreversible advance was shattered. In the next several years, the overall Communist performance at the polls showed a marked down trend: By 1988, the party's vote was cut by almost one-third from its 1976 peak.

Meanwhile, the 1979 returns had paved the way for a new phase of Italian politics featured by a revival of the center-left coalition. Compared with the governments formed after the "opening" to the PSI back in the early 1960s, the reconstituted coalition reflected some significant changes in the political landscape. It included not only a strengthened Republican party and a Social Democratic party overshadowed by the newly reorganized Socialists, but also the Liberals freed from the conservative approach and leadership which over 20 years earlier had set them on a course of strenuous opposition to the center-left policies. Even more important was the trend toward a more balanced relationship between the CDs and their lay partners, the Socialists first of all. This trend was fueled by the CD losses at the polls: in the mid–1980s, the party's share of the popular vote dropped below its earlier low of 1946 (35 percent). But it was mainly sustained by the growth of the PSI vote which powered the party's ambition to win a top role in running national affairs by overtaking the fading

Communists, developing a more and more "competitive" collaboration with the weakened CDs and eventually replacing them as the leading partner in a revamped government coalition.

Following the disastrous experience of the 1976 election, the PSI came under the control of a young, dynamic group of go-getters headed by 42-year-old Bettino Craxi. A pupil of Nenni, "Craxi intended to fulfill the old man's dream of putting an end to the CD hegemony over the government and to the Communist hegemony over the Italian left." The collapse of the "historic compromise" gave the Socialists a new opportunity to perform as "the kingpin of Italian politics" and Craxi was determined "to make the most of it." (I reviewed these developments and their follow-up in *The Commonweal*, August 28, 1981, in *Freedom at Issue*, November–December 1981, as well as in the *Wall Street Journal, Europe*, January 2, 1985, and in the Spring 1985 issue of *The Washington Quarterly*.) Craxi himself summed up the heart of the matter and pointed at the key of his party's strategy when he told the Socialist National Assembly in July 1984: "Our 11 percent of the votes gives us a decisive role in governing Italy as long as the Communists are kept out of the ruling coalition." Craxi's PSI adopted "a pragmatic approach to social and economic affairs," wholly discarding the doctrinaire Marxism which had been a strong and disastrous feature of traditional Italian Socialism. The party symbol was changed from the hammer and sickle to the red carnation. While pressuring the CDs to yield an increasingly sizable share of national power, the Socialists continued to share much local power with the PCI. Pretty soon, however, the sharpening confrontation between Socialists and Communists for control of such key cities as Milan, Turin, and Rome itself, pushed the PSI to shift from its old time alliance with the PCI in these and other towns to an expanding although very competitive local collaboration with the CDs and its other partners in the central government.

On the domestic front, the most urgent task confronting the rebuilt center-left coalition was to rehabilitate and relaunch the national economy, badly hurt by the 1979 oil crunch and still hamstrung by the all-too-slow progress in modernizing the country's productive and administrative structures. In the early 1980s, the task was made harder by a governmental instability which reflected not only old rifts and rivalries but a difficult transition to the new balance of power within the ruling coalition. The CD party could no longer escape paying a toll for a long governmental tenure that had often been uneven at best. Most of its leaders seemed tired and unable to give any sense of direction to the unruly CD conglomerate. By 1983 its losses at the polls compelled the party to yield the premiership it had first secured back in December 1945.

The new government was presided over by Giovanni Spandolini, leader of the Republican party which, like the Socialists, appeared better equipped to appeal to the expanding middle classes and more specifically to the emerging groups of managers, businessmen, and technicians. In the 1983 general election, the CD share of the popular vote dropped to 33 percent, while the Republicans' rose from 3 to 5 percent and the Socialists' from less than 10 to 11.4 percent.

In the wake of these returns and by exploiting to the full his party's pivotal position, Craxi became Italy's first Socialist premier.

Like its predecessors, the Craxi government was a frequent target of "snipers" (representatives of the parliamentary majority, mainly CDs, who backed the Cabinet on roll calls but on secret ballots voted against the government's bills and helped to defeat quite a few of them). Yet, his own determination and the rivalries among his CD rivals, enabled Craxi to remain at the helm for almost four years, the longest tenure in postwar Italy after the premierships of De Gasperi (December 1945–August 1953) and Aldo Moro (December 1963–July 1968). Thanks also to the creditable performance by CD treasury minister Giovanni Goria, significant progress was made in redressing the Italian economy. As Goria himself summed it up in an interview he gave me for the Italian language daily *Il Progresso Italo-Americano* of New York (March 1, 1987), the inflation rate dropped from 16 percent in the summer of 1983 to less than 9 percent at the end of 1984 and averaged less than 5 percent in the next several years. GNP, which in 1982–1983 had declined for two consecutive years for the first time in the postwar period, grew by 2.6 percent in 1984 and continued to expand at a faster pace than in most other major Western nations with the 1988 rise reaching 3.9 percent.

Meanwhile, a momentous change of climate had taken place. As I put it in the *Wall Street Journal* (Europe) of July 25, 1984, business was no longer a "dirty word in Italy." For a long time, I recalled, social and economic relations had been marked by "a simplistic vision of class warfare." In the early 1970s, many Italian businessmen thought that "the only way to salvage anything" was offered by a deal with organized labor which had emerged with a vengeance from an all-too-long condition of weakness in a labor market traditionally featured by chronic unemployment and underemployment. The next step, several of those businessmen felt, should be an understanding with the Communist party which was gaining ground at the polls and maintained a strong hold on the biggest labor confederation CGIL. An accord was negotiated in 1975 by Giovanni Agnelli, president of FIAT and at the time chairman of Confindustria, and Luciano Lema, the Communist leader of CGIL. A key clause introduced "rigid and pervasive wage indexation system" (as I called it in *Freedom at Issue*, March–April 1981). Big industrialists "tolerated runaway inflation as long as the bill for its magnified impact could be passed on to their customers and to the taxpayers in general." Labor turmoil, nonetheless, became a "normal" condition "in most large private and state-controlled factories and in the public services. In the newly fashionable climate of permissiveness, absenteeism rose to unprecedented peaks (up to 20 percent in some big plants)."

At the same time, there was "a mushrooming of small economic outfits and individual enterprises" which evaded "taxes, social contributions, and union control by employing millions of people who hold a 'guaranteed' job elsewhere or are willing to be paid less than the official wage rates. These 'submerged' or 'black' activities" greatly contributed to keeping the Italian economy afloat but could not spare it "a roller coaster ride" involving impending dangers of a severe recession, rampant inflation, and a large deficit in the country's foreign accounts. When they tried to contain the sweeping tide of disruptive strikes and highly inflationary wage rises top labor leaders quickly found out that they could not control "the most militant groups of workers which . . . had been infiltrated by radical grouplets and terrorist organizations. Moreover, the big unions' emphasis on equal raises for all workers, irrespective of individual skills, antagonized strong white- and blue-collar groups. Hence, the proliferation of 'autonomous' unions that appeal to the frustrations of such groups and cater to their special interests."

Things came to a head in the early fall of 1980 when FIAT management decided to dismiss some 14,000 workers as part of its strategy to cope with a crisis that affected the automobile industry all over the world but was exasperated by recent developments in the national labor field. The unions called a strike which lasted five weeks and was openly backed by the PCI. Berlinguer himself addressed the strikers in Turin, FIAT's headquarters, pledging his party's support if they occupied the plants. But the unions' opposition to any compromise collapsed when an estimated 40,000 workers, foremen, and employees marched through Turin shouting "Freedom to work!"

Organized labor had both overreached itself and failed to realize that the tide had turned. Many big and medium-sized industries felt encouraged enough to follow FIAT's example and "start restructuring their plants along lines calling for sizable payroll cuts. . . . Absenteeism dropped significantly, while productivity rose." A major move away from the rigid indexation system was undertaken by the Craxi government in February 1984. The operation of the indexation mechanism was cooled off temporarily by an executive decree. The move was backed by the unions representing Catholic, Socialist, Social Democratic, and Republican workers as well as by the Socialist wing of CGIL. But the PCI went on the warpath. "Responding to pressure from party leaders the majority of CGIL held protest rallies all over Italy and pushed to the breaking point relations between Communists and Socialists in a sector where their ties have been traditionally strongest. For four months, the PCI managed to block parliamentary action on the decree," I wrote in the *Washington Quarterly*, Spring 1985.

In the election held in June 1984 to choose the Italian members of the European Parliament and of some local administrations in Sardinia and other parts of Italy, the PCI overtook the CDs by a whisker. Some observers in the United States hastened to read much too much in this development. Joseph La Palombara, professor at Yale and an "expert" on Italy hailed the PCI's "electoral upsurge" as an event of major significance and new evidence that the party's participation in the national government was viewed by the Italians, including "many non-Communist political leaders," as far from "undesirable." These assertions were made by La Palombara in a letter to the *New York Times* (July 5, 1984) which took sharply to task the former U.S. ambassador to Rome, Richard N. Gardner. In an article in the same daily (June 22), Gardner had recalled the PCI's setbacks in the 1979 and 1983 national elections, had pointed out that Berlinguer had pursued a basically anti-American policy, and concluded that Communist entry into the government remained "neither inevitable nor desirable." In a letter printed in the *New York Times* on July 18, Gardner effectively refuted La Palombara's charges and arguments.

⌈The decline of the Communist electoral following did actually acquire further momentum over the next few years. This confirmed that the 1984 vote had been indeed "a fluke" due to an unusually low turnout at the polls as well as to the emotions aroused by Berlinguer's death on the stump and magnified by the media,⌋as I pointed out in *Freedom at Issue*, September–October, 1985, and in the already quoted article in the *Washington Quarterly*.

⌊On the issue itself of wage indexation, the PCI "projected again the image of an opposition party ready to resort to a 'the worse, the better' approach." Enactment of the Craxi decree "was widely read as evidence that a center-left government headed by a Socialist could successfully challenge the veto power long held by the PCI on major social and economic issues." Yet, the PCI promoted a national referendum to repeal the changes introduced by the decree in the wage indexation system. Repeal, I further wrote in *Freedom at Issue*, "would give back to salaried workers an average of 14 dollars a month, but the political stakes were high. . . . Premier Craxi himself pledged to resign right away if a majority came out for repeal." The Communists had the backing of the Neo-Fascist MSI and of small far-left groups. In Southern Italy, a widespread protest against long-standing economic and social depression produced a low turnout and a 50–50 split in the vote. But especially in the industrial North many workers were unswayed by the prospect of getting some money right away and were rather aware that repeal would have longer-range negative effects on the national economy. Altogether, "54.3 percent of the votes were cast to retain the cuts in the automatic wage increases." Once again, the majority of the Italians were guided by a mature and realistic appraisal of their country's requirements and priorities. ⌋

⌊As the restructuring and modernization of key sectors of the national economy proceeded under more favorable conditions, there was a lot of talk not only about a new boom but about a "second Italian miracle." The new phase of economic expansion, ⌊I wrote in the *Wall Street Journal–Europe* (August 7, 1986),⌋did start under more favorable circumstances than those which in the late 1950s had "spawned the term 'miracle.' " The restructuring and modernization process had involved not only large and medium-sized private enterprises but several important state-controlled industries while others had been returned to private ownership. The Italian economy could now rely on a "new generation" of managers and technicians who had gained "an international outlook." Most labor unions had given up or soft-pedaled many of their demands for frequent and sizable wage increases unrelated to the actual conditions and prospects of employers, and for "equal cost-of-living allowances for all workers, irrespective of individual skills and base salary.'' Economic growth, moreover, was helped by external and occasional factors such as the much lower prices of oil and other imported raw materials, by the expansion of world trade, and by the availability of capital on the international markets.

There was a reverse side to the coin, however.

The budget deficit, which had topped 13 percent of GNP, stayed much higher than in most other Western nations. The fast rising public debt might soon exceed GNP. The tax system continued to be ''socially inequitable and technically unwieldy.'' Unemployment was inching up toward 12 percent of the work force. There was still too much truth to the ''horror stories'' about the wasteful and paralyzing effects of the central and local bureaucracy.

With some notable exceptions, the gap between the South and the more developed areas of Italy and especially of the industrial North, remained very great. If anything, the gap was getting deeper in several significant ways. In the mid-to-late 1970s, I wrote in a review of the problem published in the *Wall Street Journal–Europe* (April 8, 1988), per capita income in the South, which in 1950 was just over 50 percent of the average elsewhere in the country and had risen to 62 percent in 1973, dropped back to about 60 percent. With 40 percent of the Italian territory and 36 percent of the population, the South contributed less than 25 percent of GNP. Unemployment had risen to 20 percent of the labor force compared with about 8 percent in Northern and Central Italy. Since 1950, the government had allocated more than 100 billion dollars for the development of the long-depressed Southern regions, but an all-too-great share of the monies was frittered away through waste, mismanagement, and abuses. Other sizable public funds went to finance ''cathedrals in the desert,'' huge steel, oil refining, and petrochemical plants which failed to promote clusters of smaller enterprises and to generate sizable and steady employment. In Sicily, the Mafia gained a large measure of control of the funds distribution and diverted them to the benefit of its bosses and of the political groups with which they had developed mutually profitable ties and relationships. Other criminal organizations prospered, much in the same way although on a somewhat smaller scale elsewhere in the South, notably in the Naples area and in Calabria.

Terrorist organizations operating in Italy have been dealt severe blows by more efficient police and secret services. These organizations are no longer the major threat to democratic institutions and public order that they appeared to represent in the late 1970s and early 1980s. Yet, terrorist groups, on the extreme left and also on the extreme right, are still active and show a worrisome capability to win new recruits and to maintain operative ties with similar organizations in other West European countries and in the Middle East. There is also increasing evidence of cooperation between terrorist groups and sectors of the Mafia and Camorra in Southern Italy.

Public services represent the most dismal feature because they reflect and compound, more than other sectors, the still unsolved, or only partially solved problems of a traditionally poor and underdeveloped country, and the new problems (drugs being an obvious instance) besetting a nation which, late and hastily, has become fairly affluent and demanding.

Recent surveys by respected research organizations draw a picture that is borne out by the daily experience of those who must rely on public services in such key areas as health care and railroads, social security and the mails, justice, schools, and airports. By and large, these services are more expensive than in many other Western countries while they often operate at a loss and their performance is generally well below the standards required by a modern democracy.

Another worrisome feature is the all-too-powerful and intrusive role of the political parties and notably of their chieftains at the national and local levels. Representatives of the key government parties (and to a certain extent those of the PCI, the main opposition force) have acquired effective control of all-too-many public agencies in the economic as well as in the information sectors. The result is an unhealthy relationship (to use a strong understatement) between political parties and private groups which have acquired powerful and privileged positions in those same sectors. This relationship can be too cozy or too adversarial, but the loser is always the average citizen and consumer, especially in a country like Italy which still lacks adequate and effective anti-trust laws.

Such conditions and circumstances have been often signalled, denounced, and even overemphasized by foreign observers. Yet, they are sometimes ignored or glibly explained away by some of these same "Italy watchers." A case in point is a recent book by Professor La Palombara, *Democracy Italian Style* (published in October 1987 by Yale University Press). As the author himself acknowledges, mostly in very small print footnotes, the book reflects a sharp departure from and actually a disavowal of the interpretations embodied in his earlier works. In this latest production, La Palombara seems carried away by a sweeping, almost indiscriminate enthusiasm for the nature and workings of the Italian system of democracy.

As evidenced throughout this book, I've maintained since the early postwar years that the roots of Italian democracy were much stronger and deeper than it was generally felt abroad (and in Italy herself), that in many fields the country was narrowing down the traditional distances from the leading Western democracies, and that the much maligned "political class" deserved some credit for such achievements. But La Palombara goes much further, too much so. Just to give a few samples: The factionalism within the Italian political parties "is not only logical, it is a godsend"; the spoils system as practiced in Italy "is much more nuanced and civilized than the American type" because it leaves "crumbs" and even "juicy morsels or sumptuous feasts . . . to political opponents"; there is "something fundamentally democratic about tax evasion [in Italy]: one way or another the practice is open to a very large proportion of the adult population." One is tempted to think that here and elsewhere La Palombara is pulling the reader's leg. But the professor takes much too seriously his arguments and above all himself to indulge in such pranks. Of course, La Palombara must resort to evasive action or to verbal acrobatics when his assertions and preconceptions collide with the all-too-real backwardness, inefficiency, and injustice that are still to be found in Italy to a greater extent than in the more advanced democratic societies.

La Palombara is quite consistent on one thing, though: his sympathy, not to use a stronger word, for Italian Communism (which already led him to misread the significance of the 1984 election). In his latest book, he refers almost off-handedly to the PCI's "mild electoral slide since 1979" but adds quickly that the party "attracts the support of about one out of three adults." La Palombara conveniently forgets that the string of defeats suffered by the PCI at the polls brought its share of the popular vote well below 30 percent. Nor does he mention the steady decline in the party's membership (well over 10 percent since the mid–1970s). La Palombara further uses quite unacademic language to attack all those who do not agree with his view that "the PCI, its leaders as well as its followers and voters, represent . . . mainstays of Italian democracy."

In recent years, Italy has not only emerged from a long-standing condition of underdevelopment but by many economic yardsticks has overtaken Great Britain and caught up with France. At the same time, more and more Italians have become aware that the gap between their country and the leading Western de-mocracies "remains quite large in the field of public services and institutions," as I pointed out in the *Wall Street Journal–Europe* (June 30, 1988). They have also realized that the significant progress already made especially in the economic sector can be jeopardized if the most serious of those lags and shortcomings are not corrected fairly soon. These corrections are made more urgent by the new, decisive phase of European integration which involves the removal of all trade and other economic barriers throughout the EEC by the end of 1992.

The dangers of a "widening efficiency gap" have been stressed for some time by top representatives of the economic sector, but lately the man in the street, the media, and the politicians themselves, I further reported, have become in-creasingly aware of the urgent need for corrective action. In response to mounting pressure for modern and orderly social and political structures, the new center-left coalition government, formed in April 1988 and headed by CD secretary general Ciziaco De Mita, set up a special Cabinet post for institutional reform. Several bills were submitted to Parliament and one of them, enacted before the summer recess, gives the premier's office more power to "direct and coordinate" the activities of governmental departments. More powers should also be granted to local agencies and other public bodies in order to reduce the burdens and cut delays and bottlenecks at the central level as well as to give citizens easier access to the offices handling their affairs.

Strikes in the public sector and notably in transportation services are to be regulated and restricted. Some steps have been taken and more are planned to enable Parliament to perform more speedily and efficiently by streamlining rules and procedures and by reforming the present system whereby the work of each chamber is mostly duplicated by the other.

A major battle has been fought over the issue of secret balloting. It had long been regarded as a bulwark protecting the independence of individual members of Parliament against "the rampant power of political parties" and notably of their leadership. In more recent times, however, the secret ballot had become a tool not only to promote or shelter the special interests of pressure groups but to settle scores and affect the balance of power among and within the parties making up the ruling coalition. By joining with the opposition on secret ballots, members of the parliamentary majority managed quite often to defeat government-sponsored bills, to force through crippling amendments and generally to paralyze and distort the law-making process. The overall effect was to foster political instability even when the "snipers" did not precipitate full-fledged government crises. As the main opposition party, the PCI was reluctant to be deprived of a device that helped it to multiply and sharpen the strains and divisions within the ruling coalition. On the other hand, quite a few Communists, including some party leaders, realized more and more clearly that a rigid stand against curtailing secret balloting and against other institutional reforms would promote a further political isolation of their party and expose it once again to the charge of pursuing a "the worse, the better" approach. Divided among themselves as they were, on this as on so many other issues, the Communists eventually came round to accepting to rule out secret balloting on all bills involving money outlays. This shift, however, came too late and the PCI failed to obtain in return truly substantial benefits (such as the chairmanship of some parliamentary committees).

Among the partners in the ruling coalition, the Socialists were the stoutest and most outspoken champions of reducing to a minimum the matters on which the secret ballot would still be allowed. Voting by roll call, the Socialists felt, would work as a deterrent against CD "sniping" at the governments that they (the Socialists) hope to head again in the not too distant future. Thanks mainly to Socialist pressure, the coalition parties stuck to the approach restricting the resort to secret balloting to issues of constitutional relevance (mainly civil rights) and to personal matters. The outcome appeared in doubt up to the last minute: paradoxically, the curbs on secret balloting had to be voted . . . by secret ballot! The governmental majority prevailed by only seven votes in the Chamber of Deputies where defections in its ranks reached about 60. The margin was much higher in the Senate.

The new rules on balloting were not sufficient, of course, to guarantee a smooth performance by Parliament, let alone a happy outcome for all the bills sponsored by the parties of the ruling coalition. Pretty soon, the "snipers" were replaced by representatives of these parties who failed to show up for crucial votes or who lined up openly with the opposition to introduce amendments which involved sizable increases in some of the allocations included in the budgets submitted by the government. Nor was it clear how the leaders of the parties making up the ruling coalition could or would prevent such open challenges from becoming more frequent and harmful to the effectiveness, credibility, and stability itself of Italian governments. By strongly circumscribing the use of the secret ballot, however, the Italian Parliament has greatly curtailed the scope of one of the "anomalies" which set the country apart from most other Western nations.⌐

Greater obstacles and many pitfalls, I further pointed out in the *Wall Street Journal*, loomed down the road leading to changes affecting "directly the rules of the political game." ⌐Since the downfall of Fascism, a proportional system, slightly tilted in favor of large parties, has been in effect for electing the members of the House. Somewhat more significant departures from the proportional system provide additional benefits for the major parties in the election of the 315 senators (the members of the House are 630). A majority system applies only to the election of municipal councils in the smaller towns.⌐

⌐Proportional representation has protected the survival of minor groups (Republicans, Social-Democrats, and Liberals), which embody traditional facets of Italian democracy and has enabled them to wield quite a bit of influence as important and sometimes indispensable partners in governmental coalitions. In recent years, however, local and one-issue groups, notably the Greens, have proliferated, helped by growing interest in such issues as well as by the generally more permissive climate that has developed in Italy as in most other Western countries. Out of several hundred slates of candidates fielded in the latest elections, only a few gained seats in the national Parliament. Their representatives have promoted some new legislation concerning those matters, but have also introduced additional confusion and delays in the law-making process.⌐

Several proposals have been made to extend the majority system to the election of mayors and municipal councillors in large and medium-sized towns as well as to reform the electoral system for the national Parliament possibly along the lines of the West German model, whereby a party can secure seats only if it gets at least 5 percent of the total vote. Even if this requirement should be lowered to 4 percent, several minor parties (Liberals, Radicals, the far-left Popular Democracy, the Social Democrats, and perhaps the Greens) would be excluded from the national Parliament and from many local councils. The Republicans, too, are opposed to significant departures from proportional representation, although they gather 4 to 5 percent of the votes and might be helped to make some gains at the expense of the parties which would be barred from Parliament. The PSI is the most outspoken champion of an electoral reform keyed to a middle way between the law on the books and a full-fledged majority system (which would favor not only the CDs but the PCI rather than the Socialists themselves). Such a reform would help the PSI to further expand its share of the popular vote possibly beyond 20 percent catching up with the Communists. More strength and legitimacy would be given to the Socialist challenge to the CD governmental leadership. The CDs themselves would benefit from an electoral system patterned after the West German model. As already noted, however, such a system could also materially help the PSI which is the CDs' main partner in the ruling coalition but has already grown into their main rival for the premiership. The CDs do not relish, either, the prospect of seeing some of their traditional allies (Liberals and Social Democrats) excluded from Parliament and from many local councils as well.

The Communists are divided and rather ambivalent on the issue. They know only too well that the recent Socialist gains have been made mostly at their expense and are reluctant to countenance an electoral reform likely to help the PSI's growth and standing. Following the recent PCI losses at the polls, however, quite a few Communists have begun to think that an electoral reform benefitting the larger groups might well enable their party to win votes from the minor leftist groups and thus counterbalance the PSI's gains and the CDs' long standing role as number one in Italian politics. The PCI chieftains further know that meaningful change in the electoral system (like other major institutional and political reforms) can "hardly be enacted without Communist support." For the party, "this represents," I further stressed in the *Wall Street Journal–Europe* (June 30, 1988), "a readymade opportunity to re-enter the big political game" and to negotiate some profitable deals by trying to play off the CD and Socialist parties against each other.

In many of the articles quoted or summarized in this book, I duly noted the CD party's weaknesses and shortcomings—mainly the entrenched factionalism, the failure to take strong and timely action to overcome chronic national problems, the waste of public moneys and the tolerance, bordering on encouragement, for graft and corruption (in recent years, more and more accusations of the same kind have been made against the Socialists as well as against quite a few representatives of the PCI which had long claimed to be "the party of clean hands").

Yet, even in the mid–1980s, when most foreign (and many Italian) observers predicted once again an early "disintegration" of the CD confederacy, I maintained that the party "was down but far from out. It was actually beginning to emerge from a painful reappraisal of its policies with a fresh determination to reclaim top place in running national affairs" (*Freedom at Issue*, November–December 1986). Six months earlier, I had reported in the *Wall Street Journal–Europe* (May 23, 1986), that CD secretary general De Mita, having consolidated his hold on the post, had embarked upon a determined effort to "rejuvenate" the party as well as to reestablish a working relationship with the "collateral" organizations, notably the predominantly Catholic CISL, Italy's second largest labor confederation, and other Catholic associations which since the late 1950s had been both less willing and less able to "steer their members into the CD fold."

In most local elections held in 1985–1986, I further noted in *Freedom at Issue*, "the CD vote rose again to 35 percent." De Mita played a key role in the election of CD "Francesco Cossiga to the Presidency of the Republic held since 1978 by a maverick Socialist Sandro Pertini." A significant factor in the CD comeback, I wrote, was "a more active Catholic involvement in Italian politics." The church's support for the party "is not as intense and avowed as it was most of the time under Pope Pius XII, but it is greater and more evident than under John

XXIII or Paul VI. By appealing to Catholics to be 'united' and active in Italian society, John Paul II has in effect called on them to rally behind the CDs." However, I noted in the *Wall Street Journal–Europe*, new activist groups endorsed by the Pope, notably *Comunione e Liberazione* and its political arm, *Movimento Popolare*, were looked upon "by many CDs and by older Catholic organizations as a mixed blessing at best because of their militancy" often smacking of the sort of intolerance which featured the Counter-Reformation of the late sixteenth century. While strongly opposing Communism both in Italy and abroad, *Movimento Popolare* has developed a working alliance with the CD faction led by foreign minister and former premier Giulio Andreotti. According to many observers and representatives of his own party, Andreotti has displayed in recent years an eagerness for detente with the East as well as "a sympathy, or at least a tolerance, toward Arab countries, including Qaddafi's Libya" that "on occasion have jeopardized Italian relations with Washington (let alone Israel)." By another quirk of religious-cum-political relations and alignments in Italy, Andreotti's approach has been backed and even outdone by such leftwing Catholic groups as the labor association ACLI which are strongly at odds with *Movimento Popolare* but "spurred by a knee jerk, allout zeal for the Third World . . . have long criticized the U.S. in general and more sharply and specifically the Reagan Administration for its approach to Latin America, to the problem of state-sponsored terrorism, to negotiations with the Soviet Union and to disarmament" (*Freedom at Issue*; see also *Wall Street Journal*).

In a long conversation late in 1985, De Mita defended and upheld Andreotti's performance as foreign minister, including notably his role in the events that followed the hijacking of the Italian ship *Achille Lauro* by Arab terrorists. Friendly relations with Andreotti, De Mita indicated, were an important factor in his own plans and efforts to win reelection as party secretary with a very broad majority at the CD National Congress slated for the following spring. At the same time, De Mita made a special point of emphasizing his party's "traditional and decisive role as the first and largest Italian political force committed to sustain and strengthen the Atlantic alliance and notably the ties with the U.S. This has been and this remains our basic line in foreign affairs, ever since De Gasperi's time," De Mita told me in an obvious counter to the efforts by the Socialists to claim for their party the role of the most reliable "interlocutor" that the United States could find in Italy.

At the CD National Congress in late May 1986, De Mita strengthened his control over the party. As I reported in *Freedom at Issue*, he reaffirmed the "determination of his party to operate as the mainstay of Italy's loyal and active participation in NATO." De Mita also stressed that the best way to promote a genuine detente with the East was "a strong solidarity of Italy and Europe with the U.S." and further praised "Reagan's America" for "its role in upholding the peaceful balance of power in the World."

In the next few years, the CDs continued to recoup some of the ground lost in the early 1980s. They performed better at the local than at the national level.

Yet, in the 1987 general elections the party's percentage of the popular vote inched up to over 34 percent, enough to strengthen its claim to the premiership. Former treasury minister Giovanni Goria led the new government; but in April 1988 De Mita himself took over the helm of a revamped five-party coalition.

Just as they had closed ranks time and again when confronted with strong challenges to their political supremacy, the CDs were shaken by a fresh upsurge of factional strife after this turn for the better in their fortunes. As I reported in *Freedom at Issue* (May–June 1989), premier De Mita "fueled the opposition to his leadership when he appeared all-too-reluctant to yield the party secretaryship or at least strongly determined to handpick his successor in the job." This unleashed a new bout of the CD "allergy . . . rooted in the widespread fear that any leader strong enough to get a firm hold on both the premiership and the party's helm" would "curb the power, the autonomy and the privileges of the several factions traditionally active and influential within the rainbow CD confederation." This allergy worked against De Gasperi in the early 1950s and more visibly and quickly against Fanfani in 1958–1959. At the National Congress of the party held in February 1989, several CD barons formed a coalition which controlled 65 percent of the rank and file and in effect asked De Mita to give up the secretaryship if he wanted to stay on as premier. The coalition was led by interior minister Antonio Gava, by Andreotti and by Forlani who was chairman of the CD National Committee. All of them pledged to loyally back the De Mita government after the premier accepted to yield the party secretaryship to Forlani and to succeed him as chairman of the National Committee. Yet, "the prospects for governmental stability and efficiency," I went on, looked "less encouraging than they could appear" only a few months earlier. The drive for institutional reform had begun to falter before the end of 1988. The governmental coalition seemed to find it harder and harder to deal effectively with "the negative consequences of the vigorous but unbalanced economic expansion of recent years," notably fresh inflationary pressures, the continued high level of the budget deficit and a trade balance heavily in the red.

The impatience of the Socialists over this condition of affairs was made more acute by their disappointing performance in some local elections. They benefitted much less than expected from the rifts and disarray within the Social Democratic camp and failed to attract most of the disgruntled Communists who turned, instead, to the Greens. Possibly, these returns signalized the surfacing impact of the PSI's inner weaknesses: the lack of an adequate party organization, the involvement of local Socialist bosses in unsavory deals and cases of outright graft, and the recurring feuds among those bosses only barely controlled or masked by Craxi's overwhelming and occasionally arrogant prestige and authority.

The Socialist leader, I stressed in the *Wall Street Journal–Europe* (March 17, 1989), "knows how to count and the numbers tell a very clear story"; while today and in the politically foreseeable future there is a working majority for a government including CDs and Socialists, a leftist alliance cannot expect to rally much more than 45 percent of the votes. Moreover, the defeats suffered at the polls had not yet "weakened and subdued" the Communists to the point of making them resigned to accept a junior role in a governmental coalition led by Craxi. The Socialist leader, I went on, is also fully aware that his party's hopes and his own ambitions would be dealt a deadly blow if the new PCI secretary Achille Occhetto manages to achieve at least a partial success in his campaign to stop and possibly reverse his party's unfavorable trend at the polls as well as to legitimize "its claim to supremacy over the Italian left" by securing an endorsement from several of the major Social Democratic forces operating in Western Europe. Craxi's concern over any such development erupted into the open when Occhetto was reported to have called him "the main obstacle" to that legitimization. Occhetto denied having made such a remark, but Craxi promptly charged that the PCI still "wants to be Communist" and therefore should continue to be barred from membership in the Socialist International or other similar organizations. There was no early prospect, Craxi further stressed, that PSI and PCI might work together to build "a common house" for the European left including Communists, Socialist and other "progressive-minded forces." This project could be broadened to include the Soviet party itself, Occhetto told Mikhail Gorbachev during their five-hour talks in Moscow early in March. Gorbachev himself, I recalled, had referred time and again to the USSR as part of a "common European house," an idea involving closer economic and political links between the two halves of Europe and "a significant loosening of the ties" between the United States and the European members of NATO.

At the same time, Craxi and other leading Italian Socialists seemed only too often bent on "making trouble for any government headed by a Christian Democrat." In order to wring more concessions out of the CDs, the Socialists did not hesitate to wink at the Communists and occasionally join "forces with them" and thus to keep "alive the prospect" that some day PSI and PCI may cooperate in promoting a leftist alternative to the CD supremacy in running national affairs.

The PCI was going through a most serious crisis which reflected the main factors spotlighted in several of my articles quoted in this book and published at a time when, according to most foreign and Italian observers, Italian Communism was on its way to further major electoral and political successes. As I pointed out in *Freedom at Issue* (November-December 1987), the PCI was not about "to become, like its French counterpart, a 'bunker party,' backed by only 10 percent of the votes." It could be rescued from its predicament, moreover, if the democratic forces made much bigger mistakes than they had in the past. The competition between CDs and Socialists, I wrote in the *Wall Street Journal-Europe* (June 30, 1988), might degenerate to the point of allowing the PCI to gain significant benefits by throwing "its backing to the highest bidder" on each major issue coming to the table. The PCI could also be helped, I noted in *Freedom at Issue*, by a significant and protracted deterioration of economic conditions: the big rise of domestic consumption and imports, fueled by the expansion of recent years, might produce "overheating of the economy, higher inflation and a devaluation of the Italian currency" which in turn would compel "the government and the Bank of Italy . . . to introduce restrictions and controls bound to be unpopular well before they can prove effective."

Meanwhile, the collapse of the hopes and plans for an early government role had brought to the surface the conflicting pulls and interests that operated within the composite PCI electorate. I gave specific examples in an article published in the *Wall Street Journal-Europe* (March 26, 1985) and in the May 1 national edition of the same paper. Confronted with a tax reform drafted by the Craxi government and intended primarily to crack down on large scale evasion by self-employed groups (such as shopkeepers, lawyers, and physicians), the PCI leaders felt that the party could not afford either to jeopardize the support gained in recent years among those groups or to antagonize its traditional followers in the labor unions, strongly favorable to the reform. "After many zigs and zags," the Communists "abstained in the final vote." Since the early 1970s, I recalled, the PCI leaders had committed the party to accepting Italy's membership in NATO. But this commitment was contradicted and actually voided of concrete significance as the PCI opposed any step intended to give real meaning and substance to Italy's role in the alliance, including notably the deployment of U.S. cruise missiles in Sicily as part of NATO's strategy to counterbalance the Soviet SS–20s already aimed at Western Europe. For over 20 years, the Italian Communists have campaigned for the removal of a support base for submarines operated by the United States on a small island off Sardinia. Leftwing Communist groups as well as the party's Youth Organization have gone further: they urge "an early, outright Italian withdrawal from NATO."

The strong anti-American bias, one of the main "red threads" running through the PCI's tradition and approach, continued to be reflected in the day-by-day coverage of international events by the media controlled or influenced by the party. It also emerged most significantly when PCI leaders tried to tone down at least the most shrill expressions of such a bias. These attempts have been mainly fueled by the desire to pave the way for the first visit to the United States by the party's secretary general, a "pet project" of the PCI leadership since the early 1970s. For instance, the draft platform for the party's National Congress, held in April 1986, sought to draw a distinction between President Reagan's policies, which must continue to be sharply attacked, and the "other America" which could and should be "befriended" in so far as it opposed these policies. But an amendment, denouncing the United States in much more sweeping terms, was approved by more than one third of the party's provincial Congresses and received significant support in many others. Eventually, a compromise was reached on the relevant plank of the platform and overwhelmingly ratified by the National Congress. But the episode highlighted the kind of problems that the Italian Communist leaders have fashioned for themselves (and for their party). The indoctrination campaign carried out for so many years by the PCI chieftains and spokesmen, I pointed out, "worked only too well" (*Wall Street Journal–Europe*, April 7, 1986). It has made too many Italian Communists "intolerant" both "of any substantial criticism of the USSR" and "of attempts to soften their virulent anti-Americanism." Much in the same way, the persistent campaign branding the CDs as deeply corrupted and a tool of the priests and of the rich bourgeoisie turned into a boomerang as the PCI leaders' plans for the "historic compromise" ran into strong hostility from wide sectors of the party.

The PCI rightwingers, who represent 20 to 25 percent of the cadres but command a smaller following among the rank and file, continue to press for a foreign policy approach similar to that pursued by Social Democratic parties in West Germany and in Northern Europe. The PCI rightwingers also champion a "reformist" program in domestic affairs likewise intended to pave the way for a working alliance with the Socialists which should become the cornerstone of a "leftist and democratic" coalition strong enough to win control of the government and confine the CDs into the opposition.

Quite different ideas power other sectors of the PCI. They include a small but active far left faction, led by Senator Armando Cossutta, which is militantly pro-Soviet and calls for an all-out fight against "capitalism and American imperialism." According to Cossutta and his followers, the present PCI leadership has embarked upon a course involving major and most dangerous departures from the Marxist-Leninist doctrines and has in effect "sold the party's soul to the devil." A much larger group is headed by Pietro Ingrao, veteran leader of the party's left wingers, and has the backing of almost one-third of the PCI. This group brands the Socialists as a "moderate" party that has accepted to play second fiddle to the CDs, and looks with interest to the Catholic left-wingers. Ingrao advocates a "tougher line" against the center left governments and an all-out drive to defeat the "onslaughts of Italian capitalism" which has now undertaken a more "aggressive course" within the framework of the overall approach championed notably by Thatcherism in Great Britain and Reaganism in the United States.

The crisis of Italian Communism must also be viewed within the broader framework of the rapid collapse of the myth of "Eurocommunism." As I recalled in the *Wall Street Journal–Europe* (September 15, 1988) and in the paper's national edition (September 19), back in the mid–1970s many media in the West had carried assessments and predictions by "experts" proclaiming that the Communists would soon secure key government roles in a wide arc stretching from Italy and France to Spain and Portugal. It was further asserted that the "Eurocommunist" parties were on a collision course with Moscow which would lead to a "schism" with consequences as crucially significant as the Sino-Soviet split. Actually, I noted in the *Wall Street Journal*, none of the "Eurocommunist" parties managed to secure a share of national power and most of them suffered severe losses at the polls and/or debilitating splits. Over and above differences in background and experience, the decline of these parties reflected a single and largely expectable fact: the inability to develop a new kind of "Communism" which would somehow reconcile basic allegiance to their ideological and international commitments with a "Westernization" far reaching enough to appeal to large "centrist" sectors of the electorate and thus strengthen their claim to an important government role.

Under the circumstances, I further wrote in the *Wall Street Journal*, the "new course" pursued by Mikhail Gorbachev in the USSR could represent, at best, a "mixed blessing" for the "Eurocommunist" parties and, at worst, make their crisis deeper and more tangled. To be sure, the PCI leaders have found it less difficult to "heal the rifts" produced by their strictures on the Soviet interventions in Czechoslovakia and in Afghanistan as well as by their proclaimed determination to pursue an "Italian road to Socialism" rather than continue to ape the "Soviet model." But "the devastating indictment" of the Soviet system brought about by *perestroika* and *glasnost* shattered most of the basic tenets that guided the PCI (and the other Western European Communist parties) ever since they were founded in the wake of the 1917 Bolshevik Revolution.

No wonder that at the meetings of the PCI Central Committee held in the summer and early fall of 1988 many voices were raised to demand urgent action to give the party not only "a new look" but "a new identity." Veteran members of the Communist leadership like Macaluso emphasized that in the last ten years the party had wavered between looking back wistfully to some sort of "historic compromise" with the CDs and the pursuit of leftist alliances, primarily with the PSI, which would relegate the CDs to the opposition. As a result of this prolonged "vacillation," Macaluso added, the PCI suffered several consecutive defeats at the polls, while both CDs and Socialists gained ground. Even more anguished and outspoken admissions keep coming from the rank and file of the PCI as well as of the Communist majority of CGIL: "We are neither fish nor fowl, and the voters realize it," says a party official in Turin. "We are no longer able to represent the needs of our people," adds a union leader in the same city. And some members of the PCI Central Committee are asking "whether in today's Italy there is still room and a role for a Communist party."

All Communist parties in Western Europe, I concluded in the *Wall Street Journal–Europe*, are confronted with a fundamental dilemma. They can choose not to . . . choose, accepting in effect to become a marginal force backed by a "dwindling minority of voters." Alternatively, they can decide to cut themselves off from their ideological and political roots in order to work within the democratic and modern capitalistic system. But if the "Eurocommunist" parties, or sizable chunks of them, "should move that far, wouldn't they cease to be Communist?"

The election of the Italian members of the European Parliament could not affect directly the make-up of the national Parliament or government. However, I wrote in the *Wall Street Journal–Europe*, June 9, 1989), the returns would provide an updated reading of the political balance of power in Italy at a time when strains were mounting within the ruling coalition and the fortunes of the PCI, by far the largest opposition party, were quite uncertain.

Expecting the PSI to do well in the European elections, Craxi looked forward to a state of affairs that would allow him to precipitate a general election in Italy (normally due only in 1992) under circumstances likely to enable his party to rake in further gains at the expense of both Communists and CDs. Accordingly, the Socialist leader stepped up the drive to weaken and discredit the De Mita Cabinet and thus emphasize the contrast between its shaky position and mediocre performance and the stability and achievements of his own tenure as premier in the mid–1980s. Barely a month before the vote for the European Parliament, scheduled for June 18, Craxi delivered the death blow by instructing the Socialist representatives to quit the De Mita government.

Meanwhile Occhetto was working hard to legitimize the PCI, at home and abroad, as a democratic, progressive-minded party committed to supporting Western values and policies. As part of this strategy, Occhetto travelled to the United States in mid-May, the first visit ever by a secretary general of the PCI. State Department officials most conversant with Italian affairs told me that the Bush administration did not intend to depart from the policy of opposition to a Communist role in the West European governments. "With the European elections coming up", they added, "we are most careful to avoid any move that might help, however indirectly, the PCI and hurt Craxi's Socialists at the polls." No official meetings were set up for Occhetto, Napolitano, and the other members of the PCI delegation. Two State Department officials, however, attended the dinner that Italian ambassador to Washington, Rinaldo Petrignani, organized for Occhetto and his lieutenants, reportedly on instructions from Foreign Minister Andreotti. As I further reported in the *Wall Street Journal*, Occhetto met with some members of Congress and "garnered a few statements that he exploited in Italy" as implying that the PCI was now eligible as a partner in running national affairs. Actually, this could be argued only in a few instances such as Senator Pell's remark that the Italian Communists were "like radishes: red on the outside, white and tasty inside." In his meetings and talks in Washington and in New York, Occhetto contended that his party had been committed for a long time to loyally supporting NATO. But he failed to explain satisfactorily why PCI politicians and the media they control or influence continued "to oppose every move involving a concrete contribution to the alliance and particularly to Italian solidarity with the United States (the latest instance being the transfer to Calabria of the F–16s based in Spain)." According to PCI rhetoric, moreover, Washington's call for retaining and modernizing short-range nuclear weapons provided fresh evidence that American strategy continued to be keyed to the prospect of "an atomic war to be fought in Europe and only in Europe."

The position of the Bush Administration was further confirmed by the new ambassador to Italy Peter Secchia. In his first press conference in Rome, he spelled out that, while it was up to the Italians to decide on the makeup of their government, the United States "prefers" that the PCI be kept out of the ruling coalition. In a subsequent statement, the ambassador put more emphasis on the "non interference" in Italian domestic affairs which, as reported in earlier chapters of this book, had likewise been for a long time a significant aspect of the

American approach to the "Communist issue" in Italy (and elsewhere in Western Europe).

All in all, I concluded on the basis of several interviews conducted just before and after Occhetto's visit to the United States, most Congressmen continued to feel that, while there had been "changes" in the position of the PCI, " the inclusion of Communists in governing coalitions" would still "create serious problems for the United States and the NATO alliance" (to quote Leon Panetta and Lee Hamilton, ranking representatives of the Democratic party, long regarded by the Italian Communists as more favorable or less unfavorable toward their goal of securing a government role).

A new factor was introduced in the campaign for the European Parliament when the groups controlling the Communist party and regime in China brutally crushed the students' movement. Fearful that these dramatic events would add to their party's troubles, PCI leaders gambled on a quick and vigorous counter-move. They claimed that Italian Communism had long and fully disassociated itself from "the regimes in the East." These regimes, they stressed, had actually behaved in such a way as to "forfeit" every right to be called Communist or Socialist. PCI chieftains went to extraordinary lengths to distance their party from its own past as well. On the eve of the elections for the European Parliament, Occhetto travelled to Budapest to attend ceremonies honoring Hungarian premier Imre Nagy, put to death in 1958 for his role in the insurrection against the Soviets and their local puppets. Reversing the stand taken at the time by the Italian Communists and reaffirmed ever since, Occhetto said that long time PCI leader Palmiro Togliatti had been wrong to support Soviet repression of the Hungarian insurrection and that today's Italian Communists were Nagy's children.

Long time observers of the Italian political scene recalled similarly striking pronouncements by PCI top leaders on the eve of key elections. Just before the general elections of June 1976, widely regarded as a unique opportunity for the Italian Communists to emerge as the number one political force in the country, PCI secretary general Berlinguer told *Corriere della Sera* that he felt more free and safe to pursue "a national road to Socialism" because Italy was a member of NATO rather than of the Warsaw Pact. As reported earlier in this book, Berlinguer recalled having made such a statement when I met him shortly af-terwards. But he did not repeat it later on in the same terms probably because soon after the elections it had been rebuffed by ranking members of the PCI, notably Giancarlo Pajetta. Much in the same way, soon after the 1989 balloting for the European Parliament was over, Pajetta himself and other Italian Com-munist leaders (including former party secretary Alessandro Natta) voiced crit-icism and reservations about some of the statements made recently by Occhetto in order to distance the PCI from the "regimes in the East."

At first glance, the vote for the European Parliament seemed to contradict many of the electoral trends emerged in Italy in recent years. The CDs dropped back just below 33 percent of the popular vote. The PCI received 27.6 percent for a gain of one percentage point from the 1987 general election. The Socialists, who had been credited with 15 to 16 percent of the votes, polled only 14.8 or a meager 0.5 percent more than they had received in 1987.

On closer scrutiny, however, it becomes clear that this outcome was conditioned by several peculiar factors which did not occur and are most unlikely to occur in national elections. Most important, turnout at the polls was five percentage points lower than in the 1987 general election and even lower than in the 1984 vote for the European Parliament. On that occasion, the low turnout had played a key role in allowing the PCI to overtake the CDs "by a whisker"; it was a "fluke," as noted earlier in this book and confirmed by all subsequent local and national elections (in which the turnout was again close to traditional levels). In 1989 the total of valid ballots hit a record low of some 75 percent, reflecting not only the lower turnout at the polls but the increase of blank or otherwise invalid ballots.

In the vote for the Italian members of the European Parliament, the seats at stake are 81 as against 945 in the elections for the national Parliament. Accordingly, many middle- and low-echelon representatives of the CD party are much less motivated to take an active part in the campaign and less able to impress their friends and clients with the importance and rewards of victory. And much the same is true for the Socialists and the minor democratic parties.

The PCI apparatus, although less powerful than in the recent past, proved to be once more the most disciplined and efficient in getting out the vote of party members and sympathizers (the ranks of the latter were probably swollen by voters who do not care too much for the PCI itself but feel it important to prevent an all too precipitous decline of the only large opposition party in Italy). The Communists lost over 700,000 votes out of the 10,254,000 they had polled in the 1987 election, but their percentage was up more than the Socialists', while the CDs lost in terms of percentage as well as of votes. Yet, the Communists dropped more than 5 percentage points below their 1984 performance.

The Socialists failed to achieve a breakthrough at the expense of either the CDs or the PCI. This meant that the PSI leaders must put off by some years at least the dreams of moving into the driver's seat either of a reshaped coalition with the CDs or of a leftist alliance with the PCI.

Among the minor groups, the Greens scored substantial gains, although personal and local rivalries caused them to field two separate and competing tickets which received 4.2 and 2.4 percent of the votes. A slow but steady downtrend continued to plague the neo-Fascist MSI, which polled 5.5 percent of the votes compared with 5.9 in 1987 and 6.5 in 1984. The Social Democrats lost a fraction, receiving 2.7 percent against 2.8 in 1987, but gave further evidence of their determination and ability to block Craxi's drive to attract or force them into the PSI. A joint ticket of Republicans and Liberals, which included some ranking representatives of the Radical party, polled only 4.4 percent, much less than the same parties had received in the recent national elections when they had run separate tickets. Yet, only an unlikely "grand coalition" of CDs and Communists could expect to govern without any help from the minor democratic parties. The support of these parties, notably of the Republicans, was still necessary to provide a working majority either to an alliance between CDs and Socialists or to a combination of leftist forces committed to confining the CDs into the opposition.

To sum it up: Over and above the special features and circumstances of the elections for the European Parliament, their significance in terms of Italian politics was a rebuke and a warning but not a disavowal for the coalition of democratic forces which had been in office since 1979. The voters made clear their mounting dissatisfaction over the mistakes and shortcomings stemming mainly from the tugs-of-war between CDs and Socialists and from the infighting within the CD camp. But they refused once again to "throw the baby away with the (more or less dirty) bathwater" and gave the ruling coalition still another chance. It was a further confirmation that, as I maintained over the years and spelled out most specifically in *Il Tempo* on January 26, 1976, Italian voters are "more realistic and balanced . . . and much less immature . . . than so many Italian politicians and journalists, as well as so many foreign 'experts,' seem to think." Of course, I went on, in viewing and assessing electoral returns, shifts, and trends, we must "forget about personal preferences and about those preconceived schemes within which many self styled political scientists presume to constrict the flow of facts. They operate, "I noted, "like that Greek highway robber, Procrustes, who made unfortunate travellers fit his bed by lopping off or stretching their limbs."

Some key changes in electoral behavior, notably substantial defections by PCI voters, have come later than I had anticipated. But they have come and one of the most encouraging developments has been that they have been accompanied by a decline rather than a rise of the vote going to the extreme right.

On their side, leaders of the democratic parties have managed once again to stave off the worst consequences of their own mistakes. Following the elections for the European Parliament, there were still strains, squabbles, and delays, mainly related to the settling of accounts which had been partly left open by the CD National Congress in February. De Mita's attempts to put together a new government were frustrated by an unspoken but effective alliance between Craxi and the winners of that Congress. One of them, durable Giulio Andreotti, got the inside track for the premiership and quickly formed the new government. It was again a five party coalition, based on the "competitive collaboration" between CDs and Socialists and including Republicans, Social Democrats, and Liberals. It did not differ substantially from its predecessor except, of course, for Andreotti's return to the premiership (after a ten-year interval), for the downgrading of the CD leftwingers (close to De Mita), and for the attribution of the foreign ministry to the Socialists who retained the vice-premiership as well.

The path of the new Andreotti government will not be made any smoother by the smouldering resentments and rivalries within the CD confederacy. Craxi, moreover, can be expected to look for an early opportunity to erase the memory of his party's disappointing performance in the elections for the European Parliament. He may be unwilling to wait for the regional elections due in most parts of Italy in 1990 and he may decide anyway to precipitate the holding of a general election well ahead of the 1992 deadline. Andreotti's supporters hope that his tenure will last until that deadline and that by then he will be in a position to be elected president of the Republic. The premier himself has referred time and again to 1992 but rather as the year when preparations must be completed for the full implementation of the European Single Market.

For a country like Italy, the coming down of all economic barriers within the EEC represents a major challenge. Today's Italy may be called a rich country which still has many poor people or a poor country full of rich people—and both labels would fit. Most Italians are much better off than they were a few years ago, let alone in the postwar years. They know and appreciate it, despite the frequent groans and grumbles. According to recent polls and surveys, people in Italy are both more satisfied with their present conditions and more confident they will further improve in the foreseeable future than people elsewhere in the West. Italian voters also realize that the further progress they want requires more efficient management of available resources as well as a climate of fundamental stability.

As pointed out once again in this concluding chapter, much remains to be done, just as much must be corrected. A note of special urgency is added by the impending, decisive phase of the process of European integration. Italy holds several records in reverse when it comes to implementation of EEC directives and to failure to make timely use of allocations from the Community's funds (a failure that has reportedly involved the loss of such allocations for a total of 750 million dollars in the 1978–1985 period). Some steps have been taken, however belatedly, even in the areas most resistant to change and most in need of it (political institutions, day-by-day administration, and rehabilitation of public finances). It is in these areas that more progress is particularly required to make the Italian system more similar to, or less dissimilar from, the pattern prevailing in the other major democracies of the West. Such a progress in turn is essential to sustain and further strengthen the larger and more visible role that Italy has recently acquired on the international scene.

The return of power of a center-left coalition, following the collapse of the "historic compromise" between CDs and Communists, ushered in a new chapter of Italian foreign policy. It has been featured by a more dynamic and significant participation in the Atlantic Alliance and generally by a higher Italian profile on the international scene. A by-product of this higher profile, especially with regard to the Mediterranean and the Middle East, has been to affect, at different times and occasionally in conflicting ways, the relationship between Rome and Washington.

By late 1979, the Italian government and Parliament were called upon to make a momentous decision for NATO and for East-West relations. It involved the deployment on Italian territory of 112 U.S. medium-range cruise missiles as a key part of the Western strategy to restore and uphold the nuclear balance upset by the new Soviet SS–20s capable of reaching the most important targets throughout Western Europe and in the Mediterranean basin, which had become "the arena where East-West confrontation meets and interacts with North-South problems," as I put it in the *Wall Street Journal–Europe*, December 16, 1985. There was strong and vocal opposition from the PCI, from far-out leftist groups, and from some Catholic churchmen and organizations. But the Italian commitment was clearly spelled out and firmly sustained. Concrete steps were soon taken for the installation of the first batch of U.S. missiles at Comiso airbase in southeastern Sicily. Italy's stand was crucial because West Germany had agreed to the deployment of cruise (and Pershing II) missiles on its territory only if at least one other European continental nation pledged to do so (Belgium and The Netherlands did not come through until the mid–1980s). "A middle-sized power like Italy," I summed up in *Freedom at Issue* (May–June 1982), was showing willingness and ability to "rise to the challenge" when called upon "to shoulder wider responsibilities both from the political and military standpoint."

The Italian defense budget was beefed up, although its increase did not fulfill, year-in-year-out, the 3 percent rate pledged by the NATO countries in the long-range program approved in 1979. Italian strategy was updated to meet the challenge represented by the sharp expansion of the Soviet military presence in the Mediterranean which had the logistic support of such countries as Syria and Libya. The bulk of the Italian land and air forces had been long "concentrated in the Po Valley, notably in the direction of the 'Gorizia gap,' traditionally considered the gateway for invasions from the East and Northeast." In recent years, air and sea surveillance in the Mediterranean has been broadened and strengthened in close cooperation with the United States and other NATO partners. The army, navy, and air force have received modern equipment, notably Leopard tanks manufactured in Italy under German license, Tornado fighter-bombers, new subs and frigates, as well as a "baby carrier," the 13,500-ton Garibaldi that can accommodate helicopters and carrier-type STOL-VL aircraft.

For a long time, most U.S. journalists thought it fashionable to ignore Italy's role in NATO except perhaps for calling her "the spaghetti link" of the alliance, I further wrote in the *Freedom at Issue*. Earlier in 1982, I noted, "a U.S. network broadcast a devastating indictment of the Italian authorities' 'inability to cope with terrorism.' " Yet, "a few days later, the rescue of general James L. Dozier, who had been kidnapped by the Red Brigades in Verona near some major U.S. military bases in Northeastern Italy, led U.S. media to hail with enthusiasm the skill and daring of Italian police." The country's achievements and the growing significance of its international role were at last "discovered" by some U.S. editorialists and columnists. In May 1982, the *Washington Post* called Italy "America's most undervalued and in recent times most constant alliance partner." On December 14, the same paper praised Italy "as the model among Western nations for legal correctness and political courage" in fighting against terrorism. The following June, the *Washington Post* editorialized: "Italy has proved to be one of the most stable of the Western democracies." Not bad for a paper which since 1969 had been in the forefront of doomsayers about Italy.

Yet, journalistic reports from Rome continued to be scant and infrequent. Several analyses and comments, moreover, were superficial or worse, even when dealing with developments of major domestic importance or significant international relevance. In the *International Herald Tribune* of February 11, 1985, columnist William Pfaff stated: "In Italy, terrorism was . . . in some large sense a rebellion against the experience of Italy in recent times as a museum for the rest of the world and a mausoleum for Italians." A few days earlier, the same daily carried a survey on the deployment of INF (intermediate range nuclear forces) in Western Europe. The author, Robert Kleiman, on leave as a member of the *New York Times* editorial board, asserted that installation of INF in Western Germany was "conditional on Benelux participation" in the deployment. As it was well known, the West German request that at least another continental nation accept the INF, had been satisfactorily met as far back as December 1979 when Italy announced officially her decision to deploy cruise missiles on her territory. Deployment in West Germany began in late 1983, while acceptance by the Belgians came only in March 1985, the Dutch procrastinated even longer, and Luxembourg was never involved.

By and large, leading U.S. political and military circles were quicker or much less reluctant to spot and welcome Italy's rising aspirations to a more visible international role underscored by the stepped-up dynamism of her diplomacy, by the expansion of her share of world trade, and by the enhanced relevance of her strategic position "between continental Europe, the northern rim of Africa and key gateways to the Middle East," as I put it in the *Wall Street Journal-Europe* (December 16, 1985).

Since the early 1980s, this appreciation has been more and more widely and warmly shared as evidenced by the dozens of interviews I have published in the Italian dailies *Il Tempo*, *Il Mattino* of Naples, and lately in *Il Messaggero* of Rome, as well as in the weekly *Oggi*. Just to mention some examples, such appreciation was voiced by general Bernard Rogers, then supreme Allied commander in Europe, and by admiral William Crowe, commander of Allied Forces in Southern Europe, and later chairman of the U.S. Joint Chiefs of Staff. It was likewise expressed in interviews I had with Vice-President George Bush, with the governor of New York, Mario Cuomo, with under secretary of state for political affairs, Lawrence Eagleburger, with ambassador to Italy Maxwell Rabb, and with Ambassador Allen Holmes, head of the State Department Office of Politico-Military Affairs, with under secretary of defense Fred Ikle', and with assistant secretary Richard Perle, as well as with several officials specialized in European and Italian affairs.

In the Congress, I heard similar views from ranking representatives of both parties: on the Republican side, Howard Baker, then majority leader in the Senate, Richard Lugar, for several years chairman of the Senate Foreign Relations Committee, Pete Dominici who headed the Senate Budget Committee, senators Nancy Kassebaum, member of the Foreign Relations Committee, and Alfonse D'Amato of New York; on the Democratic side, senators Edward Kennedy and Dennis

De Concini, House majority leader Thomas C. Foley, Dante Fascell, chairman of the House Foreign Affairs Committee, Les Aspin, chairman of the House Armed Services Committee, Lee Hamilton, chairman of the Subcommittee for Europe and the Middle East, as well as former senator Gary Hart, interviewed before he withdrew from the race for the White House.

In many cases, the praise and satisfaction about Italy's more dynamic performance on the international stage was coupled with the realization that it could and did involve some drawbacks. Administration officials and congressmen were disturbed when some Italian leaders seemed to go out of their way to give their country's higher profile a nationalistic bent which on occasion challenged U.S. policies. A notable instance was the refusal by premier Craxi and by foreign minister Andreotti to turn over to the United States or even detain the Arab terrorists involved in the *Achille Lauro* highjacking and in the murder of disabled U.S. passenger, Leon Klinghoffer. As I noted in the *Wall Street Journal–Europe* (December 16, 1985), this stand earned Craxi and Andreotti the applause of Italian Communists but caused a serious crisis within the ruling coalition. The Republicans, third largest party in the government, "charged that Italian foreign policy had been tilted in favor of the Arabs" to the point of hurting relations not only with Israel but with the United States. The course followed by Craxi and Andreotti was also criticized by quite a few CDs and by many representatives of the Social Democratic and Liberal parties, the two smaller partners in the government. It further emerged that most Italians were not ready, either, to respond to nationalistic appeals, but could take a "evenhanded approach to the conduct of their own as well as of foreign governments." In a poll conducted by *Corriere della Sera*, I reported in the *Wall Street Journal*, a large plurality of Italians (47 percent) condemned both the United States for forcing down the Egyptian jet carrying the Arab terrorists who had highjacked the *Achille Lauro*, and the Italian government for shielding from arrest Abu Abbas, the PLO leader accused by the United States (and later convicted by an Italian court) of "masterminding" the highjack.

Italian government leaders also voiced sharp criticism of U.S. moves against Libya's colonel Qaddafi apparently discounting U.S. charges that he supported and financed terrorist activities in Europe and in the Middle East. At the same time, Craxi and Andreotti missed no opportunity to develop and maintain good contacts with leaders of regimes and movements (from Iran to Syria and from Libya to the PLO) which displayed a more or less violent hostility against the United States. This policy reflected, at least in part, the old Italian inclination to seek to play "broker" or "mediator" in international affairs even when such mediation was not solicited by either side or when one of the sides involved was Italy's ally.

During a visit to Lisbon in the spring of 1984, premier Craxi made some statements that seemed to suggest Italian support for a moratorium on the deployment of U.S. INF in Western Europe as an incentive to the Soviets to resume negotiations on the matter. Following the negative reactions in Washington and elsewhere, the Italian premier spelled out his approach much in the same terms he had used three years earlier when he told me: "The policy of peace and negotiations with the East, to which Italy remains committed, can and must be pursued by Western Europe operating on the basis of its alliance with the U.S. and of the safeguard of military equilibrium between NATO and the Warsaw Pact" (reported in my article in the spring 1985 issue of *The Washington Quarterly*).

Other top Italian leaders affirmed clearly and vigorously that their country's higher profile in international affairs should not and would not affect its ties with the West and specifically its warm friendship and solidarity with the United States.

President Sandro Pertini told me in an interview, the only one given a U.S. newsman before his departure for an official visit to the United States and published in the Italian language daily *Il Progresso Italo-Americano* of New York, March 28, 1983: "Other nations in Europe . . . look arrogantly upon America and would like to break their ties with America . . . We Italians, instead, remember more than other Europeans that . . . the Americans, who landed twice on European shores, did not come to conquer Europe. Both during World War I and World War II, they came to prevent authoritarian regimes from dominating Europe." In the interview, the Italian chief of state further said: "Europe must look to America, it cannot isolate itself from America. . . . If we pushed the U.S. toward isolationism, we would make a tremendous mistake." Pertini concluded: "President Reagan and myself will get along well, I'm sure, because we are both aware and strongly convinced that our two countries share ideals and interests which represent the foundations of a long and warm friendship and solidarity between Americans and Italians."

The basic importance of a close solidarity between the United States and Europe and specifically between Italy and the United States is constantly reaffirmed by longtime foreign minister and now again Premier Giulio Andreotti widely regarded as the main champion of "openings" to the Soviet Union (and to such regimes hostile to the United States and to the West as those ruling Syria, Libya, and Iran). "The security of the West can be guaranteed only within a global framework and with the decisive contribution of the U.S.," he told me in a wide-ranging interview which appeared in *Il Progresso Italo-Americano* on June 7, 1987: "The validity of this approach has been specifically confirmed by the encouraging prospects which have developed recently for cutting down nuclear armaments in Europe." To a direct question about the differences that had emerged between the United States and Italy in the wake of the *Achille Lauro* affair and of the 1986 U.S. bombing of Libya, Andreotti replied: "There have been moments when perceptions and reactions have not been the same" (in Italy and in the United States). Such differences, however, were a natural feature of relations between two democratic countries and "never brought into question" the basic substance of the ties between Italy and the United States: "The roots of the solidarity and friendship which link us to the U.S. go even deeper than the fact, yet so important, that we belong to the same, defensive alliance." Like other European nations, Italy "shares key values with the U.S." In her case, moreover, a solid foundation for the relations with the United States "is provided by the presence in the United States of large, hard working, and respected communities of Italian origin."

In recent years, Andreotti repeatedly stressed that the consensus on foreign policy had remarkably widened in Italy, an obvious reference to an "evolution" of the PCI in this connection. However, I noted, many U.S. politicians and other observers felt that the Westernization of the PCI had not made sufficient progress as yet to allow contemplating without qualms a government role for the party. In the interview for *Il Progresso Italo-Americano* Andreotti replied that he could "understand these American worries." At the same time, he pointed at the "evolution" under way which had already led the PCI to drop its opposition to Italy's membership in NATO and to her participation in the EEC. The CD party, on its side, had stated recently, once again, that it was "not available for a governmental alliance with the Communists." This did not mean that "one should not pursue a 'strategy of attention' toward the Communists," Andreotti added quickly quoting an expression coined by Aldo Moro ten years earlier. "Recent progress on the road to Soviet-American accords on disarmament," the Italian foreign minister concluded, "show that an evolution is possible, in fact desirable. Yet, it is at junctures like this that one must be more vigilant."

On the eve of an official visit to the United States, Giovanni Goria, who had taken over the premiership in mid–1987 after a long service as treasury minister, told me in an interview published in *Il Progresso Italo-Americano* on December 16, 1987: "Italy's foreign policy has been traditionally keyed to two fundamental guidelines. We look with doubts and skepticism at the development in Western Europe of Directorates or subgroups operating under the exclusive guidance of a few countries . . . and we oppose firmly any attempt to pull Western Europe toward 'third force' positions or anyway to make the Atlantic wider. On the positive side, Italy continues to be strongly committed to the construction of an 'European pillar' of the Atlantic alliance, a pillar grounded in the active partic- ipation, on a footing of equality, of all the European members of NATO and on an ever closer, operative solidarity with the U.S. and Canada." Goria further pointed at the "growing attention devoted by Italian public opinion to . . . the increasingly important role played by the U.S. Congress in the field of foreign policy." Meetings with representatives of the Italo-American community were high on the agenda of the Italian premier who voiced warm appreciation for the contribution that Americans of Italian origin "have made and are making to promote an even better understanding and cooperation between the two coun- tries."

During the first several months of his tenure as premier, De Mita visited Washington (in June) and Moscow (in October 1988). President Reagan warmly praised "Italy's willingness to do her part, to share in the risks and responsi- bilities, as well as in the benefits of NATO membership." The latest instance, underscored also by other top U.S. officials, was Italian acceptance to host the wing of U.S F–16 warplanes which had to leave its bases in Spain. De Mita stressed Italy's continued commitment to the Atlantic Alliance and to European integration as well as her determination to help promote *detente* and economic ties with the East. These were also key topics in the talks between De Mita and the Soviet leader Mikhail Gorbachev. The Italian premier reaffirmed specifically the decision to host U.S. F–16s on Italian territory, a move strongly disliked by the Soviets (and vigorously opposed by the PCI). At the same time, De Mita, who was accompanied by top representatives of the major Italian private and public corporations, raised the prospect of a "Marshall Plan" to help the re-structuring and expansion of the Soviet economy. The resort to such terminology and its implications were criticized in Washington and other Western capitals as well as in Italy herself. Socialist leader Bettino Craxi, De Mita's main partner and rival within Italy's ruling coalition, seized the opportunity to attack the notion itself of a "Marshall Plan" for the USSR. This was probably intended to contribute, as it certainly did, to the warm reception given shortly afterwards to the Italian Socialist leader by President Reagan and other U.S. leaders. Both Vice-President Bush and his Democratic rival in the forthcoming presidential election, Michael Dukakis, made a special point of meeting with Craxi, and all three attended the big reception given in Washington by the National Italian American Foundation (NIAF), the leading association of Italo-Americans. Dur-ing his visit to Washington, Craxi came out once again in favor of a Palestinian state to be established in territories occupied by Israel since the 1967 war and federated with Jordan. Craxi further confirmed his plans for an early trip to North Africa, including notably a meeting with Libya's Colonel Qaddafi.

For some years, the approach to Arab regimes and movements in the Medi-terranean and in the Middle East has represented the most sensitive aspect of the fundamentally excellent relations between Rome and Washington. As already reported, administration and congressional circles were "disturbed" by the con-duct of several Italian government leaders in connection with the highjacking of the *Achille Lauro* and of the U.S. bombings of Libya. "Unpleasant surprise" and "bitter disappointment" were the main feelings that surfaced or were voiced openly in the interviews given me notably by senators De Concini, Domenici, and Lugar and by such ranking U.S. officials as ambassador Allen Holmes and Charles Thomas, deputy assistant secretary of State for European Affairs. Some of them admitted that their reaction reflected in part the fact that "we have been spoiled" by the earlier, all too prompt and deferential Italian compliance with U.S. wishes and requests. Congressmen and administration officials further stressed that, while "differences in outlook . . . are natural even between close friends and allies," the paramount matter was "to avoid looking at these dif-ferences as a reason for confrontation" and "rather work to limit their impact and thus preserve the basic motivations and the core of the alliance" (see notably *Il Progresso Italo-Americano*, May 14 and July 3, 1986, and *Il Mattino*, July 27 and August 1, 1986).

Over the next few years, such views prevailed largely in Washington and also in Rome. This constructive process was materially sustained by further, concrete evidence of the Italian government's readiness to cooperate with other NATO nations and first of all with the United States on critical issues in the Mediterranean and in the Middle East. Italy played an important role in the multilateral peace-keeping forces in the Sinai and in Lebanon as well as in the allied patrol and escort missions in the Gulf during the tense months that preceded the armistice between Iran and Iraq.

The statements I heard during my most recent visits to Washington echoed key themes of the speech given by ambassador Zellerbach back in November 1958 (and quoted earlier in this book) which spotlighted how and why a more dynamic and autonomous-minded Italian approach to some international issues, especially in the Mediterranean and in the Middle East, could benefit, rather than harm, the overall interests of the Western alliance. Thirty years later, the spirit and gist of Zellerbach's speech were best recaptured, in updated terms, by representative Lee Hamilton (D-Indiana), when he told me: "Sometimes, the U.S. and Italy do not agree 100 percent. But we look to Italy to do things that we cannot pursue in the same manner, for instance in dealing with Syria or Iran. The key point is that Italy should continue to feel that she is part of a group, the Western group, and act accordingly."

A nasty aspect continues to be the disinformation and defamation campaign against the United States and its people carried out by sizable sectors of the Italian media. Wide-ranging documentary evidence about the first stages of this campaign is given in Chapter 16 of this book where I quote extensively from my essay published in the May–June 1979 issue of *Freedom at Issue*. As I had anticipated at the end of this essay, in the following years the PCI's appeal to the Italian intellectual community was gradually weakened by the party's failure to win a significant government role quickly and by the disappointing performance of many local administrations where the Communists had gained control in recent years. Yet, the anti-U.S. campaign did not substantially abate reflecting the entrenched positions acquired by publishers, editors, and newsmen who had sparked or actively joined that campaign. Over the last few years it has emerged more and more clearly that quite a few Italian media have "enlisted, wittingly or unwittingly, in a guerrilla war of disinformation whose goals go well beyond projecting in Italy a distorted and slanderous image of America and Americans. The basic purpose is to affect a much broader framework of international relations, and the overall balance of power, to the . . . detriment of the U.S. and of the West as a whole," as I wrote in a four-part series which appeared in *Il Progresso Italo-Americano* on December 15–18, 1987.

To document this assessment, I drew again on the hundreds of clips in my files. I quoted, for instance, typical headlines and comments about recent developments and prospects in the Gulf: "USA: the ghost of a new Vietnam" (*L'Unità*); America "lacks the strength to look again defeat in the face, to admit a new, utter failure" (*La Repubblica*). According to *L'Espresso*, the United

States "has suffered a terrific loss of face" as "its powerful naval squadron . . . shuddered at the prospect of hitting a mine," while Italy and other allies "turned down flatly the American requests for help." As I pointed out, these hasty and biased assertions were belied within a few weeks.

Antonio Gambino, foreign policy columnist of *L'Espresso*, provided "further confirmation that the main thrust of the campaigns carried out by the anti-American media is to exploit all opportunities to undermine . . . and possibly break up the solidarity between Western Europe and the U.S." Italy and the other EEC nations, Gambino contended, cannot "accept the U.S. request to join its violent action" in the Gulf which "like all these taken by the U.S. in recent years, shows a worrisome lack of thoughtfulness and preparedness"; participation by the EEC countries would mean that they share "a Mid-East policy which is unacceptable because it is centered on Israel." Gambino thus brought to the fore the anti-Israeli feelings, so strong as to overflow into anti-Semitism, which animate quite a few representatives of the more or less "intellectual" and "radical" left in Italy. For them, Israel is doubly loathsome; it is a Jewish state and it is the main U.S. ally in the Middle East. Gambino himself concluded a recent series of articles on the United States (again in *L'Espresso*), I further reported, by asserting that "the Atlantic [has become] wider because by now America is 'untrustworthy,' because it feels antipathy and disgust toward any attempt to 'organize' Europe efficiently, since it looks upon such attempts as a dangerous challenge to the position of leadership to which [the Americans] feel entitled," and because the United States itself "is becoming less European."

The anti-American Italian media jumped at the opportunity that Wall Street's "Black Monday" seemed to offer them. *La Repubblica, La Stampa, Panorama* and *Epoca* played up the opinions and forecasts of those economic "experts" who asserted that a 1929-like crash was bound to take place in the near future. The same media carefully refrained from highlighting and often from mentioning altogether, I also pointed out, "the unprecedented length of the U.S. economy's expansion, entering its sixth year, the drop of unemployment . . . lower than before the 1979 oil shock, or the revival noticeable in the last few months even in some industrial sectors that were most severely hit in past years."

There "is no aspect or episode of life in the U.S. that is not used as a peg or a pretext for this campaign of disinformation and defamation. After the air crash in Detroit last August, *La Stampa*'s headline read: 'Fear of flying in the U.S.'; and *Panorama* blamed both 'Carter's liberalization' and 'the firing of flight controllers by Reagan.' *Stampa Sera* (*La Stampa*'s evening edition) emphasized 'the Russian roulette of U.S. aviation' and again *La Stampa* charged: 'Faulty engines, but no one took action.' It was left to the national news agency ANSA to conclude that the plane had crashed because of wind shearing. Meanwhile, *L'Unità* was shooting at bigger targets: 'Junk made in the U.S. . . . . weapons, missiles, extremely costly spaceships: They have only one fault, they do not work.' "

I noted the leading role played by such "professionals" of anti-Americanism as Vittorio Zucconi and Romano Giachetti. Much the same themes could be found, although developed in a somewhat different style and tone, in several of the articles written for *La Stampa* (and also for *Panorama*) by Furio Colombo (who doubled up as president of FIAT USA).

According to Zucconi, "Americans crave junk food" (*La Repubblica*). In *Epoca*, he maintained that "the shadow of desert and loneliness is lengthening again on the American cities and on U.S. society in general." In *La Stampa* Colombo drew a horrifying portrait of young Americans "ugly and violent . . . capable of extraordinarily cold and cruel crimes." Giachetti wrote in *Epoca*: "Drug addiction grows with impressive regularity. The much played up war against drugs has produced only one result—zero." Zucconi elaborated at length on the most disgusting slash movies, so liked by U.S. children that renting their videocassettes had become "one of the most explosive businesses of today's U.S. economy" (*Epoca*). Ugo Buzzolan, who writes about TV for *La Stampa*, was the author of one of the latest outbursts against U.S. serials "which spotlight the serious crisis of the TV industry in the U.S. and look like sub-products concocted for the underdeveloped countries" but "are imported into Italy (sight unseen?) against payment of a lot of dollars." It was not by chance, either, that the letters to the editor printed by *L'Unità* often echoed much the same attacks against TV imports from the United States whose broadcasting in Italy "degrades the culture of our people." In the same Communist daily, writer Dario Bellezza gave a few years ago a show of anti-American zeal hard to match: "For an intellectual, poet, and writer, Italian, as I'm proud to be, what is most horrifying is the gradual Americanization taking place in Italy and the consequent eradication of the plant 'man,' so much so that the word 'genocide' is the right one for voicing the feelings of those who, as Italians, witness in horror the invasion of that syphilis of the XX century, the American way of life. . . . The choking alliance with the U.S. has brought us to this point: to lose our national characteristics, to feel provincial and colonies of an empire founded on injustice and alienation."

Even the recent visit to the United States by Pope John Paul II was exploited to assert that he addressed "a people undergoing a crisis" (news broadcast of the Second Channel of the state-controlled TV network), "a country where the religious scene is more often similar to a bazaar of charlatans than to a temple" (Zucconi in *Epoca*), or that anyway "a good follower of this Pope . . . is a bad citizen of the U.S." (again Zucconi in *La Repubblica*).

These Italian media hammered at the sad sunset of the Reagan era "under whose sign all Western countries, Italy included, were able to delude themselves that the basic problems had disappeared under Ronnie's smile and his Hollywood-like optimism" (Zucconi in *Epoca*). Zucconi and other Italian newsmen insisted on such themes in an obvious effort to warn Italian public opinion and government leaders "against expecting anything good from the U.S. during the coming years and possibly in the more distant future as well" (as I put it in *Il Progresso Italo-Americano*).

There are still other facets to the anti-American campaign. Tireless Vittorio Zucconi extols the Soviet "primacy in space: The stars are Red and Ivan is their master" (*La Repubblica*). *La Stampa* devoted a full page to the Soviet success in overtaking the United States and to the Americans' "apathy" in the face of their defeat. *L'Unità* emphasized the USSR's contributions to the first accords for the reduction of armaments and "its pressure for further progress," while ignoring that the first concrete proposals came from the United States and were long rejected by Moscow. *La Repubblica* served up a deceptive version which had Gorbachev "calling Reagan's bluff" by appropriating the proposals that Washington had made "feeling certain that the Kremlin would have replied with the customary 'nyet.' "

The anti-American campaign reaches far into the past, I further noted in *Il Progresso Italo-Americano*: "*Panorama* turns the 40th anniversary of the Marshall Plan into an opportunity for insinuating that it was prompted primarily by the Americans' fear of losing valuable markets for their products. The dropping of atomic bombs on Japan is attributed 'to anger against . . . the yellow faces . . . which exploded even in that archetypal American, President Truman'" (Giordano Bruno Guerri, then editorial director of Mondadori, writing in *Panorama*), and/ or to the purpose of 'intimidating the USSR' thus starting the 'unfortunate nuclear diplomacy' (as asserted in *L'Unità* by Roberto Fieschi, a physicist apparently more committed to his job in the PCI hierarchy than respectful of historical or scientific facts). Another university professor, Gian Giacomo Migone, also writing in *L'Unità*, lashes out at the 'American party' in Italy as a component of 'what's left of an alignment based on the close connection between the American domination and the preservation of the traditional power setups in the individual Western states.' "

The Italian media "committed to projecting a distorted and defamatory image of the U.S.," I went on in *Il Progresso Italo-Americano*, "are only too happy to offer generous hospitality to Americans ready to speak badly of their country. The most widely quoted is Gore Vidal: 'The American political system,' he says in an interview with *Panorama*, 'is such a failure, so corrupt. . . . The Russians are ready to make an agreement with us, even tomorrow, while we spend 57 percent of Federal receipts to get ready to make war against an enemy who is not there. . . . In our schools, they are not teaching anything anymore. In the West, no one reads anything. The people beyond the [Iron] Curtain are the only ones who read.' Similar anti-American outbursts can be found in an article by Vidal published by *Epoca*." He was given a further opportunity to vent his anti-Americanism in a TV program broadcast on November 3, 1988, just before the recent presidential election, by the Communist-controlled Channel 3 of the state-owned network and put together by Furio Colombo and Andrea Barbato. Norman Mailer, I further wrote in *Il Progresso Italo-Americano*, "is not lagging behind: 'In the last 40 years,' he says in an interview carried with minor changes by *Panorama*, *Epoca*, and *L'Unità*, 'we have done many appalling things. We have carried out a useless and damaging cold war with Russia, contributing to keep that country down to a Third World economic level. We have defaced the American landscape, we have destroyed its roots.' ''

Recent books like Paul Kennedy's *The Rise and Fall of the Great Powers* have been widely publicized and interpreted as not only pointing at an already ongoing decline of the United States but at its inevitable and impending collapse.

The 1988 presidential campaign was reported by many Italian media as taking place in a nation both apathetic and deeply torn apart by social, economic, and race conflicts. Columnists like Anthony Lewis of the *New York Times* were widely quoted in this connection. When the outcome was clearly foreshadowed by the polls and after the returns were actually in, the same Italian media blamed the U.S. voters for being so reactionary and racist as to refuse to support Jesse Jackson, apparently the candidate heavily favored by the most vocal sectors of Italian journalism.

As I had done at the end of my 1979 essay, I concluded the articles in *Il Progresso Italo-Americano* by noting that several important Italian media, newsmen, and columnists did not share the anti-American slant and strove ''to portray the multifaceted American reality on the basis of facts and rational approaches.'' I reported, for instance, that ''some interesting points have been raised by Ernesto Galli della Loggia in his 'Letter to our American friends,' as well as in the debate that followed its publication. In *La Repubblica* of December 11, 1986, Beniamino Placido noted ''that Galli della Loggia is actually addressing Italian public opinion and us, who . . . focus our attention on America . . . [He] blames us for taking the wrong approach to America, an approach which is apparently progressive-minded and exacting but actually aristocratic and contemptuous, at times confused and contradictory. . . . We go wrong because we fail to realize how different America is from us, from Europe. Born from a rib of Europe, America has changed while growing, as happens to every son.'' In another article in the same daily (February 27, 1987), ''Placido writes: '[Europeans] strongly imbued with a sense of superiority . . . have always lashed out at America. But they have also acknowledged that, when confronted with the same problems, we Europeans, we Italians, were not able to do any better.' Still today, Placido concludes, 'although America is no longer ahead of us in everything, it is ahead of us when it comes to the capacity of criticizing America, to do so not by words alone, by solemn and disdainful declarations, but by actual behavior.' ''

Without necessarily agreeing with this or that statement by Placido, I can say that his writings reflect a mature and fairly even-minded approach which is not his alone and represents a welcome and important contrast with the anti-American campaign carried out by many other Italian journalists.

Most important, I pointed out in the final paragraphs of the series published in *Il Progresso Italo-Americano* ''luckily the large majority of Italians is not dazzled, let alone won over by the disinformation and defamation campaigns against America and Americans.'' Some recent articles in the media most stubbornly committed to the anti-American drive, I can now add, are beginning to reflect a frustration and a disappointment which they unleash on the Italians themselves. Here is a typical, most recent instance: Writing in *L'Unità* (October 15, 1988), Michele Serra, a devout Communist and anti-American, scolds bitterly his fellow Italians who, he charges, are so fascinated by what happens in America, so "culturally dependent" on America that they ignore what's going on in countries much closer to Italy like Algeria or Yugoslavia, and thus allow their own nation to be "devastated by Americanization."

In recent years, the growing role and influence of the Italo-American community have contributed significantly to a better understanding and even closer ties between the two countries. An eloquent and most perceptive appraisal of these developments was given me by governor of New York Mario Cuomo, notably in the interview published in *Il Tempo* of June 27, 1983. Said Cuomo: "The vision of America as a mosaic of many cultures and many different groups has gained ground and acceptance over the 'melting pot' syndrome. The Italo-Americans were among the victims of this syndrome which compelled immigrants to conform to a 'one-colored' prototype of the ideal citizen. Today, the Americans of Italian origin no longer seek to disassociate themselves from their origins. At the same time, they are becoming more aware that it is important for them to participate more and more actively in political life at the local, state, and national levels." The continuation of these trends," Governor Cuomo concluded, "opens up . . . great opportunities for even more solid links between them and Italy."

Frank D. Stella, president of NIAF, told me in a recent interview (*Il Mattino*, June 6, 1987): "The main purpose and task of the NIAF is to operate as a catalyst of all the initiatives intended to promote and strengthen the relations and ties between Italy and the U.S." Established in 1976, the NIAF has quickly made its mark as the vehicle of a new and original approach: "We do not presume," Stella said, "to grow in competition with the many associations of Italo-Americans which have long been active in the U.S. Since the beginning, we have striven to develop as an organization with a nation-wide scope which seeks to become the focus of the relations between the U.S. and Italy in every field (people to people, government to government, trade and tourism, cultural exchanges)." In reply to a question, the president of NIAF told me: "Americans of Italian origin are ready to look with sympathy upon any Italian government that is the expression of a free choice by the Italians themselves. Yet, we could not view in the same light governments that would not guarantee and promote democratic institutions in Italy as well as her active and loyal commitment to NATO, and support close ties of friendship and solidarity with the U.S." President Stella is particularly proud of his association's program for "return to our roots." It is a program, he explains, that goes far beyond its capabilities, however significant, "for giving new impulse to tourism in its traditional forms (visits to artistic and historical centers, pleasant stops in good hotels and restaurants). Now that we Italo-Americans have made so much progress and achieved so many successes in all sectors, gained a new maturity and become a fully integrated component of the national society, we must and want to find again our Italian roots, first of all by visiting the many places, especially in the South of

Italy, from which our families came to the States and where so many of our relatives still live.''

All this, however encouraging, does not mean that the anti-American bias of quite a few Italian media does not represent a problem anymore or that ''it will go away by itself,'' I wrote in the concluding section of the survey published in *Il Progresso Italo-Americano*. ''It will not be easy to dispel the shadows that have been projected and continue to be projected on relations between Italy and the U.S.'' by these Italian media and by the political and economic forces interested in loosening the ties between the two countries. There is reason to hope and expect, however, that ''a more mature approach, keyed to an even handed, thoughtful criticism (and self-criticism),'' I wrote in the same paper ''will produce and sustain a better, more perceptive knowledge and understanding of America and Americans'' by Italians—and vice versa.

Such an upbeat assessment is justified by a basic fact which, I feel, may be viewed as a summary and conclusion of this book. Over and above a far from easy transitional period in their relations, by the late 1980s the United States and Italy appeared, all in all, to be on their way to achieve an updated and more balanced partnership within the framework of their close and durable association—provided, of course, that both countries keep working at it without taking each other for granted.

Selected Bibliography

Amato, Giuliano. *Una Republica da Riformare*. Bologna: Il Mulino, 1980.

Blackmer, Donald L. *Unity in Diversity: Italian Communism and the Communist World*. Cambridge: MIT Press, 1968.

Brancoli, Rodolfo. *Gli USA e il PCI*. Milano: Garzanti, 1978.

———. *Spettatori Interessati*. Milano: Garzanti, 1980.

Craxi, Bettino. *E la Nave Va*. Roma: Edizioni del Garofano, 1985.

Del Noce, Augusto. *Futuro Prossimo? Ipotesi, guidizi, discussioni sull'Euro-communismo—Con interventi di Claudio Fracassi, Renata Pisu, Leo Wollemborg*. Bologna: Cappelli, 1978.

Di Palma, Giuseppe. *Surviving without Governing: The Italian Parties in Parliament*. Berkeley: University of California Press, 1977.

Fanfani, Amintore. *Da Napoli a Firenze (1954–1959)*. Milano: Garzanti, 1959.

Galli, Giorgio. *La Sfida Perduta (Biografia Politica di Enrico Mattei)*. Milano: Bompiani, 1976.

Gronchi, Giovanni. *Discorsi d'America*. Milano: Garzanti, 1956.

Horowitz, Daniel L. *The Italian Labor Movement*. Cambridge: Harvard Univeristy Press, 1963.

La Malfa, Ugo. *Contro L'Europa di de Gaulle*. Milano: Edizioni di Comunita', 1964.

Lange, Peter and Tarrow, Sidney (eds.). *Italy in Transition: Conflict and Consensus*. London: Frank Cass and Co., Ltd., 1980.

La Palombara, Joseph. *Democracy Italian Style*. New Haven: Yale University Press, 1987.

Saragat, Giuseppe. *Quaranta Anni di Lotte per la Democrazia*. Milano: U. Mursia & C., 1966.

Sartori, Giovanni. *Parties and Party System*. Cambridge: Cambridge University Press, 1976.

Schlesinger, Arthur M., Jr. *A Thousand Days*. Boston: Houghton Mifflin, 1965.

Willis, F. Roy. *Italy Chooses Europe*. New York: Oxford University Press, 1971.

Index

About the Author

LEO J. WOLLEMBORG has been a writer on international relations and a news correspondent since 1942, when he served as a news editor and script writer for the Office of War Information, Italian section, during World War II. He also served as an analyst for Allied counterintelligence activities from 1943 to 1947.

Mr. Wollemborg was born in Loreggia, Italy, in 1912, and became a U.S. citizen in 1943. He received a Ph.D at the University of Rome in 1933 and taught history there from 1936 to 1938. Two years later he began lecturing on international relations at Columbia University.

The author of several books on Italian foreign policy and politics, including *Italia al Rallentatore* (*Italy in Slow Motion,* 1967), he has contributed widely as a columnist and writer with both U.S. and Italian journals. These include *The Wall Street Journal*, *The New Republic*, the *Washington Post*, and the Italian newspapers *Il Tempo, Corrierre della Sera, La Stampa,* and *Il Mondo.* Mr. Wollemborg resides in Italy.